Classroom Voices

Language-Based Learning in the Elementary School

Classroom Voices

Language-Based Learning in the Elementary School

David Booth
UNIVERSITY OF TORONTO

Larry Swartz
SCHOOL CO-ORDINATOR

Meguido Zola
RESEARCH CO-ORDINATOR

HARCOURT
BRACE
CANADA

Harcourt Brace & Company, Canada
Toronto Montreal Orlando Fort Worth San Diego
Philadelphia London Sydney Tokyo

Canadian Cataloguing in Publication Data

    Booth, David

        Classroom voices: language-based learning in the
        elementary school

    Includes bibliographical references.
    ISBN 0-7747-3151-6

    1. English language–Study and teaching (Elementary) I. Title.

    LB1576.B66 1993   372.6   C93–093684–1

Publisher: *Heather McWhinney*
Acquisitions Editor: *Christopher Carson*
Developmental Editor: *Elizabeth Reid*
Copy Editor: *Wendy Thomas*
Director, Art and Design: *Patricia Garbett*
Cover and Interior Design: *Landgraff Design Associates*
Photography: *Cathie Archbould*
Cover Photograph: *Alex Murchison*

Acknowledgements

This book is called *Classroom Voices* for good reason. Many people contributed to the picture of language-based learning that is reflected in these pages:

- *Meguido Zola*, who through research and dialogue, directed me towards the ideas and structures that support good teaching;

- *Larry Swartz*, who co-ordinated the contributions of the teachers and students at Queenston Drive Public School and who did so much of the collecting of bibliographic information;

- the principal, *Paul Shaw*, and the teachers at Queenston, who chronicled their education experiences honestly and openly so that others can learn;

- the children at the school, who volunteered their conversations and writing;

- the parents, who gave permission for their children's contributions and who themselves offered views and suggestions;

- the friends and colleagues of the teachers at Queenston who contributed their expertise to the project;

- *Carol Thornley-Hall* and the team of teachers who created the Peel TALK Project;

- *Jo Phenix*, who has proven herself an authority in literacy education;

- the editors who helped put various parts of this book together–*Wendy Cochran, Nancy Ennis, Jackie Isaac, Kaila Kukla, Diane Taylor;*

- *Arn Bowers, Alison Preece, Judith Cassady, Barbara Mischio and Arthur Smith*, who reviewed the manuscript and offered their sugestions;

- and *Elizabeth Reid*, whose commitment to the book grew far beyond that of editor and who became the polisher of ideas as well as of words, smoothing the pages with her love of language.

David Booth
Faculty of Education
University of Toronto

The author and publisher wish to thank those whose copyright material has contributed to *Classroom Voices,* in particular

- the excerpts from various publications and booklets from TALK, a Medium for Learning and Change, the Peel Board of Education project TALK, a Medium for Learning and Change;
- Arlene Perly Rae's letter to Liza and Heidi, reprinted by her permission;
- excerpts from "The Teacher Disguised as a Writer, in Hot Pursuit of Literacy, by Mem Fox, which first appeared in *Language Arts,* Volume 64, Number 1, January 1987, pp. 18–32, copyright 1987 by the National Council of Teachers of English, reprinted by permission;
- the excerpt from *Bill Martin's Instant Readers: Teacher's Guide.* by Bill Martin Jr, copyright 1972, published by Holt, Rinehart and Winston, reprinted by permission of Bill Martin Jr.;
- excerpts from "An Interview with Jo Phenix" by David Booth from *Growing with Books,* Book 3, adapted by permission of the Ontario Ministry of Education;
- the excerpt from *Readers and Writers with a Difference: A Holistic Approach to Teaching Learning Disabled and Remedial Students* by Lynn Rhodes and Curt Dudley-Marling, copyright 1988, reprinted by permission of Heinemann Educational Books, Inc.;
- the excerpt from the report of the External Review Team for the Vancouver Board of Education, the Vancouver Board of Education;
- the excerpt from *Any Child Can Read Better: Developing Your Child's Reading Skills outside the Classroom* by Harvey Wiener, copyright 1990, reprinted by permission of Bantam Books, Inc.;
- excerpts from *In the Middle: Writing, Reading and Learning with Adolescents* by Nancie Atwell, copyright 1987, by permission of Heinemann Educational Books, Inc.;
- the poem from *Maniac Magee* by Jerry Spinelli, reprinted by permission of Little, Brown and Company;
- "Yukuto Chung," by Lisa Katz, by her permission;
- the poem "Construction" by Virginia Schonberg from the anthology *Subway Singer,* copyright 1970, reprinted by permission of William Morrow and Company, Inc.

A Note from the Publisher

Thank you for selecting *Classroom Voices: Language-Based Learning in the Elementary School* by David Booth. The author and publishers have devoted considerable time to the careful development of this book. We appreciate your recognition of this effort and accomplishment.We want to hear what you think about *Classroom Voices.* Please take a few minutes to fill in the postage-paid reply card that you will find at the back of the book. Your comments, suggestions, and criticisms will be valuable to us as we prepare new editions and other books.

Contents in Brief

Contents

Introduction

C LASSROOM VOICES grows from observing the classroom work of professional, dedicated teachers; from conversations with colleagues at work and at conferences; from reading the reports of researchers who have come to grips with the complexities of learning to talk, read, and write; from writers who have chronicled the progress educators have made in teaching language arts; from student teachers struggling to turn theory into practice; and from the children in schools everywhere. It is in the stories teachers tell as they strive to develop the language potential of young people and attempt to articulate their ideas about their work. Some of these voices will confirm your beliefs about language and learning; others will extend your understanding of teaching with a language-based philosophy; still others may jar you into looking at language arts from a different perspective.

The focus of this book is Queenston Drive Public School in Mississauga, Ontario, where 600 children and 30 staff members form an educational community. I became involved with Queenston through the Peel Board of Education's research project *TALK, a Medium for Learning and Change*. As I wanted to write this book around an actual school functioning in a real community, Queenston was a natural choice for me. Time was my toughest obstacle: these are busy teachers committed to their children. The principal's organizational scheme, however, allowed me to meet them as groups and individuals, to observe in their classrooms, to read their journals articulating their thoughts as teachers, and to share children's writings and project work. Some teachers bravely audiotaped or videotaped their classes and transcribed tapes of children talking for later analysis. Others collected data and observations from thematic units and special events.

The children at Queenston are using language for real purposes, with no "dummy runs." Not only are they communicating but they are able to talk about the language they use to do so. Their teachers have individual styles of teaching but share similar beliefs and goals. Thus my understanding of a language-based school is found in the excitement and chaos of one school building full of real professionals and real children struggling to grow and change. Through journal writing, collaborative talk, and classroom observation and research, their stories are the glue that binds my thoughts together. The voices in this book are those of the principal, teachers, resource personnel, parents, and students of Queenston, of the visiting educators suggested by staff members, and of the dozens of writers on language teaching who have inspired the framework for this undertaking. To these voices, you will add your own and those of the children you teach—all in together.

Queenston Drive Public School accommodates children from four to fourteen years of age in classes from junior kindergarten to grade eight. The children come from a wide mix of families, many new to the country. Some walk to school from the modest three-bedroom homes that surround the school; others ride school buses from large suburban homes, apartment buildings, or townhouse developments farther away.

The teachers are as multifaceted as the children, in age, background, and teaching experience: a few teachers have been at the school for close to a decade; four are just beginning their teaching careers; three acted as language arts resource teachers for the Peel Board of Education before joining the Queenston staff. Two ESL (English as a second language) teachers help service the large immigrant population, and special education teachers assist students in their regular classrooms, withdrawing children at times for a session or two; two resource teachers from the field office are available to help plan programs, visit classrooms, and present special lessons, such as storytelling, drama, or science experiments. Music and French are part of the regular program.

As we walk through the corridors at Queenston, we see teachers having conversations with their colleagues: "Look at this building Matthew made out of Lego." / "The kids didn't like the poem I read to them today." / "Sharon and Stephanie took over and conducted a meeting of environmental experts." / "I had four kids decide that the room should be made into a castle." / "You should have heard Carson's response to the legend I read." / "How do you get your kids to work so co-operatively in groups?"

The school is a maze of additions: No one area is devoted to a specific grade division. To the right of the front door are two large classrooms of junior and senior kindergarten children. On the left is the office where the school secretaries accommodate most requests with efficiency and humour. Two junior family groupings and grades seven and eight classes share a corridor; the basement houses a grade one class, a grade two class, and a large double pod that holds a grades one-to-three family grouping; ten more classrooms occupy the second floor, along with a music room, an art room, and a science room; two junior classes and the English as a second language program use the portables at the south end of the school; down a few stairs from the main floor is a kindergarten-to-grade-two family grouping and across the hall from this is the library—the hub of the school. In the summer of 1990, a computer lab was installed at the west end of the library, and students and teachers of grades four to eight use it freely.

Primary (junior kindergarten to grade three), junior (grades four to six), and intermediate (grades seven and eight) division meetings are held monthly for teachers to discuss budget plans, share curricular materials, organize trips, plan special events, and present classroom inquiries. The principal, Paul Shaw, has introduced professional growth sessions in which teachers meet once a month to discuss programs and share stories and research from their own classrooms. The staff is divided into two teams, an arrangement that allows one team to cover classes while the other attends a session. The principal's enthusiasm and the normal sharing and discussion that takes place with colleagues next door and across the hall have led many teachers, including some who might be considered "traditional" in their approach, to move more and more toward language-based programs.

Time for Professional Growth
Paul Shaw

I think I reached my way of thinking before I had actually read about the concept of empowerment. I wanted somebody to give me the right—the power—to be responsible for the kids in my classroom, to respect my views as a professional. I wanted to be treated as if what I had to say counted. I wanted to create an environment in which each student would learn and grow. But suppose you're a teacher. Think about how you work. There are so many practical things you have to deal with. In the morning you have your 25 to 35 children to look after, and at the end of the day you want to go over what happened, to reflect, to question assumptions, and to identify beliefs. But it's time to go home, and you're too tired to do anything else. So how can we change that way of working? The issue first of all is time.

At Queenston, we've dealt with that very simply: we've put it right in the schedule. We take teachers out of classrooms, give them time to sit down, talk, examine certain procedures that they use in their classrooms. Our commitment is to find 70 hours a year. We take about half of that out of prime teaching time, and the other half comes from professional development days, staff meetings, and a few extra wine-and-cheese gatherings.

Once we've created the time, there is the question of how to bring about the culture of inquiry and reflection. That's a little more difficult, but these are the guidelines I use. First of all, I think you have to recognize the background and experience that teachers bring to the classroom. You want to enable teachers to look at what they're doing but in a non-threatening way. I try to demonstrate that I value their views, that I respect their ideas, that I welcome them to talk about their

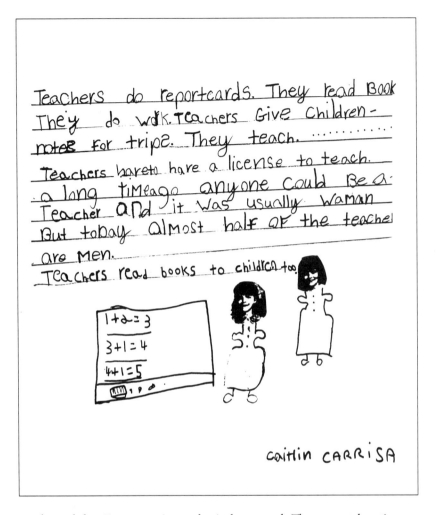

Teachers do reportcards. They read Book
They do work. Teachers Give Children-
notes for tripe. They teach.
Teachers hareto have a license to teach.
a long timeago anyone could Be a
Teacher and it was usually Waman
But tobay almost half of the teachel
are Men.
Teachers read books to childrea too.

1+2=3
3+1=4
4+1=5

caitlin CARRISA

work, and that I'm not going to be judgemental. That trust takes time
to build—for some teachers, just a matter of weeks; for others, at least
a year before they come to be part of the sharing and exploring
process and are ready to talk about their classes, about their successes,
about their values, about doing things differently.

On the first day of school, I sent the teachers something to read
along with a personal note suggesting that if they found it interesting,
they might find somebody on staff with whom to share it. I asked them
to respond, and about 75 percent did. I was beginning with the idea
that we need to be informed. From this, we went on to create our own
professional growth team. The seven members each interviewed about
four or five teachers about their values, beliefs, and future plans and
brought that information back for the entire staff to reflect on.

When we started this, people seemed a little hesitant about this process, but in two to three months, the dialogue became sustained and focused. We read; we reflected; we went back to our classrooms and did some things differently; we shared those experiences with our colleagues. And what we had was a demonstration that we can work with one another, that our classrooms are rich with information—both data and resources—that we can come to trust each other, to talk, to share, and to grow.

These are some of the formal things that go on with developing a culture of inquiry, but you have to understand that what happens in that 70 hours is really the tip of the iceberg because you're promoting a way of looking at the job of teaching that is very different.

The language arts philosophy described in this book creates a picture of the teaching and learning dynamic in progress. Each chapter follows a similar structure, beginning with a brief summary of the research and writing that supports these observations and findings, and then focusing on a particular facet of language arts explored through personal experiences. The chapters are laced with essays by and excerpts from interviews with the staff at Queenston, transcripts and written work by the children, and relevant statements by recognized authorities in the field, Each ends with an essay about memorable books for children, an annotated list of professional resources for further reading on the focus of the chapter, and a series of questions and topics for discussion relevant to both new and experienced teachers.

Chapter One is a holistic overview of language and learning, alongside images of the teachers and students at Queenston Drive Public School. Chapter Two examines the organizational strategies involved in carrying out a language-based program and presents several planning models for different divisions. Chapter Three discusses young children's emerging awareness of print and proposes frameworks for assisting the children in their desire to become readers and writers. It describes the literacy environment that will supply the resources required and techniques for promoting the use of authentic children's books throughout the curriculum. Chapter Four looks at the developing reader and offers a series of response modes for helping students reveal their understanding of text and for modifying and deepening their attempts at constructing meaning.

Chapter Five focuses on the writing process, from the initial act of composing through to revision and editing for classroom publication, and the various modes of writing children will be doing across the curriculum. Chapter Six examines the complexities of transcribing language—spelling, punctuation, capitalization, usage and handwriting, all the problems inherent in writing words down.

Chapter Seven proposes incorporating speaking and listening in all aspects of learning, from group talk in science to interpreting a poem with a partner.

Chapter Eight compares dramatic play and drama in education and outlines the value of improvisational drama and role playing as a way of learning about life by seeing it through the eyes of others.

Chapter Nine discusses assessment techniques in a language-based classroom that enable teachers to gather information about individual children's language needs and then develop programs for assisting their growth in areas of concern. Examples of useful assessment tools are offered, as well as suggestions for reporting progress to parents.

Schools are most effective when theory and practice are joined together by teachers committed to the best education possible. In Chapter Ten, I take the opportunity to suggest ideas for our continued professional growth as teachers, as learners ourselves, and ways we can put our professional knowledge into action.

Developing a Language Arts Program

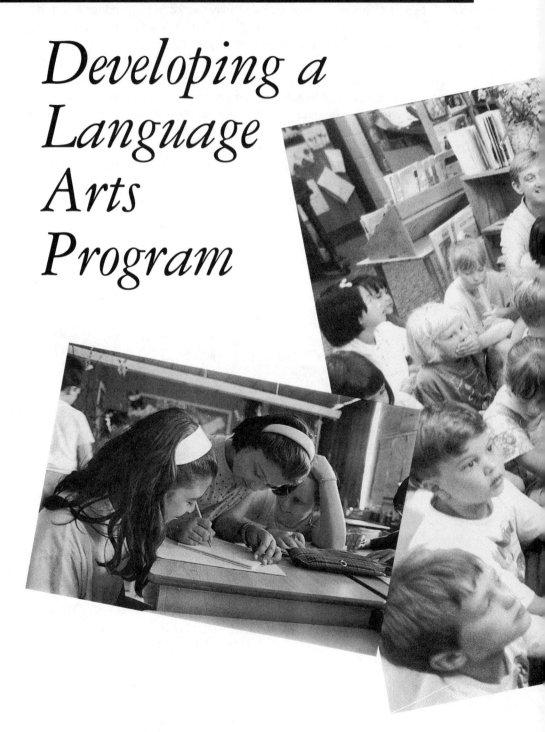

I N MY 35 YEARS as a teacher, I have seen a phenomenal growth in what we know about how children develop power with language, from how they learn to talk as babies to how they learn to read and write. The teaching of language arts has changed radically, based on well-researched educational theory as well as teachers' intuitions about children, literacy, and effective classroom practice. We now have a body of books, journals, and research documents that provides a background for shaping and articulating our language curriculum as we come to understand the complexities of language development in young people.

M.A.K. Halliday (1975), Frank Smith (1973), Kenneth Goodman (1986) and other linguists and psycholinguists have given teachers an awareness of cognitive psychology, or how children develop intellectually, and how they find meaning in everything and everyone around them. Ethnographic studies by Shirley Brice Heath (1983) alerted us to the social context of learning and the importance of a child's home culture. Gordon Wells (1986) described how a child's experience with significant adults in the early years affects future literacy competence. We now recognize the need for teachers to establish links with the home (Baskwill, 1989), both in order to learn about children from their parents and to allow parents to be partners with the school in helping their children learn (Griffiths and Hamilton, 1984). As Myra Barrs (Barrs and Thomas, 1992) puts it, "Each child arrives with different experiences and understanding, and these must form the basis of their continuing learning."

Our attitudes to the teaching of reading began to alter. Sylvia Ashton-Warner (1965) pioneered teaching reading through the words that are significant to a child; Jeanette Veatch (1986) created reading programs for individual children; Don Holdaway (1979) and Robert and Marlene McCracken (1987) took a new look at the possibilities of "choral reading" and developed "shared reading" strategies; Jerome Harste (Watson, Burke, and Harste, 1989) focused on children as authors. Yetta Goodman (1990) helped us understand the child's development as a reader through the mistakes or "miscues" made while reading. Educational writers began to question traditional practice from their own observations and research. Donald Graves

(1983), Lucy Calkins (1991), and Nancie Atwell (1987) reviewed the teaching of writing and restructured our understanding of the writing process. Teachers in Canada, Australia, New Zealand, and the United States formed grass-roots organizations to come to grips with the need for change in helping children to become readers and writers.

As we built a picture of the attributes of an effective language arts program, a curriculum based on language development took shape. Pre-service and in-service courses for teachers began to incorporate these new approaches. In 1988, the Peel Board of Education set up the TALK Project, in which teachers determined their own enquiries, and staff at the University of Toronto Faculty of Education and Ontario Institute for Studies in Education acted as consultants and co-researchers. As part of the TALK Project, I began in 1989 to work with some teachers at Queenston Drive Public School on a classroom-based research model to develop a sound understanding of how language learning takes place in the elementary classroom.

In this first chapter, we look at the varied backgrounds of some of the children at Queenston and present a rationale for a language arts program centred on children growing as language users through activities that require them to read, write, listen, and speak for reasons that are actual and authentic to them.

Who Are the Children We Teach?

There are 600 children attending Queenston, each with individual needs and potential for language growth. I asked three teachers each to tell about one child to demonstrate the variety of background and experience that children bring to school and the need for a philosophy of teaching and learning that will allow all of them to develop their potential as users of language.

Nyssa's Story
Jan Bayes

Nyssa came to Queenston at the beginning of her grade one year after a somewhat unsuccessful first school experience in a French immersion senior kindergarten. She entered my kindergarten-grade one classroom wearing a walking cast to correct shortened tendons in her foot. Her fingers were also slightly webbed. Nyssa had a congenital heart condition, and her lips and fingers were visibly blue. Her parents suggested that Nyssa herself should determine how far she should participate in normal classroom activities; they wanted her to function as normally as she felt able.

Nyssa was a warm, loving little girl whose ready smile endeared her to all. From the beginning, she showed an avid interest in books, loving to be read to, gravitating to the listening centre where she could look at the books with accompanying tapes, and pretending to read aloud as she sat on the classroom couch. I felt sure with all these attributes, Nyssa would soon be reading!

However, I soon discovered that she had not yet developed a sense of narrative. She was unable to recount familiar, simple, highly repetitive stories such as *The Three Little Pigs*. The books she "wrote" consisted of individual scenarios on each page—none related to another in any logical or sequential order. She had no intuitive sense of the relationship between sound and symbol; her attempts to form letters for anything other than her own name were very rudimentary. Abstract mathematical concepts were also beyond her; she had no real concept of one-to-one correspondence and would impulsively blurt out an answer, smiling and hoping that she had pleased me.

Doing up zippers and putting on boots, especially over the cast, were difficult for Nyssa because of her slightly misshapen fingers. But it became clear that Nyssa had learned to play the role of a sweet little girl who required the assistance of adults. I soon came to recognize the helpless little smile and "I can't," when it came to other life-skill problems such as finding lunch bags and keeping track of winter garb.

Nyssa remained at this academic and social plateau for most of her grade one year. I discussed her progress with her family on a regular basis, and we all supported each other's efforts.

The following year, I was working in a team-teaching situation, and Nyssa was placed in grade two in our family-grouped classroom. At our request, the In-School Review Committee arranged for psychological testing for Nyssa to ensure that we were in fact meeting her needs. A parent volunteer and our special education teacher worked with her individually, the latter for about half an hour each day. Her parents offered to have her tutored privately, but we recommended against it as Nyssa was obviously physically tired at the end of a school day. She adjusted fairly well to the larger classroom environment of 47 students, although in the early fall of that year she complained more frequently of fatigue, headaches, and stomachaches. We kept in close touch with her parents at these times. We provided a special resting place for her on our classroom couch and carried her up the three flights of stairs to the music room. These bouts disappeared part way through the year. By the end of grade two, Nyssa had clearly made progress, but she could still not be considered to be "reading" and continued to have difficulty with math concepts.

Although we modified her program to meet her specific learning difficulties, at no time did we alter our philosophy. We read to her constantly. We provided her with real purposes for writing, such as notes to friends, scribing for her when she was too frustrated.

Nyssa is now back with us as a grade three student. She has formed a close friendship with another girl in grade three, an above average student—an encouraging sign of social progress. Nyssa recognizes that she cannot do many of the tasks expected of grade threes, but she cheerfully accepts our suggestions that she might join them for gym, library, or in specific small teaching groups. And this fall, Nyssa has begun to see herself as a reader and a writer! She is a happy student and is revelling in her new-found prowess.

Working with Nyssa has been proof for us that teachers are first and foremost facilitators who through the day try to capture the moments when children are ready to be taught in the belief that all children can and do learn.

Siu Pang's Story
Brian Crawford

Siu Pang has been at Queenston since his arrival from Hong Kong three years ago. He entered grade two as an enthusiastic but quiet boy who said little but "Hello, my name is Siu Pang." A daily 30-minute withdrawal period for ESL (English as a second language) instruction was arranged for Sui Pang, but the rest of the time, he found himself immersed in a language-based, activity-centred program. He was encouraged to listen to stories, read and write with other students, and speak with his friends during activity time. Much of his writing was modelled on pattern books. Soon his journal entries reflected the way that he spoke: "I have brother. We go to park." "I go swimming with my class." He usually drew pictures to explain what was happening in his stories and his spelling reflected the way he pronounced words.

Siu Pang was lucky to find a friend in his class who spoke Chinese fluently. Claire often translated instructions for him and communicated his ideas to his teacher. She soon had Siu Pang repeat what was being said to him in English to help him feel more comfortable in his second language. Claire would also transcribe for him when he presented in Chinese ideas that he couldn't write in English.

Siu Pang's teacher was in charge of music for the primary division and led his own children in singing every day. He found that Siu Pang loved singing. The rhythms and repetition in such songs as "A Sailor

Went to Sea Sea Sea" and "Miss Mary Mack Mack Mack" were ideal vehicles for him to practise "out-loud language." By the end of grade two, Siu Pang was conversing happily with his peers at the sand table or the cut-and-paste centre.

In grade three, Siu Pang was placed in a family grouping of children from kindergarten to grade three. Siu Pang enjoyed his status as one of the oldest in the class and felt confident because he was ahead of the younger ones. Reading was not a problem; Siu Pang was able to understand short novels. As his English speech improved, his syntax and spelling became as well-developed as other children's of his age. He was encouraged to write for real purposes and often shared his work with his peers.

Now a grade four student, Siu Pang is comfortable with the routines of reading and writing that he is meeting in a new situation: my grades three, four, and five family grouping. I have noticed that he is hesitant to take risks with his writing; Siu Pang wants to present his work with perfection. He writes very neatly, using simple sentences and familiar words. But he was able to move away from this comfortable mode during a drama lesson on a medieval community when he wrote a letter in role as an apprentice to the manor lord. I have encouraged him to share his journal with a partner, and with this "buddy," he is becoming more adventurous with his writing. Siu Pang is somewhat reluctant to share ideas in whole-class discussions, but he expresses himself well in small-group situations. During an investigation of electricity, Siu Pang built a flashlight and explained his work as a scientist to his peers. He also wrote about the process.

We continue to read to Siu Pang and encourage him to read for real purposes, to write, and to find audiences to share his growth. By now, Siu Pang sees himself as a reader and writer. He readily takes part in small groups and is beginning to enter discussions when he has a larger audience The consistency of the language arts program at Queenston has allowed Siu Pang to take more and more risks.

Liza's Story
Larry Swartz

Reading and writing have become very important to Liza, a grade six student at Queenston. It wasn't always so.

Liza's parents are both teachers. Since infancy she has listened to stories, attended plays and concerts, travelled, and shared outdoor and science experiences with her family. She was very strong orally, but the transfer to print was slow to come. Her mother told me that Liza had begun grade one with a teacher who taught through a structured, phonics-based, "ditto-sheet" program, and her next teacher had used a radically different approach. Liza seemed to be getting mixed messages about language. Although she enjoyed drawing and illustrating, she was very nervous about putting words down on paper. Spelling was always a struggle, and her writing often showed several attempts at a word. Liza entered my classroom in grade four, and it turned out to be the right environment at the right time.

Both home and school were encouraging a love of books. Liza was very aware of authors, recognizing names such as Katherine Paterson, Patricia MacLachlan, and Betsy Byars. She would frequently ask me to recommend books. Silent reading time in class was precious to her and her daily routine at home also included reading. Her family visited the community library and the local children's bookstore regularly. Soon Liza was building her own library. Her parents often asked me for suggestions for books for Christmas and birthdays.

Because spelling was difficult for Liza, she was somewhat intimidated about expressing her thoughts in writing. Her ideas were not always articulated clearly. She often felt the need to confer about transcription problems as she revised. Yet she was determined to experiment. She enjoyed writing stories and poems, which she usually based on ideas from literature. One of her early attempts in grade four was to create a new version of *Sidewalk Stories from a Wayside School* by Louis Sachar.

Liza also took the opportunity to write with her friends Laurie and Johanna, who were proficient writers. The three would brainstorm ideas and compose stories for "publication" together. Liza often chose to revise her work on the computer, either in the classroom or at home, doing three or four versions. She seemed to feel better when she presented a "neater" finished piece.

Liza stayed with me for grade five, and I watched her become a very independent reader. She enjoyed folk tales and poetry and became interested in the author Gary Paulsen and novels about the holocaust (*Number the Stars, The Devil's Arithmetic, The Upstairs Room*).

Liza's notebook includes comments on books she had read, poems about the environment ("The wind of March is crying / as the end of nature nears. . . .") and drafts of letters, such as one to the prime minister sharing her thoughts about the the conflict in the Middle East. A letter to the editor she wrote to complain about a critic's review of a novel was published in the newspaper.

No such thing these days as boys' or girls' books.

This is Heidi and Liza. As you can tell by our names, we are girls. We are writing this letter to complain about a headline in the Saturday Star on March 16: Newbery award winner compelling read for boys.

We are reading Maniac Magee and enjoying it and we are not boys.

The critic, Arlene Perly Rae, seems to think that only boys would enjoy this winning novel. Do you think this critic is stereotyping? We do. In our Grade 5 class there is no such thing as boys' or girls' books. The fact is that half of the population is female. The author would lose a lot of his profit if his book was sold only to boys.

LIZA
HEIDI
Mississauga

Dear Heidi and Liza,

I didn't notice your letter to the editor but asked for a copy this week after a friend mentioned it. I'm so glad you enjoyed Maniac Magee. I too thought it was a terrific book for boys and girls.

When I wrote about it, I was also responding to a problem that had emerged in letters some parents had sent me at the Star. They wrote that their sons, aged about 9-12 had given up reading! They asked for help. Many young people (like you) enjoy reading. All you might ask for, from time to time, are recommendations. I agree with you that most books are not written just for girls or just for boys. I wanted to emphasize that this particular book was so good it might tempt even those averse to reading (perhaps you have friends like them?) to try it out. I needed a book so tempting it could lure them away, at least once, from TV and the great outdoors. Maniac Magee with its impressive lead character -- a legend and sports hero to boot -- well written and with a strong plot, fit the bill perfectly.

If the column implied in any way that others (girls? grown ups?) shouldn't read it or wouldn't enjoy it too, that was a mistake, and I'm sorry. My 9 year old daughter, a voracious reader, read the column and then read the book. She loved it. I hoped my enthusiasm for the book would bubble up to include all young people interested in a good read.

What made you read the book? You might want to discuss with your teacher why some people like certain books, and others don't. Do some books appeal more to people with certain interests -- what about mysteries, fantasies, history? What is literary taste?

By the way, you complained in your letter about the headline: I don't write the headlines. I just see them in the Saturday paper, the same as you do.

Yours sincerely,

Arlene Perly Rae

Liza's spelling gradually improved, and her love of books grew by leaps and bounds. On the last day of school, Liza slipped a card on my desk. Inside was the following message:

Dear Mr. Swartz,
Thank you for 2 whole years of Books and poety.
Love Liza

The stories of children in this school lend support to research suggesting that a program based on the children's own language development appears to offer most support to most students. Our job as teachers is to promote activities that require children to speak and listen, to read and write, for reasons that are important to them and thus grow and develop as users of language. Children must be willing participants in endeavours that have them both using language to learn and learning about language.

Successful teaching builds on what children already know. The language that they bring to school is the basis for all further learning. As teachers, we must respect and value the linguistic competencies of all our students and design curricula through which they can continue to grow.

Children with Special Needs

We have been aware of our responsibility to provide education geared to the needs of exceptional students for most of this century. Such provision has varied from period to period, district to district, and school to school. Today, the policy is to place exceptional students as far as possible in a classroom setting that integrates them with the general school population and at the same time attempts to meet their special needs. It is true that schools that cater to students with a specific range of needs may be able to provide more resources and special equipment, and in a few cases, children may be better off placed in such schools. Most often, however, the social and cognitive benefits of including exceptional students in a "normal" classroom with people of differing abilities, differing aptitudes, and differing talents outweigh the disadvantages. An inclusive classroom enables all children to know the individuals who belong to the wider community, understand their needs, respect their rights, and contribute to their well-being and sense of self-esteem.

The Education Act for Ontario says, "An exceptional pupil is one whose behavioural, communicational, intellectual, or physical needs, or a combination of these, as determined by a committee of the school board, in consultation with the parents, are such that the pupil may benefit from placement in a special education program." We have many terms and classifications we apply to exceptional children: low vision, blind, orthopaedic, learning disabled, speech and language impaired, autistic, gifted, hard of hearing, deaf, behaviourally disabled, multiply disabled, educable retarded, trainable retarded. Is it any wonder that advocacy groups would prefer us to look at the person first and see the particular condition as no more than that: a condition that affects how this person relates to the world?

Schools in Ontario have four modes of classroom placement for children with special needs: full integration (placement in a regular classroom for the entire day with support services provided within the regular classroom); integration/withdrawal (placement in a regular classroom with specialized instruction outside the regular classroom for a portion of the school day); partial integration (placement in a special education class with integration in a regular classroom for a portion of the school day); and self-contained (placement in a special education class, a special school, or even a special residential school). Though a range of such placement options will continue to be required, research indicates that integration offers greater value in both social and intellectual development for most exceptional children (Rhodes and Dudley-Marling, 1988).

For example, in the early 1960s, I was involved in the first program in Hamilton, Ontario, for "gifted" children. The children were brought by bus from their own neighbourhoods in various parts of the city to attend my school, and while my memory is full of the wonderful experiences I had with them, I now realize that they should have grown up inside their own social network, not in a distant classroom where they were labelled as "different" from other children. As teachers, we need to rethink our beliefs about all children with special needs and our programs for them in order to provide them enriching opportunities for intellectual growth in a socially healthy atmosphere.

At the time of our project, Queenston Drive Public School was working on a partial withdrawal model for children with special needs. All children found themselves in regular classrooms most of the time, and I saw interesting friendships, deeper insights, and new approaches to making meaning spring up simply because the class was not a homogenized group but a variety of individuals, all special. Today, Queenston is moving toward full integration. More and more, the teachers who offer specialized teaching are joining their students in the home classroom rather than having the children come to them.

Bill Wanted to Be a Teacher
James, grade five

Bill wanted to be a teacher so he was sent to our school to see if he could be a teacher. He was with us for two months. Then he went back to Woodlands. He stayed for the afternoons only.

Bill is 18 years old. I think when Bill grows up he will be a very good teacher. Even though he is blind he can remember things very quickly. He also works well with kids. I think that on his farewell the poem Cindy read was really fitting. When he was here I got used to him.

The poem goes something like this . . .

> *I loved my friend*
> *He went away*
> *And now the poem ends*
> *As softly as it started*

Language and Learning

We are the "meaning makers"—every one of us: children, parents, and teachers. To try to make sense, to construct stories, and to share them with others in speech and in writing is an essential part of being human. For those of us who are more knowledgeable and more mature—parents and teachers—the responsibility is clear: to interact with those in our care in such a way as to foster and enrich their meaning making (Wells, 1986).

Sixty years and more of research on child development have contributed to our understanding of children and their language abilities. Working in Russia in the early 1930s, Lev Vygotsky (1962, 1986) described the relationship between the development of thought and the development of language, which he believed are, in the first place, separate processes: once children discover that everything and every action has a name, their thoughts take new and more complex form. Vygotsky's theory is that teachers should be aware of the child's "zone of proximal development" and prepared to promote new concepts when the child is ready for them: "The only good kind of instruction is that which leads it; it must be aimed not so much at the ripe as the ripening function" (1978). Jean Piaget (1969), who relates his work to Vygotsky's, suggested that children acquire language by using it as they participate in activities that are meaningful to them; they learn to speak because the need to express themselves and to understand others drives them.

If children are surrounded by people who provide a rich language environment, their language potential will continue to develop. They become active members of society through language, sharing the experiences that bind them to others. As they use language, they discover that it can represent their thoughts. They acquire the rules of language from inside language. As their awareness of society extends beyond the here and now, they begin to appreciate that written language conveys lasting meaning and taps the memory of the community.

As teachers, we need to be aware of some of our subjective assumptions about language. What we know as English may not be English at all to a child from a home where a different dialect is spoken—and vice versa. Even within what we call "standard" English, different groups develop special words to communicate common interests—consider the jargon used by engineers, sports fans, and even teachers—and different generations may use some words and idioms in different ways. A further complicating factor for teachers at many schools is that many children are from homes where the language of the classroom is not spoken. Yet the need to communicate is common to all: we all understand the functions of language. At

Queenston, several dialects of English and more than 30 other languages are spoken by the families that make up the school community; about one-third of the children come from homes where "standard" English is not spoken. The teachers try to ensure that this language diversity provides a rich setting for language experiences.

Humans learn to speak without formal instruction. Even as babies, we make verbal sounds when other people are talking, using language to learn and learning to use language at the same time. If we are surrounded by people who use words to tell stories, express feelings, convey ideas, and ask questions and who expect the same of us, we will continue to develop as language users.

Although they are unaware of it, most children understand a great deal about language long before they come to school: "Their language and culture at home has structured for them the meanings which will give shape to their experiences in classrooms and beyond" (Heath, 1983). By building on this understanding and working with their interests and abilities, a teacher can motivate children to extend their use of language and their knowledge about language. The school can provide a sense of community that comes from participating naturally in activities that incorporate the functions of language.

The needs of children as learners are recognized when language is taught through authentic occasions for using language rather than through practice runs. When the focus is on using the many functions of language for real purposes, oral and written language skills will grow across the whole curriculum. When children are interested in what they are hearing, reading, or writing, they will develop control over the medium of language—as well as explore the context of each experience. In other words, children need to find themselves in situations that require real language for real communicating.

Children learn language not by giving the expected answers to formula questions, but by risking, attempting, failing, responding, and inventing. The way in which those around them respond helps shape their language development. They test hypotheses about the way language works as they interact with others in conversation. They learn to control the ways they use language as their understanding of the rules of the system grows. They struggle to find vocabulary with the power to communicate their message. They experiment with the form of language to make it do what they want it to.

Babies do not "practise talking"; they struggle to make meaning—calling for "ma-ma," demanding juice, distinguishing between "dog" and "cat," and identifying "me" in a precious moment of self-assertion. The social context of language is vital to children's meaning making—which is not only conveying their own meaning to others but discovering how what others say has meaning for them. Parents—and, by implication, teachers—must follow their children's interests, bridge the gaps in their understanding, discern and extend their intended meanings. Children need the support of persons who treat them as partners in conversation. When children grasp the symbolic thought processes embedded in language, they become the constructors of their own knowledge.

We need classrooms that continue to support the children's attempts at becoming "meaning makers." Is it possible for one teacher with several curriculum areas to cover to provide learning opportunities that promote language growth for each of 30 students who have varying abilities, needs, and proficiency in English? At Queenston, not only have many teachers found that it is possible, but by building language-based, collaborative, and interactive programs, they have turned theory into practice.

A Language Arts Program

The philosophy of the language arts program at Queenston is based on the children's own language development. Children negotiate with compassionate and constructive teachers a curriculum with language at its heart. School districts have described this type of program as "integrated language arts," "whole language," or "holistic learning."

These labels, however, can mean various things to various people. For example, the term "whole language" has been used to describe every type of methodology, from working exclusively from "whole language basal readers" to teachers' withdrawing from the children's activities for fear of interfering. Neither practice illustrates what "whole language" is intended to be. Good teachers choose from a range of strategies to help children "fulfill a variety of personal intentions in a range of social settings" (Dudley-Marling and Dippo, 1991). But such ambiguities and contradictions regarding philosophy and practice lead to confusion for parents and principals as well as for the teachers who are trying to teach. How well we explain what we do may determine what we are permitted to do in our classrooms in the future.

I use the term "language-based classroom" in an attempt to encompass not only the theory of language learning and the teacher's background in it, but to highlight the centrality of language in all aspects of learning. The language-based classroom is not concerned with what is known as "the language arts" to the exclusion of other areas of knowledge. It is, rather, a shorthand for assumptions, values, and theories not only about what language is and how it is learned, used, and taught, but more generally and pervasively, about the essential role of language in all curriculum and all learning and teaching.

A language-based classroom stresses the unity of learning through language. It looks at how children learn and how our teaching practices affect their learning. Language exploration is a necessary part of mathematics, the arts, social studies, and the sciences, and language learning takes place naturally and continuously as the children approximate, explore, and evaluate. These "subjects" can provide the context for much of the language use and growth that occurs. Instruction and skill development evolve better in context than on practice sheets.

Education is a process of helping children decipher the unfamiliar and relate it to the patterns of what they already know—and often changing those patterns (Piaget, 1964). Whether in informative or entertaining contexts, children must see language as a source of personal satisfaction. "When children are doing more talking, writing and reading about what matters to them, to someone who matters to them, they will be back to the basics of learning" (Britton, 1975).

Language is acquired through use, as those who have learned a second language well understand. Language-based teaching grows out of building the curriculum on the way children actually acquire language proficiency: talking, reading, and writing through need and desire. A program based on language growth frees the teacher to choose from a range of curriculum options for various children.

Whatever the label we give language teaching, it can become a metaphor for change, a call to question, examine, and reassess our assumptions, and to reflect on what we are doing as teachers. Teachers need to engage in dialogue with learners and be open to learning about children, about reading, about writing, about learning itself. Though we teach our students, our students are also our constant teachers. We must also engage in dialogue with one another, observing, coaching, and learning from other teachers—creating a community of teachers, just as in our classrooms we work to create a community of learners.

Talk, Literacy, and Visual Communications

The traditional focus of language arts programs has been literacy: reading and writing. A complete program, however, has three interdependent modes: talk, literacy, and visual communications.

We cannot take talk—the integration of listening and speaking—for granted just because children arrive at school with some development in this area. Listening is perhaps the most important skill a good business manager, a doctor, a salesperson, not to mention a student, can possess, yet traditional programs often failed to recognize the need to foster listening skills at all. They acknowledged speaking by including "public speaking" on an occasional basis.

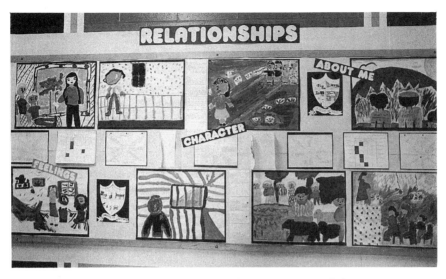

Many of us remember the counter-productive agony of these once-a-year events. There was no emphasis on regular dialogue with the teacher and other children to clarify thought and extend meaning. In a language-based classroom, talk is fundamental to the program as children respond to the story they have heard, discuss with a small group a draft to be written, or design an experiment in science.

Communication is more than a matter of words. Indeed, visual images—the view of the street, the picture in the advertisement, the action on the screen—often convey the larger part of the message. Parents, teachers, and book publishers have long recognized that pictures are important for young children, but only recently has exploration of "the media"—television, film, magazines, and so on—been seen as an integral part of the learning continuum. Children of all ages need opportunities to be critical viewers to ensure that they become "media literate." The expressive side of visual communication is representing thought through art and drama. Most children "write" their first stories in pictures, and many will continue to use pictures as an aid to their writing if the program is unified and does not put "art" and "composition" into separate compartments. Similarly, rather than putting on a play for an audience once a year, children use improvisation and dramatic play regularly to explore a story or situation in greater depth.

These aspects of language arts are cyclical and continuous: listening to a story leads to talking about it, illustrating it, reading similar stories, writing a new version, acting it out—which can lead to further reading and writing, perhaps within role, and more talk as children share and reflect on their own and others' dramatic insights. The language-based classroom reflects this interdependence of all modes of discourse and provides the context for it. Discovery, expression, and communication are the outcome.

We don't read reading, we don't write writing, we don't talk talking; we use these language processes as a natural part of learning and communicating. Teachers can create language programs with real purposes, programs that will support each child in developing his or her language potential. They can monitor the children's progress, assess their efforts, and regroup their forces when necessary. If teachers value the language abilities of the children in their classrooms, recognize the social context in which the children live, and accept the background and experience they bring to school, they will be able to help them grow and learn. No single teaching methodology suits every child; teachers must bring all their knowledge and understanding to each new class. They must be judicious in their choice of the strategies they use to develop language skills, whether in whole-class, small-group, or individual teaching situations. In other words, the children must determine the curriculum the teacher develops.

Teachers and Children: A Partnership

In the classrooms I observed at Queenston, learning occurs as the result of a positive partnership between teacher and children. An enabling and supportive teacher pays attention to individuals, offers help until they can proceed alone, encourages them to compete with themselves rather than with others, makes certain all are involved, explains and discusses classroom and school rules, listens with interest to their experiences, acknowledges their feelings, and creates an atmosphere in which it is safe for them to take risks. He or she may participate in an activity; ask open-ended questions; arouse the children's curiosity; supply new materials, resources, and information; help the children solve problems; teach new techniques; or review what has been learned. The goal is to build a curriculum that addresses both what each child wants and what each child needs. Skills are not ignored; they are taught as children need them in their quest to communicate and make meaning.

Teacher education programs are beginning to require personal awareness of and reflection on what makes a good teacher. Teachers must feel that they can effect change in the classroom (Fullan and Stiegelbauer, 1991). They must also realize that their own learning does not end when they leave university. They must be ready to explore new approaches to learning, classroom planning, effective practice, and continuous assessment of how the children are learning rather than looking at test results. Supportive administrators, colleagues who share their convictions and work with similar approaches in their own and other schools, can help build on successes and examine failures. Support groups provide opportunities for sharing concerns.

Newsletters, journals, books can inspire. Teachers should see their class-rooms as research laboratories and themselves as researchers into how children learn language. They should continually connect theory and practice, trying out theoretical concepts and adapting them according to what actually works. We cannot, then, expect all language arts teachers to work in the same way. Each teacher will develop a program that fits his or her personality, the needs of the children, the prescribed curriculum, and the dynamics of the classroom.

In the classrooms at Queenston, all types of activities come under the umbrella of language arts. The topics may be chosen from science, literature, or history. Children help decide what is to be studied and how it is to be carried out before the activity begins. They help organize the classroom, plan effective groupings, and assess what they have learned about the topic and what they have learned about language. The classroom is home to all kinds of print—from posters to books; all kinds of writing implements—from crayons to fine ink pens; and all kinds of writing paper—from large sheets of newsprint to elegant parchment. Areas are designated where children can proceed with their own interests at their own rate, spots where groups can share an activity, a place where the classroom community can meet together. Because children help determine the rules, they tend to follow them. There is organization, not chaos (Cambourne and Turbill, 1987).

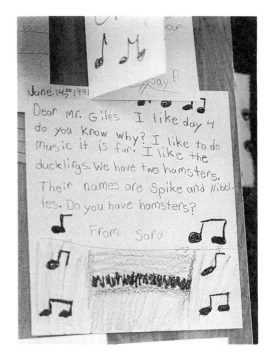

Each day includes large- and small-group activities, some planned and monitored by the teacher, such as shared reading, music, and drama games, and others selected by the children, such as painting, writing, reading, and dramatic free play. There are many opportunities for children to work on their own. The teacher supports the children's choices by helping to plan and organize, motivates by asking questions, assesses their progress by listening and noting what they are doing, and leads them in exploring new concepts by providing challenges for them to pursue.

Children grow inside and outside the classroom. Teachers learn a great deal about the experiences and backgrounds of the children through parent interviews, home visits, orientation sessions, observing the children's interactions, and simply talking to them. Teachers strive to develop self-esteem and trust in their students and to create an environment in which they feel secure and able to take risks with their learning. Because rules for classroom behaviour are developed with the students, they can be held accountable for their actions, not only by the teacher, but also by their classmates.

My Journey to Language-Based Teaching
Doris Bryce

If anyone had said to me several years ago that I would be a proponent of active learning and the holistic language approach, I would have scoffed at the idea. I had been a successful "traditional" teacher for many years, so why change a good thing? As I look back on my last few years of teaching, I realize that I have, in fact, changed—not only in my own beliefs and methods, but also in my understanding of how children learn and how to create the necessary environment for them as learners.

I have had to revise my behaviour as a teacher, learning to "let go" of my students and give them the freedom to make decisions about their learning and to try new ideas and the encouragement to express and share ideas. I've learned to give the students opportunities in both group and class discussions to ask questions, to share knowledge, to draw conclusions, and to interact with each other, not just with me. I have seen them become more independent learners and take more responsibility for their daily agenda.

The students and I have been more like partners in establishing the purpose of an inquiry, in setting goals, in discussing strategies, and in monitoring progress. Not all activities are elective, but I have learned not to focus overly on language conventions, particularly in written work.

By necessity, my assessment methods have changed. I have become more used to gathering data on language development from the full range of subjects and activities in the classroom. The students themselves join in the assessment through discussion and individual conferences.

I can see benefits to this new teaching style: learning is taking place in a more relaxed environment; the students are immersed in situations where they take charge of their learning and make necessary decisions. And we have learned together that the teacher is there to encourage, to interact, and to confer with when necessary.

Parents and Teachers: Another Partnership

Cooperation between parents and teachers in children's learning is a comparatively new field, although the research findings and examples of good practice are accumulating. The one clear direction in which such cooperation does take place is away from the traditional split between home and school and towards a genuine sharing of responsibility for children's education. We believe that this could signal a real turning point for children and their learning. . . . Whatever the future holds, we are now convinced that parents must be included as partners in their children's learning (Griffiths and Hamilton, 1984).

Parents are a child's first and most important teachers. In a language-based program, parents can be the teacher's strongest allies. Books such as *Reading Begins at Birth* by David Doake, *Family Storybook Reading* by Denny Taylor and Dorothy Strickland, and *Writing Begins at Home* by Marie Clay help explain how parents who read for their own interest, read aloud to their children, and talk with them about reading and writing promote literacy by conveying that reading is an important, and normal, activity. Schools should make determined efforts to encourage and broaden parents' reading with their children.

Parents will be allies, but only if they know and understand what goes on in the classroom. Keeping in touch with the home through interviews, conversation, reports, and co-operative projects is now common practice. Articles and books such as those just mentioned can also be made available to parents so they will be aware of the activities and goals of integrated language-based learning. Many teachers at Queenston send home a monthly newsletter to inform parents about the upcoming month's assemblies, fund raising, excursions, birthdays, and other celebrations. An accompanying calendar highlights classroom and school events. Parents have responded enthusiastically to this monthly correspondence as it helps them to plan and to discuss what goes on in school with their child. Teachers who take the time to prepare these letters feel that they form a significant bridge between school and home.

A Letter to Parents
Jan Bayes and Jim Giles

Here we are nearly into May! We're sending the newsletter out early so you can prepare for some of the exciting things happening next month. If you have any questions or concerns, please feel free to contact us at school.

Science Experiments: Many thanks for your contributions—especially to Mrs. Morgan for the wonderful equipment she provided for our experiments with bubbles and to Mrs. Nugent and Mrs. Campbell for the potting soil and numerous yogurt containers. Our sunflowers and popcorn plants are growing extremely well. Now we are experimenting with two kinds of peas.

Education Week: Education Week is from April 29 to May 3. The primary classes and choir have planned a special presentation as part of our Spring Concert on Wednesday, May 1, at 7:00 p.m. in the old gym. On Friday, May 3, we are inviting younger brothers and sisters (with their moms and dads) to join us for a "Let's All Play Together" morning.

All our parents are special, but we are extremely honoured that Mrs. Dianne Cummings has been recognized by the Peel Board of Education with an Education Week award for her phenomenal contribution over the past five years. Congratulations, Dianne!

Teaching Partner: Ms. Julie Wilkins from York University is joining us for three weeks. She has planned an exciting environmental studies unit based on the theme "The Sea." We would really appreciate any materials such as shells, nets, or lobster traps that you have at home.

Endangered Species Mural: Our wildlife mural is on display at the Food City supermarket at Deer Run. We hope you and your family will check it out!

Duck Eggs: Spring is a time of birth and growth, so we've planned to incubate and hatch duck eggs. We'll be sending out "birth" announcements.

Report Cards: We hope you have read over our draft for the report card form. Some parents have already presented questions and constructive comments to the Report Card Committee. Please feel free to submit your views—the report card is for you, and we want it to tell you what you need to know.

Physical Activity: A schoolwide "Run Across Canada" starts May 1. Each class will jog around the school's tarmac and log the distance covered. We are also planning primary swimming for June—more details to come!

Rabbits: Mickey, Minnie, and Laura will be needing a summer home and are still available for weekend visits in May and June. If you can take our class rabbits, please send a note to school with your child.

B & B: Book and Briefcase in its many forms was a HUGE success due to the commitment of the parents and the children! We hope to continue this program next year. Thank you for making it so much fun.

During May, our class will be focusing on

Language
- reading with our buddies (children from older classes)
- shared and individual reading
- communicating with our pen pals
- writing parodies of familiar fairytales

Environmental Studies
- hatching eggs
- experiments with seeds
- the sea
- a visit to the Science Centre

Math
- money: the relationship between various coins; making change
- measuring things over a metre long in non-standard and standard metric units
- operations with three digits
- investigating symmetry

Art
- paper-crafted animals
- making puppets
- making pictures with shells

Physical Education
- skipping
- soccer baseball
- Run Across Canada

As teachers, we must demonstrate to parents how children learn language and develop as language users. The staff at Queenston is very aware of the difficulties that can arise when parents do not know about the school's philosophy of language teaching. The teachers are constantly informing parents about the strategies they are using with their children and providing careful documentation of each child's growth. Parents need to understand how language is the basis of our curriculum, so that when they see their children reading silently and aloud, revising, explaining, and researching, they will know that they are learning about language as they work with it.

When parents hear children read aloud chorally, see them create a poetry anthology, or receive from them handwritten invitations to classroom events, they will recognize language learning and language growth. When parents help in the classroom, taking part as storytellers, scribes, or assistant librarians, they will see children involved in real language experiences. When parents see the teachers' plans—with long-range goals set out—and

A B & B sharing session.

observe careful records of children's progress, they will grant teachers the support they need to make a curriculum based on the children's own language development successful.

Book and Briefcase
Jim Giles and Jan Bayes

We have found "Book and Briefcase" (or B & B) is a stimulating way to take classroom activities into the home. B & B consists of a plastic briefcase containing paper, crayons, markers, a parents' journal, and a book chosen by the child from the classroom library. Each child takes home a B & B once every two weeks.

The most exciting component of B & B is the journal, which invites parents to comment on the family's experiences with B & B. The journal is addressed to the children, the teachers—and other parents. Each day, the class has a B & B sharing session to report, raise questions, and evaluate the experience.

This is the letter that introduces B & B to parents:

Dear Parents,

This is our B & B (Book and Briefcase). One child in our class will bring it home each day. It contains a book that your child has chosen and materials with which your child can write and draw. Parents are asked to read the articles about children and education in the Parents' Journal and to write their comments, observations, and questions in this journal.

Please encourage your child to take good care of the contents of our B & B and to return it to school without fail the next day so that the next student can take it home.

Writing can be long or short—plain or fancy. We just want something to share with the class the next day. If your child would like to write a "rough draft" for you to edit for spelling and so on, that's okay! We're happy with invented or guessed spelling. The idea of B & B is to have fun with it! Enjoy the book your child has selected to read or have you read to them, and enjoy writing together.

Thanks for your support for B & B.

Jim Giles
J. Bayes

Ideas: Send us stories, letters, poems, riddles, jokes, recipes, advertisements, invitations!

The following are some entries in the parents' journal.

Nov. 8
Satsuki enjoyed B & B last year.
As she can bring B & B home again this year, she is happy.
I think that B & B is good for her to practice spelling and to make stories.
I also enjoy B & B.

Nov. 13
B & B needs no introduction to me as Jenna's sister, Vicky, had it home last year. Jenna was very excited to have it home and she already had planned in her mind earlier on in the week what she was going to do, so I really didn't help her too much this time. I asked her what she thought about it and she said, "It's fun."

Nov. 21
I'm sitting here at our family table with Meaghan and Matthew, discussing the concept of "B & B." While we have always spent time talking and reading, this "forum" has been very useful in providing a project we can all participate in. Meaghan is "pretend writing" a story and colouring a Dinosaur picture. Matthew is trying to find the name, weight, and kind of food of the Dinosaur he brought home, and I'm attempting to

write coherent thoughts with punctuation. It's like the joke about walking and chewing gum at the same time—so far I'm stumbling!

I think your "B & B" idea is wonderful. I've just read the article you included, "On the Home Front," and believe it should be required reading for all parents. The point about providing "material and support" while not overwhelming your child is well taken. I hope I can remember it. Lynne (mom) is home now and we're going to read Matthew's book by the fire.

P.S. "JUST PLAY YOU SAY" should be on everyone's refrigerator!!

Over the year, we extended B & B to science (S & B), poetry (P & B), jokes (J & B), and math (M & B).

Dec. 10
Unfortunately, we don't have much to show to the class today—we got a little carried away playing the car game and with the attribute blocks. However, we did have fun and were very pleased to see how quickly Chris solved the math problems in the car game and spotted (correctly) all the differences between the blocks.

Who says the discovery method doesn't work?

Dec. 14
This time working with M & B was great. The story about Dr. DeSoto was wonderful considering Tara just lost her first tooth. Tara invented a game with the shapes. We talked about the shapes and their names. Then she traced them and played the morning away working with all the material and shapes.

Dec. 20
Here we are again around the family table! If I'm late for school today it's because I told Matthew we would figure out the "enrichment only" puzzle. Twenty minutes later we have solved it, using all triangles. I think it would be fun to see how many different ways you can solve this problem. We could have an M & B contest with parent and child or in class.

Mothers and fathers find the briefcase device opens communication with the school and gives them insight into their child's learning. And when they read the articles and other parents' entries in the journal and write in it themselves, they are modelling for their children the processes of reading for a real purpose and writing for a real audience.

Booktalk: The Classroom as a "Borning Room"
Meguido Zola

I take pleasure in leafing through children's books that, like Bill Martin Jr.'s *Knots on a Counting Rope*, serve to remind me of who I am as a teacher—what I believe, aspire to, hope for. I find affirmation of my worth as a teacher, of my potential to make a difference in the life of every child in my class in M.B. Goffstein's *An Artist:* "An artist [for which read teacher] is like God but small."

As painting a picture or writing a story is for Madeleine L'Engle "an act of creation and of incarnation," so, for me, teaching is midwifery and birthing—not only truth and beauty and learning but, above all, people. In this sense, I liken my classroom to the olden days' "borning room," a metaphor Paul Fleischman subtly explores in *The Borning Room*, in which he tells the story of several generations through the events that take place in the borning room of one house.

Teaching is also nurturing, creating conditions for growth. At the heart of my teaching are the children's needs. As Florence Parry Heide's *I Love Every People* reminds me, perhaps the single most powerful way I can begin to meet children's needs is by building their self-concept—through acceptance, through respect, and through unconditional regard. I must help children meet their needs in such a way that the children remain at all times responsible for and in charge of their growth and learning. This, for me, is the pedagogical point of John Burningham's *The Blanket*, which concludes: "Mummy looked in the washing/ And Daddy looked in the car/ But I found the blanket under my pillow and went to sleep."

To teach, I must, in Margaret Donaldson's words, "de-centre": that is, dwell in the world of the children, be present to them, and place them at the centre of the learning experience. This is the lesson for me of Daniel Pinkwater's *I Was a Second Grade Werewolf*, the story of the imaginative would-be werewolf that nobody wants to recognize. Of course, this is not easy. But when the going gets tough, as M.B. Goffstein's *School of Names* reminds me, I have to have faith in the children. And I have to trust their natural need and ability and desire to learn and to know.

Sometimes all that is needed is a little time—which is the point of Rosemary Wells's *Max's First Word*, the story of Max, "whose one word was 'Bang!'" His older sister could not teach him to say anything else. Until Max was ready . . . and the occasion, biting into his first apple, called for the perfect response: "'Yum yum, Max. Say yum yum.' 'Delicious!' said Max." And I must allow the children not only time to grow but also space. Morris Lurie's *The Story of Imelda Who Was Small* is the fable of a girl who was so tiny she slept in a shoe box. No doctor's advice helped her—not eating long foods like spaghetti, runner beans, or licorice sticks; nor even avoiding short, dumpy foods like porridge, potatoes, and pancakes. Imelda is cured only when her parents listen to the common sense of the old lady in the park: "'Buy her a bed. A proper bed. Something she can wiggle her toes in. A nice, big bed with plenty of room. That's the way to grow.'" In the metaphor of Hiawyn Oram's *In the Attic*, creating conditions for growth may be nothing more (and nothing less) than finding the right ladder for the right child at the right moment.

Easier said than done, of course. As David McKee's *Not Now, Bernard* reminds me, in the classroom it is nearly always "Not now, Bernard." For a characteristic of teaching is its immediacy and coerciveness. Arthur Miller tells us, "The word 'now' is like a bomb through the window and it ticks." For this reason, I need always to remember this about teaching: that while some things are important, others are merely urgent. And I need always to distinguish between the two.

Suggested Reading for Teachers

Baskwill, Jane. *Parents and Teachers: Partners in Learning.* Toronto: Scholastic, 1989. In this candid account, the author describes her growing concern about the lack of communication between home and school and the positive action it inspired.

Botrie, Maureen and Pat Wenger. *Teachers & Parents Together.* Markham: Pembroke Publishers, 1992. This volume is a guide to implementing parental involvement in all aspects of their children's learning.

Crafton, Linda K. *Whole Language: Getting Started. . . . Moving Forward.* Katonah, N.Y.: Richard C. Owen Publishers, 1991. The author demonstrates how whole language affects children and teachers, home and school, theory and practice, teaching and learning.

Edelsky, Carol, Bess Altwerger, and Barbara Flores. *Whole Language: What's the Difference?* Portsmouth, N.H.: Heinemann, 1991. As teachers, researchers, and teacher educators, the authors attempt to clarify the term whole language through a discussion of theoretical constructs, historical context, and relationships between whole language and writing.

Froese, Victor, ed. *Whole Language: Practice and Theory.* Toronto: Prentice-Hall Canada, 1990. This book is designed to help teachers learn how to structure, plan, and execute a whole language program.

Heald-Taylor, Gail. *The Administrator's Guide to Whole Language.* Katonah, N.Y.: Richard C. Owen Publishers, 1989. This book is for principals interested in learning more about whole language. Although the issues for teachers and administrators are the same, the approaches to these issues may differ, and this book takes these differences into account in its presentation of whole language philosophy and implementation.

Pappas, Christine C., Barbara Z. Kiefer, and Linda S. Levstik. *An Integrated Language Perspective in the Elementary School: Theory into Action.* London: Longman, 1990. This book explains integrated language theory and provides examples demonstrating how it can be translated into classroom practice. Included are eight detailed thematic units or prototypes for grades K-6.

Stephens, Diane. *Research on Whole Language: Support for a New Curriculum.* Katonah, N.H.: Richard C. Owen Publishers, 1991. This book provides an annotated bibliography of whole language resources, with discussions of the history and philosophy of whole language.

Vacca, Richard T., and Timothy V. Rasinski. *Case Studies in Whole Language.* Orlando: Harcourt Brace, 1992.

Watson, Dorothy, Carolyn Burke, and Jerome Harste. *Whole Language: Inquiring Voices.* Toronto: Scholastic, 1989. This book is the vision of all three authors for the future of whole language, from a definition for the classroom to the need for political change.

Weaver, Constance. *Understanding Whole Language: From Principles to Practice.* Toronto: Irwin Publishing, 1990. The author applies the whole language philosophy to the entire school culture, explaining that this process requires a sustained, long-term effort by all parties involved.

Wells, Gordon. *The Meaning Makers: Children Learning Language and Using Language to Learn.* Toronto: Irwin Publishing, 1986. This study follows the development of a representative sampling of children from their first words to the end of their elementary education.

Reflections

❶ Language arts teachers are all part of the network of educators who are contributing to the knowledge base and developing the rationale for approaches to language teaching and learning. Books, journal articles, and research reports support good classroom practice. Read an article on an aspect of language growth, such as emerging reading or journal writing, and discuss it with a group of teachers or student teachers. With a team of teachers, conduct a school-based inquiry on, for example, ways of assisting young readers in need of remediation. Plan a professional development day around such an inquiry, or prepare an outline for a journal article or research report on it.

❷ How can your school present its curriculum for language growth so that parents will understand the program and support the teachers? What articles and books have you read that you could make available to parents to provide background in the language development of children?

❸ Children in any classroom come from a variety of linguistic, cultural, and social backgrounds. How can the school honour each family's way of life and at the same time develop a sense of school community? What changes may be necessary in the so-called "traditional" classroom to promote multicultural awareness and respect in children?

❹ Children come to school with wide and diverse backgrounds as language users. How can schools build on these early language experiences in developing a language arts curriculum? How can "kid-watching" help teachers to build a profile of each child's language development, respecting growth and honouring potential? Observe a few children at work or play with others and note aspects of their language use that you feel are significant.

❺ What resource staff does your school provide the teacher for working with children with special needs in the regular classroom? How can you structure your program to make best use of their help in a classroom of children with different abilities and experiences? Can you design a timetable to allow for both planning for and teaching those children who special educational needs? What strategies will help you integrate them fully in the life of the classroom? How can resource staff help you develop programs for children in difficulty throughout their years in the school so that each year builds on previous experiences?

❻ A study in New York State (*The New York Times*, October 17, 1992) revealed that students labelled "learning challenged" improved amazingly when placed in specially created "enrichment" classes for "gifted students." What changes must we make in our own personal attitudes and approaches to children branded with such labels if we are to create a school environment that engages them in significant learning events?

❼ Do we always teach the way we were taught? What does your own language background bring to you as a teacher? How can you examine your own teaching methods in order to identify your biases and build on your strengths? If possible, video or audiotape a classroom session and analyze the classroom strategies used with a group of teachers. What methods can be implemented in your school to help teachers reflect on their own teaching practices?

A Language-Based Program

ORGANIZING A language-based program that implements the most effective strategies for helping children learn demands, in the first place, a flexible approach to timetabling. Large blocks of time allow children to conduct sustained investigations, both singly and with others (Harste, Short, and Burke, 1988). Teacher and children also need time for planning together (Goodman, Hood, and Goodman, 1991). Such a program requires mutual respect between teacher and children and among the children themselves. As children take on responsibility for classroom routines, they begin to direct their energy toward tasks and activities (Brownlie, Close, and Wingren, 1990). Meanwhile, "freed from the demands of managing resources, teachers are able to spend considerable periods of time with individual children, giving assistance when it is really needed and helping them to reflect on what they are doing and to see how to extend it in various directions" (Wells, 1986, p. 121). Lucy Calkins's *Living Between the Lines* (1991) describes how flexible timetabling in her approach to the language-based classroom takes advantage of every opportunity for true learning.

Mention "classroom" to most of us and we'll conjure up a memory of rows of desks with a teacher standing at the front. In some schools, the description may still apply (Goodlad, 1984), but in a language-based program, each teacher will organize the classroom according to his or her personality and the needs of the children (Johnson and Louis, 1987). Most teachers arrange a meeting area for large-group or whole-class discussions, specific work areas for group interaction, and private spaces for independent work (Schwartz and Pollishuke, 1990). They find that the physical classroom environment has a profound effect on the way children carry out their tasks. To accommodate learning needs, effective teachers rearrange classroom furniture at various times during the day.

If children are to become readers through reading real books, classroom resources must play a vital part in building an environment in which literacy is valued (Booth, Swartz, and Zola, 1987). The children will develop a sense of story as they find the teacher reading aloud and telling stories that they can add to their own literary storehouses through personal reading. The classroom book collection should include picture books for sharing with the class, anthologies for small groups, poems for shared reading, non-fiction books for projects, pattern books for beginning readers, longer storybooks for developing readers, and novels for mature readers. In addition, the school library will be an important adjunct to classroom activities, for both teacher and children.

Organizing a language-based program is a complex and difficult task. In this chapter, several teachers from Queenston Drive Public School outline aspects of their school day and the role language arts play. We can derive from their observations, and the readings and research now available, some general principles for creating a true literacy environment.

Time in the Language-Based Classroom

I am often asked how teachers find time for the student-centred teaching that a language-based program demands. The answer may lie in a reorganization of not only time but also of our own resources. Some things we expect to do need not be done at all or can be done as well or better by others—such as the students themselves. Rather than only lecturing at the front of the room, we can guide children in small groups, confer with individuals, and observe them at work. We can use preparation time for more than organizing elaborate lessons that will never run as planned; we can plan units and themes that integrate various aspects of language growth; we can share ideas with other teachers; we can have the children help organize the day so that their responsibility will free us for other duties; we can use "buddies"—children from older classes—and senior-citizen or parent volunteers to enrich and supplement the time we can spend with individuals and small groups; we can have children presenting their own research to the class as knowledgeable experts; we can take the time to read to our students, taking them to distant places and unusual times.

In the past, teachers often spent as much as an hour and a half each day (Weaver, 1990) listening to children read aloud in groups, with no real reason either for the reader to want to read or the others to listen. Rather than assessing in a vacuum that wastes the children's day, teachers can observe reading skills as the children use language to grow and to strengthen their abilities as communicators. We have to recognize what truly matters in the classroom and how we can make the time for true teaching/learning situations. Rather than covering the curriculum, we should be helping the children to uncover it (Boomer, 1982).

The important thing about organizing time is that the children should know what to expect and what is expected of them. In this sense, organization is a vital component of a successful learning environment. For example, Jane Hansen says of time for writing,

Students can plan their writing because they know on which days they will write, at what time, and how they will spend their time during writing; whether, for example, they will write first, have a small group conference, or have an all-class conference. Whenever the time to write arrives, the children either start new pieces of writing, continue on with yesterday's, or return to an even earlier draft (1987, p. 6).

Negotiating the Curriculum

Setting up a language-based classroom can be achieved only with the under-standing and co-operation of the children. A well-organized classroom cre-ates contexts in which children want to get work done. Orderly activity emerges as the children begin to feel responsible for the set of rules and structures that govern behaviour. They require careful support and guidance until they accept the ground rules and can work at ease in situations that they help determine. They need to understand that reading, writing, and talking all have a legitimate place in the context of language-based learning. It takes time for a language-based atmosphere to evolve—an atmosphere in which the children "take ownership" of their activities and see the teacher as a moderator, assistant, motivator, and co-ordinator rather than just as an authority figure.

When the teacher moves from being the disseminator of knowledge to becoming the facilitator of the learning process, teachers and students move into partnership and share the responsibility for selecting and organizing tasks. The daily program can allow various types of learning to go on simultaneously so that teachers can meet individual needs. A range of instructional strategies, resources, teaching styles, and activities will accommodate the interests, abilities, and backgrounds of both the teacher and children and will provide opportunities for children to work alone, in flexible groups, and as a whole class. In short, choice should be an integral part of the language arts program.

Choice in Learning
Paul Shaw

When I came to Queenston, I felt our first task was to know about our students. I sat down with the teachers and I said, "Tell me about your children, tell me about their needs, tell me about what we could do that would help them to really make a difference." And the teachers responded with ideas. I know that successful schools are focused on their students and have come to understand what's really important for them. In our professional growth sessions, we decided there were things we needed to know. We began to gather data.

Literate people read and write voluntarily, out of choice. We chose a day and asked each teacher to keep a classroom list and to record every time any given child or group of children had an opportunity to choose something to do with their curriculum. For example, if the child got to select a book during reading time, that was a choice; if the child chose a topic to write about, that was a choice; if the child chose some aspect to explore in science, we recorded that.

We then took our lists and put them in order from kindergarten to grade eight and posted them all across the staff room. We were interested not in what one class did as opposed to another but in the range and opportunity for choices across each age group. We discovered that as the children got older, their opportunities to choose diminished. The children who had the most choice were in kindergarten. Those with the least were in grade eight.

That made us think about our image of the learner. Obviously our children were not self-directed. That was quite a revelation. It sparked all kinds of discussion and provoked a lot of reading and a lot of talk, in particular with respect to the older students. Out of that experience grew a discussion paper about the grades seven and eight students, summarizing the data that we had collected and including a series of recommendations. Some of the staff took this extremely well because they were very excited about the possibilities for change. Some were tentative, but willing to look at the report. A very few staff members found this inquiry culture overwhelming.

We decided to focus on choice and the self-directed learner through the vehicle of literacy. We wanted students to become more independent, more in control, and to make better choices. Out of that came a range of decisions: about how we build a timetable; what our priorities are; how we spend our money; what we want to communicate to parents. We established a personal reading time for every child during the school day, and we worked with the expectation that each teacher would share literature with every child at least twice a day. We decided each child would have a writing folder.

Today at Queenston, teachers are beginning to inherit children who've had three years of choosing their own literature, responding to books, choosing their writing topics, sharing and celebrating the books. These are a very different kind of student: they are comfortable making choices; they are used to buying in; they would be very concerned—and would voice their concern—if they didn't have some control and some ownership over their learning.

Setting up a Classroom
Brian Crawford

I teach a family grouping of junior grade children. Looking back at my journal entries for the past year, I can see how important "choice" is for me. The day before school started, most of my comments revolved around how much influence I would have in setting up the classroom:

I'm trying to strike a balance for the creation of our classroom. Will I have too much influence? Will the fact that I am one of two adults (myself and a student teacher) in the classroom result in an assumption by the children about who controls what happens?

When the children entered class in September, they found a room piled with furniture and boxes. It could be someone's definition of chaos. Through brainstorming, reflection, discussion, and organization of ideas, we came up with a plan for our classroom. This process occurred individually, in small groups, and with the large group. This was our early encounter with choice. That night, I wrote in my journal:

The organization of the room went better than I had anticipated. In the brainstorming sessions, the children gave excellent ideas of what we needed. They have a very good awareness of what they require in a classroom. When they worked, they were in focus. They were able to discuss the merits of why things should be placed where they were. They challenged each other. They were able to take the information from the six groups and use it to come up with a class blueprint.

This was only the beginning. As I indicated earlier, I feel choice is important. I demanded choice as a child. My parents have filled in the gaps of my memories and have reminded me of how they negotiated with me as I explained why I was going to do what I had chosen. In a way, I was negotiating my curriculum—one of the main thrusts of choice in the classroom. I think of the children discussing their interests with me and how they were going to carry out these journeys. More often than not, their choices coincided with provincial and board "curriculum." Once they decided on an area of exploration, my main role was to provide possible strategies to help them examine it as fully as possible. The most significant result is that the children took on more and more responsibility for their learning.

Learners having choices usually results in their setting goals that are important for them and in more of the learning being meaningful to them. The very concept of choice inspired some children to write about it.

Choices Are Important
Sharon , age 9

Choices are very important to me. Mr. Crawford was the first teacher to give me a lot of choices. We get a choice of what we want to study in Social Science, we get choices on who our partners are going to be, we get choices about almost everything!

In the beginning of the school year, Mr. Crawford let us design our own room. . . . Everyone agreed it was our room, not Mr. Crawford's. We all share it. I think if I didn't get choices, I wouldn't participate in a lot of things. Kids should have choices because if they don't then they might not be interested in what the teacher want them to do but they might be more interested in what they like.

There are choices to make in life everyday: from the least important, such as what to have for lunch, to the most important, such as refusing to take drugs. Sometimes choices are hard to make because things could be tempting. For example, stealing a piece of candy from a store. When you have difficulty making choices you have to think of the consequences and discuss it with other people. If you make the wrong choice then you have to learn to live with it and never make the same mistake again.

A Place Where You Get to Choose
Sarah, age 8

I spend most of my days in a classroom. That classroom is 109, a place where you get to choose. My year started with choosing about our room and what we need. We set up the room well with everything we needed. And the room became ours. We moved into reading and writing, slowly at first, but I think choosing your book and story helped the new people. It certainly helped me when I was new. I worked hard to put it on paper. Math, Social Science and art revolve around choice. Choosing how to explain yourself, or which way to do something.

As our year goes by we become ourselves when there is no teacher making you live the life they want and not your own. Not all classes have choice, but I'm glad mine does.

Timetabling Language-Based Events

The teachers at Queenston organize the language arts program in a number of ways, but each approach encompasses the common elements of shared community time, group activities, and individual assignments.

Community Time (Whole-Class Activities)

Each day, the whole class gathers together. This shared time builds a community. It is often used to organize—to set the theme for the week, to build a web of ideas for future exploration, or to establish the focus for the day. Sometimes it is devoted to the most traditional of classroom activities: instruction, explanation, and direction.

Brian Crawford and Jan Bayes and Jim Giles prepare letters on large sheets of chart paper to greet the children in their primary and junior family groupings at the start of each day. These may reflect something that happened in the class the day before, give an overview of the coming day's timetable, or congratulate certain children on specific accomplishments. The letters often prompt discussion during the morning class meetings that follow the opening exercises. If the children have something to add, they are encouraged to continue the message. The classes become a real audience for the teacher's writing, and the letters serve as models for the children's journal entries.

Community time is a perfect setting for reading aloud. The teacher may read a chapter from a novel or one of a series of stories in a set, introduce new books or excerpts, talk about authors or illustrators, or relate the books to specific curriculum topics. A story may introduce a theme, go beyond it, or reflect upon it as it is completed. All the time, the teacher is modelling the satisfaction to be gained from a good book.

The class can join in shared oral reading, using "big books" or stories, poems, and songs written on chart paper. They may watch relevant films and videos or respond to an invited speaker. They may use a story to set the stage for discussion, drama, or other activities.

Small-Group Activities

Children at Queenston spend a large part of their day working in groups, but these groups are continually changing. Sometimes, they are of the children's

Today is Monday, June 24, 1991
Good morning How was your weekend? Do you have any news you would like to share with the class? Today we have an awards ceremony in the gym. We will also be making "thank-you" cards for Cora our cleaning lady. Julie Got a Haircut It Looks Great Andrea. W. Got scratch scratch and Andrea.w went to her mom's friends house and the cat Scratched her.

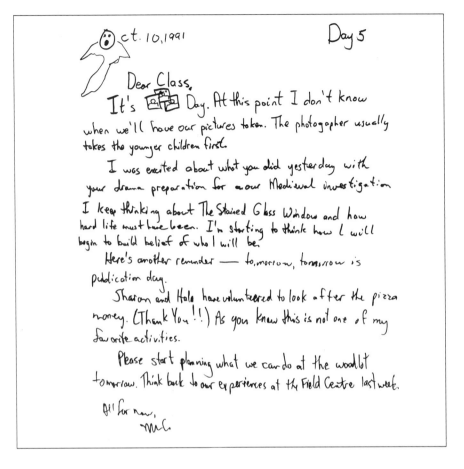

Oct. 10, 1991   Day 5

Dear Class,
It's 📷 Day. At this point I don't know when we'll have our pictures taken. The photographer usually takes the younger children first.

I was excited about what you did yesterday with your drama preparation for our Medieval investigation. I keep thinking about The Stained Glass Window and how hard life must have been. I'm starting to think how I will begin to build belief of who I will be.

Here's another reminder — tomorrow, tomorrow is publication day.

Sharon and Hala have volunteered to look after the pizza money. (Thank You!!) As you know this is not one of my favorite activities.

Please start planning what we can do at the woodlot tomorrow. Think back to our experiences at the Field Centre last week.

All for now,
MrC.

own choosing, based on friendship or common interests. The teacher may also assign children to groups to ensure a range of skills and approaches to learning. In such heterogeneous groups, those with more developed skills guide and instruct others directly or by example, thus consolidating their own understanding. Occasionally, the teacher creates flexible and temporary homogeneous groups in order to teach a particular skill or concept.

Groups vary in size depending on the task. Pairs may read a story, making meaning together from the narrative and pictures, discussing new concepts, and helping each other with the "difficult" words. Groups of four to six may create a poster, build a model, or take part in dramatic play. Larger groups may prepare a shared reading selection or join in discussion led by the teacher.

Group work can grow from the whole-class preparation time, from pre-established activities at learning centres that children choose or to which they are assigned, or from projects they initiate themselves. These activities may continue for several days. Group time allows the teacher to conduct conferences—leading a discussion about the books one group has been reading, or helping another establish the direction that a piece of writing might take.

Working in co-operative groups helps develop the students' problem-solving and decision-making strategies. The children gain respect for each other and learn to appreciate different points of view. Group time also allows the teacher to conduct "mini-lessons" only with the children who need the instruction.

Individual Assignments

Teachers in this school expect all children to work on some tasks individually, but it is hard to find a classroom where every child is working alone. When children want advice about their work, they are just as likely to turn to a classmate for help as to the teacher. And some children will be involved in group activities while others are working independently.

One daily timetabled event in every classroom is independent silent reading, when the children read books of their own choosing. This may last from five to thirty minutes, depending on the maturity, interest, and involvement of the children. The emphasis is on reading whole books, not just excerpts, though children freely discard material they find too difficult, too easy, or simply boring. The teachers use this period to confer with individual children, for some need guidance in selecting books that they can and want to read. Others need to be encouraged to use the strategies that effective readers use to read for meaning, rather than simply decoding individual words.

Most teachers expect children to record in reading journals the books they read. This often leads to personal writing as the children are encouraged to give their impressions of what they have read. Younger children often draw pictures in their journals and then write or dictate a caption. Other response activities may include role playing, art, or storytelling. Reading one story may lead some children to undertake projects investigating other stories on similar themes or other books by the same author. And students who find they have enjoyed similar books will share their ideas and questions and recommend further reading to one another.

Learning centres, or work stations, enable the teacher to address the needs, interests, and learning styles of individual children. The opportunity for choice that centre activities provide helps the children assume responsibility for their own learning. The teacher also assigns tasks at various centres to children who need to develop or strengthen particular skills. Children choose (or are directed to) a particular work station where they can explore an overall classroom theme through various media such as paints or modelling clay; work on special tasks, such as with manipulative blocks; conduct a science experiment by following an assignment card; dramatize the story they have heard that day at the dress-up centre; or work with the teacher on a particular skill. Teachers help children balance their choices of centre activities, challenge them to risk new experiences, or encourage them to contribute to a collaborative activity.

Possible learning centres include

- a reading centre (picture books, novels, anthologies, child-authored books, magazines, comics)
- a listening centre (tapes of stories and songs for reading along with, tapes of instructions to follow, tapes made by the children)
- a writing centre (plain and lined paper, pencils, crayons, markers, erasers, stapler, paper clips, book covers, alphabet cards or books, word banks, word lists, dictionaries)
- a viewing centre (films, filmstrips, magazines, comics, picture books)
- an art centre (paints, modelling clay, paper, scissors, glue, fabric, yarn, needles, thread, crayons, markers, chalk)
- a play or games centre (dress-up materials, props, puppets and puppet stage, construction toys such as wooden blocks or Lego, stuffed animals, dolls, model cars, trucks, machines)

Sharing Time (Whole Class or Large Group)

In the classrooms that I visited at Queenston, the community atmosphere is evident when children share the results of their activities and projects. The time allocated for reporting research findings or responses to literature to the class provides an occasion for celebrating what the children have accomplished, for reflecting on what has been done, and for considering what direction to take now. The act of presenting information to a genuine audience poses a number of questions for the children to consider: What is the purpose in presenting this material? What will be interesting, important, and relevant to those receiving it? What form should the presentation take (a diagram, a note, an illustrated talk, a written report)? The community's store of common knowledge and understanding grows as other children respond to presentations with questions, comments, and discussion, revealing their insights and feelings in a safe and focused atmosphere. The sense of community these teachers build in their classrooms fosters collaboration and co-operation.

A Primary Family Grouping
Jan Bayes and Jim Giles

The primary family grouping at Queenston is home to 42 children in grades one, two, and three—and to two teachers. Our aim is to maintain a stable and consistent environment in which a child may stay for up to three years. As teachers, we come to know the individual children and their needs, abilities, and interests really well. As ours is a "child-centred" program, we've tried to keep our double classroom as "open" as possible, making it colourful, inviting, and warm. The children work at tables instead of desks.

The children value books and their reading time. We have a large collection on display, including picture books, chapter books, non-fiction books, and even joke books. A calendar above the couch in the reading area lists the books we will read aloud each day.

Writing is also important. The students have displayed their versions of *The Three Little Pigs* and *The Enormous Chocolate Pudding* on the walls outside the classroom. Their individual language bags hold their writing folders, along with their crayons, pencils, and other implements. Students often use the art or other "hands-on" centres to make pictures or models based on stories and display their representations on a table near the bookshelf. Students were anxious to share their creations with a recent visitor: a bug box made from scrap boxes, puppets from paper rolls, a spacecraft from Lego, and an airplane made at the woodworking centre.

We schedule activity time in large blocks over the week. Students choose activities from among the sand, water, computer, drama, painting, listening, science, fix-it, and woodworking centres. We draw up group and individual contracts for activities to ensure that every child fulfils the prescribed curriculum. Some days, then, students choose their own activities while other days, we may select activities for them to extend their classroom experiences and promote risk taking. Books, paper, pencils, scissors, and hands-on and audio-visual learning resources are within easy reach. Each child is assigned a centre to keep in order. Thus we give the children responsibility not only for their own learning but also for the care and upkeep of the room.

Our aim is to motivate our students to become "independent" learners, but that certainly doesn't mean we leave them alone! During activity and language time, we are both moving about the room, encouraging one group of children, sharing the discoveries of another, reflecting our interest and respect for each individual child. The children help us assess their learning by keeping careful records indicating

Weekly Contract for - Name: Belinda
- week of:

Monday	Tuesday	Wednesday	Thursday	Friday
activity:	activity:	activity: Sinc	activity: rabbits	activity: train set

Monday — activity: puppets

I went
to Puppits
I was
a coml
with two
hums we
were
abot to
do a play
But it
vas to
hard

Wednesday — activity: Sinc

I went
to Sinc
we yosd
watr
and tide
It Into
plotid
watr
and then
we startid
to wundr
whot wood
hapin

Thursday — activity: rabbits

I went
to rabbits
I tryde
to get
mice ut
But He
did not
I suew
him woshi
ng his
face
and his
fet

Friday — activity: train set

I went
to train
set @ I
had fun
I wrkt
ubn —
I went
thar
for an
awre
I t flet
like
It

tasks they have completed in their individual "record books" that we can refer to along with work samples, observational checklists, and our own notes on day-to-day progress.

We have developed classroom routines and expectations with the children so that they have a sense of ownership and responsibility. Sometimes we need to demonstrate and discuss problem-solving strategies, especially when resolving peer conflicts. But the sharing and discussion of work each day promotes co-operative learning. The family grouping allows children to learn from each other, with the older students being models for the younger ones. Thus every child is challenged yet able to experience success. We want our children to develop life-long learning skills so that they can call upon these strategies throughout their lives. The positive reinforcement we offer when children accomplish tasks leads to a good feeling about school and learning. We believe the family grouping provides a worthwhile experience for these children.

Language Growth across the Curriculum

We read to find the story, not just the facts; we talk and write to "make sense" of the story, not just to report those facts. Children use language to process their experience and give meaning to it all day, not just during a period labelled "language arts." They need to practise and develop language competencies particular to each area of the curriculum. When children choose a topic for investigation with their teacher, exploratory talk and writing allow them to recall and share what they already know and to generate questions they would like answered. This gives them a personal investment in their learning and a language base from which to proceed to organize information and solve problems. It also provides guidelines for the teacher in planning appropriate reading, writing, drama, art, and historical, mathematical, or scientific research. True learning has occurred when the children can express concepts and describe experiences in any curriculum area in their own words (Graves, 1991).

Discovery Boxes
Brian Crawford

My grade three-to-five class used "discovery boxes" in a two-week investigative science unit that provided opportunities for both inquiry and interaction.

To begin, I held a discussion, asking the children to consider things that they wondered about in the scientific world: how something works, how something was invented, what was the effect of one substance on another. Once they had decided on their personal topics of interest, they prepared lists of questions that aroused their curiosity, narrowing down to focus on a single question for investigation. They then gathered the necessary materials, conducted an experiment, and reported their conclusions.

When the research had been done, all the necessary apparatus and instructions on how to carry out the experiment were placed in a shoe box. The child wrote the question on the lid of the box. Each child then exchanged boxes with a partner, who conducted the experiment by following the instructions, thus "discovering" the answer to the scientific question.

As the children gathered their equipment, collected data, and shared in each other's work, the classroom became like a science lab. As in any good laboratory, the planning, speculation, and revision led to a continuous exchange of information and ideas. Greg wanted to discover whether pulling an elastic band farther makes an object go

farther. David wanted to discover how much two toy boats of different shapes can hold before they sink. Hala wanted to find out how many seconds it takes for marbles of different sizes to go down a ramp. Michael wanted to discover if pulleys really make it easier to lift a heavy load. Stephanie examined the relationship between weight and air pressure.

The children talked as they planned their experiments, questioned one another about procedures, described their work, and reported their findings. Having them write the instructions caused more talk as they helped one another clarify the various steps required to do the experiment. Because the second phase invited other children to work alone without the assistance of the researchers, the instructions had to be very clear. After the individual work, there was more discussion as researcher and experimenter shared their discoveries.

In the following conversation, two girls discuss an experiment that involved smelling different substances.

Sara: I'm not sure why you wanted to do this experiment.

Sharon: I began to think about the way things smell. Then I wanted to find out if people could guess what different smells were. Because I knew that I was going to do the experiment with nearly everybody in the class, I decided to compare the difference between the sense of smell of boys and girls.

Sara: Why did you want me to be blindfolded?

Sharon: I didn't want anyone to see the jars I had.

Sara: I read somewhere that if you take away one sense from somebody, then their other senses become stronger. Like a blind person can hear better. I think that by being blindfolded I was able to smell better.

Sharon: How many of the smells did you guess correctly?

Sara: I wasn't sure about the cinnamon.

Sharon: Most kids had trouble with that one.

Sara: Do you really think it makes a difference whether you're a boy or a girl?

Sharon: I don't want to be sexist, but I think that most of the girls did better on the survey.

Developing a Thematic Unit

Themes can be useful tools for organizing the classroom program. Relating activities and experiences within a given period of time to an overarching theme helps children make connections and see relationships not only among the events in the classroom but also to the experiences in their lives. The essence of good planning is to incorporate the children's particular interests and enthusiasms. Themes that capture their imaginations may continue over many weeks, while others may not receive the same response. Sensitive teachers will know when to move on. Themes are pegs on which to hang learning experiences, not inflexible devices for delivering the curriculum.

Relevant books—poetry, fiction, non-fiction—can expand children's horizons and present opportunities for sharing discoveries with those of different abilities and interests. A challenging theme can bring together diverse books into a frame that develops connections. As children explore perceptions in various books, they can begin to compare and contrast facets of the theme, see patterns between content and style of presentation, and draw conclusions about their own taste and preferences.

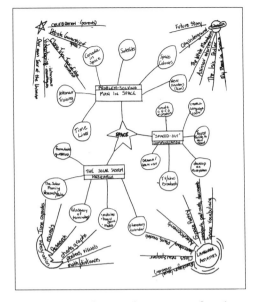

A theme integrates aspects of the work and provides reasons for sharing learning. Teacher and students can develop an extended unit of study that starts from interests the children already have. We can help children create a list of possible topics that they can explore within the theme through strategies such as brainstorming to build a "learning web." As ideas are related to the theme and are added to the web, they will open up new areas of interest, pose questions that inspire new learning, direct children to new resources, suggest activities for whole-class, small-group, and individual exploration, and provide both informal and formal ways for the children to present their findings to each other. Children can volunteer to explore ideas that challenge and interest them. Of course, as they work, new questions will arise, and they will redirect their efforts.

The demonstrations that follow show how science can be the basis of an integrated thematic unit at two levels of development. First, Jan Bayes and Jim Giles tell us about one part of their class's study of a unit on flight. Next, Lois Roy describes how her grades five-and-six class were so fascinated by their study of space that they continued to work on it for three months.

Owl Study
Jan Bayes and Jim Giles

During January, our grades one-to-three family grouping explored the theme of flight in a science unit. We visited the Mountsberg Wildlife Sanctuary to take an "Owl Prowl." Birds are housed at the sanctuary because they have been injured or because they were "imprinted" on

We Want To The owl prowl in theiTr Time

we lerned aBut the bored owl. it is gray and Has Bick ies. won They eat Ther pray They SPit out a pﬁit. won They FiD Ther proy They Put Ther wing ovr it, They have one ear HiYr And one ear lowr becos if Things go uP in The orey They Can Her Them And if Things go on the grond

The coh Her Them. They Coh't move Ther ies BuT They Can Move Ther Nacks ezilee. if Your NoT wring a Spocul glove Theyl cuT ih to Your arm.

> *We went to the owl prowl in the wintertime. We learned about the barred owl. It is grey and has big eyes. When they eat their prey they spit out a pellet. When they find their prey they put their wing over it. They have one ear higher and one ear lower because if things go up in the air they can hear them and if things go on the ground they can hear them. They can't move their eyes but they can move their necks easily. If you're not wearing a special glove they'll cut into your arm.*

humans as fledglings and never learned to forage for themselves. The children watched a puppet play and slide show that demonstrated the concept of the food chain and the owl's special adaptations as a bird of prey. They next met a great horned owl named Chomper. The children also toured the sanctuary in a horse-drawn sleigh to visit other birds of prey, a snowy owl, a barred owl, and even a bald eagle.

The excursion proved significant to the children and it sparked further discussion back in the classroom. Many children marked the occasion through art, writing, or reading. Jordan and Tara created scenes of owls at the painting and drawing centres. Colin used modelling clay and cardboard to make a diorama showing a habitat for a bald eagle and a snowy owl. Spurred by Colin's idea, Ian created out of modelling clay a number of owls and other bird figures that he proudly displayed on the classroom tree.

Besides recording their impressions of the trip in their journals, many children chose to write stories about Chomper with such titles as *Mr. Owl Went to Hoot, Owl Prowl,* and *Tyler and the Owls.* Kelsey, a grade one student, found an article on the snowy owl in *Owl* magazine and decided to use the pictures and information to create her own book about owls. A stream of children went to the library to gather reference books on owls and returned to record what they learned on a classroom chart. Sara brought in *Owls of the World,* a book that she had found in the public library, and others began to look for information there and in their homes.

Ashley's father, who works on a farm, brought owl pellets into the classroom, and Ashley and her friends used toothpicks to dissect them under the magnifying glass at the science centre. They used the bones they found in the pellets to demonstrate to the rest of the class what animal the owl had eaten. Steven also built a bird stand and feeder at the science centre after he discovered a reference book about how to take care of birds. When they saw Steven's work, others wanted to create bird feeders, and so the class took pine-cones, rolled them in peanut butter and bird seed, and hung them in the woodlot a ten-minute walk from the school.

The study of owls was complemented with the sharing of poems and picture books: Jane Yolen's *Owl Moon,* Eve Bunting's *The Man Who Called Down Owls,* and Tejima's *Owl Lake.* The children also listened to us read aloud their first novel of the year, *Owls in the Family* by Farley Mowat.

A Tour of Space
Lois Roy

On a typical morning during our exploration of space, the students were preparing for parents the presentation that would culminate their study; notebooks, booklets, diaries, logs, charts, diagrams, itineraries, space postcards, pictures, and profiles adorned every nook and cranny of the classroom. Groups of students were deep in conversation; one was compiling and categorizing pictures for a slide presentation on

"Man in Space"; a lively foursome outfitted in shirt aprons was painting a mural of the solar system; two students, in charge of narrating their group's demonstration, were practising on tape and critiquing their delivery. Meanwhile, I was consulting with the group who was planning the logistics of the parents' open house.

The classroom had been transformed into a space ship, and the students had become space colonists or explorers. I had let the teacher-librarian, Sue Checkeris, know about the unit, and she had helped the students gather books, films, and other resources. They had used local libraries and galleries to obtain further materials and information. The class library was filled with resources relating to the theme, both fiction and non-fiction, and I was grateful I was not running it—the student "librarian-in-charge" was busily checking books in and out and keeping track of each item's whereabouts more effectively than I ever could have. At a research centre, students were combing through *National Geographic, Owl, Chickadee, Time,* and *Maclean's* for historical information on the space shuttle and the Kennedy Space Center. Some students were using theme-based picture books for story-telling and drama.

Students moved from one group to another sharing information, asking questions, or exchanging books. Over the course of the theme, the groups had developed a smoothly operating structure. This morning, one recorder was consulting her group's members for a progress report. She gently chided one member for forgetting his file at home and reminded him of the very real deadline created by the date for the open house.

I find theme-based learning integrates language arts with science, social studies, mathematics, and the arts. The students and I choose topics from various areas of the grades five and six curriculum—Japan, Egypt, Flight, Space, The Sea, and Birds. A thematic unit may last from one month to four, depending on the interest and commitment of the students. Working on a theme offers them the opportunity to branch out in directions of their own choosing. To begin each unit, we create a web to discover where the unit may lead us.

A theme the students have chosen provides a stimulating and dynamic atmosphere for focusing learning in language and communication, as well as in the subject of the theme. To participate, students need not only to read, write, listen, and speak, but also to think, negotiate, plan, organize, evaluate, and socialize. They work in large and small groups to research, solve problems, keep records, and present their learning.

The highlight of each theme is the evening when they share their

knowledge with their parents, a celebration of learning totally planned and executed by the students. About 75 parents, grandparents, and friends enjoyed the recent "Tour of Space" with their young space explorers.

Creating a Literacy Environment

If we had looked inside the desks in an elementary school classroom thirty years ago, we would probably have found in each the same controlled-vocabulary basal reader, the same few textbooks designed solely to fulfil curriculum requirements—and little else to read. Today's classrooms are filled with books of all types—picture books, easy-to-read stories, folk tales, novels, anthologies, science books, histories, mathematical puzzles, games, pop-up books, poetry collections. We see teachers telling stories to their classes, letting them absorb story patterns, literary structures, the sounds of language, the power of narrative.

What draws children to print is the sense of story (Hardy, 1977). Some stories take children where they have never been, while others offer them reflections of their own worlds—their families, their society, their culture. Recent children's books of quality often reflect themes and issues from multicultural settings in today's urban communities, ensuring that children from different backgrounds can find themselves in stories in their classrooms.

Young children come to print ready to read, with a background of story experiences that they can apply to text. Children who can read on their own continue to build their story repertoires, listening to teachers interpret books that stretch their minds, building vocabulary and storing expressions for future use. They meet text face to face in their individual reading, in discussion with children who have read the same selection, in group reading of poster-sized "big books" and wall charts, in sharing information from books with their peers, in using reference materials to check facts.

Teachers strive to select the best books for their students' classroom libraries and for their own personal collections. They look for materials that face up to contemporary social issues and that draw children to authors and books beyond the popular bestsellers. Classrooms are full of resources for readers beginning to feel success, mature readers, interest groups, individuals with particular concerns, gifted students needing enrichment, and children beginning to work in English. The presence of books found in the wider world rather than just textbooks found only in classrooms helps children to see what they read in school as "real" and reading as a lifelong activity.

Selecting Books for the Classroom

Some children meet books in their homes from babyhood, and for them, sharing books with loving adults is a normal experience. Others meet books for the first time in school, and if they are to become lifelong readers, these students in particular need to read more than school texts.

The classroom collection of books tries to offer each child a satisfactory reading experience. Other places will provide a wider selection—the school library, public libraries, the home bookshelf—but a nucleus of books chosen with the varying backgrounds and stages of development of the particular children in mind is central to a classroom reading program. Children recommend to each other titles they enjoy, discuss their personal reading with others, return to favourite titles and authors. As sharing responses is a daily occurrence, children begin to recognize many of the books and authors in the core collection. Being familiar with the classroom library, the teacher can recommend books and discuss them with the children. The collection can be viewed as the "class text," and its importance and relevance in learning to read can be discussed with parents.

There are tens of thousands of books for children today. The challenge is to choose wisely. What should our selection criteria be? Should the teacher have read each selection? Should we choose children's favourites, critics' favourites, or our own? How can we represent positive role models, children with special needs, the multicultural diversity of our communities? How can we balance classics from the past with modern selections? The answer to most of these questions is that children need to experience all types of books: classic and brand new, predictable and challenging, hardcovered and soft-covered, poetry and prose, fiction and non-fiction, popular and little known, short stories and novels, single works and series, picture books, anthologies, books for boys and books for girls, folk tales from their own and other cultures, books by award-winning authors and books by classmates, books related to the curriculum and books irrelevant to it, magazines, talking books, films of books, books about books.

A Classroom Library
Jim Giles

I consider my classroom library an extension of the school library and the public library and draw from these two valuable sources regularly. At the same time, I try to ensure that my classroom library does not undermine the school library or divert funds from the library budget.

Sue Checkeris, our school librarian, has been my "partner in action." I have arranged with her to take out a monthly selection of books; I advise her of the themes I will be covering in class and suggest specific books I would like to have in the classroom. Often, I choose books I might want to use for drama, read aloud in class, or present to my class in a book talk. I also ask for a number of books by the class's "author of the month" so that students can read and compare the works of a single author. Sometimes I include books I feel will be of particular interest to individual students. During our regular visits to the school library, I encourage my students to recommend books that they would like to have in our classroom library. The books I sign out usually remain in the classroom unless a student seeks special permission to take one home. This keeps me in good standing with the school librarian so that she will let me sign out another 40 books next month.

We use the public library in much the same way as the school's—to extend and enrich the classroom library. We set set aside a special area for public library books and mark them with masking tape for ease of identification. I arrange a class trip to the local public library each term so that the students will become familiar with it and the books and resources available there.

We also have a permanent book collection in the classroom. Here the first hurdle, as always, is obtaining funding. At Queenston, we have found three sources: the school, the students, and the parents. The principal, Paul Shaw has allocated funds for classroom libraries from the school budget or other administrative sources. We have established a book fund to which students can contribute. We have presented a classroom library proposal to the parent-teacher association and found that parents are eager and willing to help raise funds for something of such benefit to their children.

For the permanent collection, I asked the students to select the books. I allotted each child a small amount of money, and we arranged a visit to a children's bookstore. There the students each chose one or two books that they thought we needed. My job was to screen the selections and encourage them to find books that the whole class would enjoy. Most students were eager to share the books they chose with their classmates. We left the bookstore with more than 30 paperbacks at various reading levels.

Visiting a reputable bookstore gave the children a large variety of high-quality books to choose from. If the trip had been impossible, I might have tried one of the "book kits" offered by various bookstores. These contain a range of books from various publishers and cover the range of reading levels in primary and junior grades. They are good starters, making it easy for teachers to acquire a variety of books. Many teachers also encourage reading and increase their classroom library at the same time by registering the class in a book club. Students can buy books from a monthly list, and teachers select free books based on a percentage of the students' total purchases. Another place to acquire books is at teachers' conferences and workshops, where publishers stage exhibits and sell books suitable for classroom libraries.

We could have built our library from second-hand books or discards, but we wanted books that are interesting, attractive, and current, books that the children would use rather than outdated ones in poor condition and with no appeal. Books are consumable products and eventually have to be replaced. I try to renew the classroom library to some extent each year.

I feel books should be the focus of a classroom. They should be visible, accessible, and properly stored and protected. Tiered book racks are ideal for displaying and storing classroom books. Fold-up book racks display books nicely and use little space, but small paperbacks often slip through the elastic bands meant to hold them in place. Boxes are good for storing books but tend to make them invisible. Younger children in particular will not use books they cannot readily see and have to dig for. An unused chalkboard ledge or a table is an ideal location for short-term book displays. Our classroom library is a carpeted, quiet area that invites students to make use of the books; cushions and stuffed animals add a welcoming note. Stories that the students write and "publish" are part of the library, too, giving them a genuine reason to write.

Setting up the classroom library has been challenging and rewarding for all of us. The time and effort put into it communicate to the students how I feel about reading and books. Some students have followed our example and set up their own libraries at home. The classroom library invites students to enjoy books now while sowing the seeds for a lifetime interest and joy in reading.

Because the students feel genuine "ownership" of the books they helped to purchase, they are motivated to use and maintain their classroom library. I ask my class to care for the library as though it were a living creature. Students know to report damaged books immediately so we can repair them properly to prevent further damage. They are proud of their library: they keep it clean; they treat it with respect; and in turn, it serves them well.

The Significance of Poetry

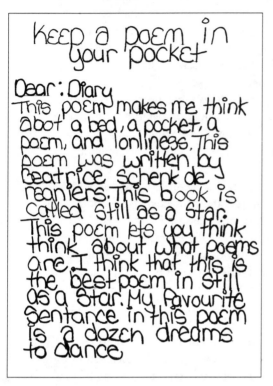

Keep a poem in
your pocket

Dear: Diary
This poem makes me think
abot a bed, a pocket, a
poem, and lonliness. This
poem was written by
Beatrice Schenk de
reaniers. This book is
called Still as a Star.
This poem lets you think
think about what poems
are. I think that this is
the best poem in Still
as a Star. My favourite
sentance in this poem
is a dozen dreams
to dance.

Poetry is a special part of childhood. Children grow through poetry as they do through painting, drama, movement, and games, because artistic experiences are both cognitive and emotional. As teachers, we must trust the arts and the educational power that lies within them. We don't need to use poetry simply to introduce a topic on this month's curriculum, to set a desired mood, or to round off a theme—although it can do all of this. A poem is a work of art and should be allowed to stand on its own merit.

A poem is a concentrated teaching package, its effect far-reaching and long-lasting. It demonstrates language in unique patterns and forms, triggering new meanings and vivid perceptions. It tells a story in a special, compact fashion, intertwining plot, emotion, and images. It stays in children's minds to be remembered.

Poetry also provides stimulating and satisfying experiences with oral language. Children can read poems chorally—the rhythm and rhyme attracting readers of different abilities, even non-readers. The language patterns first learned by ear will later be understood in print. Poems demonstrate the musicality and lyricism of language, as it twists and turns tongues, lips, and vocal cords around unfamiliar yet intriguing language patterns. Readers look closely, think carefully, and make different meanings with each reading.

Most poems demands response. Children grope toward their own private meanings and share communal meanings. Poetry opens up histories and cultures different from their own and lets them see through different eyes and feel with different sensitivities. It touches the spirit and draws them into perceptions that transcend day-to-day life.

A rich store of poetry encourages children to manipulate words and ideas in their own writing, exploring patterns of language and reworking thoughts in potent ways. It bequeaths a private and personal strength to be called on in lonely or difficult times.

A Poem a Day
Larry Swartz

I read Felice Holman's "Who Am I?" from *Voices in the Wind* (Booth, 1990) to my grade five students on the first day of school to begin our journey into poetry together. I chose it not only for its theme of curiosity but because for me, the classroom, like life, is the whole being greater than the sum of its parts. We have met two or three hundred poems on our journey since then.

The students were greeted with a display of 30 to 40 poetry anthologies assembled from the permanent classroom collection, the school library, and my own books. After sharing Felice Holman's poem, I asked each student to select an anthology to read during our first silent reading session. I told them that we weren't going to "do" anything with the poems, but I invited them to discover what they might have in common and perhaps consider which their favourite might be as they browsed through the anthology.

I explained to the students that one of my goals was to feature "poems of the day" in the classroom so they would meet a variety of forms, a range of poets, and a banquet of words through the year. Each day we would read a poem written out on chart paper. I agreed to choose the poems for the month of September. For the rest of the year, the choices would be their responsibility. The next month, the students each selected one poem that they felt "spoke" to them and copied it on a large sheet of chart paper. We then had 28 poems to share.

On Friday afternoons we chose a favourite out of the five or more poems that we'd met over the week. "Hurt No Living Thing" by

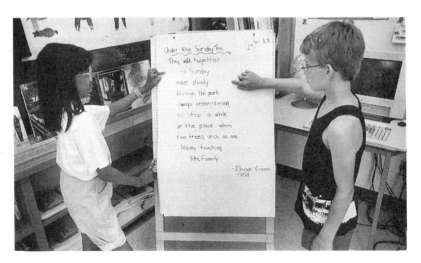

Christina Rossetti, *The Hunter I Might Have Been* by George Mendoza, "Louisa, Louisa" by Jean Little, "Keepsake" by Eloise Greenfield, and "Michael Built a Bicycle" by Jack Prelutsky have been among our choices. In December and in March, we reviewed the poems to select the "poem of the term." The winners were "Santa and the Reindeer" by Shel Silverstein and "Lazy Liza Briggs" by Dennis Lee.

In the second term, we moved on to "the poet of the week." Each day, one student or a pair of students was responsible for transcribing a poem by the chosen poet. Not only did the students choose the poems that we met, but we could explore our favourite poets, Eloise Greenfield, Dennis Lee, Eve Merriam, Jack Prelutsky, and Michael Rosen, in some depth.

On some occasions, the "poem of the day" activity lasts only moments. On others, we linger over the poems for longer periods of time. The children may close their eyes as I read the poem aloud, join in chorally, clap to the rhythm of the poem, repeat it several times in different tones of voice, raise questions about it, highlight a wonderful word or phrase to savour—or just laugh.

A day does not go by that we do not meet at least one poem, though often I slip in a few extra. Though I have been faithful to the use of handwritten poems on chart paper, we have also read poems from overhead transparencies, from "big books," from posters, from photocopied sheets, and from many anthologies. Occasionally, I buy a new book to add to the classroom collection, and sometimes, the students bring in poetry books from the library.

"A poem should not mean/But be," says Archibald MacLeish. Taking a moment to pour a poem into their heads demonstrates to the students that poetry matters far more than my telling them that it does. By experiencing many poems in many ways, students come to discover those that have meaning for them and, just as important, those that don't.

Non-Fiction as Literature

How can we connect love of language to other curriculum areas? Last winter, I set out to relive the lunches of my childhood by cooking a big pot of potato soup. I reached for my gift set of Julia Child's cookbooks to find the recipe—and found myself entranced by her description of the history and romance of this old-fashioned pottage.

How strange and fitting that even directions for soup can become a literary experience—that words labelled non-fiction can draw from me the reader a response both cognitive and aesthetic and bring back all those past years of comfort food and secure noon hours. Such is the power of writing when writer and reader connect, and torrents of meaning rush back and forth between the print and the eye.

What is the curriculum if it isn't story: stories of other times; of people we never knew but want to; of places that no longer exist but in the mind; of fin, fur, and feather; of trees that were here by the thousands and are now all but gone; of volcanoes that wipe away villages; of rivers ten million years old; of spiralling strands of genetic information that alter our concept of life; of telescopes that let us look back to the birth of the universe. When did we forget that everything is a story? (Even the Dairy Bureau of Canada calls its presentation to children *The Story of Milk.*) Was it when we decreed that non-fiction writing be devoid of emotion in order to balance more imaginative "creative" fiction? Did this lead us to drain factual information of excitement and passion by creating curriculum materials that were lifeless?

It makes more sense to see "literature" as a vehicle for making connections to the curriculum: a novel of pioneer life as part of a social studies unit, a poem about the mysteries of the deep as an introduction to a science lesson. These linkages certainly help children to form the collage of stimuli and information that surrounds them into a connected "learning web." Yet at the heart of the curriculum, I prefer to see the very words the experts use: the scientist's appeal for ecological courage on the basis of experimental findings and their implications; the historian's blend of the hardships of pioneer life with the traces of their journeys across the prairies; the sociologist's discussion of urbaniza-

tion and the charts and figures that illuminate the multicultural complexities of the neighbourhood; and the home economist's guide to a bowl of soup through a look at a cultural heritage.

All good writing is literature and opens windows for learners in every area of the curriculum. The child who listens to powerful stories and poems cannot help but connect the widened world they illuminate to whatever is being studied. Teachers may label a book "history" or "science" or "health," but the child sees it as a contribution to the maelstrom of ideas and feelings whirling in the brain and heart.

Every subject should be literature-based, and every literature experience part of the whole curriculum of life. We must use only the best in print to open up, extend, and enrich every topic. This means the non-fiction in our classroom must be written by authors who see themselves as storytellers, just as the poems, novels, and songs we use must have something to say about the real world. Such connections will develop a sense of story in our children and the realization that writing and reading apply to every discipline under the sun.

Sharing Literature with Children

We no longer flinch when the principal walks in to find us reading aloud, sharing a powerful selection from the myriad of choices offered by contemporary literature for young people. The modern classroom is now an accepted setting for the age-old story tribe. Mothers, fathers, teachers, older brothers and sisters—all have led the story tribe. Children of all ages snuggle on the couch, gather on the rug, sit around the table, or nestle in their beds, to listen to that most ordinary and fabulous of all constructs—the story.

We can read to children all kinds of stories that they can't handle on their own, that they might not choose, that at first seem beyond their range of experience. A story can take children outside their own culture, past life, and experience into other worlds—stranger, different, unsettling, or fantastic—and introduce them to characters they didn't know existed or that stare back at them from the mirror. Listening requires no reading strategies, word recognition, or attack skills—story is all, meaning is at hand.

Children who are immersed in story begin to read earlier and progress more quickly. They know story; they are story; they will read and write as a normal part of story, of school, of life. Listening to stories teaches children to imagine and to read. As the reader brings the words to life, the listeners consider events, characters, motivations, and connections. They create pictures in their minds, shadows as background to future reading. Their vocabulary grows; they learn about sentence structure and literary patterns. They discover genres of books—poetry, non-fiction, biography, folk tales—that they might not on their own.

As teachers read aloud, they become models of how to read, in phrasing, characterization, dialogue, and nuance, and demonstrate how print holds rich meaning. As they listen, the students will create their own stories in their minds.

Teachers can put together story sets. An author such as Jane Yolen provides a folk-tale series with a dozen wonderful stories for reading aloud. Richard Chase and Alvin Schwartz are there to support a collection of tall tales. Developing a repertoire takes time. Try stories, adapt them, discard them, try them again. Different audiences, moods, settings, prior experiences can affect the response to a story. Let the children take you to the next story set. Read several short stories on some occasions; on others, share longer, continuous stories. You will find some stories work for all ages; some have special relevance for particular groups: children with special backgrounds, various book experiences, differing sensibilities. Some stories are most effective when read to a small, intimate group; others are better with large audiences. Matching text to audience is an artistic skill honed through practice. A record of what you read may help develop a read-aloud program in your classroom and plan suitable read-aloud stories at different levels in your school.

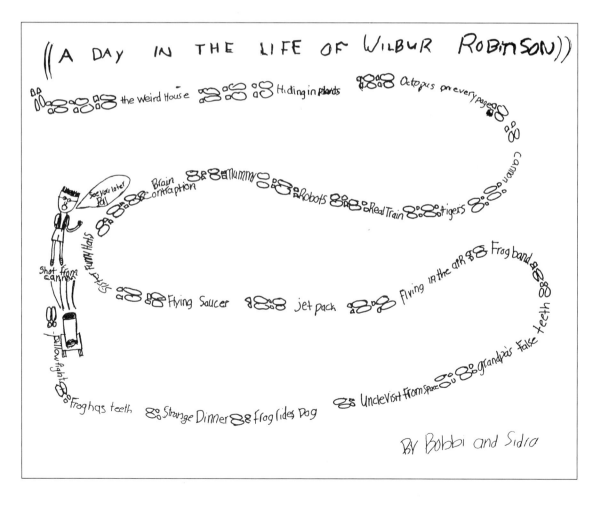

Reading a story aloud to a group of children is, in essence, a performance. The community of learners can benefit from this shared literary experience in a thousand ways. Sometimes a careful introduction will set the time, place, or mood. Sometimes the story will fit inside an existing thematic unit. The teacher can work with the class after the story, extending and exploring issues inside and outside it. After listening to the teacher read *A Day in the Life of Wilbur Robinson* by William Joyce, a grade three class brainstormed events and images that they considered to be humorous or unusual. They examined the surrealistic fantasy elements presented by the author and at the same time gained an understanding of one technique a writer can use to create humour.

The importance of reading aloud does not diminish as children grow older. Young adolescents still need to listen to stories. When adults share literature aloud, they reveal their literary choices, demonstrate their appreciation and taste, and bring alive the words on the page. The impact will influence what young people choose to read and expose them to books they might not choose or are unable to read on their own.

When we read aloud, the shared experience binds the group together in a moment of growth in which the book, the story, and the author form the focus for feelings and responses. We read aloud what we've written ourselves, excerpts from stories that we loved or wondered about, words that touch us or puzzle us, tales from before, now, and hereafter, episodes from people's lives, poems that cry out for sounds in the air, letters from friends, stories about places where we have never wandered, stories about dogs and horses and mothers and grandads and eccentrics and school and the city, stories of hope and death and wonder and fantasy. We read short stories and long stories in chapters that build up the tension for days. We read stories from album covers, blurbs about writers from book jackets, titles, and reviews. We fill the classroom with the voices of our ancestors, our friends, our researchers, our journalists, our ad writers, our novelists, our poets, our records, our native people.

Storytelling

A special magic is created for the story tribe when we tell stories rather than read them. Storytelling may be a scary prospect at first—it seems so much easier to disassociate oneself from the story, to take refuge in the printed page, but as Judy Caulfield, a resource teacher at Queenston, points out, we all use the narrative form to make sense out of our lives. And so do our children.

Sharing Stories the Age-Old Way
Judy Caulfield

The teachers at Queenston are all storytellers in their own right—sometimes without realizing it! The kindergarten teacher spontaneously dramatizes *The Gingerbread Man* to the delight of her children as they join in on the refrain "Run, run, as fast as you can . . ." When the junior teacher gives a summary of a novel, he pauses for effect and chooses phrases that carry the most impact. In the staff room, another teacher tells how, while on vacation, he tackled a thief in his hotel room in the middle of the night. (I wonder if he told that story to his class? He certainly kept the staff spellbound.) When the teachers meet in Paul Shaw's workshops, they tell fascinating stories of their classes and of their teaching experience.

Why tell rather than read? There are many fine novels and beautiful picture books. But storytelling offers different opportunities. It invites the children to bring their own personal experiences into play. Place, shape, texture, scent, colour, and size are all pieces of the puzzle that the listener adds to create a unique vision of the story. For example, when I told *The Three Little Pigs*, we discussed the story, drew about it, and played it in the home centre. Then I showed a filmstrip of the story. One child was very adamant: "The filmstrip is wrong. That wolf was brown and our wolf was black." Yet I had not given the wolf a colour in the telling of the story. I knew then that I had to keep telling stories. I knew I wanted my students to experience their own images.

In picture books, illustrators are so masterful that children often consider their view of the story definitive. But if they have first listened to a story and played with it, children are often fascinated to see a picture-book version. Does the illustrator's view match theirs? How is it different? This way, the children's own aesthetic response is validated as they take the illustrator's view as merely one of many possibilities. It also encourages them to take an active role when they view the many sophisticated images from today's variety of media.

How do you start storytelling? Begin with a folk tale that has been shared across generations, a story that you loved as a child, or one that is a current favourite in your classroom. If you feel that you can tell the story without turning the pages, you probably can. Storytelling is not a memory test. Learn the opening and closing for confidence' sake, and then use your own words. As you become more at home with a story, you may wish to include some of the author's rich or particularly evocative phrases. Remember, eye contact is a direct invitation to each listener. No book acts as a barrier between you and the child. As you re-create the story between you, parts of it grow or diminish in importance in accord with the moment and mood.

There are many styles of storytelling. Sonja Dunn uses a "storyskirt" with a built-in felt board and many pockets to hide objects that will trigger a story. When Alice Kane tells stories, she stands straight, still, and calm, adamant that she stay out of the way of the story. Helen Porter often combines storytelling with movement and music. Some tellers use puppets, felt figures, or chalk. Storytelling can be as informal as a whisper between two friends about an event of the day. You need to explore to find your own approach. The first time I told a story to my class, I put on a large red badge with three apples on it and told them the Armenian saying, "Three apples fell from heaven: one for the storyteller, one for the listener, and one for the one who heard." We talked about the saying and then I launched into the story. About a week later, when I next put on the badge, they crowded around in anticipation and delight.

Oral language carries a lilt, inflection, rhythm, and cadence that written language cannot. Children learn this as they join in for refrains and chants and incorporate these phrases with their own language when they tell the story. They often use the rich phrases of story to make a point at play.

Indeed, children use many of the elements of story in their lives. They bring story and story form into their games, their dramatic play, and their writing. Older students will connect historic events with stories they have heard and will use story and drama to make sense out of events. The chants and patterns found in stories will appear in the speech of students learning English as a second language.

Conversely, telling stories can validate other cultures, and some children who come from an oral tradition can contribute stories of their own or versions of stories that they have heard. Others will share family lore. Children learn best when they make connections between themselves and the story, or between stories.

Storytelling builds the sense of "tribe" that Bob Barton and David Booth talk about in *Stories in the Classroom*. Seek out opportunities to hear storytellers: experience the wonder, chills, laughter, and tears as you listen to a story and share it with your friends and with your class. Many communities now have storytelling groups and local libraries often plan storytelling events or visits from guest storytellers. Last year, several teachers from Queenston attended the annual Toronto Festival of Storytelling, which is held the fourth weekend of February. They came back revitalized—and with stories to share.

Media Literacy

Television, radio, and tape recordings are part of every child's life. We have to consider the effect of these media and their influence on the thinking, reading, and writing proficiencies of children as we develop our school curriculum. Viewing—the observing process—is an essential component of communication. The technology of the future will bring an ever-increasing flow of visual information, which children will need to learn to comprehend, analyze, and apply to new situations. The critical strategies that we hope to develop in children as they interact with print are just as necessary when they interact with television, film, communications media brought to us by the computer screen, or technologies yet unknown and undeveloped. Therefore, listening and viewing are vital elements in any integrated language arts program, and the children at Queenston are as familiar with responding to a film they have seen together as they are in discussing a story they have all read.

Yestr day My class soo a Moveiy It wos a adot SICiS one wos a wotr SiCl and the wotrGows UP and thin it G W2 NdiWN

> *Yesterday my class saw a movie. It was about cycles. One was a water cycle and the water goes up and then it goes down.*

The Library Resource Centre

In the school library at Queenston, children can find books and other reference materials such as data bases, pictures, films, and videos that go beyond their classroom collections. The professional librarian can assist the children in making use of the fiction and non-fiction resources and work with the teacher in curriculum development. The children themselves are the best source of what the library means to them.

In an interview for the school newsletter with Lisa, a grade six student, teacher-librarian Sue Checkeris said that her favourite thing about being a librarian is that "I get to work with children of all ages. I get to meet every student at Queenston and find out what they are interested in. Also, I love books and especially love sharing them."

Lisa also wanted to know how Sue chose what to buy for the library.

Sue explained, "Sometimes I buy books because I am familiar with the author. I also consult with teachers to find out what curriculum they will be covering so I can decide what kind of materials to buy. I ask for recommendations from students, from teachers, and from other teacher-librarians. I visit many bookstores to see what's new and what's popular. I also read reviews in journals, such *The Horn Book*, and newspaper columns."

One particularly telling question Lisa asked was "Do you expect your library to be a quiet place?"

Sue replied, "Not really. I think it is a place for talking and meeting and working. I really like when children talk about books with each other. When a group is doing research, there is a need to share ideas. I think lots of important talk goes on in the library." Perhaps Sue's approach has a lot to do with the enthusiasm Queenston students have for their library.

Ten Great Things about Our Library
Lindsay and Sidra, grade three

1. There are tables, chairs, a computer, slide shows, videos, stuffed cats, a bath tub to read in, and lots and lots and lots of books.
2. Miss Checkeris helps you choose good authors and good stories. She knows them well.
3. My favourite thing in the library is seeing Miss Checkeris and listening to her laugh.
4. When Miss Checkeris reads us books she looks at the pictures VERY closely. She reads with the voices that are in the story, and when she is done she tells you her feeling of the story.
5. Children use the library when they need to exchange books or when they need to work quietly.

6. In our library you can talk to someone about what you are reading or what you are working on. In some libraries, talking is not allowed.
7. There are lots of posters in the library. There is one that says "Books are windows to the world."
8. Whenever you go to our library, Miss Checkeris always has new books. She must buy a new book every day.
9. There are all kinds of kids in the library all the time.
10. Miss Checkeris said she thinks of the library as a house. We are like visitors in her house.

Booktalk: Non-Fiction Can Fascinate
Sue Checkeris

Listening to the librarian read aloud is an important ritual when a class comes to visit the library. I am finding that more and more I read non-fiction to the children when they come and gather around the reading chair. And yet I hardly think of many of these books as non-fiction in the traditional sense, because authors today choose to convey information in a variety of intriguing formats.

In the fall, I love sharing *Red Leaf, Yellow Leaf* by Lois Ehlert. The children want to do more than examine the illustrations; they want to touch the pages. *Red Leaf, Yellow Leaf* is an ideal starting point for having the children share their own lore about autumn as they learn more about seeds, leaves, and trees. This October, the picture book particularly attracted those children who had visited the neighbourhood woodlot to collect leaves and adopt a tree.

Ken Robbins imparts more botanical knowledge in *A Flower Grows*. After listening to this picture essay, Matthew, in grade two, went home and asked his mother to buy an amaryllis that he could bring to school so that he and his classmates could observe and record the growth of a flower.

Tara, who is in grade two, listened to her teacher read *Waiting for the Whales* by Sheryl McFarland and Ron Lightburn, and *The Whales' Song* by Dyan Sheldon and Gary Blythe. She appeared at my door to collect "all the whale books there were in the library." Joanne Ryder's *Winter Whale* gave Tara the information she wanted in an unusual way. In the series *Just for a Day*, Ryder writes in the second person to help the children see and feel from the animal's perspective. Other books in the series transform the reader into a polar bear in *White Bear, Ice Bear*, a Canada goose in *Catching the Wind*; and an anole in *Lizard in the Sun* ("You are a lizard / small and thin / as light as a pencil / as light as a handful of popcorn"). Taking their cue from these books, the children in a grade four class presented their own research about animals in the second person.

I purchased Daniel San Souci's *North Country Night* for the library without hesitation because I loved the detailed paintings of the animals and the calm blue colours that appear throughout. As I read the book aloud to a primary class, the silence in the room seemed to match the silence of the woods, so I knew that *North Country Night* was one of those "special" books. But I didn't really know how special it was until the children said that they learned more about animals from it than they had from an encyclopedia. After listening to the story, the children brainstormed a couple of dozen facts that they had learned about night creatures. In the process, however, they raised even more questions about the animals, and that prompted them to further research.

Children often develop an interest in non-fiction material when their curiosity has been aroused by books such as *North Country Night*. In one grade three class, Lindsay investigated salamanders after reading *The Salamander Room* by Anne Mazer, and Samuel wrote a picture book entitled, "Ten Facts I Learned about Crickets" after reading *The Cricket in Times Square* by George Selden.

Non-fiction resource books may inspire children to investigate other materials on a topic. *Samuel Todd's Book of Great Inventions*, by E.L. Konigsburg, invites children to wonder about the discovery and importance of items in their everyday lives such as zippers, Velcro, and mirrors. In one grade five class, it became a springboard for research on machines and other inventions. From *Samuel Todd*, the children went on to explore *The Stoddart Visual Dictionary of Everyday Things, The Way Things Work* by David Macaulay, and *The Invention Book* by Steven Caney.

Many appealing books provide children with alternative formats for presenting information for projects on diverse themes. For a project on medieval times, Karen, a grade five student, said, "I think I'll take the magic school bus there." *The Magic School Bus* series, by Joanna Cole, describes the adventures of a class whose teacher takes them on field trips to the solar system, to the waterworks, and through the human body. The series combines narrative with facts, lists, charts, and diagrams. Karen borrowed this concept for presenting the information she found about knights and castles.

The classroom teacher and I presented factual information on the explorations of Christopher Columbus to one junior classroom in a variety of forms. *I, Columbus* by Peter and Connie Roop describes the voyage in journal form; *I Discover Columbus* by Robert Lawson tells the story from the parrot's point of view. Rich illustrations by Peter Sis for *Follow the Dream* provide a visually appealing account of the discovery of America, and Jane Yolen's *Encounter* presents the events from the point of view of an aboriginal chief.

Kids Can Press publishes some excellent information books, such as the *Amazing Milk Book, Amazing Dirt Book, Amazing Egg Book, Amazing Apple Book,* and *Amazing Paper Book,* Pam Hickman's *Plant Wise, Bug Wise,* and *Bird Wise,* and the Ontario Science Centre's *How Sports Works, Have Fun with Magnifying, Scienceworks,* and *Foodworks.* These popular, informative references appeal to many children. Camilla Gryski's *Cat's Cradle, Owl's Eyes, Many Stars and More String Games,* and *Super String Games* challenge children to learn new games and tricks using string by following written and graphic instructions. String games have become contagious in the schoolyard, and Gryski's books seem to be out of the library more than they are in it.

The most successful non-fiction materials have a good balance of visuals and text that will absorb the children in a particular topic. Throughout the day, junior and intermediate children are in the library looking for information on topics of current interest in the *Eyewitness* books from Stoddart Publishing: *Seashore, Bird, Sports, Tree, Arms and Armour;* younger children seem to enjoy the Kids Can *Amazing World* series. It is particularly exciting to see these references being pored over by a small group of children discussing, describing, and questioning the information they find inside the covers.

Suggested Reading for Teachers

Barton, Bob. *Tell Me Another: Storytelling and Reading Aloud at Home, at School and in the Community.* Portsmouth, N.H.: Heinemann, 1986. This comprehensive guide to finding stories, choosing the right story, and telling a story well is based on the experience of Bob Barton, one of Canada's most popular storytellers.

Bird, Lois Bridges, ed. *Becoming a Whole Language School: The Fair Oaks Story.* Katonah, N.Y.: Richard C. Owen Publishers, 1989. The author describes the evolution of one shool, Fair Oaks, as a microcosm of the history of whole language.

Booth, David, Larry Swartz, and Meguido Zola. *Choosing Children's Books.* Markham: Pembroke Publishers, 1987. An annotated list of more than 600 of the best children's books at all grade levels to guide teachers, librarians, and parents.

Brownlie, Faye, Susan Close, and Linda Wingren. *Tomorrow's Classroom Today: Strategies for Creating Active Readers,* Writers, and Thinkers. Markham: Pembroke Publishers, 1990. These teachers view specific learning strategies through the words of a classroom teacher, examples of student response, analysis of teaching and learning styles, and a brief review of each strategy for easy reference.

Cambourne, Brian. *The Whole Story: Natural Learning and the Acquisition of Literacy in the Classroom.* Toronto: Scholastic, 1988. For the past decade, Brian Cambourne has been researching how learning, especially literacy learning, occurs. His book presents an alternative view of learning and an approach to teaching literacy.

Carletti, Silvan, Suzanne Girard, and Kathlene Willing. *The Library Classroom Connection.* Markham: Pembroke Publishers, 1991. Topics addressed include classroom instruction, special library programs, and issues including building an awareness of bias-free materials.

Forester, Anne D., and Margaret Reinhard. *On the Move: Teaching the Learners' Way in Grades 4-7.* Winnipeg: Peguis Publishers, 1991. This book describes negotiating the curriculum with students in the junior grades.

Gamberg, Ruth, et al. *Learning and Loving It: Theme Studies in the Classroom.* Toronto: OISE Press, 1988. The authors explain the theme studies approach to education using case studies from the award-winning Dalhousie University Elementary School in Halifax, N.S., demonstrating how teachers can set up theme studies programs in their classrooms.

Goodman, Yetta M., Wendy J. Hood, and Kenneth S. Goodman, eds. *Organizing for Whole Language.* Portsmouth/Toronto: Heinemann/Irwin, 1991. In this collection, classroom teachers, administrators, parents, and teacher educators share their experiences organizing time, space, materials, people, and ideas to turn the philosophy of whole language into classroom realities.

Graves, Donald H. *Build a Literate Classroom.* Portsmouth: Heinemann, 1991. Graves presents his philosophy for helping teachers and children in making reading/writing decisions in the classroom in order to build a program to improve learning.

Harris, Violet J., ed. *Teaching Multicultural Literature in Grades K-8.* Norwood, Maine: Christopher Gordon Publishers, 1992. An informed look at multicultural literature for children, including an excellent bibliography of children's books.

Harste, Jerome, Kathy Short, and Carolyn Burke. *Creating Classrooms for Authors. The Reading-Writing Connection.* Toronto: Irwin Publishing, 1988. A practical reference guide to organizing process-centred classrooms, presenting a curricular frame around which teachers can plan classroom activities.

Mills, Heidi, and Jean Anne Clyde. *Portraits of Whole Language Classrooms: Learning for All Ages.* Portsmouth, N.H.: Heinemann, 1990. The authors, concerned about misconceptions about whole language, have invited a group of whole language teachers to share their personal experiences by highlighting a typical day in their classrooms.

Rosen, Betty. *And None of It Was Nonsense: The Power of Storytelling in School.* Toronto: Scholastic, 1988. Betty Rosen describes her years of teaching a group of multi-language, multicultural boys using a wealth of stories as the core around which she helped the students create their own, through storytelling and story writing.

Routman, Regie. *Invitations: Changing as Teachers and Learners K-12.* Toronto/Portsmouth: Irwin/Heinemann, 1991. *Invitations* provides specific strategies for putting whole language theory into practice.

Schwartz, Susan, and Mindy Pollishuke. *Creating the Child-Centred Classroom.* Toronto: Irwin Publishing, 1990. A practical resource book for teachers K-9, combining the philosophies of whole language and active learning with practical strategies and sample activities.

Ward, Geoff. *I've Got a Project On . . .* Portsmouth, N.H.: Heinemann, 1988. This book will help teachers rethink how and why they might use projects and ensure that children and their parents understand what they are being asked to do.

Reflections

❶ Children themselves can assess the dynamics of the classroom and their own learning behaviour. How can we enable classroom discussions that focus on the effectiveness of the children's own participation in events that occur during the day and ensure that their suggestions are followed up in future sessions? What activities can we design to promote collaboration and co-operation and to establish a classroom community where the students feel a sense of ownership and control over their learning?

❷ Language arts timetables broken into short periods allow for little integration of language processes. How can we organize our days so that children can learn about language as they participate in classroom activities? Draw up a tentative program that will allow children to read, write, and talk about things that matter to them.

❸ How can we include volunteers in the classroom to assist us and the children with various activities? Consider in what ways parents, student teachers, high school students, older student buddies, and invited guests can participate in your classroom. What will be the benefits for your children, the volunteers, and your own work as a teacher?

❹ Classroom resources need to be replenished during the year. Plan strategies that your school might use or review those in place for ensuring that both children and teacher have access to learning materials that are appropriate to the development of the children, useful at various work centres, and related to changing themes that may be the focus for learning.

❺ Many classrooms are supplied with class or group sets of textbooks. How can we ensure that these multiple copies of books in various curriculum areas are an effective resource? In language-based classrooms, what difficulties may they pose and how may these difficulties be accommodated? Choose a text in language arts or a related curriculum area that is in current use and consider how you might use it to foster language growth as well as mastery of content. What changes might you suggest for a revised edition to the authors and publisher of this text?

❻ Michael Fullan (1991) says that although change may be messy and although some aspects of it will appear to confuse the issue, teachers must persevere and continue to adapt to new learning and research. A teachers can alter language and learning programs in his or her own ways, always moving toward integrated and holistic teaching. In every teacher's classroom, some teaching approaches work well. It is these that form the basis for expanding and enriching the teaching/learning relationship. Assess the way you organize your language arts program:

- What aspects already demonstrate a language-based approach?
- Do you build the program around content of real interest to the students, perhaps organized into thematic units, rather than around sets of skills?
- Do the children feel responsible for deciding what they will read and write and how they will interact with others during group activities?
- Are the children helping to plan their activities? Are they themselves monitoring and assessing their growth?
- Do classroom activities appear to the children as significant and important learning events or as time spent in practice or "dummy runs"?
- Is the classroom an environment that assumes and encourages literacy, filled with books, children's writings, posters?
- Does your organization of your time allow for individual conferences and interviews, small group mini-lessons on particular skills, and whole-class information and sharing sessions?
- Are the children helping each other become better readers and writers, leaving you more time to work with individuals and groups?

Does the learning environment in your classroom lend itself to you as teacher being not only a motivator and assessor but also a participant who works and learns with the children from inside the learning events?

Emerging Literacy

S TUDIES BY PARENTS, teachers, and researchers of children in their own homes (Bissex, 1980; Butler, 1980) and in preschool settings (Paley, 1990; Clay, 1988) reveal that most children begin to notice how print works long before they start formal schooling, though the grasp of the concept will vary from child to child (Clark, 1976; Harste, Woodward, and Burke, 1984). As teachers welcoming these children to the school environment, we must plan a program that builds on this emerging understanding of the function of print. In order to offer the developing young reader continual support, we need to record our observations of early language behaviours in the classroom from the child's sense of story to awareness of the significance of print.

We know that satisfying stories provide children with the best possible background for literacy (Wells, 1986). Favourite books that draw children back again and again play a major role in learning to read. Don Holdaway (1979) and Bill Martin Jr. (1972) showed us that children can "read with the ears first," building a repertoire of stories from predictable patterns and entertaining "real books." Liz Waterland (1988) and Jill Bennett (1979) describe children as apprentice readers learning about meaning and print when they sit beside adults reading to them from the best of picture books. Young children need to preview books, take part in reading, and talk about books with others in order to enter the world of reading.

It is important that children see themselves as successful readers from their very first experiences. As teachers, we need to demonstrate a full range of reading strategies, supporting their initial attempts and imparting to them a confidence with print. Individual children progress at their own speed through a well-defined series of stages in reading, and we need practical ways to monitor their progress if we are to help them become true readers.

We can build a community of readers in our classrooms and develop individual children's reading potential by reading aloud to them, reading along with them, helping them read both independently and in groups, using their own writing as reading material, and providing situations in which they can read orally for real purposes (Smith, 1986). The literacy programs we develop for young children will determine their future as readers (Clay, 1988). We need to continue to examine both theory and practice as we find out more about how children learn to read.

to MSS. HiLL JAn. 21st 1991
HOW is your CLASS?
GrAD one is fun
We Lern Aer tAKAWAS
AND PLUSis
i cAn NTAcK STores Now
You Aer A Good tycHer
fromM MArk

To Ms. Hill. Jan. 21st, 1991. How is your class? Grade one is fun. We learn our take-aways and pluses. I can make stories now. You are a good teacher. From Mark.

Young Children as Readers and Writers

When they begin school, some children are already fascinated with print and are aware of the basics of reading and writing; others do not yet understand that print carries meaning. Some already appreciate books and what they do; they have listened to storybooks and can retell their favourites as they look at the pictures. Some children in the class may recognize a few words, be able to print their names, or have started to experiment in producing their own pretend writing, which they may also pretend to read back. These

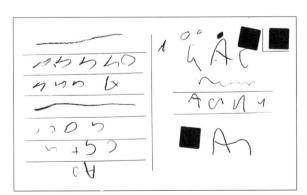

"postcards" from grade one students to their kindergarten teacher indicate that Mark looks at writing as a way of making meaning. Another child is still pretending to write. At this stage it is important for children to see their own words written down in a form that others will understand. When they see a reason to read and a reason to write, most children want to become literate. The early classroom years should concentrate on awakening a recognition of the function and power of print rather than on the mastery of particular elements of reading and writing.

The ways in which children encounter print in the first years of school may determine their view of reading and writing for the rest of their lives. Classroom experiences with printed words should be a natural part of the play and learning that arise from the need to communicate. Children who talk, model, paint, paste, and draw are already using codes and symbols to represent thought. They will see words and letters as just another code that lets them explore and communicate. Our job at this time is to convince children that print is meaningful, that print embodies thought, and that written language can help them make sense of their experiences.

As the children focus on the reading and writing processes, we work to expand and extend their language development, to help them make sense of what they are reading and of what they are writing. They need to assess their writing through their own reading to discover how what they want to say can be fully realized by the reader. We can build on the knowledge of literary patterns the children already possess and let the children take charge of the meaning making in ways they understand, as they build narratives, add dialogue, and discuss the essentials of a story.

Language-based teaching capitalizes on what children can already do with language and extends literacy as part of a natural process. In the language-based classroom, the environment is full of print—signs, books, magazines, and stories. When they see their names around the room, on their belongings, on charts, and on bulletin boards, children become aware of written messages—how they help us communicate, give us information, direct us. They notice the teacher using print—on memos, lists, and charts; it becomes an active force in their lives, as they dictate their stories to others or write them with their own invented spelling. They experiment with the forms they need for various functions of writing—labels, lists, stories, captions, letters, and journals. As the teacher reads aloud to them, the children experience the power of print and the joy of story. They grow into seeing themselves as readers as they join in the shared reading of texts they can follow, listen to older children read aloud, choose what they want to read at some times, and read assigned texts with a group at others. They grow into seeing themselves as writers as they keep private journals, engage in group record keeping, and reflect in print on their own pleasures and concerns so others may read their thoughts. They learn to revise their writing so that readers can understand what they want to convey, moving toward the use of conventional spelling and punctuation and control over form.

Through all this activity, we help the children grow metacognitively—in understanding what they know about how language works and how they can manipulate it. They become aware that they can rely on print to carry a message. They discover, subconsciously at first, that a book is used in a particular order—from front to back; a page is read from left to right and top to bottom; the message is revealed line by line, word by word, and letter by letter, the style of print and the punctuation giving clues to intonation; pictures can be used to predict or demonstrate what the print has to say; word-attack strategies and spelling skills can help in making meaning from text. As they become familiar with various functions of print, they will find that good readers are always making predictions and connections. They see how stories, poems, lists, and instructions "work" as they absorb the flow of language and the internal patterns and structures.

We must find ways of working with children that support this developing understanding. We want emergent readers to learn how print functions and to understand that different types of reading material demand different styles of reading. As the children become more fluent and experienced as readers, they will be willing to take on more extended and more challenging books, becoming more critical of what they read, and of what writers have to say. They will become more able to question and admire aspects of content, form, and function.

Just as children learn to talk through conversation, they learn to read through interaction: listening to a story, commenting about the pictures and the print, discussing their ideas, learning what it is to act as readers. We can read with children as we talk with children, interactively, valuing and encouraging both tentative and carefully considered responses. Good stories seep into the mind and enhance all future comprehension. By building a classroom atmosphere that nurtures positive attitudes to reading, we create situations where literacy is welcomed and cherished and, most important, continued for life.

Literacy in Action
Jan Bayes and Jim Giles

We make a ritual of reading aloud to the children several times a day. The first opportunity comes after we have sung "O Canada" and made morning announcements. One day, when the children gathered on the rug, Ashley handed a recent birthday gift, *The Wretched Stone*, to Jim and told him he was to share it. The children were captivated by the illustrations and raised many questions and hypotheses about the strange stone aboard the sailing ship.

The read-aloud session is a prelude to the children's own reading time. Several big books in the classroom encourage them to join in and read together. Sarah was thrilled to read *Each Peach Pear Plum* on her own. The predictable pattern of the story gave her enough confidence to read it aloud to the grade two class across the hall. Three grade two students practised reading aloud "Three Tickles" as a round and presented their choral dramatization to the rest of the class during sharing time.

Some students found a private corner of the room to look at their books. Michael was curled up in the class bathtub reading *How to Dig a Hole to the Other Side of the World*, while Ashley sat on the couch with a large teddy bear on her lap reading *Fox and His Friends*. Julie was enjoying being by herself at the far end of the room and could be faintly heard reading aloud *The Quilt Story*.

We had just added some new books to the classroom library. Anthony, a grade one child who is struggling with reading, attempted to read aloud *I Took My Frog to the Library*. Even though he couldn't read all the words on the page, he became familiar with the pattern "I took a ___ to the library" and used the pictures as an aid in telling the story to others. Caitlin, who had just lost her tooth, chose *Martin and the Tooth Fairy*, and Kelsey grabbed *The Principal's New Clothes* to take home for her parents to read that night. Matthew chose a book about magic tricks and read the instructions carefully so that he could perform tricks for his friends during activity time. The joke and riddle books were particularly popular: together on the couch, Andrea and Jordan read a collection of animal riddles entitled *Belly Laughs*. Each time they laughed, they would run up to one of their friends, book in hand, to read the quip aloud.

Steven, Ian, and Michael helped each other with *20,000 Baseball Cards Under the Sea*, a challenging book for them but one they all wanted to read. Steven assumed the role of leader and pointed to the words as Ian and Michael attempted to find meaning.

Some children particularly enjoy what they call "finding books." A group of grade one students, inspired by a visit from author/illustrator Phoebe Gilman, shared her *Little Blue Ben*. Each participant read a page and pointed out to the others where Blue Ben was hidden. Children like to read pop-up and lift-the-flap books in pairs. Diane and Julie were reading *Going on a Lion Hunt*, and each took a turn reading a page and lifting the flap. Grade one girls, Robin and Alison, fascinated by *The Blue Balloon*, soon had a crowd of six children join them as they lifted the pages to see how the balloon got larger and larger.

Sometimes, children want to read a story that is too challenging for them and they seek assistance from older, more experienced readers in the class. Chandini consulted Belinda in grade three for help with the words in the pattern book *I Wish I Had a Pirate Suit*. Belinda was very much the teacher and had Chandini cue in the repeated phrase "I wish I had a pirate suit."

Chris, Bobby, and Kenny had read and rehearsed a short script, *Captain Bumble*, earlier in the week. The three boys each took the part of one of the pirate characters and shared it with the class. This inspired other children to try reading aloud other pieces of literature as plays.

Throughout the twenty-minute reading period, Martina and Diane were busy adding to the morning letter, which noted the day's events, people who had overdue library books, and people who had news to share. Later, the two girls read the revised chart to the class and invited further revisions or editorial comments on their message. Bryan chose this time to read his own story to the class, about a striped boy with striped hair as well as striped clothes.

The Process of Reading

A reader interacts with the text, using a variety of strategies to build understanding. Different purposes demand different reading techniques. The material being read, the background of the reader, the reason for reading, the responses of others involved, what will happen after the reading, all are part of making sense of print.

If we are to help students become better readers, we must understand the many facets of the reading process, from the choice of text through to the grasp of the larger themes raised by the author. Reading materials, which, of course, the readers should help select, should draw upon their expanding abilities, relating the present to their prior knowledge and experience. They can then anticipate and predict what will come next. Support from adults and other readers while they are reading the text, not merely after they have completed it, will ensure that they make as much meaning as possible. Children need to think about what they are reading, make their own discoveries, and share their understandings to extend the meaning they make. Literary understanding grows as children begin to grasp the many reasons why authors write and the many choices made in the writing, not only of topic and story line, but also of style and technique. Their world view expands as they relate an author's concerns to their own lives. The reading process is all of this; "understanding" words on a page is only a small part of it.

Novice readers need extensive opportunities to work with a variety of materials for a variety of purposes, both in school and at home—stories, poems, non-fiction, manuals, newspapers, magazines, and cartoons. They must see reading as a satisfying, purposeful endeavour that brings pleasure, knowledge, and discovery, not as a task required in order to answer the teacher's predetermined list of questions. They need time both to read and to respond, privately or publicly, free from ridicule or any sense of failure. If reading is to become a lifelong habit and books a vital part of their existence, their early interactions with text must result in success. Our aim is to make children's experiences with print so positive that they will continue to read without us.

The Cueing Systems

Readers of all ages use the same overall strategies in making meaning from print. First, they prepare, often intuitively, considering the author, the type of material, or the topic. During the act of reading, they sample the text, confirming or rejecting possible meanings, looking for answers, and forming new questions. They respond to both the intent and content of the print, developing a personal interpretation that reflects their own linguistic resources and world experience. They apply the necessary strategies—reading along, pausing to consider meanings accrued so far, hypothesizing, rereading, omitting words until they have more information, reading ahead to build additional context to modify or clarify meaning, or simply stopping because the material is unsuitable or too difficult.

Readers read to comprehend. While reading a text, they subconsciously ask if it makes sense. When children attempt to read print, they draw on many different kinds of knowledge to make meaning; they go back and forth, hypothesizing about and confirming ideas using cues found in the print—the semantic context, the syntactic structures, and the visible features of the words and letters. Everything matters when reading; the reader must bring all kinds of information together in order to grasp the sense of the text. Effective readers balance and integrate the various cues into the broadest possible construct for comprehension.

Pragmatic Cues (Knowing about Books)

Written material is organized in practical ways, ways that work. Chinese and Hebrew are laid out differently on the page and in the book from English. Shopping lists are different from statistical tables, just as instructions are from novels. As teachers, we must help readers understand these pragmatic contexts within which all the other cueing systems function.

Mem Fox (1987), the Australian author of such fine children's books as *Possum Magic* and *Wilfred Gordon McDonald Partridge*, claims she has "hunches about reading from my observations as a parent, as a storyteller, and as a woman, all of which have influenced the way I teach reading—disguised as a writer." She points out that

reading one book teaches us how to read another. It's one of the "prior knowledge" factors in reading. So, along with our knowledge of the world, and language, and print, children need to develop a knowledge of how books work. That's why Possum Magic *starts with "Once upon a time," because children have heard it before and will hear it again. That's why* Possum Magic *is an archetypal quest story; it prepares its readers for Victor Kelleher's* Master of the Grove, *Tolkien's* Lord of the Rings, *the Arthurian legends, and the* Odyssey *of Homer.*

Semantic Cues (Knowing about the World)

Being able to read the words correctly does not necessarily result in comprehension. Readers must be able to relate these words to what they signify; they need some prior knowledge of the subject matter. Semantic cues relate the reading material to known facts, ideas, or concepts so that readers can integrate new information with what they already understand. Mem Fox calls semantic cues "knowledge of the world":

I was aware of that when I wrote Possum Magic. *I built on the familiar . . . but I also felt a duty to extend the horizons of my readers by including all the state capitals of Australia and by making it clear that Tasmania was an island state:*

> *"You look wonderful, you precious possum!" said Grandma Poss. "Next stop, Tasmania!" And over the sea they went.*

It was done on purpose. I was teaching reading by providing information that would become prior knowledge in their subsequent reading of other texts.

Syntactic Cues (Knowing about Language)

Syntactic cues allow readers to transfer their knowledge of oral language to printed material. A knowledge of common sentence patterns and the functions of words within sentences enables readers to predict upcoming words. In the sentence "The angry dog chased the frightened cat," readers can choose the type of word that follows the second "the" from a limited range of alternatives—adjectives and nouns. As they develop, readers become familiar with the language patterns used in writing rather than in speech and predict successfully through these more sophisticated syntactic cues. Mem Fox comments:

The children I write for are so young that they're still immersed in the rhyme and rhythm of nursery and playground rhymes. I wanted to build on that background, to connect that world to the world of books, so I included rhyme in Possum Magic, *right there, in the middle of the prose:*

> *She looked into this book and she looked into that.*
> *There was magic for thin and magic for fat,*
> *magic for tall and magic for small,*
> *but the magic she was looking for wasn't there at all.*

Phonographemic Cues (Knowing about Print)

Phonographemic cues, often called "phonics," are the relationships between the sounds (phonemes) and written symbols (graphemes) of language. Readers use them mostly to help confirm guesses: "As all reading teachers know implicitly, phonics is easy if you already have a good idea of what the word is in the first place. Children who can predict that the next word is likely to be either cow, horse or sheep will not need much knowledge of spelling-to-sound correspondences to decide which it is. In fact it is through such prediction that a mastery of useful phonics is acquired" (Smith, 1986). Thus, phonographemic cues are probably used in reading less often and to less purpose than many people suspect. English has no simple one-to-one correspondence between spoken and written forms; there are often many ways to represent the same sound. Readers use semantic and syntactic cues to develop generalizations about letters and sounds. Mem Fox doesn't simplify vocabulary because, as she says, she doesn't feel hidebound by the phonographemic cueing system:

I know that meaning isn't difficult to grasp because we read in chunks, so I never worried about the apparently long words in Possum Magic *such as "invisible," "pavlova," "lamington," or "Vegemite sandwiches." (A "laming-*

*ton" is a delicious, typically Australian, chocolate-and-coconut sponge cake.)
When I read* Possum Magic *to five year olds, I have to prepare the muscles in
my face not to smile when I come to the sentence: "In Hobart, late one night,
they saw a lamington on a plate," because there's nearly always a heartfelt
chorus of "Arrh, yu-u-u-m!" It's the "Arrh, yu-u-u-m!" that teaches the kids
how to read, not the length of the word "lamington."*

The Cueing Systems at Work

In reading, all four cueing systems are constantly at work and the
effectiveness of one is increased by the use of the others. When readers
have sufficient background experience with the type of reading material,
prior knowledge of the subject matter, and familiarity with the language
patterns, they use detailed visual information only occasionally, relying for
the most part on an ability to predict accurately. This lets them read fast and
fluently. When the subject matter or the vocabulary and sentence structures
are unfamiliar, the reader is less able to predict and must look more closely
at the print. The reading rate slows down and more rereadings may be
necessary. Thus a letter from a friend is easier to read than an involved
technical manual. Proficient readers use a minimum of cues to derive the
maximum of meaning from print and are continually compromising between
speed and accuracy.

Emergent readers, however, are restricted in the cues they can use.
They may even rely on a single cueing system at a time. Independent
readers slow down to analyze a particular word every once in a while, but if
emergent readers are confined entirely to, for example, the phonographemic
cueing system, they are relegated to the impossible task of decoding every
single word. Meaning making occurs when children recognize most of the
words in the selection that they are reading instantaneously and automatically
—when they read words at sight. Having to analyze letters or word particles
too frequently retards fluency and comprehension. The emergent reader
who is forced to spend time simply identifying words seldom understands
the story.

Marilyn Jager Adams describes phonics as "a system of teaching reading that builds upon the alphabetic principle, a system of which a central
component is the teaching of correspondences between letters and their
pronunciations" (1990, p.12). Some children, perhaps those of a more analytic frame of mind, rely heavily on phonographemic logic. They need to
know what sounds a particular sequence of letters makes. If they cannot see
how the letters build to form a word, they cannot read it—indeed, they may
not be able to read at all. Children who seem to be drifting in reading yet
have a firm grasp of analytic skills in other areas, such as mathematics, may

need more support in carefully examining words and word particles than those who approach reading from a more holistic perspective.

Phonics, therefore, certainly has a place in language-based instruction, even though it is only one of the cueing systems that young readers need. But worksheets and workbooks intended to teach phonetic decoding seldom promote reading growth for either limited or mature readers. Children in trouble rarely understand how the seatwork will help them develop strength as readers. Good teachers, however, are aware of the need for drawing children's attention to words and letter combinations and are adept at offering children strategies for generalizing principles of sound/letter correlations. At the same time, there is no substitute for children's own reading of real books and their own questions about how words work.

Children cannot become skillful decoders by memorizing generalizations or rules. For neither the expert nor the novice does rote knowledge of an abstract rule, in and of itself, make any difference. Rules are useful only as far as they pertain to experience. Rules are intended to capture the patterns of spelling. But productive use of those patterns depends on relevant experience, not on rote memorization (Adams, 1990, p.83).

Phonic rules and generalizations are, at best, of temporary value. Once a child has learned to read the spellings to which they pertain, they are super-fluous (Adams, 1990, p.126).

Obviously, children who can recognize the letters of the alphabet and are familiar with their function are better prepared for reading. They learn the names, shapes, and sounds connected with letters through games, songs, books, and activities that draw attention to the significance of letters. (A large part of *Sesame Street's* success is its constant promotion of alphabetic awareness.) Through print in context, children begin to conceptualize what a "word" looks like and to appreciate the relationship between sound and shape.

Teachers can help children notice how words work. Sight-sound presentations and word games with partners and in small groups promote an awareness of how syllables blend into words and highlight commonalities and irregularities in groups of words. In every story or poem, some words jump off the page and attract attention. Skilful teachers can emphasize a particular word or group of words—its complexity, sound, shape, connections, incongruities, odd spelling, roots, history, connotations, use, and misuse. Word-attack skills grow as children explore the print characteristics of words—blends, vowels, compounds, and plurals—that they meet as part of a literature experience. They can then apply these attack skills to newer, more complex words and sentences, and the teacher will have promoted a healthy, inquisitive approach to learning how words work and what they mean.

Children find out how stories, poems, and sentences work by experimenting and verbalizing. Similarly, they should choose their own ways to find out how words work. Children enjoy analyzing a word they have discovered in the context of a meaningful language pattern. With further experience, they will be able to apply their independent word-attack skills to longer and more complex words and analyze them for triple blends, root words, prefixes, and suffixes. They can discover general rules and apply them in their reading and writing, verifying the word-attack process with phonic and structural information. (It is in writing that most children find they must learn the relationship between phonemes and graphemes in order to produce words and sentences that others can read.)

It is not just the presence of a variety of activities that makes a program of reading instruction effective or ineffective. It is the way in which its pieces are fitted together to complement and support one another, always with full consideration of the needs and progress of the young readers with whom it will be used (Adams, 1990, p.122).

The teacher's task is not just to understand the significance of each cueing system but to enable children to recognize the need for employing all of them as they attempt to make meaning with print. Reading is a complex act, and children need to use every bit of information at hand in order to interact fully with printed text.

Margaret Mooney (1990) says that children learn to read just as they learn to talk—by seeing others read, by listening to others read to them, by reading with others, and by reading by themselves and to others. In a language-based classroom, then, observers would see the teacher reading to children, the teacher reading with children, children reading silently on their own, and children reading aloud with their friends.

Reading with a Developing Reader
Larry Swartz

Erin is a grade three student who feels quite confident reading pattern books, such as *Would You Rather . . . ?* by John Burningham, but becomes nervous when she meets new vocabulary. She was reading Faith Ringgold's *Tar Beach*, a more difficult book than she is usually comfortable with. She stopped on the word "lifted" and looked to me for help. I suggested that she keep reading as she often found that when she finished a sentence, she was able to go back and understand the word.

When I encouraged Erin to start again and reread the sentence, she corrected "when I stars fell down around me," to "when the stars . . ." When she read that the brother was "leaving still on the mattress," I asked her if that made sense. She looked at the picture and saw that he was "lying" down, so she corrected her miscue. For "floodlight" she began by sounding out the "f" and then the "fl" and made the sounds "flo," "fight," and "flooding" before saying each syllable separately and reading it correctly.

As she read, I frequently asked, "Does that make sense?" For instance, when she read, "I owned all that I can't see," I asked her to reread the sentence and look carefully at the word. Erin tried the following guesses: "can," "couldn't," "can't" again and finally "could." I asked her if that made sense and she agreed that it did. Then she realized that there was no "t" in the word and understood.

"Sleeping on Tar Beach was magical" led to these attempts:

Erin: Sheeping . . .
Teacher: Sheeping? . . .
Erin: (self-corrects) Sleeping on Tar B— (stops).
Teacher: Do you remember the name of the book?
Erin: Sleeping on Tar Beach was a ma (stops and spells) mag (then guesses words that make no sense) mag, magicking, makal . . .
Teacher: Skip it.
Erin: (still guessing) magal, make believe . . .

When Erin finished the page, I asked her to retell what she had read and she answered that the girl was playing "make believe," which was her interpretation of the word "magical."

Sometime miscues or errors made sense to her, and she didn't correct them. Instead of "tracking me through the sky," she read "taking me through the sky," which was semantically and syntactically correct. At the end of the reading, we might have taken the time to go back and examine some of these words.

Erin used her knowledge of the phonographemic cueing system to confirm her guesses. When she substituted "look" for "like" in the phrase, "just like I told him to," she recognized that what she said didn't sound right and on closer inspection, she sounded out the "ike" sound:

Erin: Just look I told him . . .
Teacher: Does that make sense?

Erin:	Just look—like I told him . . .
Teacher:	One more time . . .
Erin:	Just like I told him to.

Though Erin often stumbled over words, we didn't overuse the sounding-out-and-guessing strategy. Sometimes I helped with certain cues (the "wash" in "Washington") and sometimes I pointed out picture clues for her to use (What game are the next-door neighbours playing?).

After a few pages, I asked her to retell what had happened so far in the story. She answered, "The girl was flying all around every- where . . .the next-door neighbours and her brother . . .she told him to lie down on the mattress. . . ." Her ability to recall details indicated appropriate literal comprehension. She even remembered details of passages that had caused her some difficulty when reading the words aloud. She was not so lucky with the following passage:

Daddy said that the George Washington Bridge is the longest and most beautiful bridge in the world and that it opened in 1931, on the very day I was born.

To assess whether she understood what she had just read, I asked her to name two things that happened in 1931. Erin answered, "George Washington had a baby," and when I asked what the second thing was, she said, "The baby was born."

Erin had trouble with the word "bridge," and it appears five times on the first six pages. When I asked her to look at the picture to help her, Erin could see only that the girl was flying over the buildings. Sometimes when she came to the word "bridge," she would say "build- ing," but sometimes she would mumble some gibberish with a "br" sound. On the seventh page, however, the illustration shows the father standing on a platform over some water and Erin read, "'Daddy worked on that bridge . . .' Hey! It's the George Washington Bridge, not building," thereby recognizing and correcting her former miscues.

Erin needs texts with pictures on every page. Gradually, she is being introduced to books that have more text and smaller print. For reading time, Erin chooses to read riddle books or stories that have been read aloud in the classroom (for example, *Polar Bear, Polar Bear, What Do You Hear?* by Bill Martin Jr. and *Owl Moon* by Jane Yolen). Several children around her are reading novels, so she also attempts easy-to-read books such as the *Kids at the Polk Street School* series by Patricia Reilly Giff or the *Pee Wee Scouts* series by Judy Delton. Because the vocabulary is simple and the plots are appealing, these books are luring Erin into becoming a stronger reader.

Ways to Explore the Cueing Systems

There are many techniques teachers can use to help children gain proficiency with the cueing systems. Some are directly related to the reading experience, but opportunities to raise awareness also occur as the children write, talk, paint, or sing.

Using language—oral or written—for many purposes—to describe, give directions, report, complain, ask questions—lets the children discover a variety of pragmatic contexts for language. Reading aloud daily from a wide range of authors, topics, and genres builds familiarity with how print works and the variety of language structures and patterns used in books. The children can also explore different purposes for reading, such as to find information, follow a plot, proofread, make judgements, or appreciate style or mood.

To provide a semantic context, real-life situations such as field trips, nature walks, and hands-on activities can extend the children's background of experiences. Vicarious explorations through television or radio programs, movies, drama, and discussions can also add to their store of knowledge about the world. To build semantic cues for the text the children are about to explore, teachers can ask them before reading to recall and share what they know about a subject. Similarly, asking children to respond to the text in expressive modes such as writing, drama, art, discussion, and music helps clarify and deepen their comprehension.

Children will become aware of syntactic patterns when we encourage them to make predictions before and during reading and move them from word-by-word reading to searching for meaning within the text. Children should read silently most of the time, since reading out loud forces them to focus on each word, rather than on the meaning. We can draw attention to syntactic patterns in literature and encourage the children to experiment with these patterns in their own writing.

Children should hear language both before seeing it in print and while seeing it in print if they are to make the best use of the phonographemic cueing system. The connecting link between sounds and print symbols may be clearest when children see their own words in print. As they attempt to invent spellings to match their speech, they extend, consolidate, and display their knowledge of sound/symbol relationships. Generalizations about sound/symbol relationships will also emerge through playing word games, reading alphabet books, noting rhyming patterns, and looking for words in literature that start with the same sound. Children can tell the group about special words that interest them, scrutinizing the printed form, making generalizations about spelling, and considering exceptions. They can also become aware of the patterns to be found in the syntactic and graphemic pieces of words—the prefixes, suffixes, roots, and plurals and the beginnings and endings, middle letters, unusual letter combinations, silent letters, double letters, and irregularities.

Children should engage in extensive independent reading, in the knowledge that we read to make meaning. They should write frequently, since encoding meaning connects all of the cueing systems. Always we stress the wonder, the puzzles, the surprise, the joy of words. Indeed, we should not forget or fear to teach vocabulary, but rather highlight words in story contexts and through response activities. As children use words, play with them, embroider them, taste them on their tongues, and record them on paper, they will become word people who treasure the sounds and squiggles that give us language.

The Stages of Reading

Most children proceed along a recognizable continuum as they learn to read. The rate of progress from one stage of development to the next differs from individual to individual, and some children may begin to acquire characteristics of the next stage before assimilating all the major characteristics of the one they are in. When assessing children's reading abilities, we should also be aware that the type of text can influence which stage a child appears to be in. Children cannot be hurried through a particular stage, but we can assist their progress by providing appropriate types of reading material. It is important, therefore, to understand the general characteristics of readers as they grow from emergent readers to developing readers to independent readers.

The Emergent Reader

Emergent readers know that books are a source of information and enjoyment and expect to learn to read successfully. They can identify and name most letters and understand common words as well as some of the print they see in the environment, such as street signs and advertising logos. Emergent readers enjoy listening to literature and have favourite stories that they want to hear repeatedly. They look at books voluntarily and attempt to read. They realize that the function of print is to preserve and transmit meaning and that its meaning is fixed, they understand the directionality of print (left to right, top to bottom), and they can follow a line of enlarged print. When they read, they can make meaningful predictions using context and syntax clues.

They use oral language as writers use print—to describe, explain, report, or justify. They can retell past experiences and relate a sequence of events. The literature they read or hear becomes the basis for dramatic play or painting, and conversely, their art is often the basis for their own stories. They want to see their stories written down and like to read them back when they are transcribed by the teacher, a parent, or a friend. They also attempt to write, representing many words with invented spelling (often initial consonants only).

We can build on the enthusiasm of emergent readers by helping them discover that print can be a source of enjoyment, information, and personal enrichment. If our classrooms are filled with lots of environmental print such as the children see in their daily lives, we connect reading to the real world. Related activities before reading will place printed material in a semantic context. Reading materials with repeated syntactic patterns, strong context cues, and vivid illustrations give readers confidence. Familiarity also helps: we can read a story or poem aloud; let the children read along as they listen to it on tape; then have them reread it with a partner.

We can create situations in which children need to use language for various purposes and involve them through discussion, drama, and choral speaking. The shared reading of well-known rhymes and poems from big books, overhead transparencies, or chart paper can bring print to life. Writing the children's own words down for them demonstrates the link between written and spoken language. Publishing the children's writing in books for other children to read lends a real purpose to the writing.

The Developing Reader

Developing readers are beginning to understand sound/symbol relationships and recognize some phonic generalizations (rhyming words, words that start or end the same, digraphs, blends). They pay close attention to the print in order to decode words, sometimes fingerpointing or subvocalizing. (In the past, such behaviours were often frowned on, but for readers at this stage, they are genuine aids to the use of phonographemic cues that will disappear spontaneously as the readers gain proficiency.) Oral reading is often slow and meticulous. Developing readers use all four cueing systems. As they look for meaning, they correct themselves or make meaningful substitutions when the text does not make sense to them.

Developing readers read some things independently. They comprehend what they have read and can retell a story. They have a store of sight words to draw on in both reading and writing. When writing, they represent all syllables with invented or standard spelling and use some conventions of print such as capitalization and punctuation.

Many of the teaching strategies for emergent readers can also be used with developing readers. As the children read, we can draw their attention to various features of words and sentence patterns and encourage them to use context clues to predict words. Silent, independent reading can be established as the norm.

We can involve the children with literature through discussion, drama, choral reading, painting, and writing. Group writing activities with an adult acting as scribe allow everyone to participate in the writing process.

The Independent Reader

Independent readers are able to read material at an appropriate level without assistance. They read silently but occasionally subvocalize when the text is difficult. They use all four cueing systems, make predictions about unfamiliar words, and self-correct when the reading does not make sense. They adjust their reading rate to the material and purpose and comprehend not only at the literal level but also at interpretive and critical levels. When writing, their invented spellings approximate standard spelling.

We can provide a variety of reading materials and types of reading experiences for independent readers—shared reading, rehearsed oral reading, silent independent reading, reading to assist emergent and developing readers. All these will foster an appreciation of literature. As the need for self-esteem is constant, and children need to know their work has meaning, we should continue to publish the children's writing.

When Learning to Read Is Difficult

Some children, like Nyssa, whom we met in Chapter 1, do not easily gain even the incipient understanding of the reading process that most emergent readers exhibit. It is important that we identify these children as early as possible in order to provide them with appropriate support. Leaving them to drift may mean they never catch up with their peers and may doom them unnecessarily to functional illiteracy as adults.

How do we distinguish children who are truly floundering from those who are slow developers, like Larry Swartz's student, Erin? We work mostly by observation. Techniques and check sheets to record such observations are discussed in Chapter 9. Standardized diagnostic tests may also pinpoint specific difficulties. The call for help to school psychologists and special education advisers is not admission that we have failed with a child, but a way of ensuring that that child receives the special help required.

Reading Recovery is an early intervention program for children who are experiencing difficulty during their first year of reading instruction. Reading Recovery is a remarkably successful remedial program developed in New Zealand by Marie Clay. It has recently gained popularity in North America. Children having trouble learning to read are withdrawn daily for individual 30-minute lessons with a specially trained teacher; during these sessions, the children read real books and write and read their own stories. The teacher's response will vary according to the individual child's strengths, needs, and interests. He or she finds opportunities to draw attention to the details of print and to the letter-sound associations and spelling patterns that arise within those activities. Children learn to use their literacy knowledge and to recognize the functions of print. These tutorials do not take the place of regular classroom instruction and the intervention is not intended to be long-term. As soon as a child has successfully caught up with peers, the program is discontinued, and another child is able to receive the individual tutoring.

Reading Recovery worked for Dante, a grade one student for whom everything seemed difficult (Pinnell, Fried, and Estice, 1990). Dante was chosen to participate in the program because he was one of the lowest achieving students in his class. In the Reading Recovery Diagnostic Survey (Clay, 1985) in October, he could write his first name, *a*, and *cat*, and he could hear and record the sounds for *b, s, t,* and *l.* He demonstrated that he did not understand that the words on a page should match spoken language. Twelve weeks later, he had made some progress: he could write fifteen words, most of which had been introduced in the basal reading program his teacher was using, and he could hear and record 21 sounds, but he did not apply these skills in the real task of reading.

Dante began receiving Reading Recovery lessons in January, starting by reading many short books with repetitive patterns and clear illustrations with his teacher. They also wrote stories together and used these for rereading. He learned to check his reading, to self-correct, and to search for cues. He learned to write high-frequency words, to listen for sounds in words in order to analyze unknown words, and to write useful letter chunks, such as *-s* and *-ing.* By April, his new-found abilities and confidence were evident throughout the school day. His classroom teacher said she knew Dante had become a reader the day the librarian from the public library visited to explain the summer library program and she and Dante greeted each other on a first-name basis.

When the researchers last caught up with Dante, he was in grade five and, according to his teacher, a strong reader and writer. He performed extremely well on various diagnostic and achievement tests. Because he had caught up by the end of grade one, he had been able to take advantage of later learning opportunities. The researchers believe that without a program like Reading Recovery, he probably would have remained a low achiever, year after year, as so many similar students do.

In these times of economy and retrenchment, teachers at Queenston do not have access to the extra financing that a program like Reading Recovery requires. Queenston teachers have noticed, however, that Reading

Recovery is based on the same philosophy of teaching and theory of literacy development that they use in their classroom practice. Therefore, they offer students at risk as much as possible of the intensive one-on-one attention of Reading Recovery during reading and writing conferences; they call on the help of special education instructors and teaching aides; and they arrange for these students to work with volunteer helpers and parents, whom they tell what to look for and what to celebrate.

A Frame for Developing Literacy

As effective teachers working with young readers, we have many strategies to support emerging literacy.

Reading Aloud to Children

Although one of the long-term goals in reading aloud to children is to encourage literacy and promote reading skills, the primary, immediate goal is to share the joy of literature. Successful stories and poems contain action, suspense, surprise, and characters with whom the children can identify. As they listen to lyrics, ballads, myths, fairy tales, folk tales, and stories of their own time, children gain literary background and develop imagination and awareness of language.

The language of books is not the same as the language of talk. Listening to literature introduces the children to vocabulary, sentence patterns, and story forms that are quite different from those they meet in conversation. They collect ideas, words, and language patterns with which to begin their own reading and writing.

Children who are read to frequently are likely to come to love books and to want to read themselves. When they see teachers and other adults reading to gain information and enjoyment from print, they will perceive reading books not only as a childhood pleasure, but as a desirable lifelong activity.

Young children want to hear the same books again and again. They enjoy retelling the stories from memory and from picture clues. They may also develop their own tastes in literature and art, preferring books by particular authors and illustrators. An appreciation of representational methods, style, and artistic media is valuable in its own right, as well as developing an eye for detail that is useful in analyzing print.

As they watch and listen to an adult read, children become aware that books are read in a particular fashion; they begin to look carefully at print; and they come to understand that the story they are hearing was *written* by someone. As children listen and respond to literature, they predict, make inferences, hypothesize, identify with characters, respond critically and creatively—and develop a sense of story. They will later use these skills in their own reading.

Reading with Children

Using text in a big book, a chart, or a projected visual for shared reading allows us to build on preschool experiences with print and gives the children immediate success in their reading. Poems, songs, and stories that are worth repeating will become favourites. The use of repetition, refrain, rhythm, and rhyme, and repeated syntactic patterns applies the children's extensive experience with listening and speaking to the task of reading. As they hear and see a well-known selection over and over again, the children begin to synchronize their voices with the print.

The print itself gives children opportunities to pick out specific words or letters, match words, find words with similar beginnings, recognize frequently repeated words or phrases, ask questions and make observations about what has been read, and anticipate and predict what will come next. The children can retell the story or parts of the story to each other. They will continue to read "through the ear" in later years as they are read to in school and at home, listen to tapes and records, and hear their own voices as they read to younger children and take part in singing, choral speaking, and other shared experiences.

We must begin by giving children "sufficient prior knowledge of what they are expected to read" (Smith, 1986). Alphabet books, counting books, books based on culturally significant sequences such as days of the week or months of the year, books that use simple patterns from one page to the next— all allow children to enter the print world with confidence. When we read such books to children, they can often join in on the second or third reading. They begin to feel that they are readers and that they can take pride in demonstrating real reading behaviour.

The literary power of a reading selection provides the greatest opportunity for a young reader to make meaning. The story, the images, the sounds, the rhythms, the words—all come together to make "literary sense." Reading power grows from worthwhile print experiences. Bill Martin Jr. (1972) invites us to consider "the ingenuous, cumulative coupling of sequences" in his *Brown Bear, Brown Bear:*

> *Brown bear, brown bear, what do you see?*
> *I see a red bird looking at me.*
> *Red bird, red bird, what do you see?*

I see a yellow duck looking at me.
Yellow duck, yellow duck, what do you see?
I see a blue horse looking at me . . .

The coupling has nothing and yet everything to do with reading. Momentarily banished are the restrictions of print, the preoccupation with eye movements from left to right, and "today's new words" drill. The literature creates its own life. The linguistic dance of the question and answer in Brown Bear *is so pervasive and appealing that the reader is caught up in it and responds without labored awareness of technicalities and rules.*

The important meaning of these and other [books] is not the story facts. It is irrelevant which animal Brown Bear saw or what trick was performed on which floor of the apartment house. The humanly worthwhile meanings are found in the playfulness of the language, in the interrelations of color and design and story evolvements, and in the inculcated awareness that life is worth living.

Independent Reading

Children need large blocks of time for silent reading. They need to know that making sense of print is what reading is all about; that we read to understand and to reflect upon what we have read. Children learn to read through regular and active engagement with meaningful text. Therefore, the number and quality of the books children read will influence their success. As Marilyn Jager Adams reminds us, "Research indicates that the most critical factor beneath fluent word reading is the ability to recognize letters, spelling patterns and whole words, effortlessly, automatically and visually" (1990, p.14). Such facility does not arrive overnight.

The books we select for young readers must support their reading growth. Their comprehension of the text is determined by the ease with which they are able to perceive words. Successful word recognition promotes independence in reading and supports the understanding of the ideas in the text. "To maximize achievement, children should be given texts that they can read orally with 90-95% accuracy" (Adams, 1990, p.126), or as Liz Waterland puts it,

Children should know what they are going to read before they read it. This is not the same as teaching the words of the first primer on flash cards so that all are known before the book is tackled. It means letting children hear where the story is going and why, so that they can predict the sense and the language. Yet, somehow, there is an uncomfortable feeling that this is "cheating," that children ought to tackle a text cold or they aren't really reading. This is like saying the toddler isn't really speaking when repeating the name of something after us, or chanting a nursery rhyme. It is the firm expectation of what is likely and possible that is built up by this approach. Once children know a poem or story it is surprising how quickly they can locate its parts on a printed page and read it (1988, p. 14).

With the reading of familiar texts, the reader begins to take risks by making informed guesses. The language cues begin to mesh, and the child takes on more of the reading, making the text meaningful.

Through engaging in the lifeblood of a real book, children are not practising for reading: they are reading. They are also adding thousands of words to their language storehouses. Words have no meaning outside a given context, and a story is a meaning-referenced collection of words. Since language works in chunks of meaning, a good story provides an invaluable source for learning useful and powerful words. This reservoir of words embedded in meaningful structures is part of a lifelong building process: the acquisition of language. The more significance a word has as a literary structure, the greater the hope of adding that word to the reader's storehouse.

A classroom library needs to cater to a wide readership and should include a selection of quality books from a variety of cultural settings. Children need help in learning to select books that are useful and appropriate. Those in difficulty need a great deal of encouragement, and others may need assistance in reading more books or more difficult books. We must be supportive and nurturing of children's choices and try to modify the books children choose without implying criticism.

Reading in Groups

If all children have experienced a text in depth, they can come together to discuss it. They can look at events in the story that touched them as they read, ask questions, and discuss puzzling aspects. They can share possibilities, create new meanings, and rethink their own interpretations by listening to the ideas of others. Individuals can then work on their own with features of the story that seem important to their understanding and bring back their new findings the next day—perhaps a chart of the actions in the stories or a floor plan of the characters' house. The study group helps them realize the depth of experience each story brings.

Each person's talents, experiences, and perspectives are unique, and the members of the group soon begin to value the contributions of the individual to the general discussion and to see mistakes as part of the learning rather than as "wrong." As group members find out what each other thinks, the group sharing leads to more meaning making for the individuals. They

The Book contest

We had a contest in our class to choose a favourite Book. First everybody got a picture Book. Then we into partner and read the book to each other. We both chose which book we like. the most. After that, we got into groups of four and chose another book. The finalists were "professor Noahs Spaceship", "The Great Kapok Tree," "Lulu and The Flying Babies" "Were Back", "Giant", and "A Day with Willbur Robinson" LaLu and The Flying Babies was the 1# winner.

Jeffrey
by Jamie

find out that interacting with print means interacting with a text, the author, the members of the group, and their own experiences as they explore the multiple facets of literacy.

Reading in groups requires multiple copies of the same stories, but the average classroom library cannot afford such duplication. This is where a reading series comes into play. Graded "readers" are regarded as anathema by some language arts specialists, but it is often not the books themselves that are the problem, but rather the uses to which they are put that "destroys their impact for most children" (Holdaway, 1979). A reading series does not replace a large number of fine children's books at various reading levels in the classroom; an anthology can comprise only a fixed number of pages. However, anthologies of good materials can support a balanced classroom reading program in a number of ways: children can follow common reading experiences with discussion and joint activity; they can read together chorally and share literary moments aloud with each other; they will enjoy reading a well-chosen anthology of stories and poems; anthologies "provide easy, unseen reading which is so important in developing the 'I-can-read-all-by-myself' feeling" (Holdaway, 1979); and parents may relax if they know their child has "mastered" an approved text. Anthologies may include selections that are otherwise unavailable to children—fine stories that may be out of print, stories with hard-to-obtain illustrations by great artists, examples of the best in children's literature. A literature-based reading series can provide teachers with supportive structures for developing programs, along with suggestions for other books and media to extend and enrich the themes begun in the anthologies. "A whole group of children of different abilities [should not be] forced to progress through the series, willy-nilly" (Holdaway, 1979).

Connecting Writing and Reading

Children should begin to write as soon as possible. Attempts at making meaning with print—groups of letters, sounds represented by consonants, whole words—often appear in preschool and kindergarten amid the usual pretend or scribble writing. Independent writing activities help children appreciate the reciprocal nature of making meaning with print: that they can record messages as well as receive them. Early writing—formulating, organizing, and expressing their ideas on paper—encourages them to think actively about print and sound/spelling relationships. "Classroom encouragement of invented spellings is a promising approach to the development of phonemic awareness and knowledge of spelling patterns" (Adams, p.126).

Some children who have wide experience with print, both in books and in the environment, may make the connection between sounds and symbols early and try to incorporate this knowledge into their own writing. Such attempts should be encouraged. Growth can happen very quickly if the teacher shows an interest in what children have written. Not all children will experiment in this way. Drawing, mapping, tracing, modelling, and constructing are all representational activities that foreshadow writing for children who are not yet ready to work with print, just as looking at pictures foreshadows reading. It is enough for many children to enjoy the literature,

Once there was a mother bird. One day the mother bird had a baby. Everybody was there. The baby bird had 14 brothers and 30 sisters and 50 cousins and 80 aunts and uncles and dads and moms. A couple of years later the bird was eighteen. It was her birthday. She had every present in her family (to go). When it was over it was time to go to bed. The end.

participate in oral activities, and be involved in group composition. There will be plenty of time for them to focus on print when they are ready to do so. The teacher's role is to provide materials, opportunities, and purposes for writing and to respond to the children's efforts.

Children who read and listen to a wide variety of books begin to understand how writers work; learning to read and learning to write are connected processes. By adapting language patterns, by borrowing words and structures from stories, by writing about ideas suggested in a book, and by using books to model their own writing, children can develop as "print users" who read and write to make meaning.

The teachers at Queenston use many of the techniques that Jo Phenix, a resource teacher with the Peel board, has used in her own grade one classroom. The children's own writing is part of the classroom collection of reading materials and helps children become a part of what they read, hear, and view. Jo takes children beyond straight word recognition. She encourages them to imagine, to picture what the words say, and to seek out and play with the patterns inherent in the language. Children in Jo Phenix's classes are actively engaged in their "own words" as well as the "words of others."

Readers as Writers, Writers as Readers
Jo Phenix

At the beginning, most children's writing is just a one-word label. For example, in Colleen's book on Hallowe'en, each page has a single picture: "pumpkin," "ghost" "bat," "witch." Janet uses a sentence on each page in the same kind of repeated pattern:

I like hearts on all kinds of things. I like hearts on swing sets. I like them on cars. I like hearts on pictures. I like hearts on clowns. I like hearts on games.

Angie's "I Was Walking at the Forest" is a bit more complex.

I was walking at the forest, I saw the sun. He said hello, and my friend said, "Hello, Mr. Sun," and the sun said hello back to us. I was walking at the forest. I saw trees. They said hello to me. I was happy. I said, "Did you say something?" They said, "Yes." Then I woke up with my sister. We went to the forest, I saw flowers. The flowers said hello to me, I said hello back to them. One day I woke up. I went to the forest. I went by myself. Then my friend came. I went to the forest. The sky said hello to me. I said hello back to him!

In the children's writing you can hear all kinds of literary and linguistic structures that have come from the literature they have read and heard. This is particularly true of group writing. We brainstorm different ideas, different settings, different concepts for the pattern; we collect words and ideas and develop new ideas around the same pattern. The groups then take turns in a story circle to read their work aloud.

For example, once they worked with a poem called "Over There" by Cynthia Mitchell. Here is an excerpt.

*Over the rice fields, over the kites,
over the top of the northern lights.*

Over the ice fields, over the snow,
right to the ends of the earth we'll go.

Groups of four children working together wrote pattern books. One group chose to write about the bottom of the ocean:

Over the rocks, under the fish,
beside a whale, through the seaweeds,
near the starfish, around an octopus,
on top of the sand, across a submarine,
past some shells, on top of the seal,
beside an otter, at the end of a shark,
right to the bottom of the ocean we'll go.

Another group chose the rainbow:

Under the sun, on top of a house,
through the clouds, under the clouds,
behind some clouds, across the jet,
over a fence, around the children,
in the pond, on the driveway,
past all the bright colours, near a pot of gold,
right to the end of the rainbow we'll go.

The pattern is the same but the concept is different.

The visuals the children create are also important. When they work individually, some of the children illustrate before they write and others after. A group can work both ways, too. If it's a pattern that they are using, usually the words come first. If it's an idea, very often the pictures will come first.

I encourage the children to use invented spelling, so they get their ideas down on paper. Most of them put letters down on paper right from the start, and when they read the story to me, I transcribe for those who can't write enough letters for the work to be readable. So sometimes the writing in the group books is my printing.

You'll notice that their word choice is not monosyllabic "basal reader" style It's their own language, or that of the literature they are working with. It's interesting that when they are reading their own stories aloud, they read with meaning, "chunking" the words into groups. In fact, that's the only way they can read them—the way they wrote them. I think they learn to read for meaning by reading their own stories, because they are used to putting meaning in these stories. Therefore, they expect to find meaning in a story written by someone else; they expect it to make sense. There's no real transition from reading their own writing to reading the words of others. They go side by side, growing together.

I can hear the literary and linguistic patterns and the ideas they use in their writing in the stories I read aloud to them. The counting book below is patterned on "One, One, Cinnamon Bun" by Clyde Watson (*Catch Me, Kiss Me, Say It Again*, 1978). I printed their own ideas for the counting rhyme on chart paper, and they used this as reading material for their choral reading. Here, the oral words came before the writing; the children did the illustrations for the story and published it in a book, "One, One, Elephants Come."

One, one, elephants come,
two, two, kangaroo,
three, three honeybee,
four, four, lions roar,
five, five, sea lions dive,
six six, baby chicks,
seven, seven, a bear called Kevin,
eight, eight, monkeys wait,
nine, nine, porcupine,
ten, ten, start again.

They brainstormed to find the rhymes for each number and tried several themes before they settled on one for which they could find the right rhyming words. My contribution was to put the numbers in black and the rhyming words in red. It made it easy for them to read. You can also do a choral response by writing alternate lines in different colours and asking groups to take either the red ones or the black ones.

The care artists take in the graphic design of children's books— how much goes on a page, the size of the print—is equally important for classroom publishing. When children write their own work, they should be able to read it easily. This is a pattern book based on the nursery rhyme "A Was an Apple Pie." The brainstorming of the story line was done as a group, and individual children then chose pages to illustrate.

A was an airplane.	*H heard it take off.*
B built it.	*I iced up the wings.*
C cleaned it.	*J just landed it.*
D dusted it.	*K kept the key.*
E entered it.	*L looped the loop.*
F flew it.	*M made the engine.*
G gassed it up.	*N named it.*

O opened the door.	*U unfastened the seat-belt.*
P piloted it.	*V vacuumed it.*
Q quit the job.	*W watched the movie.*
R rode in it.	*X exited.*
S stopped it.	*Y yawned on it.*
T towed it.	*Z zoomed into the air.*

An interesting point about alphabet books is that the children do a lot of research using the ABC books in the classroom. They don't know many words beginning with Q, and they find it interesting to make a list and decide which one they can use in their story. Then they start looking for words they can use for X and other more difficult letters. Here they were starting from a book called *Q Is for Duck*. It didn't take the children long to catch on to the pattern of that one.

A is for trampoline.	*Why? Because the trampoline has acrobats.*
B is for house.	*Why? Because a house is built.*
C is for baby.	*Why? Because the baby cries.*
D is for fire.	*Why? Because a dragon breathes fire.*
E is for volcano.	*Why? Because a volcano erupts.*

The answers are written upside down, and it's interesting to watch which children bother to turn the page and which ones just go ahead and read upside down. This one required much more thought. They were really fooling with the language, working with the concept, and building a whole new pattern.

This next story also started with brainstorming and illustrating all the things the children do in the snow. Then, working as a group, they put the illustrations in sequence and dictated the story, which they then cut and pasted together. It starts in the morning.

One day I woke up, I looked out of the window. It was snowing. I put my clothes on, I put my shirt and my sweater and my leg warmers and my pants on. (This is illustrated with cut-and-paste collage like Ezra Jack Keats's A Snowy Day*) I put on my snowpants, my boots, my mittens, my coat, my hat, my earmuffs, and my scarf. I was ready to go. Then I picked up my friend. She came outdoors. We rolled a big snowball. (That's a direct copy from John Burningham's* The Snow. *They liked that idea.) We made a snowman with buttons out of raisins, a carrot nose and a licorice mouth. We dressed him in a scarf, mitts, and a hat. We fed the birds some bread, crackers, popcorn, and bird seed. We made some angels in the snow. And dug and dug and dug and made tunnels in the snow. We went in to see what it felt like. It felt freezing and wet. We made an igloo. We made a big pile of snow and* *dug out the insides and crowded inside and played. We saw bird tracks, dog tracks, stick tracks. We made sculptures. The snow has to be hard. We took a sharp stick and carved it. We skated on the pond and I fell down. It felt cold and I bumped my head. My friend and I fell down together. I went down the hill with the sled with my friend, I held on to my friend. When we came home we saw the Christmas lights on the house. They shone on my face. I felt bright and happy as it was almost Christmas. I took off my winter clothes. We had hot chocolate; it was hot and sweet and it smelled chocolatey. I liked the marshmallows, it made me feel happy. We warmed our hands in front of the flaming fire. We sang carols and watched Christmas specials. It was night. It was still snowing. My friend went home. I went to bed. I felt tired. I would dream about everything I did today. I hope it snows tomorrow.*

They ended the story the same way John Burningham did. We have here a compendium of two styles rather than two syntactic patterns. They are beginning to apply the style of authorship to their own work.

Here's a counting story:

One rainy Tuesday morning, while on my way to school, I saw two shivering geese flying away, one wet puddle freezing, near the little path through the woods. One windy Wednesday morning, while on my way to school, I saw three shivering geese flying away, two wet puddles freezing, one yellow leaf falling, near the little path through the woods. One thundering Thursday morning, while on my way to school, I saw four shivering geese flying away, three wet puddles freezing, two yellow leaves falling, one cold squirrel gathering nuts near the little path through the woods. One foggy Friday morning, while on my way to school, I saw five shivering geese flying away, four wet puddles freezing, three yellow leaves falling, two cold squirrels gathering nuts, one chilly child wearing a warm coat, near the little path through the woods. One snowy Saturday morning, while on my way to the synagogue, I saw six shivering geese flying away, five wet puddles freezing, four yellow leaves falling, three cold squirrels gathering nuts, two chilly children wearing warm coats, one soft snowflake swirling, near the little path through the woods. One freezing Sunday morning, while on my way to the church, I saw seven shivering geese flying away, six wet puddles freezing, five yellow leaves falling, four cold squirrels gathering nuts, three chilly children wearing warm coats, two soft snowflakes swirling, one cheerful snowman grinning, near the little path through the woods. One cloudy Monday morning, while on my way to school, I saw geese flying, puddles freezing, leaves falling, squirrels gathering, children wearing coats, snowflakes swirling, snowmen grinning. Why? It's winter.

A lot of things went on during the writing of this one. At first it was just a bare list of geese and puddles and leaves and squirrels. On a second draft, the children added some of the other words. It was by chance that someone noticed the alliteration in "chilly children," and then they went back and changed some of the other words to make it happen in other parts of the story, too. Their word awareness came after the ideas. This is really quite a sophisticated story: it has a climax and uses cultural patterns, days of the week, and counting backward. Everything that is listed on the page is shown in the illustrations, so if it says "six shivering geese," there are six shivering geese in the picture. It really forced them to put the detail into the illustrations, too.

The children like to hear the same stories over and over, and they memorize the story patterns. This is Andrea's story, "The Beanstalk."

Once upon a time in a faraway land, there lived a princess and all around they were poor. One day there was a storm and the palace's window opened and the princess was gone. Then one day Mickey saw the cow between the beans. Mickey ran home. "I got one bean." "Beans, beans?" said Donald. "They're not ordinary beans," said Mickey. Donald threw the beans out the window. That night the beans started to grow and grow and grow. The next morning Mickey woke up with a surprise. He called to Donald and Goofy. They climbed and climbed and climbed until they came to the top. And then they saw a big castle.

She has the foundations of fairy tale, the qualities of fairy tale, the story grammar embedded in the writing. She really likes things like "to grow and grow and grow, and they climbed and climbed and climbed . . ." She uses that a lot in her writing. It ends with the Disney characters finding the princess:

"How did you get there?" "A giant captured me," she said. "A giant?" said Mickey. "Yes," she said. They all heard her. Then the giant made her sing a song and he fell asleep. They quietly took her. Then they were at the bottom. Mickey hurried, and the giant was dead, and they put the princess back in the castle and they lived happy ever after.

This next child has a firm grasp on literary form. Paris comes from a Greek family and his mother tells him the Greek stories, over and over again. When Paris came to school, he knew them well. Paris will go for quite a long time without writing very much at all, or anything of much value. Then, when he is ready, he starts to write one of his stories, such as "Hercules," which he wrote when he was just seven.

Once upon a time there was a boy called Hercules. One day Hercules was in his crib. Two poisonous snakes went there. Hercules strangled them with his hand. From that day Hercules was a hero of all making. Hercules grew up and went to school and learned many things. Most of all Hercules liked to help people. The people believed Hercules was a son of God, or God because he was so strong. Goddess Hera was very jealous and made Hercules do something bad. When Hercules realized what he did, he prayed to God Apollo what he could do to purify himself. Hercules was commanded to do the twelve labours that were impossible for any other ordinary man.

Paris has amazing structures and vocabulary and formality of language because storytelling is an old tradition in his family and because he is an avid reader. He is a boy who likes to be by himself, and any spare moment that he's got he goes out by himself and he reads. It's interesting that the other children recognize the quality in his writing. Paris has a lot of respect in the class as a writer.

"Prince of Troy" took him a long time to write because he was a little embarrassed about his own name being in it. The story structure, the detail, and the sequence in the story are just phenomenal—Menelaus and the Trojan war and the wooden horse, and the story of Achilles are all there. Paris ends his story saying:

Prince Paris fought until death for his country and his love. The army won the war by the clever scheme of the wooden horse. This is the end of the Trojan war and the most beautiful love of Paris and Helen.

No other children in the class can write this way, and it's interesting that in between stories like these, Paris will spend maybe two or three weeks writing things of very little quality. This is something that's important to him, it matters, and he seems to put all his writing energy into it.

Children express their own intuitive emotional feelings and ideas best when something really does concern them. That's something you can't plan for. When they are ready to write something personal, they do. Sometimes what they've read, or I've read aloud, triggers a personal emotional response. The children will talk to each other about the story and apply it to their own experience. This is "When I Was Sick" by Anita.

One day I was sick. My friend came over. She brought me some flowers to make me feel better. I said, "Thank you." She said, "You're welcome." Then my other friend came over too, and she gave me flowers. And I said, "Thank you," and I feel better from the flowers my friends brought.

They knew that I would feel better. I was happy. I felt better and I was very surprised. When one of my friends just went home, my other friend was surprised too. My friend said, "Maybe it's because she catches your germ, because she catches all of her friends' germs. So I guess she doesn't want to get a cold." And she said, "I think I should go home too so I don't catch your cold." "But then who will play with me?" "Play with someone else that's sick too." Then my mom gave me some hot chocolate and I felt better. But I had very much fun at home. I even had lunch in bed. I never knew that when you're sick it's still good fun.

She's taking her own experience and giving it a literary format. And she's putting some humour in there, too.

The use of dialogue often happens right from the start. Sometimes they're not aware of it as dialogue, and it's just a thought stream. When you mention that somebody is talking on their page, they can soon recognize it, and they seem to learn about quotation marks very easily. In fact, it's the first punctuation they usually learn. Once they've used it, they never forget it.

This kind of reading and writing combination seems to make them better at choosing books. At the beginning, they choose either books that have good pictures or ones they think are easy to read. But suddenly, they choose books because they are interested in the content, in what's in the book. And I think that's the breakthrough for them in reading. They even go after particular authors. We used to have an author of the week, and we have author collections. Arnold Lobel was a favourite, A. A. Milne for a while, John Burningham at present. The style of the author comes through in the children's writing, too.

I think that this kind of literature approach also affects their development as human beings because their reading and their sharing of their own writing leads them to become aware of audience, different points of view, and what other people think about things. They sometimes start off very critical of each other, but they grow more sensitive to the kind of things you say to others about their writing and their ideas. It's hard for little children to accept other people's ideas and to listen when other people talk, and I think this kind of experience in sharing helps them.

This kind of embedded language play and usage remains with them throughout the school. You see it in their writing, you see it in the games they play, you see the patterns going out onto the playground and the patterns from their games coming back into the classroom.

Oral Reading

Traditionally, in a reading lesson, children read aloud so the teacher could check pronunciation and reading fluency. Such unrehearsed oral reading was usually a painful time for troubled readers—and an embarrassing one for their more proficient friends. "Round reading," with each child reading a sentence or paragraph for the class, may even decrease a child's appreciation of the meaning of the story; it tends to be merely an exercise in pronouncing words. Children should not be required to participate in such meaningless activity. Without the opportunity to think about what they are reading and to notice how others are feeling and what they are wondering, children will be sharing print aloud for no real reason, often decoding phonetically and comprehending almost nothing. Children need the opportunity to come to grips with the meat of the story before attempting to share it.

And yet oral interpretation, when done well, can improve comprehension skills, lead to revelation for the reader, and strengthen the grasp of a particular interpretation for the listener. Reading aloud in pairs or in small groups is a pleasant way to enjoy a story. Reading to parents and older siblings lets children demonstrate favourite stories. Shared reading of texts in big books or on chart paper is a confidence-building group experience, in which the group's efforts carry the individual along. Beyond taking part in activities such as these, children should be asked to read orally only for specific purposes such as to verify an answer; to show they have located a specific detail; to share an enjoyable part of a selection with others; to dramatize parts of a story; or to re-create dialogue. If they are going to read orally for an audience, they should be given a chance to rehearse. Oral reading then has a legitimate purpose that the children can understand.

Retelling

Retelling a story is far more valuable than simply reading aloud words that lose their context in the process. Many of the strategies we employ in teaching children to read involve asking them to retell to improve their comprehension, fluency, and word recognition. When children retell a story to make sure they know it before reading it to another child, their growing familiarity with all aspects of the text clarifies and modifies their ideas and understandings. When a group of children tape the dialogue of a story as a script, they are practising skills of interpretation and using the responses of peers to deepen their own understanding of the meaning of the text.

Retelling becomes a vehicle whereby reading and writing . . . can be explored and developed. It is a powerful strategy for enabling children to transform a text into their own words, taking in what is only truly comprehended. By so doing, not only are they transforming information, they are unconsciously, and painlessly, learning to write in a particular genre, using style and sentence patterns, vocabulary and all other accoutrements of different forms of text (Cambourne, 1988, p.41).

Jane McGarvey, a primary teacher involved in the Peel TALK Project, has established a storytelling centre in her classroom. The children tell their stories on tape so others can listen to them at a later time. They also use the tapes as a basis for their writing.

Laura Tells a Story
Jane McGarvey

I started trying out formal storytelling lessons after the students listened to *Strega Nona* by Tomie de Paola. They told stories in role to convince Strega Nona they were in need of her help. When we read Judith Viorst's *Alexander and the Terrible Horrible No-Good Very Bad Day* together, they detailed their own very worst day to a partner (embellishing as necessary). Such activities were met with enthusiasm and success. But, this wasn't quite what I was interested in any more.

I thought about my own childhood and what I expected of my grade one writing program, and I felt it was important that I learn about storytelling as an art. I am told I had lots of stories to tell as a young child, and we ask primary students to retell personal experiences in journals and to create books in their writing folders. So, together, the students, our friend the librarian, and I identified sources of stories. We studied the work of one storyteller (Robert Munsch) and told stories we knew by heart.

By October we started to look at ourselves a little differently. We discovered real-live storytellers among us. Laura, a small, at times quiet, grade one student, was the first to try audiotaping a story she knew by heart. After reviewing how to load, record, pause, stop, rewind, and play the tape recorder, Laura went into the hall to tape a story she had learned at summer camp. She was gone a *long* time. When she returned, her smile signalled success. Her only problem had been interruptions by passersby in the hallway. We both put on headphones, listened, and laughed! Here is a transcript of Laura's story:

This is the story about The Baby and the Oatmeal. It is being told by Laura.
Once upon a time there was a family and the baby wanted something to eat. (So she sent her little . . .) The mother sent the little girl

downstairs to get some oatmeal. And she got half way down the cellar
stairs when she heard a voice say, "I . . . I am the ghost with the one
black eye." So she ran upstairs, told the mother, "There's a ghost down-
stairs in the cellar." So baby couldn't eat her oatmeal.

Does your teacher let you be here?

Quiet!

(So she went) So she sent (her brother, the brother) the little boy
downstairs to get some oatmeal. Then, then he got half way down the
cellar stairs when he heard a voice say, "I am the ghost with the one
black eye." He ran upstairs and told the mother that the baby couldn't
have any oatmeal.

So then the father came home. (He said) The mother said, ("You're
going . . .") "Baby wants some oatmeal so you're going to have to go
downstairs to get some oatmeal." So he got, he got half way down the
cellar stairs until he heard a voice say, "I am the ghost with the one
black eye." He ran upstairs, told the mother (he couldn't) baby couldn't
have any oatmeal. So the mother went downstairs by herself. (So, and)
And then she got half way down the cellar stairs . . .

What are you doing?

Be quiet!

. . . she got half way down the cellar stairs when she heard a voice
say, "I am the ghost with the one black eye." She ran upstairs, told baby
he couldn't have any oatmeal. (So she ran) So the baby jumped out of
her high chair and ran downstairs. He (went) got all the way down the
cellar stairs when he heard a ghost say, "I am the ghost with the one
black eye." (Baby told the ghost) Baby said, "If you don't give me my
oatmeal, you'll have two black eyes!"

As fall progressed to winter, interest in taping new stories

by Laura age 6

fluctuated. Then something happened spontaneously that rekindled the excitement. Laura's story became a favourite choice at the listening centre. During our not-necessarily-quiet activity periods, a voice might be heard to boom, "I am the ghost with the one black eye!" I asked Laura if she would consider teaching the rest of the class her story. Laura played off the tape, asking us to "pair and share" after each short segment, and we all learned the story by heart.

Storytelling had a positive effect on story writing that jumped off the pages! Laura's own written version of the story indicates her growing awareness of the feelings of the ghost and its voice. A version written by a grade two classmate who had been struggling with language arts clearly shows how her active involvement in learning to tell the story has allowed her to make it her own.

In spring, when warm temperatures returned, we finally came up with a solution to our recurring storytelling/taping problem. An extension cord allowed storytellers to sit outside the classroom window and tell their tales without interruption.

Teaching Exceptional Students

The principles of fostering language development for children with special needs are consistent with those for regularly achieving children. Research by specialists working with such children indicates that they learn best in real language situations, exploring new meanings and integrating them into what they already know, just as "normal" children do. The teacher's task is to find ways of matching language competency with the demands of the curriculum in the classroom to ensure the child's language growth—and delight.

Debate over how to teach reading and writing to students with learning disabilities continues between those who teach reading and writing as a sequence of component skills and those whose teaching is based on a holistic theory of instruction. The behavioural model—training the child to give the desired response to a particular stimulus through drill and practice—has perhaps been even more prominent, and persisted longer, than it has in classroom teaching in general. Rhodes and Dudley-Marling (1988) explain that teaching methods and attitudes may be especially crucial for these children. What they eventually learn and how they learn it will be even more affected by their previous experiences, by what they already know, and what they know is expected of them.

Current identification practices, which stress academic underachievement, have produced a heterogeneous population of LD [learning disabled] students, students who are as different from each other as they are from normally achieving children. Although we favor holistic approaches to reading and writing instruction with all children, they may be especially valuable for LD and remedial learners. Behavioral approaches to written language instruction subject LD and remedial students to years of meaningless drill and practice. Additionally, the constant barrage of drill and practice focuses on students' deficits, or weaknesses. This deficit model, with its constant reminder to students of their inadequacies, has had a devastating effect on the lives of many LD and remedial students (Poplin, 1984). Finally, drill and practice encourage passivity in learners. The teacher decides what is to be learned and how it is to be learned. Because of the focus on isolated skills, students are unable to take advantage of previous learning.

It's our view that reading and writing cannot be learned by breaking written language down into fragmented parts. We are firmly committed to holistic approaches because they are consistent with our view of the world and of learning. For us the world can be understood only by examining whole systems, not by analyzing fragmented parts. We also believe that, except in cases of adult interference, children learn holistically. They learn about their world by confronting their world in natural settings and actively trying to make sense of it. They do not make sense of their world by first focusing on isolated, meaningless bits of information.

Reading and writing, like other higher forms of human learning, must be learned in natural contexts. Fragmenting written language into skills and subskills does violence to the very nature of written language.

English as a Second Language or Dialect

As the racial, ethnic, cultural, and linguistic diversity of a community changes, so do the educational needs of its children. In recent years, the number of children entering our elementary schools who speak English only as a second language, or who have little proficiency in English at all, has increased dramatically. In some schools, "ESL/ESD" children make up a majority of the school population. Queenston Drive Public School is in an area that has attracted a large number of immigrant families. Teachers and administrators at schools like Queenston have made significant changes in their classrooms, their schools, and their programs to serve their students.

Although children who do not speak English are welcomed into a reception classroom, those of us who have learned a second language know from experience that we do not gain true mastery until we are immersed in the language environment and truly need to communicate. We also know that children placed in the regular classroom as soon as possible will feel part of the community sooner and learn language much faster from real interaction with native speakers..The ESL teacher can then move through the school working with the children and assisting the teachers by offering special strategies for working with ESL children.

While we encourage children to integrate with the life of the classroom and the wider community, we have learned that we must give due weight and respect to the first language and cultural background of the children and their families. Research indicates that, while most school settings do not provide for it, children should be able to learn to read and write in their first language (Barrs and Thomas, 1992). However, multicultural themes are now part of most classroom curricula, and books in children's first languages are included in classroom libraries so that children are encouraged to think, speak, read, and write in their first language as well as in English. Queenston is committed to the concept that the child's home culture is to be accepted and valued in the school setting.

When children who speak little English arrive at Queenston, they are paired, usually with other speakers of their home language, as Siu Pang, whom we met in Chapter 1, was paired with Claire. The first-language buddies welcome the new students and orient them to the school, smoothing the transition and creating a feeling of belonging; buddies can help each other in their own class; older students can serve as tutors for primary grade students. As well, the teachers ensure that content, resources, and activities for these children will be appropriate for their age and grade level—they don't attempt to teach twelve-year-olds to read English using a grade one primer. As they find themselves in social situations where a variety of real-life demands are placed upon them, the children soon discover the need to use English and begin to function in it as their second language.

A teacher who went to Vancouver for a conference brought back to Queenston the following summary of the needs of and appropriate programs for ESL students. It was prepared by an External Review Team for the Vancouver School Board in 1989. Queenston teachers were interested to see how these findings paralleled their own beliefs and practices.

1. *The educational and personal experiences ESL students bring to Canadian schools constitute the foundation for all their future learning; schools should therefore attempt to amplify rather than replace these experiences.*

2. *Although English conversational skills may be acquired quite rapidly by ESL students, upwards of five years may be required for ESL students to reach a level of academic proficiency in English comparable to their native-English-speaking peers; schools must therefore be prepared to make a long-term commitment to support the academic development of ESL students.*

3. *Interaction with users of English is a major causal variable underlying both the acquisition of English and ESL students' sense of belonging to Canadian society. The entire school is therefore responsible for supporting the learning and interactional needs of ESL students, and ESL provision should integrate students into the social and academic mainstream to the extent possible.*

4. *If ESL students are to catch up academically with their native-English-speaking peers, their cognitive growth and mastery of academic content must continue while English is being learned. Thus the teaching of English-as-a-second-language should be integrated with the teaching of other academic content that is appropriate to students' cognitive level. By the same token, all content teachers are also teachers of language.*

5. *The academic and linguistic growth of ESL students is significantly increased when parents see themselves, and are seen by the school staff, as co-educators of their children along with the school. Schools should therefore actively seek to establish a collaborative relationship with minority parents that encourages them to participate with the school in promoting their children's academic progress.*

Winnie's Story
Peter Jailall

Winnie, a quiet, shy, six-year-old whose first language was Cantonese, came to Queenston in September. She did not utter a word to me during her time in reception or to her classroom teacher, Katie Thurston, for three months. We were beginning to worry, but we decided to wait.

On October 8, Winnie printed her name; then she drew a picture of herself. During November and December, she used picture making to represent significant others in her life—her mother, father, sister, and friend. I talked to Winnie about her pictures, her family, her friends. At the same time, I helped her to label her pictures and provided opportunities for her to share her work with others. All along she was free to set her own agenda, to decide what she wanted to draw and label. I intervened judiciously. She drew and we labelled together—the sun, a house, an ice cream, a tree, a book, a pizza.

Through January and February, I continued coaching and supporting her in her writing endeavours. After the completion of each piece of writing and artwork, I praised Winnie for her efforts, which I valued very much. I had confidence in her ability to create pieces of writing, and I tried to be patient with her small efforts to succeed.

She worked with a group of other ESL writers like herself, and they supported each other, talking about pictures, ideas, and the possible spelling of words. They often giggled as they exchanged writing in their own scripts. During this process of sharing, they came to understand that they each had their own unique form of writing—Chinese, Japanese, Portuguese, Punjabi, and Hindi. I encouraged them to write and to talk both in English and in their mother tongue.

It was mid-April when Winnie suddenly started to put strings of words together to make meaning in her own way. She wrote:

I like my mother to me.
I like my father to me.
I like my sister to me.
I like Kyoko (her friend)
to me.

She began writing and reading longer texts in English and in Chinese. and to share her pieces of writing with her classmates in ESL and in her home-room. She also brought her parents to our Parents' Night. She was now excited about drawing, writing, reading, and talking about her work. As teachers would say, she "blossomed." Winnie had

discovered the joy of sharing with others. But most of all, she suddenly found out how writing can make others listen, respond, and recognize her ideas. Winnie became a new student—talking, laughing, enjoying school, making friends, learning language skills, and gaining enough confidence to launch out further afield into other areas of the curriculum.

Winnie continues to develop new understandings every day in her drawing, writing, talking, and reading. And she is doing it by herself with full support from me, her classroom teacher, and her classmates. She has been truly empowered through her new-found ability to communicate.

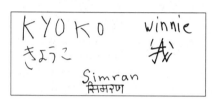

Building a Community of Readers

All children in a classroom must feel they are part of the reading community. Even prereaders can sense that they are part of the print world—listening, joining in, rehearsing the reading process with well-known stories that they select and hold and turn the pages of. Belonging to the literacy club requires success with print at every age and stage of development. Children who cannot yet read need support for their belief that they too can become readers. They need all kinds of materials in their classroom to gain access to the world of print, and these resources must connect to the satisfaction of reading, not just to "reading readiness." We learn to read in the pursuit of genuine purposes. To build a community of readers, we must create an environment for literacy, not just with print resources but with support systems that encourage children to accept literacy as a needed and desired way of life.

We model the reading process when we read aloud and read along in shared reading. It is especially important that we are seen reading our own materials, not simply supervising as the children read theirs (Hornsby and Sukarna, 1986). Teachers should talk about authors, publishers, illustrators, covers, new books, reviews, reissues, versions, series—all the "book" aspects of reading as well as the connections to "real life."

We can set up conditions in which the children can see themselves as readers by providing regular private reading times, when children select books and read silently; group reading times, when several children discuss the same book or a number of books connected by author, theme, culture, or pattern; times for shared reading, when the whole class participates; and times for audience reading, when individuals read aloud to a buddy, a group, or even the whole class if they have rehearsed and volunteered to do so. The classroom should include places to read alone and together, a gathering spot for the whole class, space for displaying books, bulletin boards for children's responses, posters, and paper jacket covers of new or favourite books.

Flexible grouping strategies will allow children to read together in ability groupings and as partners of differing ability as they share a text, each gaining insight into the reading process. Group work can free the teacher to work privately with an individual child.

A timetable and organization that encourages children to become immersed in appropriate books promote extended involvement and engagement with a printed story. If we want children to become lifelong readers, to see reading as a natural process in learning, and to recognize books as part of the fabric of life, they must be encouraged and coaxed into accepting responsibility for their own reading, setting their own expectations for themselves. Tracking and organizing are important when children can choose their reading material from a wealth of real books. Children need to record what they have read, and teachers need to observe both the material read and the students' responses to it. Reading logs can track progress; dialogue journals can promote interaction between child and teacher.

Where are the resources for a "real" reading program to come from? The classroom library of appropriate and suitable books can be augmented and enriched by materials from the school and public libraries and by books children bring from home. Other print materials besides books will support the varied interests and abilities of the children: magazines, child-authored materials, reading texts approved by the Ministry of Education, and tapes and films of books. We can help children to connect their classroom reading to the world of story they will meet throughout their lives.

Children need time to respond to and reflect upon what they have read and to explore various modes of response. They need to feel that these activities connect the story to themselves and to their own private worlds. They need time and opportunity, alone and with others, to make their ideas and concerns explicit, to discover forms in which to express their thoughts and take them further, thus increasing their ownership of the reading experience. Their responses must be as embedded and as authentic as the stories they read.

Booktalk: Emergent Readers' Favourites
Jim Giles

When the children in my class voted for their favourite book of the year, *The Very Quiet Cricket* by Eric Carle was easily declared the winner. I remember the first time I read the book aloud to them. There was a fascinated silence in the room as I read about the creatures that the cricket meets from page to page. But interrupting that silence was the chanting of the children's voices as they joined in on the refrain: "So he rubbed his wings together. Nothing happened. Not a sound." These young children treasured *The Very Quiet Cricket* not only for the cricket's search for friendship, the unusual collage illustrations, the repetition that let them participate in the reading, but for the magical cricket sound that emerges at the conclusion. I won't easily forget the audible gasp that came from 42 children when I reached the end of the story. Nor would they soon forget the book, which allowed many of them who were at the emergent stage of reading to say, "Hey, I can read that!" just as they could with Carle's earlier books, *The Very Hungry Caterpillar, The Busy Spider, The Grouchy Ladybug,* and *Do You Want To Be My Friend?*

In our family grouping classroom, there are children at various stages of reading development and when choosing books to engage the children, I look for a wide range of genres: books that lend themselves to chanting, music, drama, visual arts, storytelling, or story writing. A child who is learning to read will usually find a book memorable because it has a repetitive pattern, because of appealing illustrations that help make meaning on the page, or because it invites the reader to join in by answering questions or making predictions.

Having achieved success when they read aloud *Brown Bear, Brown Bear, What Do You See?* by Bill Martin Jr., the children were thrilled to see a sequel, *Polar Bear, Polar Bear, What Do You Hear?* Like the classic original, this story gave them the satisfaction of being able to decode the words on their own. In *Chicka Chicka Boom Boom* (Bill Martin, Jr., and John Archambault, illustrated by Lois Ehlert), the letters of the alphabet try to climb to the top of the coconut tree; once all 26 letters are up the tree, they all fall down. The colourful illustrations, the rhyme, the play with the letters, and the refrain "Chicka Chicka Boom Boom / will there be enough room?" appealed to many children and they wanted to read it over and over and over again. I am also a music teacher and I think it important to fill children's heads with rhythms, rhymes, and refrains. Similar predictable patterns found in such books as *Each Peach Pear Plum* by Janet and Allan Ahlberg, *The Wheels on the Bus* by Maryann Kovalski, and *Mr. Gumpy's Outing* by John Burningham help build young readers' confidence. These books, like those by Bill Martin Jr. and Eric Carle were among those most often taken home for the "Snuggle Up and Read" part of our Book and Briefcase program, in which the children shared books with their parents.

Some books invite the children to take part in the story by answering questions or making decisions. *The Sneeze* by David Lloyd and Fritz Wegner asks them to create the sequence of events by choosing on each page the way they think the story should evolve ("Did the man jump over the dog?" "Did the girl jump over the suitcase?" "Did the dog jump over the girl?"). *The Sneeze* reminded the children of John Burningham's *Would You Rather . . . ?* which had inspired drama, storytelling, and pattern writing. *In Once Upon a Golden Apple* by Jean Little and Maggie De Vries, illustrated by Phoebe Gilman, children are invited to identify familiar fairy-tale characters and call out yes or no answers. The children are stimulated to read because they participate in the text, making predictions and decisions about questions raised in the story.

The great success of the *Where's Waldo?* books by Martin Handford had the children looking and talking together with classroom buddies as they searched for clues to find Waldo and other objects within the densely illustrated pages. Similarly, Ann Jonas's *The Trek*, Graeme Base's *Animalia*, and books by Anthony Browne (*Piggybook*, *Gorilla*, and *Look What I've Got*) offer opportunities for reading text as they linger over illustrations. Currently a big favourite is *Hide and Snake* by Keith Baker, in which a brightly coloured snake challenges readers to a game of hide and seek.

To this day, I remember Ludwig Bemelmans' *Madeline*. It was one of my favourite childhood treasures. I remember those girls "who left the house / at half past nine / in two straight lines / in rain / or shine/ the smallest one was Madeline." I'm sure it was the first book I read "on my own," and I remember sitting in my bedroom reading it aloud to my younger brother. Years from now, if I should happen to meet some of my children on the street and asked them which books they remembered best from those days with Mr. Giles, I am sure that Belinda would say it was Phoebe Gilman's *Jillian Jiggs*, and that Ashley would recall *The Name of the Tree* by Celia Lottridge and Ian Wallace, and Michael would remember putting his face into the hole of Frank Asch's *I Can Blink* and becoming a different animal on each page. Stories such as these and others about brown bears, quiet crickets, and wheels that go round and round help children like Belinda, Ashley, and Michael become independent readers, and I'm sure will be as fondly remembered by them as a row of girls in two straight lines is by me.

Suggested Reading for Teachers

Adams, Marilyn Jager. *Beginning To Read: Thinking and Learning about Print. A Summary.* Urbana: University of Illinois, 1990. A thorough review of all aspects of phonics and early reading, covering the past twenty years of basic and applied research in education, linguistics, and psychology.

Allen, JoBeth, and Jana M. Mason. *Risk Makers, Risk Takers, Risk Breakers: Reducing the Risks for Young Literacy Learners.* Portsmouth, N.H.: Heinemann, 1989. An edited collection of essays about emergent literacy, addressing both policies and practices in early language learning.

Bissex, Glenda. *GNYS AT WRK: A Child Learns to Read and Write.* Cambridge, Maine: Harvard University Press, 1980. The documentation and discussion of Paul, the author's son, and his growing literacy from ages five to eleven includes a look at invented spelling and writing at home compared with assigned writing at school.

Clay, Marie M. *The Early Detection of Reading Difficulties.* 3rd ed. Toronto: Irwin Publishing, 1988. This third edition provides for the systematic observation of young children's responses to classroom reading instruction and contains a set of Reading Recovery procedures for use in an early intervention program with young children who have difficulty with beginning reading.

Dunn, Sonja. *Crackers & Crumbs.* Markham: Pembroke Publishers, 1988. This book contains 80 new original chants created by the author to involve children in drama, music, art, mime, play, and reading aloud.

Graves, Ruth. *The RIF Guide to Encouraging Young Readers. Reading Is Fundamental.* Garden City: Doubleday & Company, 1987. A sourcebook of more than 200 reading activities, plus an annotated list of books and resources.

Harste, Jerome, Virginia Woodward, and Carolyn Burke. *Language Stories and Literacy Lessons.* Toronto: Irwin Publishing, 1984. The authors describe their study of preschool literacy learning and its considerable implications for teachers, researchers, and the curriculum.

Hart-Hewins, Linda, and Jan Wells. *Real Books for Reading: Learning to Read with Children's Literature.* Markham: Pembroke Publishers, 1990. A comprehensive guide to using "real" books to nurture a love of reading and language in four- to eight-year-olds, with examples of children's responses to literature. An extensive bibliography of recent children's books is organized around ten levels of children's reading development.

Holdaway, Don. *The Foundations of Literacy.* Toronto: Scholastic, 1979. Based on research and theory of how children develop literacy, Holdaway's book discusses educational practices in New Zealand, including the use of shared book experiences and "big books."

Johnson, Terry D., and Daphne R. Louis. *Literacy through Literature.* Toronto: Scholastic, 1987. Original ideas for including literature in the classroom as a part of a whole language/literacy program, with practical suggestions and routines for promoting healthy response models for children when reading and listening to real books.

McCracken, Robert, and Marlene McCracken. *Stories, Songs & Poetry to Teach Reading & Writing.* Winnipeg: Peguis Publishers, 1987. In this practical book, the McCrackens demonstrate techniques for using stories, songs, and poems as the basis for children who are learning to read and write.

Mills, Heidi, Timothy O'Keefe and Diane Stephens. *Looking Closely: Exploring the Role of Phonics in One Whole Language Classroom.* Urbana: National Council of Teachers of English, 1992. This book demonstrates how one teacher helps children learn about sound-symbol relationships in language through the context of authentic reading and writing.

Schwartz, Judith I. *Encouraging Early Literacy: An Integrated Approach to Reading and Writing.* Toronto: Irwin Publishing, 1988. This book describes how to implement a whole language approach to literacy with the young child from K-3, concentrating on school programs for different developmental levels, on establishing a literacy plan for children as young as three, and on ways of engaging children in experiences with written language.

Strickland, Dorothy, and Lesley Mandel Morrow, ed. *Emerging Literacy: Young Children Learn to Read and Write.* Newark, Del.: International Reading Association, 1989. An edited collection of information about emergent literacy, using photographs, oral and written language samples, and descriptions of children.

Temple, Charles A., Ruth G. Nathan, and Nancy A. Burris. *The Beginnings of Writing.* Toronto: Allyn and Bacon, 1982. A guide to young children's discovery of writing through the scribbling, spelling, and composing stages, the book includes the beginnings of writing, spelling, composition, and playing with literature and language. Observations and samples of children's writing are included.

Wason-Ellam, Linda. *Start with a Story: Literature and Learning in Your Classrooom*. Toronto: Pembroke Publishers, 1991. This book of stories and books suggests ideas ranging from reading and writing to listening and talking, viewing, art, music and drama, and activities that incorporate the use of a variety of books—from wordless picture books to poetry, from novels to non-fiction.

Waterland, Liz. *Read With Me: An Apprenticeship Approach to Reading*. 2nd, revised ed. South Woodchester, England: Thimble Press, 1988. In this volume, Liz Waterland recounts her continuing classroom experience of the ways that real books can make real readers. She clarifies and extends points made in the first edition of her influential booklet, answering some of the questions asked by other practitioners of the apprenticeship approach.

Reflections

❶   What can teachers, day-care workers, and others do to involve parents of preschool children in building a foundation for literacy? Once the children arrive at school, how can we explain our philosophy and our program to parents and invite them to promote similar strategies at home?

❷   How can we increase and strengthen the variety of approaches young children bring to making meaning with print? How can we help them to use these reading strategies on their own, so that they become independent readers? How can we best help those children for whom reading remains difficult, or even a mystery? What opportunities can you find in your program for the direct teaching of those techniques a particular child has yet to acquire?

❸   What types of intervention programs for young readers "at risk" should we develop? What reading strategies can we suggest for those children who do not grasp that print holds meaning and therefore have trouble learning to read? Do different children require different types of support?

❹   Does your school subscribe to professional journals and periodicals that can add to teachers' understanding and aid their practice? Do you have access to new books discussing emergent readers? Does the school hold seminars and workshops with leading educators who can help the teachers effect change in their classrooms? Do you share ideas for classroom organization and curriculum with colleagues in order to develop a school-wide philosophy for language arts teaching?

❺ Which curriculum areas lend themselves to a language-based approach to learning? How can teachers begin to integrate the language processes of reading, writing, speaking, and listening with these other areas of learning so that children have opportunities for working in longer blocks of time?

❻ Is your grasp of the theory and practice of language teaching such that you can explain your program to administrators and parents? Can you counter the often polarized arguments about such aspects as "phonics" versus "whole language"? How else can you help the wider community recognize the holistic needs of young readers so that you will gain support for your attempts to build an environment for literacy in the classroom?

Children as Readers

ODAY'S ASTONISHING rate of functional illiteracy among adults in North America has made everyone—not just teachers—concerned about the teaching of reading. Teachers want to know the most effective techniques and strategies for helping young children develop as literate language users on the path to lifelong reading. What can a teacher do to enable literacy in every child? We have all met adults who choose not to read, others who read anything in sight. We have seen many types of readers in the classroom—non-readers, would-be readers, might-be readers, refuse-to-be readers, accomplished readers, critical and creative readers. What *is* reading? What type of program will assisst each of these children?

Jeanette Veatch (1986) advocates individualized reading programs as the chief means for promoting literacy, and Constance Weaver (1988) outlines the research and methodology necessary for reading development. Terry Johnston (Johnston and Louis, 1987) has designed activities for responding to print. Robert Protherough (1983) and Jack Thomson (1987) help us to put reader response theory into classroom practice.

The teaching of reading has altered. "Real books" are a familiar component of many classrooms in today's schools (Hart-Hewins and Wells, 1990). With simplistic basal readers now in decline, we see young people engaged in the sort of reading that promotes a lasting love of reading. Beverly Kobrin (1988) reminds us of the importance of non-fiction—"books about real people, places and things"—in the literary lives of young people. Jim Trelease (1989) stimulates parents and teachers into making time for reading stories and poems to children, not just at bedtime, but as a vital component of the regular home or school program. Bob Barton (1986) brings storytelling back into our lives and presents teachers with strategies for developing a story sense in children at every age level.

Young readers need to be engaged in actual reading, with time for response and interaction through journal writing and discussion that enable co-operative, reflective meaning making. We want children "to read extensively, to extend themselves into the world of literature, connecting in personal ways with the story world, and to read intensively, the emphasis on mindful or deliberate interpretation, with attention focussed on the act of constructing meaning" (Peterson and Eeds, 1990).

The Act of Reading

Today, attention is shifting—in university lecture halls and literary magazines, as well as in elementary school classrooms—from the text as an autonomous object that in itself contains meaning to what happens in the minds of readers as they engage with it. Louise Rosenblatt (1978) regards reading as a transactional process, a kind of conversation between reader and writer, who together shape the ideas captured by the words on the page. The writer contributes words, sentences, and paragraphs to represent his or her views; the reader brings personal experiences, attitudes, thoughts, and feelings.

The reader thus takes considerable responsibility in making meaning—inferring, generalizing, distinguishing fact from opinion, and making judgements. The reader brings to the print all of life's experiences and uses all the features of printed material—headings, diagrams, photographs, and captions as well as words, paragraphs, ideas, and imagery. Reading is only guided by the text; it is also influenced by the reader's personal and cultural history, current representation of the world, and internalized knowledge of reading conventions. Because children come from varying backgrounds with different attitudes, values, and circumstances, the responses they have to a text are all individual—and all legitimate. Each reader must paint his or her own story picture. Two readers may read the same book, but the stories they read will never completely match.

Some story worlds are easy for us to enter: we have seen that mountain; we have lived in that city; we have known those bulrushes; we have owned a dog like the one in the book. Others are more difficult: we need the deft author who invites us in, the clever storyteller who draws us along, or the perceptive teacher who builds for us a context. As we hear or read the words, we transform those symbols into startling pictures that let us see into the story.

Reading

James, grade five

Without reading is like . . .
An airplane without wings,
A baby that doesn't cry
A person without a heart
Going to sleep without a dream
That's what it is like without reading.

Reading a book is like travelling through a tunnel
First is the beginning of a story like a train going into a dark tunnel.

Second is the middle of the story when you are in the middle of your
   journey but still more adventures lie ahead and it is like the middle
   of the tunnel where light is coming in.
Third is the end of the story, the end of the tunnel but not the end of
   the journey adventures are still ahead.

Reading is like a neverending journey.
You may finish a book
But the story will live on
But the journey goes on

Helping Children Become Readers

How do effective readers make sense of what they are reading? What strategies do they employ? Can mapping these strategies direct us in helping
struggling readers? Even before reading, good readers think about the text,
preparing themselves for reading by drawing on prior knowledge, analyzing
the sort of text to be read so they will know what particular approach to
take. As they read, they build for themselves a coherent, personal interpretation of both the selection and its real-world connections. They look for
important ideas, paraphrase, predict, anticipate, and read ahead for additional context. They look back and reread to clarify a confusing part or to
relate new knowledge to existing knowledge. They test hypotheses and
understandings and create mental images to visualize description. They look
for interconnecting details and monitor their own reading to ensure understanding. (Effective readers know to stop reading if the material is too difficult.) After reading, they reflect upon what they have read, relate what they
can to their own experience, and respond in a variety of modes to enrich
and extend the meaning-making process.

Good readers rely on context to understand a word or an expression
and construct meaning from every bit of information the total print environment provides. Noticing the syntactic value of the place of the word in the
sentence, looking for other words and phrases that will help define the
word, analyzing it for roots, prefixes, or suffixes, drawing the context of the
selection into play, even omitting a word until more information is acquired,
are all educated guesses that good readers make, confirm, or change while
reading or during response activities.

Traditional teaching methods that focused on the mechanical and linear aspects of reading tended to frown on practices such as skipping words.
If you didn't understand a word, you were supposed to plug away at it until

you figured it out—either using "phonics" (sounding it out) or "look-and-say" (being told what the word was and "learning" it). Older readers were expected to stop and look up an unknown word in a dictionary. Good readers have consistently ignored such precepts, which interrupt the flow of reading and the making of meaning, resorting to them only when context really fails them. (Fortunately, in silent reading, the teacher never knew what sins the reader was committing.) Poorer readers, with less confidence in their ability to make meaning, could be utterly stymied by this approach. By the time they had "read" the problem word, they had lost all sense of the author's intention.

Harvey Wiener(1990) provides us with a good example of the need for context as an aid to comprehension:

Did you know that ground *has almost thirty—that's right, thirty—different meanings enumerated in a dictionary? Without knowing which definition the writer might have intended, you shouldn't even try to guess at an answer to your child's question. You've got to know what the context is. Let me show you some of the various uses for the word* ground.

- *The submarine moved slowly along the ground.*
- *The farmer leveled the ground and then tilled it for planting potatoes.*
- *Speak softly when you approach the Indian burial grounds.*
- *His strange behavior gave us grounds for suspecting that he stole Manny's wallet.*
- *I poured the coffee grounds down the sink.*
- *Father grounded the wire before plugging in the old hair drier.*
- *He grounded his opinion in many years of research by scientists all over the world.*
- *His eyesight was weak, and as a result the company grounded the pilot permanently.*
- *The catcher grounded out to the shortstop.*
- *During our trip out west we covered lots of ground.*

Unless you had a clue about the intended meaning, guessing at the word ground *in the abstract makes no sense. You need to consider the context. I've simplified this presentation somewhat by building pretty clear clues into the ten sentences containing the word* ground, *but the print environment does not always create such conditions. Often you have to consider information in surrounding sentences, paragraphs, sometimes even pages in order to know the writer's intended meaning.*

Readers do not work through literal levels, move to inferential predictions, and conclude with critical generalizations. Instead, they work in a non-linear fashion, changing their judgements as they glean information and discover implications, anticipating and adjusting their predictions as the context deepens. All these processes are components of higher order thinking, the guesswork that leads to broadened consciousness. We must design classroom activities that will provide opportunities for using various thinking processes when children engage in print.

A reader's fluency is dependent on practice—lots of reading (Smith, 1973). For children in school, time for reading must be a major focus of the language arts program. Readers bring their individual and personal concerns to interact with the text on all levels. The teacher's role is to empower children to wander inside and around the selection, to wonder about it, to make meaningful connections, to deepen their picture of it. With the teacher as lifeguard and coach, children can safely explore the text and relate the ideas they find in it to their own lives, the author to the text, what other students see to what they see in their own minds, the patterns in it to those in other texts, its world to the world of the moment. Forging such links to learning helps children become readers.

Developing a Sense of Story

James is a reader and readily talks about the books in his life. Meaningful stories, whether fiction or non-fiction, become part of the "landscape of the mind" of those who read them. They are for "living through," not just "knowing about." They draw children in, giving them new points of view and reinforcing the developing framework of their imaginations. Stories validate important feelings and help children deal constructively with inner experiences.

Stories have been told and retold over generations, and children instinctively relate them to other times, other places—and other stories. Stories let children stand in the shoes of people in the past, present, and future and to tune into the archetypes of human wisdom. Reading a story is a developing relationship. A story is a means of filtering experiences through the mind's eye, of making sense of them, of tapping into the universals of life.

Each reader also needs to realize that others reading the same text will find different ideas and understandings—different stories—in it. Through discussion and analysis, readers absorb the diversity of meanings their classmates have taken from the text, and this modifies and develops their understanding of the meaning they themselves have made. Sharing story experiences helps children come to know how they read, how they listen, how

James
Grade 5

Books I have read

Seven parts of Ball Team And other Sports Stories
The TV Kid   The Demon's Den (Hardy Boys)
Matilda
The Whipping Boy   The Scattertrain Booky
General Butterfingers   With Love from Booky
The Boy Who Owned the School As Ever Booky
The Island   The Codebreakers Kid
Patoose   Good Work Amelia Bedelia
Ice Magic   The Italian Spaghetti Mystery
Robin Hood   Rookies 1# Play Ball
Me and thy Wardos   Rookies 2#
Number the Stars   Rookies 3# Spring Training
The Burning Questions of Bingo Brown Rookies 4#
The Voyage of the Frog Rookies 5#
Dear Mr. Henshaw   Rookies 6# World Series
Throwing Heat   Bunnicula
One Day I'll be Perfect Howliday Inn
Everywhere   The Celery Stalks at
How to Eat Fried Worms Midnight
The White Mountains Nighty - Nightmare
The City of Lead and Gold 7 for Zombie
The Pool of Fire   The Book of Three
Football Fugitive   The Black Cauldron
Darksword 1 Search for the Darksword
The Kid who Only Hit Home Runs
Dirt Bike Runaway   The Castle of Llyr
The Book of Three   Taran Wanderer
Nicobobinus

they make meaning, and what their own personal perspectives are. By sharing meanings with others, they build a stronger and bigger world for themselves.

At the same time, teachers must reassure students of the validity of their own reconstructions. We must watch our own enthusiasms: if we, as teachers, set out to impart a particular truth about a story, the story we share is ours, not the children's. We cannot rob children of their own stories in an attempt to make a single, common story: to do so renders learning insignificant and turns pleasure into drudgery. Our goal must be the deepest reader response, not the solving of a puzzle that we have designed and to which only we know the answer. We must share our wisdom to help children through their own story mazes, sustaining them in their own struggles to become independent readers.

Beyond the reading of stories, children need to create and re-create stories to make their own meanings. They need to imprint their representations of their worlds on their conscious and subconscious minds by telling their stories of life to themselves and to one another. Teachers should foster the communal making of stories in a supportive environment. Children can look for fresh possibilities in the stories they read, borrow from them, remould them, tell them anew. When they are immersed in stories, children develop a sense of narrative and how it works in all its forms.

As children weave their personal stories into the classroom fabric, they develop a sense of the worth of each person and of each person's story. They become actively engaged in making meaning through language—the syntactic patterns, the idioms, the imagery, the multiple meanings of words. When children meet and use a variety of story structures and styles, they learn about genre and form. They know which sentences, which words, which images they want to remember and savour as they add the ideas, motifs, values, and language of the story to their own literary storehouses. They recognize the story because it connects them to all humanity and illuminates past and future.

The Reading Environment

Obviously, children's reading environment must include plenty of raw material. It must embrace not just a range of types of texts and genres from many cultures, but also old favourites to be dipped into again, books about their current interests, and reading that is challenging but still within their grasp. All kinds of books, magazines, and reference materials must be available. In this setting, children must have generous opportunities to read, to become lost in a book.

Knowing the children and their interests is absolutely essential if we are to provide the material they need. As teachers, we can demonstrate care and concern for individual children during reading time, advising, motivating, encouraging the child who is developing, and enriching the print world of the gifted reader. We must be conscious of what takes place as the children read: how they "get at" stories; how they depend on certain patterns to structure their interpretation; how their views change. We can help children use a variety of reading strategies to facilitate comprehension, offering in-depth explanations, and devising appropriate techniques for particular problem areas. Above all, a pleasant and friendly atmosphere will lead children to seek out the materials they want to read.

The years between eight and thirteen are the "quantity" years, when children gain reading power through in-depth experiences with biographies, with science books, and especially with novels. Children often enjoy reading several books by a favourite author or a series of books about a familiar set of characters. Common themes link the most widely read books—humour, school, friends, mystery, fantasy. Yet readers' tastes may shift—and develop—almost from day to day. Boys and girls may prefer different types of books, and peer group pressures may influence their reading choices. While children should be given as many opportunities as possible for choice in their independent reading, we can still bring fine stories to their attention that will interest them, fill their needs, and present a wider view of the world, free of stereotypes and sexist portrayals.

The range of reading levels in the middle years varies widely. Those children who have developed into mature, independent readers need to deepen their reading experiences by moving into quality alongside quantity rather than to "adult" fiction. There are many novels at an appropriate intellectual and emotional level that will present these young readers with problems and situations of greater complexity, subtle characterization, and multi-faceted plot structures than today's paperback bestsellers. Stories from other countries, other cultures, or other contexts can challenge their concepts and ideas. We must also remember that even the many readers who have reached a level of independence have listening abilities that still outreach their reading abilities; it is still important to read to them.

The lives of young people are full of friends, homework, sports, lessons, and chores. At this stage, reading may get squeezed out of the daily schedule. However, success in school—and in life—is greatly determined by literacy skills, so adults must help young people find time for reading. Children who are not fluent or independent readers need special support if they are to choose books wisely. Many authors today are writing books for readers who prefer, for whatever reason, to stay with "easy" reading material. These books have a reading range that allows the readers success and an interest level that makes them want to continue reading. For example, Arnold Lobel has created prize-winning stories for younger children featuring Toad and Frog; the stories use a set list of 45 words. Similarly, some novelists have created stimulating "high-interest–low-vocabulary" books for older readers. But as teachers, we must be wary of simplistic books that rely on word count rather than good stories as their reason for publication. Authors with talent and the needs of young people in mind create novels that give children the chance to become literate people who want to read well.

Novels allow the reader to engage in dialogue with an author on a wide range of topics and at a deep emotional level. Personal and private reading gives the youngster the security to delve into situations that may touch his or her life and to identify and reflect upon human traits and behaviour.

Responding to Text

Responding to story is as important as meeting story. When children express their personal ideas, feelings, and preferences freely, they demonstrate their literary growth. They can talk about a story; read the dialogue aloud, create their own versions; paint, model, and role-play characters and events; write about ideas sparked by the story; read other stories of the same type or by the same author. With the teacher's careful intervention, collaborative responses can extend each reader's personal response and help generate a wider and more thoughtful appreciation of the story.

Response activities should cause children to read carefully, extend their knowledge, elaborate upon first understandings, and discover new patterns of thought. Children will respect and respond to helpful teaching. In the past, we often depended upon "approved texts" with elaborate manuals that left us little reason to think for ourselves. We became dependent on predetermined activities and questions for the children that did not grow from their own interests in and puzzlings about what they had to read. Do we need manuals on a specific book, for example, *Charlotte's Web*, purporting to lead children through the story by way of lock-step "creative activities"? Sometimes children can select from a range of follow-up suggestions that accompany a story, and this can help focus their ideas in directions that may lead them to interesting discoveries. But if we take the time to listen to their initial responses, activities can spring from their needs and desires.

We do not always ask for an external response. Sometimes the reading of a story is a complete experience in itself. The children may call upon it later but have no need to respond at the time. Usually, though, children should *do* something with what they have read—whether through discussion, writing, drama, or art. Helping children go beyond the text requires techniques that relate the concepts in the text to the children's experiences and tap fundamental memories brought forth by the intensity of the reading experience. We can promote and develop the children's responses by opening the text up for discussion, encouraging them to make their viewpoints and opinions known—opinions that are relevant to, but not necessarily identical with, those in the story:

When you conduct a discussion with one child, a small group or with the whole class the atmosphere should be relaxed, uninhibited and informal. No child is likely to reveal his deep down beliefs to anyone he does not trust or in a situation where his opinions are not respected. By using open-ended questions, children are released from the traditional notion that every reader is expected to obtain the same meanings and the same ideas and feelings about a piece of literature. By comparing responses and activities with others and with themselves, children are learning to weigh their own understanding of themselves and others by becoming more aware of their own values and the values of others (Reasoner, 1972, p.103).

A sense of trust during response time allows young readers to reflect on the story experience and to modify their understanding. If we help the children decide what modes of response are appropriate and when they want to respond individually, when in groups, and when in a whole class sharing, the children can go a long way toward selecting and directing their own learning. As they articulate their own interpretations and learn from the different viewpoints, wisdom, and experience of others, they begin to appreciate the complexities of a good story or poem and notice the appropriateness and effectiveness of particular words and expressions.

The activities that children engage in following their reading should extend and enrich the print experience, not take the place of actual reading. In the past, some children spent five minutes reading and two days completing worksheets. Yet reading growth requires plenty of time for a story to seep into children's minds. Children may need to be jolted into interaction and involvement with a selection after reading it, and time spent with them in the selection of response activities that provide true reasons for a close reading of the text will lead to significant dialogue.

As children respond to specific stories, they will begin to explore the more traditional elements of literature—plot, characterization, setting, and so forth. Teachers seldom need to introduce these concepts; the children usually bring them up in their own questioning or research. When such terms of reference are useful, they can be explained. The knowledge about story thus grows from need and context.

When I asked eighth graders to be specific about their literary knowl-edge, to spend a few days reading through our letters and making cate-gories of the kinds of things we talked about, they named over 150 liter-ary topics, including how authors wrote—how they began and con-cluded books, developed characters, used dialogue, selected a narrative voice, pointed themes, structured chapters, followed or overthrew formu-las and conventions. We also talked about authors—their lives, their other books, the ways they researched their subjects, their last reviews. We talked about concepts of genre: what makes a novel a novel and a short story a short story; how poetry differs from prose and how we clas-sify fiction, non-fiction, and all their various modes. We talked about readers' process—when we skimmed, skipped, and abandoned books and how we made these decisions; when and why we reread; how we planned and predicted and revised in our heads the ways books should have been written; how we learned to read and what we are learning about ourselves as readers. We made and followed up on recommenda-tions. We gossiped about the world of publishing, about editors, agents, advances, royalties, remaindering, how and when hardcovers become paperbacks and books become films. We noted format—jacket copy, cover illustrations, copyright dates, type size, and length. We made con-nections between published authors' styles and subjects and those of our own writing. And we made connections between books and our own lives (Atwell, 1987).

Talk as a Way to Meaning

Talk is probably the main tool in teaching reading. As the children dig inside the narrative, they revise and remake their own stories in the light of what others reveal about their own attempts at making meaning. In a small group, discussion is spontaneous and individual children can put forward their own concerns. Before reading, children can meet together to predict, anticipate, and set the stage for the narrative. During and after reading, they can use talk—invisible print that can be edited and re-formed so easily—to make both personal and collective meaning. Talk can be the starting point for story projects of all kinds—research, role-playing, writing, storytelling, read-ing aloud, painting. Some discussions can be tape-recorded for playback as clarification and consolidation or for another group to hear. Sharing thoughts and feelings with others who have read some of the same books can lead to quite sophisticated literary generalizations and understanding.

Books Need Readers
Larry Swartz

If books could have more, give more, be more, show more, they would still need readers who bring them sound and smell and light and all the rest that can't be found in books. The book needs you (Paulsen, 1989).

In my grades five-and-six classroom, I arrange for groups of children to discuss stories they have read together. In the following transcript, a group of grade five students respond to "Tuning," the prologue to Gary Paulsen's *The Winter Room*, and share some of their ideas about reading.

Teacher: What do you think Gary Paulsen means when he writes "The book needs you"?

Janine: I think the author means that without you the book is nothing except for all kinds of words.

Miranda: A book doesn't make any sense if nobody's reading it.

Sunny: It's sort of like the book and the person need each other.

Teacher: How does the person need a book?

Sunny: Without a book they wouldn't learn anything. And the book without a person is just words on paper.

Christi: All that's in a book is words. You have to picture what you think would be in your head, matching the words, the noise that it would make would be in your head and the pictures that you thought should be in your head.

Sunny: No—I think that a book does have sounds and smells . . . but only you need a reader . . .

Christi: No—you imagine them.

Teacher: What does a reader do for a book?

Heidi: Because when the author writes a book, he gets all his enthusiasm and puts it on paper.

Sunny: He puts his imagination on paper.

Ryan: So you can read his mind.

Sunny: . . . read his thoughts . . . A book is nothing without a reader.

Heidi: . . . until you understand it and like it.

Liza: A book is just black and white lines on paper.

Sunny: A person is nothing without a book either.

Teacher: Why do you say that?

Sunny: Because we wouldn't know anything. Because you pass on things you know to your sons or something by writing it down. You can't tell them when you're dead.

Heidi: I think books can't have light.

Sunny: They do have light!

Heidi: They have light when people read it.

Sunny: They have light when the sun shines in.

Liza: Or when your eyes shine on it . . .

Sunny: But it won't shine by itself—unless it's a really good book.

Teacher: How does a reader help a book come alive?

Janine: The reader helps the book come alive because you give it sort of like a light.

Christi: Everyone has a question in their mind . . .

Janine: . . . and the book gives them more thoughts . . .

Sunny: The reader is part of the mind of the book . . . the thoughts and the mind of the book . . .

Ryan: When he reads it, a person makes pictures in his mind.

Teacher: Is it the person's imagination that does that or is it the author's writing?

Ryan: It's the person's imagination . . .

Sunny: It's the author.

Ryan: I'd say it's both . . .

Sunny: It's both. The author uses his imagination and gives you sort of like a plot and you can think about the theme or what happens.

Ryan: So he puts his thoughts on paper to put thoughts in your mind.

Georgette: I think books do have light. Sometimes a person is mad or miserable or something. A book sometimes lights them up and brings them into another world instead of this one.

Sunny: But he has to read it . . .

Georgette: Yeah . . . they read it.

Sunny: A book has everything it says in here—it can smell, it can see, it can have light—just as long as the reader is there.

Christi: A book can have plot, it can have words, it can have pictures, but it can't have light.

Sunny: It can have life.

Christi: It can have life in your head because you're thinking about it.

Janine: You can be the characters. If the book's so good, you want to be the character, the book has life in your head.

Sunny: Mr. Swartz wrote something in my notebook about a poet who said "I like to wander in other men's minds," or something like that. When you read you go into the author's mind. The author writes it down and you read it so you go into his mind . . .

Heidi: When you read you take the character's personality . . . Sometimes you have to read the whole book to understand it.

Teacher: Do you always have to read the whole book?

Heidi: Well, it depends what kind of book it is. Sometimes I skip parts.

Teacher: Why would you skip a part?

Liza: It's boring . . . they lose you, you don't think you need that part because it's not interesting.

Sunny: Or you don't think it's necessary. In *The White Mountain*, he said that they were cutting the small part from his armpit and the author describes an ant crawling on the ground—you don't think that's important—but I think the author writes that because the character wants to get his mind off the pain and so he sees the ant.

• • • •

Georgette: Reading books could have sound . . . what does that mean?

Sunny: If a book has a reader . . . it can have all those things that Gary Paulsen talks about because you can make it happen.

Liza: Books teach you stuff—more than probably your teacher does.

Teacher: Sometimes . . .

Sunny: The teacher only teaches you about math and stuff like that but books teach you more.

Liza: . . . how life can improve . . .

Sunny: . . . how other people are feeling . . .

Teacher: Books do more than teach you things, don't they?

Christi: It helps your thoughts and you travel wide. It makes you think of things you never knew before . . . bad people and good people . . . In *Where the Red Fern Grows* . . . that made me think . . .

Heidi: He talks about the boy's feeling and how the animals felt toward each other.

Georgette: I read *Sister* and that book gave me life . . . it made me think that you should always be nice to friends, even though you're not relatives . . .

Heidi: I read books that I could relate to the people and their problems.

Teacher: What about the words the author uses?

Christi: One word in a sentence makes you think about what was just said. In *Where the Red Fern Grows*, as soon as I read that they both died and the fern came . . . I thought about it a long time. I felt really sad because the dogs died and I liked the dogs in the story.

Liza: In *The Ugly Little Boy* everybody goes "ahh" and thinks that the boy is so ugly . . . but the word can mean other things.

Heidi: Christi read me this newspaper article about how these animals kept dying in plane cargoes.

Christi: . . . because there's too much pressure . . .

Heidi: When they wrote that in the paper it kind of gave you the feeling of how the animals felt.

Christi: . . . the feelings of how you should feel about them . . . if you should feel happy or sad or mad . . .

Heidi: There are all kinds of animals that are dead and when they wrote the article, they made it sound . . .

Liza: . . . terrible.

Heidi: It really is terrible. You could have the feelings of the animals. I could just picture them . . . you could smell . . .

Liza: Like they say a new baby's in the house and you smell the baby powder and it's really nice.

Heidi: . . . and when you smell stuff like pie baking, you think of cinnamon. When they write in books "The apple pie was in the oven" . . . you think of the smell.

•   •   •   •

Teacher: Okay. So is it your mind or what the author writes?

Christi: It's our mind.

Sunny: Actually it's the author that makes us think about it.

Liza: Because the author thought about it and he gave the thought to us . . .

• • • •

Teacher: What makes a book really good?

Sunny: The way the author writes it.

Georgette: Sometimes they have an introduction that gets you interested. Just like "Tuning" is the introduction to Gary Paulsen's story.

Liza: A lot has to do with the writing of the author and the way he makes your mind work and you imagine and stuff.

Sunny: No, the reader makes the book come alive. If the reader doesn't have any imagination, when he reads the book he won't feel how good the book is. You need imagination.

• • • •

Miranda: After you read a good book and you like it . . . you enjoyed it—then you never forget it.

Christi: I read *Say Goodnight* over two months ago and I still remember it. It was such a good book.

Heidi: Whenever people die in a book, it's usually at the end of a chapter when they stop because I think they want you to put down the book and think.

Liza: You don't want . . . after everything you've done in your mind with the character, you don't want it to die.

• • • •

Teacher: When you read a book do you hear a voice in your head or do you just hear the words?

Miranda: If you get into the book you do, but if you don't really like the book, you just sort of read it and leave it and you don't think about it.

Sunny: When I was reading *The Hobbit*, there were so many parts that were boring. It took me so long to get through it because I would always fall asleep. I always read at night.

Liza: Me too!

These children are making meaning from the printed word, as they explore the ideas of the author and interweave them with their own thoughts. In this transcript, we see the connections they make to the text, to the comments of others, and to their own previous experiences. We can see that readers make meaning all the time they are engaged with print—and long after.

Readers—that is, people who willingly pick up books and read because they value the experience—do not materialize overnight. It takes time to build a frame of reference for literature and to become confident as a reader. True readers are always in a state of "becoming."

Readers as Writers

In most classrooms, writing is a common mode of response. Many children spend hours answering comprehension questions, retelling, inferring, and judging—oblivious to the way they are structuring and recording their answers. Even when discussing the answers, few teachers draw attention to the writing processes, focusing exclusively on content. Yet such writing can be true composition. By linking the story and its patterns and ideas to the process of writing, the teacher can help children deepen their response to

When the Stars come Out

There was a boy named Jim
He had only 2 weeks to live
He had cancer
One day a boy told him if he looked
up in the sky each night and altogether
he counted at least 2000 stars he
would live
Jim counted 1347 stars altogether
Then he died
Jim died peacefully, gently, and happy.
And his spirit floated to the stars
and danced with them everynight that
they came out.
In the night even though you
can't see him he will be always

print and give them reasons for writing down their thoughts and feelings. Too often, response projects such as "book reports" lead the child away from real thought about the story to mere concentration on the mechanics of completing a writing task.

Children who learn to read with real books see how writers represent experience. They borrow structure and vocabulary for their own writing. They learn how to describe characters and places and how to emphasize what is significant in a plot. They learn how to present factual information, how to write captions for pictures, and how to inform their readers of the main idea. To demonstrate the worth of the students' writing, we need to integrate their own publications—books and poems they have written, projects they have completed—into the reading and sharing experiences of the classroom. Reading and writing are learned hand in hand, the one enriching the other. We cannot teach writing without providing the best possible examples of how it is done. Jane Hansen and Shelley Harwayne (1992) outline some of the possibilities of story as a springboard for writing. The link between the reading and writing processes is discussed further in chapters 3 and 5.

We should not discount the responses of children whose sole means of conveying thoughts and feelings is through the visual arts—drawing, painting, collage, papier mâché. Children who are unable to respond orally or in print—because of anxiety, poorly developed skills, or low self-esteem—can and often will represent their ideas visually in a non-print medium. The results can be used like written notes as points for group discussion or valued simply as a personal expression of response. The teacher can observe what the child chooses to "say"—the significant details, the style, and the suggested emotions.

The Reading Response Journal

The reading response journal (also called a dialogue journal or literature log) is a convenient and flexible tool that students can use to reflect on their independent reading. The journal allows children to communicate and explore the ideas and feelings that they find stories evoke. The teacher can then enter into written dialogue with the children, commenting on their responses, pointing out other connections to their thoughts, expressing feelings about their viewpoints. We can also respond to the journal in conversation during a conference to help clarify thoughts about a story or perhaps relate the story to the child's own life. A reading response journal makes the connection between reading and writing. In Larry Swartz's classroom, response journals provide him with a record of reading conferences, the books that each student has read, and the understandings that the children have brought to their reading. Larry invites his students to track their reactions, make connections, and ask questions about any text they have read. Journal entries can be answers to the open-ended prompts he provides when he writes in the journal, or spontaneous comments about the impressions a reading has inspired.

When students begin to use the response journal, they may simply retell what they have read rather than make inferences, analyze a text, or comment on the author's style. As they become more comfortable with the journal, their responses to what is happening in the books they read will grow more varied. The author's description of a character, an object, or a scene may evoke a strong mental image, or the text may arouse strong feelings or memories. Students can record what they liked or disliked about a book, predict what they think might happen next in the story, question the story line, or register their approval or disapproval of the way a character thinks or acts. The text may remind children of other stories, films, or real-life experiences, and when they choose to record these connections in their journals, they are reflecting not only on their reading, but on how it applies to their own lives.

Children should be encouraged to write in their response journals regularly—as they begin a novel, while they are reading it, or once they have completed it. Entries may appear in point form, as questions, as webs, as illustrations, or more commonly, as comments to the teacher. It may be necessary to set aside a special time for journal writing, but once they come to appreciate the journal's purpose, some children may begin to make entries spontaneously.

Reading response journals place children at the centre of their own learning. The journals are a record of the children's thoughts about literature, their reactions as readers. They serve learners by having them reflect upon, interact with, and find personal meanings in works of literature. They encourage narration, questioning, imagination, and speculation. We read journal entries to discover what the children do as they read, and to help them learn about themselves as readers. Journals provide information about thinking and learning—for children as readers and for the teacher as audience and guide. The reading response journal is a medium for interaction among teacher, text, and learner.

Readers and Their Journals
Larry Swartz

As I read my grade five students' journals from the first term, I tried to make sense of the information I was collecting. The following are some observations that I noted:

In the beginning I found that students seldom ventured far from summarizing the plot:

I have read another chapter of Borrowed Children *and Mandy's mother almost dies while having the baby. So now Mandy has to quit school and take care of her mother and baby brother. Mandy has to clean, cook and make dinner. In the book Mandy said it's hard work but she can handle it*
 Miranda

In this book its about a boy how cames from Washington D.C. to a new school and he meets a boy called Bradley and everybody does not like Bradley at all.
 Cindy

I am reading a book called Beans on the Roof. *There is this girl named Anna Bean and she is on her roof and writing a roof poem. But then this boy named George ask's Mrs. Bean if he could go on the Roof and write a poem. Mrs. Bean said ok but don't bother Anna. So he goes on the roof and say's "hello" Anna. I'm here to right a roof poem. But he think's a roof poem is if you write a poem on the roof. Look at the poem he wrote:*
The cat was fat
It sat on a hat
The hat got flat.
 Jagpal

When asked to talk about their reactions to a book, the students might say, "This is a really good book," or "I like it because it's funny." I attempted to stretch their thinking by asking in reading conferences what it was about the book that appealed to them, or how they thought the author made the book funny, suspenseful, or sad, but many wrote little more than Ryan's "I dont' know why I liked it. I just did."

During September and October, for the most part the students continued to retell the bits of the story that they had just finished reading. I invited them to be more specific and explain what they liked or disliked about the text, and a few began to offer their opinions and share their feelings:

The author did not put too much detail in this book. What I mean by that is Matt Christopher would write, "The little white pellet came in like a speeding bullet." But the author of this book would write "the ball came in very fast." On a rate from one to ten, I would give it an eight because it was funny and exciting but a little bit boring.
 Ryan

I chose The Boy Who Wanted a Family *because it make you think why can't god give everybody a place to live. That why I choose this because: I want to see how it felt to want a family. I like books that tells about some things that's really going on in the world today. If I was that kid I would think I'm a unwanted foster kid feeling unlove.*
   Shannon

I am enjoying the part when they were journeying to Bridgeport. This taught me how somebody would feel if their mother walked away without a goodbye. Because I wouled be so so so so so so so sad.
   Christi

I am enjoyed Park's Quest. *I think Park's mom should tell Park about his father. I think he should try and find some relatives other than his mom. He should look for his fathers father or I mean his grandpa. His mom (Randy) should be more open with him becauce Park should know what his dad was like before he became a name on the wall.*
   Janine

Although I encouraged them to discuss how they see themselves as readers, only a few students were able to comment on their reading behaviours:

I am not that big of a reader but on the other hand I like books. Becuase some are funny, sad, mad, OK Books. But when I was in Grade 1–3 I use to hate Books. Then I descoved the joy of books. I think of some people who can't read so I want to read when I grow up.
   Shawn

I love reading and I always will when I was in graed 1 and 2 I didn't know how to read but in gread 3 4 5 I new how to read. Thank you, Mr. Swartz. Last year I read 30 or 40 books. This year I have read 4 books. I want to read 140 books. Mr. Swartz you were the one who helped me read and so did Johanna and Laurie. Thank if it wiest for you and my mom and dad I would not be in graed 5. I will to read 140 book if you will do more drama.
   Liza

The most insightful entries seemed to be those that were made in response to a poem, a picture book, or a novel that I had read aloud to the whole class. These entries usually were written as follow-up to a discussion, and the students tended to be more involved and critical

than in their private reading, as these entries to *The Wall* by Eve
Bunting reveal:

*If my name were on The Wall I would like the people who visit the wall
to think about what I did to put my name on the wall.*
Sunny

*That book was very touching. I am all American and I think the war
was to save the country. The book made me want to go back to the U.S.
I think my great Uncle fought in that war.*
Matthew

I didn't really like the book The Wall *because I hate hearing about people that have died. I have two questions: How do they know the person's
name if he/she is dead? Are girls alowed in the war?*
Miranda

*I think that the Wall is a very emotional place. How did they get all these
peoples names into one place? That's cool. The people who made up the
idea of the wall is great. If there was one more Vietnam person from the
war I would give them the biggest gold and place it on their heart and
say you earned it because they are the one who fight for your country.*
Georgette

Two students responded to the book by writing poems:

The wall is a   *The wall The wall*
very sad place   *It's for the dead and*
to go to when I   *It's for the live*
go I woe "Why   *I hope I can see it*
for us, Why   *I'll look at it*
why not"!   *Till it comes to an end.*
Charlene   Ricky

When I made comments, opinions, and questions, in response to
theirs, the students were sometimes reluctant to "dialogue" back. Many
times my responses would be much longer than what they had written.
They didn't answer my questions, so if my comments stimulated a
thought, they generally didn't articulate it. Nevertheless, they were
often aware of me as audience:

*Mr. Swartz do you think the world was more safe when you were little or
when we were little?*
Heidi

Last time you asked me if I want to go to the future. Yes, I would really want to go for two weeks. P.S. Thank you for introducing me to the book The White Mountain *and finding the sequel* The City of Gold and Lead *for me.*
  Sunny

Yes, I do like sports, Mr. Swartz. I think Matt Christopher books are popular. I don't think girls would read them. I like to read books by different authors.
  Harveen

Mr. Swartz, sometimes I have a picture in my mind from the story you are reading. I have read Phantom of Fear, Portal of Evil, Stealer of Souls, Vault of the Vampire, Sword of the Samurai. *I would like you to recommend some more books.*
  Robbie

What is your favourite book these days?
  Lisa

Often I encouraged the students to consider what they were reminded of as they read the books. I particularly looked forward to reading these entries to discover if they were making connections from the text to both fictional and real experiences:

Here is something I thought about when I read Dominic *today. It remind me of* Abel's island *because Dominic had to survive to meet his fortune.*
  Alan

Where the Red Fern Grows *made me think about . . .*
1) how a dog is man's best friend
2) how love can be precious
3) how there is always hope for love between friends
4) how hope can provide love
5) How hope can turn into true love
  Sunil

I like Tucker Countryside *because it about friends and it remind me of Johanna and Laurie from last year because they were there when I need someone just like Tucker and Harry and Chester.*
  Liza

I am reading Eva. *I thought about when my cousin had an accident and he got hurt. He was driving out from a restuarant into a crossroad and this green car was coming out from the side and crashed into them.*
    James

The more I was able to establish myself as a person in dialogue with them, the deeper their responses became. I realized that the strength of the response journal lies in the relationship between teacher and child. It seemed that students seldom wrote spontaneously in their journals without having structured class time to do so. Most students needed a prompt or a question or a mini-conference before they would write an entry. As they continued to write in their journals during the term, entries increased in length, and in the later part of the term they were beginning to write more about episodes from their own lives conjured up by the story.

Students need practice in talking and writing about literature in order to gain confidence in themselves, to realize that their ideas matter to me, an adult engaged in dialogue with them.

More Response Journals

Dear Mrs Collinson,
    I read Hansel and Gretel. *I like when Gretel pushis the wicked witch in to the oven the best. What do you like in the book? I think the book is very good. I wondr if there stepmother was the witch? Do you no if she is? I like Gretel the best because she is afrad of alout of things I am afrad of. Are you afad of aney thing? PS. I have not read any of the small potatoes club books are they chapter books? I read little apple books.*

Dear Megan,
    I like *Hansel and Gretel* but I'm always sad a father would take his children in the woods and leave them. That stepmother was mean! Lots of kids in real life have really great stepmothers because their dad married again.
    When I was young I was afraid of fire because my best friend almost died in a fire. Today I worry about my family and whether they'll get sick or hurt in an accident. What things do you worry about?
    Bye for now!
    Mrs. C.

Dear Mr. Crawford

I just fineshed reading the childrens Story book for the Perfect Child. *It was pretty crazy sort of like Roald Doal's revolting ryms. I like the story that one of the charecters sneaks bubblegum.*

Dear Greg,

I agree with you. This book is very much in the style of Roald Dahl. It's unusual in books to have characters that are "revolting" as the heroes. I guess *Rotten Island* is like this too

I think that it would be fun to write in this style.

All for now,

Mr. C.

Reading on Their Own

It makes sense that children should have opportunities to choose books that are of interest to them and at a reading level with which they feel comfortable. This "quality" reading gives children time to hone their reading skills and to become discerning in their choice of books that suit their interests, needs, and abilities. For many children, school is the only place that provides books and nurtures reading. The long-range objective of an individualized reading program is to ensure that children don't need "teacher motivation" to read.

Children should feel secure that when they read books of their own choice they are doing so for their own purposes. Personal reading should not be followed with demanding or artificial activities. The teacher can monitor the children's progress by observing their reading behaviour, talking to them about their books in informal conferences, having them record the books they have read in a reading log or response journal, and giving them opportunities for rehearsed oral reading.

Reading from a broad spectrum of sources helps children become discriminating readers. The teachers at Queenston aim to give children confidence in reading material from their own "popular" culture at home—series books, comics, and so forth. In school, the teachers try to take the children as far as possible to meet the best of books to balance their literary diet. During the year, the teachers add new titles to the classroom library to pique interest, often giving "booktalks" to introduce them. As their interest in reading grows, children will look for books on a favourite topic, by a favourite author, or in a preferred genre. In response to their reading, they may choose to pattern a story, represent it through painting or drama, or simply file it away for future reference.

Silent Reading Time
Larry Swartz

At the beginning of the year, I stressed to the children that every day we would have a silent reading time. First thing in the morning when they entered the classroom, they chose their books before the opening exercises. They then read for fifteen or twenty minutes. Some months later, I asked the students whether they would like the reading period to be in the morning or the afternoon, and they chose to finish the day with reading. Just as writing something and listening to me read a story or part of a novel are daily activities, so is silent reading.

The children make their own choices on what to read each day. If they don't wish to read novels, they can choose from a collection of picture books and short stories. I strongly encourage them to choose novels, and most of the time, they do. Some students, of course, simply will not yet read novels. If they wish, they can go to the library for non-fiction materials—if they want to read about hockey during the reading time, they certainly may do so. When a student finishes a book, we hold a conference, and I learn something about what he or she enjoyed about the book. Often students will choose to share their enjoyment with the class. After reading time, I might say, "Who is reading something about food today? Would you like to tell us about it?"

I have found that if books are there, the children will read and grow with reading. I make books generally available, and particular books available to particular children. I suggest books that they might want to read, but I never give a book to a student and say, "I want you to read this." I think reading has to matter to them. Instead, I try to find out their interests and suggest a book. I may give them time limits, saying, "You should have this finished in three weeks, and we are going to have a discussion during the week."

The Reading Conference

We can set the stage for reading conferences by establishing a routine in which the child feels comfortable and looks forward to discussing privately with us what he or she has read. In a typical conference, the child reflects on the story, retells it, explains personal views on why things happened as they did, gives opinions about the content, and makes some judgements about the style and quality of the selection. We can close the conference by helping the child decide what to do next: whether to begin a response activity or to choose a new book.

We can use the conference not only to help the child to explore further meaning making but also to assess the child's reading progress. By noting how the child responds and contributes, we can assess the child's attitudes, interests, and level of comprehension. During the year, patterns in the child's reading will emerge that can help us build a complete picture of the child's reading growth.

Conferences can take ten seconds or half an hour, depending upon the situation. Often a special corner or seating arrangement will encourage a child to open up. We may want to discuss a book with a child before reading begins, relating other books to the new one, explaining the background, the author, the time, or the place. It may sometimes be important to confer with a child while he or she is reading a book to clear up misconceptions or to bring the child's prior knowledge into play as an aid to understanding. The child may also request an interview during the reading of the story to discuss the background of the story or the ideas in it.

During conferences, children can present their reading logs or response journals, where they may have raised issues worthy of discussion. Some children may benefit from lead-in activities before a conference. As the children reveal what they feel and think, we can harness and extend their insights. This close, intimate situation gives us the opportunity to listen to a child read aloud in order to share in the child's interpretation of a worthwhile reading selection—and at the same time assess the child's reading performance on a technical level. Together, teacher and child can discuss a further response activity and plan the next book experience.

When we confer with an individual child, that child receives the teacher's full attention. Story concerns may be shared in one-on-one conferences and may, indeed, arise only in this trusted relationship. Stories can trigger very powerful responses in children, and we can seize the opportunity to relate perspective and compassion in the literary situation to the real world.

Reading in Groups

As we know, we should organize groups in response to students' learning needs, and so that no child's self-confidence is damaged, we should form and re-form groups constantly for reasons beyond the need for direct instruction. Several children's common interests may suggest reading groupings where students can share ideas and feelings growing out of a story they have heard or read and learn to appreciate the points of view of others. Group conferences with the teacher can focus on creating a web of characters, plot, and subplot; works in a particular genre or style; the language (words or patterns) of special images or effects; the content, theme, setting, or mood of a selection and how it relates to other works by the same author or illustrator or to other stories, films, or television shows. Members of a group can read the same selection, different selections by the same author, or different selections that have a similar theme. Students in the group should have some responsibility for their own learning; they should help design the activities and determine the time frame in which to accomplish the task.

For example, a group of grade three children who had been reading *The Comeback Dog* by Jane Thomas prepared a web to show their understanding of the relationships among various characters in the novel. They made one character, Daniel, the central focus. They drew arrows from Daniel to the other characters in the novel and wrote statements next to the arrows that describe feelings that the characters have for one another. For example "Daniel cares for Lady. He is frustrated because she doesn't show any love back." "Lady doesn't trust people because she has been mistreated." "Lady doesn't know Daniel."

Group conferences can lead to further response activities—a readers' theatre presentation (see "Reading to Others," p. 167), a research project on the historical background to a book, a sharing of responses written in journals, a discussion of how ideas from different books appear to relate to each other.

Retelling the Story

One activity that children can find highly stimulating is to retell a story they have read. As they rethink the material, it grows in their imaginations and they come to understand more fully its nooks and crannies, subtleties and surprises. Their ideas about the story and what it means to them emerge in the retelling. Staying with the story in this way thus facilitates the comprehension process.

We should not expect a retold story to remain the same; it will be a resynthesis. Consciously or unconsciously, the teller will make changes to create what seems a better, or more appropriate, story. Listening to others retell the same story helps children examine their own responses with more objectivity. They begin to recognize that their own perceptions are valid, but not absolute. Skilled teachers help young readers build imaginative re-creations of stories in many ways. We must understand both the sensitivity that children bring to a text and the connotations that any story carries for them.

Parallel Reading

Children can read other stories that illuminate, clarify, or open up the original story experience. Teachers can help children classify or categorize stories by genre, type, theme, or story attributes. Consider some of the possibilities: cultural variants of the same folk tale; other stories from the same culture;

stories with similar structures (for example, ballads); books by the same author or illustrator; the same story illustrated by different artists; stories with similar themes; stories with the same characters.

The children often initiate parallel reading. We may begin with one particular story, and before long, they have found a dozen more, some hidden in the recesses of their minds, some unearthed from the library. Children should be encouraged to share the insights they gain from parallel reading. They, the teacher, and their classmates will soon find that one thing leads to another.

Cynthia Voigt
Sharon, grade five

My author is Cynthia Voigt. I' ve read *Izzy willy Nilly*, *The Callendar Papers*, and right now I reading *Homecoming*. So far I think Homecoming is the best cause of her plot about abandoned children and how they survive and her choice of words. For example, when the kids asked Dicey to tell them about their father, Voigt said "Dicey gathered her few memories, like scattered marbles." I thought it was a very good choice of words cause I could really picture Dicey trying to remember things about her father. My prediction is her grandmother is going to take care of them. I think Voigt has influenced me as a writer cause by reading description it's starting to rub off on me. Voigt doesn't describe the charecters straitforward she would say Dicey brushed her sandy brown hair or something. So far the similarities in the books I've read are, all the main charecters are girls and they all have problems to deal with. I enjoy reading Voigt's pieces of writing cause it matches my reading level perfectly. I found *Callendar papers* a bit on the dry side, but Sarah thought it was great! Oh well. I hope this is enough cause I've run out of things to say!

Ivey's Story
Barbara Dixon

The Y.O.U. (Your Own Uniqueness) Club at Queenston is a program for gifted children in the upper grades. As special education teacher, I meet with the club once a week or so both during and after school hours. Ivey, a student in Diane Carter's grade eight class, had been identified as a gifted student by the special education department. She was a quiet student who joined the club in October. For several weeks she contributed very little to the club, but when she chose to elaborate on discussion points, it was obvious that she stated her views only after reflection and deliberation. It may have been this "reflection-before-response" or her unique journal entries that intrigued me. Whatever the reason, I wanted to know more about a grade eight girl named Ivey.

In November, she started working with me after school, writing quotes and poems for my classroom. I wanted the "environmental print" in the classroom to be powerful, and Ivey had beautiful handwriting. During these weekly calligraphy sessions, Ivey would answer questions but ignore my attempts to engage her in conversation. I offered hot chocolate and cookies at breaks, but for a long time, her reserve persisted.

My classroom was full of children's books as well as those of professional interest. I had often thought about being a librarian, and I guess it showed in the way I set up a classroom. Ivey began borrowing books from me. She was very interested in King Arthur so she borrowed *The Once and Future King* and the Mary Stewart versions of the Arthurian legends. She returned all four within ten days. I also love those stories, and we talked at length about them. Ivey's reaction to the books was one of what the French critic Roland Barthes calls *joissance*—joy and ecstasy.

Ivey was now engaging in animated conversation when we were alone but remained relatively quiet during club meetings. I decided it was time to involve her in additional writing. I encouraged her to look through some of my writings to see if there were any models or themes she would like to follow. We also listened to an audio tape I had made in which I had set one of my short stories to jazz. Ivey subsequently wrote a short story about an old man who sold watches on the streets of Hong Kong and Toronto. He eventually became too old to run from the police. Her story is told with the sensitivity of a natural writer. The fact that I was often reading or writing when Ivey was around helped establish a literary climate that piqued her interest and made her feel more comfortable about her own love of reading and writing.

In January, the club members watched a film that depicted various ways of viewing the future. I asked the students to write a response to the film and the discussion surrounding it. The following week, Ivey read two responses to the group. In one, she described humans of the future as a species whose problem-solving abilities allowed them to adapt and survive changing conditions. In another, she delineated the number of technological inventions that had made our lives easier. I told Ivey how pleased the principal and her classroom teacher were with these writings.

I asked Ivey if she was interested in interviewing Farley Mowat. She pondered the invitation for a few moments before declining because her schedule was too busy. However, she enjoyed listening to the tapes made by her fellow students when they interviewed Mowat and Pierre Berton. She also listened to "Writing Down the Bones," a tape in which writer Natalie Goldberg explains her craft. It seems that it was during these sessions that Ivey began to perceive herself as a writer as well as a reader. She writes in her journal, "But it was through that club that she [Barbara Dixon] found out about my hobby of calligraphy and decided she could use my services. During the evenings when I worked on various things, she found out about my ability to write [creatively] and drew my attention to that ability also."

One of Ivey's many poems portrays her as a true reader—and demonstrates that she is a true writer.

In double rows upon my shelves
Impressed on pages, tucked in covers,
Familiar friends and precious worlds,
Eager to be known, but without a whisper.
I am a reader
A traveller of sorts
So I must possess the key.
Books are worlds where I wander,
With the key
Unhindered,
Free.

For Ivey, I have been what Aidan Chambers calls "an enabling adult." Ivey states, "I never used to talk to anyone about my readings because nobody was interested." Here she gives voice to the vulnerability of the gifted child who is so out of sync with her environment. Many of Ivey's elementary-school "peers" would be unable to discuss *The Lord of the Rings* or *Les Misérables,* or even the Arthurian legends, for the simple reason that they hadn't read them. In *Interwoven Conversations,* Judith Newman writes, "Teachers must also ensure that children have access to reading materials that are relevant to the kinds of writer they are interested in becoming at a particular moment; teachers must recruit the authors who will become the unwitting collaborators" (1991, p. 370).

A child with Ivey's love of the worlds that reading presents to her perceives, thinks, and feels the images that the author presents and becomes, as C. S. Lewis states, "a thousand different people" while remaining herself.

Reading to Others

As discussed in Chapter 3, children should be asked to read aloud only in the interest of real communication rather than simply to comply with the teacher's wishes. In Larry Swartz's junior classroom, the children develop their abilities to read aloud when they visit with their buddies in the grade one class. Before the twice-monthly visit, they each choose a picture book and prepare to read it aloud. The younger children also practise reading a favourite story to share with their older buddies. As Larry's students help their buddies with their miscues, they learn more about the cueing systems that we all use as we read. They can later bring these new understandings to their own reading.

Larry uses a similar buddying strategy within the classroom. Children work with partners; each pair receives two copies of a novel. During scheduled reading times, the students often read aloud parts of the novel to each other, allowing the more developed reader to practise reading aloud and at the same time assist an emergent reader. Once again, metacognitive awareness about the reading process can only increase for both participants.

The children often enjoy a more formal approach to reading aloud. A small group can present a story as "readers' theatre." In readers' theatre, the children read aloud the dialogue of a story in role. Sometimes one child will read aloud the narration that surrounds the dialogue (leaving out the extraneous "he saids"). The presentation can be simple or elaborate: the children may read a dramatic incident in readers' theatre simply for their own satisfaction; they may add simple gestures or improvised costumes to their reading; they may read it into a tape recorder as a sort of radio drama for others to listen to later.

Poems displayed on the overhead projector provide another training ground for techniques of oral expression and interpretation. "Bleezer's Ice Cream" by Jack Prelutsky, "Clickbeetle" by Mary Ann Hoberman, and "Sounds of Water" by Mary O'Neill are some of the children's favourites. Poems of the day written on chart paper, big books borrowed from the primary division, and poems from anthologies offer further opportunities for reading poems aloud. For a school concert, the class worked in groups to present a choral reading of poems about the environment. The whole class prepared a choral reading in which they wove together the words of the song "What a Wonderful World" and the poem "There Was Once a Whole World in the Scarecrow." In this exercise to show the contradictory themes about nature, each child was responsible for one or more lines of text.

The Story through Drama

Drama brings the meanings of a story into the children's own worlds as they enact personal responses. By joining story and drama, children can combine their interest in the story characters with an exploration of their own struggles for control over their lives. Drama that evolves from story is an organic process of role playing, decision making, problem solving, verbal interaction, mime, movement, and group dynamics. Drama is discussed in more detail in Chapter 8.

Celebrity Authors

Teachers should look for feasible ways of asking professional storymakers to help develop the children's sense of story. Some authors will also correspond with their young readers. Some authors and illustrators enjoy visiting with schoolchildren, but they can seldom handle all the invitations they receive, so we must ask our students to show consideration and understanding when they are fortunate enough to meet them in person.

When it can be arranged, meeting an author, illustrator, poet, or storyteller is an exciting and motivating experience. Children who recognize professional authors as real people see themselves as writers and the writing of stories in a new light.

The teacher should glean as much teaching potential as possible from the occasion. Once the visit is arranged, the preparation with the children should begin—locating the author's works, finding sources of biographical information, helping the children to create a list of significant questions for an interview. After the visit, the children can write thank-you letters and plan follow-up activities.

Classroom visits by authors can be arranged through organizations such as CANSCAIP (the Canadian Society of Children's Authors, Illustrators and Performers). Grants may be available to cover the cost of bringing an author to the classroom. (Check with your board about funding.) Budgeting for authors' and artists' visits is one of principal Paul Shaw's priorities at Queenston. Further support for the program comes from the parents' association, which donates a generous amount to invite authors, storytellers, artists, and performance companies to the school.

Gordon Korman, author of *This Can't Be Happening at Macdonald Hall, Fifth Grade Radio*, and *The Twinkie Squad*, has spoken to students from grades four to eight about his early experiences in publishing and has shared some personal stories, telling how he incorporated them into his novels. Phoebe Gilman invited the primary children to join in as she read her book *Jillian Jiggs* and gave them a preview of her new story *Something from*

Nothing. She donated to the school some drawings she created on the spot and they went on display in the library. Ruth Ohi, who illustrated Hazel Hutchins's *Nicholas at the Library* and *Katie's Babbling Brother,* brought in some of her original drawings and gave a workshop for the older children to help them illustrate their own stories. After Camilla Gryski, the author of *Super String Games* and *Cat's Cradle, Owl Eyes,* came for a visit, string games became very popular with the children.

Reading with the Whole Community

The language events the class takes part in together form a powerful dynamic that affects how students work alone and in groups. To build a caring community, where each individual is part of the whole, we need to find opportunities for reading in which children from different backgrounds, with different life experiences, and with different abilities and interests can participate. At Queenston, children gather each day to inform each other of the happenings of the morning, to share discoveries and celebrate achievements, and to read together. I have seen children sharing with the class a poem they have found; they let their classmates join in reading it from a copy they have transcribed onto chart paper. Sometimes the children will all read a brief selection from a class text and respond to it together through drama. Presenting songs, chants, and dramatic prose on overhead transparencies allows all children to see the same material so they can raise their voices together in a shared reading.

One way for the teacher to bring the class together as a community is to read stories aloud. This way, we introduce the students to material they might never pick up on their own. When our pleasure in sharing literature by reading it aloud is apparent, we bathe our listeners in the richness of language and draw them into the fascination of the story. Good novels, read a section at a time, can bind together the common threads of a theme or unit that the class is exploring over a period of time. A poem can illuminate the mood of the day. A topical article in the newspaper can reinforce the role of reading as an interesting activity through which people gain access to knowledge outside or beyond their direct experience.

A Novel for My Class
Larry Swartz

I read *Maniac Magee* aloud to my grade five class as part of a theme on survival. This novel by Jerry Spinelli won the Newbery Medal for best book of 1990. It is the story of Jeffrey Lionel "Maniac" Magee, a young white boy famed for his athletic feats, who tries to bring a city's segregated East Side and West Side together. As I read sections from the book, I encouraged the children to keep a listening log or response journal to record their thoughts about the story or its writer.

When we finished the book, the class explored the plight of street kids and the issue of segregation through a number of activities.

Revisiting the Novel

In response to four questions that I asked, the class raised the following points, which I recorded on chart paper:

Q: *What did you like about the novel?*
- untangling Cobbler's knot
- the baseball episode
- Amanda's toughness
- Mars Bar's invitation to visit his home
- running the race between Mars Bar and Maniac
- Amanda's gift of the book
- butterscotch krimpets
- the author's description "before the story"
- football throw/frog
- Fishbelly
- chant "Maniac, Maniac . . ."
- story about illiteracy/Maniac teaching Grayson
- Grayson's kindness
- birthday party
- "Don't get the facts mixed up with the truth."

Q: *What bothered you in the novel?*
- allergic to pizza
- the fact that there was segregation
- Amanda and Mars Bar's fight
- stealing—Piper and Russell
- "I'll let you be a white."
- war games—"I'll let you be a white."
- running backwards
- "I feel so bad I'm half black."
- Amanda's argument/library card
- Fishbelly; Honky
- Grayson's death—no tears
- pallbearers didn't care to show up
- pitching frog incident—believable?
- black/white issue—not clear if it has been solved

Q: *What patterns did you discover in the story?*
- Maniac is with a home . . . then he goes to streets . . . with a home . . . then streets again . . . with a secure home . .
- white side/black side . . . alternate settings
- buffaloes—slept with them at the beginning and at the end
- No matter what happens to him, Maniac never gives up.
- Maniac feels that every family he goes to gets in some sort of trouble.
- always achieving things
- hero—caught the football, untangled string, won race
- took anything he could get
- In the end, people always cared for Maniac.
- hero by bringing whites and blacks together
- Maniac was never racist, never bragged, never complained.
- always searching for a home

Q: *What questions or puzzles do you wonder about?*
- Why did he run away in the first place?
- Whites and blacks—did they really get together?
- Why would somebody want to write a book like this about blacks and whites?
- Sometimes I was confused whether the story was taking place on the black side or on the white side.
- How did Maniac get the blacks together? Was it one event?
- Why did he stay in that town?
- Why did Mars Bar invite him to live with him? Why didn't Maniac accept?
- Before the story—was Beale's house still there?
- What happened to the aunt and uncle? Did they seek out Maniac?
- Why wouldn't Maniac go with Amanda unless he was forced to?
- What was so special about being a "white" when you were playing a game?
- Why did he leave Beale's house if they were so good to him?
- How did Mars Bar "suddenly" become a good friend?
- Is Maniac happier on the streets or being home?
- What will Maniac's future be like?
- How did the blacks get their opinion of the whites in the first place?
- How did the whites get their opinion of the blacks in the first place?

Storyboard

After explaining how storyboards are drawn up by artists to depict episodes that appear in a film, I asked the class, "Which scenes might you expect to see if the novel *Maniac Magee* was to be made into a movie?" We laid out a sheet of mural paper about ten metres long in the hallway outside the classroom and I invited the class to create a storyboard depicting events, characters, and images that they felt should be featured in the movie.

As the students planned, they continued to discuss what happened in the book and the pictures that came to mind when they listened to the story. They used crayons and pastels to create the illustrations, and the completed storyboard was taped to the wall so that everyone could revisit and interpret the story through the illustrations.

Writing

Jerry Spinelli begins the novel with a prologue entitled "Before the Story" in which we first learn about "Maniac" Magee in a little girl's skipping chant:

Maniac Maniac
He's so cool
Maniac Maniac
Don't go to school
Runs all night
Runs all right
Maniac Maniac
Kisses a bull!

In their discussion after we had finished the novel, the children wondered about Maniac Magee's fate, whether he would live happily, and whether racism still erupted on the East Side and West Side.

Since the author did not include an epilogue entitled "After the Story," I invited the students to write their own. They could write what took place the next day, the next week or month, or years into the future and from Maniac's or any other character's point of view. They could also choose to write the epilogue as an interview, a poem, a newspaper article, a narrative, or a journal.

Independent Parallel Reading

I offered the students a selection of novels that they could read independently. I chose these titles because they dealt with the theme of prejudice and/or because the protagonists shared some of Maniac Magee's heroic strengths.

- *Roll of Thunder Hear My Cry*—Mildred Taylor
- *The Devil's Arithmetic*—Jane Yolen

- *Winners*—Mary-Ellen Lang Collura
- *Sounder*—William Armstrong
- *Summer of My German Soldier*—Bette Greene
- *Park's Quest*—Katherine Paterson
- *Nobody's Family Is Going to Change*—Louise Fitzhugh
- *Listen for the Singing*—Jean Little

I invited each student to keep a fictional journal for a character in the novel he or she was reading, encouraging them not just to retell what happened in the book but to imagine the character's feelings, the problems the character faced, and his or her relationship with others. I suggested they make comments, raise questions, and argue as the character might. They could write journal entries after reading a significant episode or while reflecting on large chunks of the story.

This activity let the students write in the first person as they were propelled into thinking and feeling as their chosen characters. Lisa said that it helped her understand the book better because she had to "be" the character, and James commented that this type of book report was interesting because he could still be himself while becoming somebody else.

I found the fictitious journal to be a significant medium for assessing the level of comprehension of the students. Some of the more literal-minded merely retold the events of the story as Joey did for *The Voyage of the Frog*. Others, like Georgette, writing from the point of view of Willie Sheridan in *Nobody's Family Is Going to Change*, were more reflective about actions and attitudes. As Willie, Georgette felt the power that parents can have over their children and the frustration of having ambitions squelched.

The journal was a useful tool for promoting discussion about the book during a reading conference. I would ask the student to assume the role of the character and answer questions in role, thereby elaborating the ideas recorded in the journal. The interview situation let the student deepen his or her appreciation of both the role and the book. Sometimes I suggested students conduct such interviews with a partner, in small groups, or even with the whole class.

After the Story
Heidi, grade five

That walk to my new home felt like it took a whole day as we passed through the street leaving our hot foot prints in the light of the moon. Our laughter echoed through the streets where only the black people frist walked but now two black people and one white boy walked together. When we finally were at Home I stared at the 3 numbers over the garage door. At last I had an address. For one time in my life I had everything a wonderful family the best address and people who would let me stay here in the black territory. When I woke up the morning Hester and Lester were laughing and giving me kisses and lots of love. If I was to make a time capsule and I was to put everything that happened in that one year I would put all the good things—the baseball glove from Grayson or cobbler's knot or the book that I used teach Grayson to read or Beale or Mar Bar to remind me of my black enemy who be came my friends. If some one opened that time capsule one day I wonder what they might say. They might say that there was a boy who brought a black boy to a white boy's party or they might say that the white boy who lived with a black family. May be no one will even find my time capsule may be the blacks and the white will never come together despite the efforts of the one they called

Maniac Magee!

Books: An Author Study
Larry Swartz

As children become independent readers, they learn to choose a book by more than just the cover. They become very aware of the authors they like. A study of the work of a particular author can take children beyond a bunch of good stories and pleasant reading experiences; it can yield an understanding of theme, style, plot, and characterization.

Over the past decade, Gary Paulsen has become an important and popular author for pre-adolescent and teenage readers. Three of his novels, *Hatchet, Dogsong,* and *The Winter Room*, have been chosen as Newbery Honor books. Paulsen's work always states his beliefs strongly, yet the story remains of prime importance. Because he has lived in the woods of Minnesota, travelled to the northern wilderness, and competed in the Iditarod dogsled race in Alaska, experiences with nature occur and live again and again in his writing.

The theme of coming of age runs through each of Paulsen's novels. His protagonists (usually male) go through some type of metamorphosis, usually as a result of being thrust into survival situations where they begin to question themselves and the world around them. Brian Robeson in *Hatchet* survives a plane crash in the northern Canadian wilderness and returns there in a sequel entitled *The River* to relive his experience. In *The Island*, Wil chooses to abandon his family and go to live on an island in northern Wisconsin. In *The Voyage of the Frog,*

David's uncle has died, and the boy goes out in his sailboat to scatter his ashes to the wind; he is caught in a fierce storm and must survive many days on the ocean. *Dogsong* and *Woodsong* tell of dogsled journeys: in the former, an Inuit boy travels to find himself and his past; in the latter, Paulsen describes his own breathtaking adventure on a dogsled race in Alaska. Though physical survival seems to be the centre of each of these stories, the protagonists must work out their feelings about others, about growing up, and about the power and wonders of nature.

In several of the novels, the protagonists confront their problems and learn about the world through association with an adult other than a parent. In *The Crossing*, Manny, a street kid fighting for survival in a Mexican border town, develops a strange friendship with a disturbed American soldier who decides to help Manny cross the border. In *The Foxman*, an elderly disfigured man teaches a young boy about surviving in the wilderness when he finds himself lost in the woods. In *Tiltawhirl John*, a runaway discovers that working in a carnival doesn't protect him from the cruelties of life.

Often the protagonists come to find meaning in their own lives through another's experiences. In *Dancing Carl*, the appearance of Carl on the local skating rink has a great impact on the lives of two twelve-year-old boys. In *The Night the White Deer Died*, Janet, who lives in an artists' colony in New Mexico, is drawn to Billy Honcho, whom she meets when he begs money from her. In *The Monument*, Rocky's life is changed by a remarkable artist who visits her small Kansas town to design a war memorial. Sometimes, an animal helps the protagonist understand the meaning of life and death (the frog in *The Island*, the dog in *Woodsong*, the deer in *Tracker*).

Nearly all of the main characters in Paulsen's novels are separated from their parents for some reason. In *The Cookcamp*, a young boy goes to live with his grandmother during wartime. In *The Monument*, Rocky's mother left her as a baby in the back seat of a police car. In *Popcorn Days and Buttermilk Nights*, Carley's parents send him off to live with his uncle on a farm in Minnesota in order to keep him out of reform school. We learn mostly about parents from the viewpoint of the main character. Often the protagonist is dissatisfied with the parents' lifestyle in some way (Brian's anger at his parents' divorce in *Hatchet*; Wil's decision to live on an island when his parents moved to a new home in *The Island*).

Other than the two brothers Eldon and Wayne who listen to their Uncle David's stories in *The Winter Room*, siblings do not appear in Paulsen's books. Similarly, peer friendships are not strongly developed nor are boy-girl relationships, though they are suggested in *The Boy Who Owned the School* and *The Island*.

Gary Paulsen's *Hatchet* became almost contagious at Queenston. A grade six teacher first chose the novel to read aloud, and it has since passed on to teachers of grades five to eight. *Hatchet* tells of Brian Robeson's escape from a plane crash and his struggle for survival in the wilderness. The adventure, the battles with nature, and Brian's growing maturity as he comes to terms with his parents' divorce greatly appeal to young adolescents. As the students listened to sections of the story each day, they were encouraged to share their thoughts and opinions of Brian's story and the way Paulsen tells it. One teacher had the students write a letter that Brian might have written to his mother or father if he had had the chance to do so. This strategy invited the students to step into the shoes of the protagonist, enabling them to come to a better understanding of the conflict in the novel and to reflect on it from the main character's point of view.

After the whole class had listened to *Hatchet*, many students were stimulated to read other novels by Gary Paulsen independently or in small groups. They began to compare the novels on such points as characterization, the role of nature, how the character grew and changed, and the problems they had to overcome. After one group had read several of the novels, they brainstormed features they had found in the books. They used these ideas to compare the characters, thoughts, actions, and style of writing in Gary Paulsen's work and changed and added to the list as they progressed further in their exploration of the author. Here is their final version.

weather	*conflict with nature*
descriptions of nature	*coming of age*
loneliness	*characters learn about themselves*
journeys	*mostly male characters*
characters go through a change	*chapters end with a punch*
loves animals	*sometimes short sentences*
bravery	*conflict with self*
death	*optimism*
reflective	

Paulsen's protagonists are usually the age of the intended audience. What gives them strength is a sense of determination and optimism. They are curious and observant, with the ability to assess their problems and confront them directly. Paulsen brings alive their thoughts about the circumstances in which they find themselves and about the people in their lives. These reflections help make the characters very real to the readers and lead them to ask themselves questions about their own lives. As one grade five girl wrote in her reading response journal, "Gary Paulsen makes you think that the characters are alive and that you even are that character."

We often tend to worry that children get stuck reading the same type of material over and over again. But children who have taken the time to discover why they like the work of one particular author have acquired a key to intelligent literary criticism that they can use to unlock the work of others. They become more discerning readers, ready to find pleasure and meaning in new books, new authors, and between new covers.

Suggested Reading for Teachers

Barrs, Myra, and Anne Thomas, ed. *The Reading Book*. London: Centre for Language in Primary Education, 1992. *The Reading Book* surveys what we now know about reading, in chapters corresponding to the four major partners in the reading process—child, parent, teacher, and text—and includes issues that feature in a primary school's reading policy.

Benton, Michael, and Geoff Fox. *Teaching Literature, Nine to Fourteen*. Oxford: Oxford University Press, 1987. In this book the authors address three fundamental issues: what happens when we read stories and poems; what experiences do different types of literature offer children; what are the best ways of handling literature in the classroom?

Booth, David, and Bob Barton. *Stories in the Classroom: Storytelling, Reading Aloud and Role-Playing with Children*. Markham: Pembroke Publishers, 1990. Teachers learn how to find, choose, and use specific stories with students of all ages and abilities. A special "story response repertoire" includes activities from basic story talk to reading, writing, dramatizing, thematic projects, and more.

Booth, David, and Bill Moore. *Poems Please*. Markham: Pembroke Publishers, 1988. A valuable handbook for reading and writing poetry, including an annotated list of 200 useful poetry anthologies.

Chambers, Aidan. *The Reading Environment: How Adults Help Children Enjoy Books*. South Woodchester, England: Thimble Press, 1991. This volume is a collection of practical advice and comment on what can be done in schools to help children become thoughtful, willing readers and is a convenient summing-up for teachers and librarians wanting to review their practice.

Cullinan, Bernice E., ed. *Children's Literature in the Reading Program.* Newark, Del.: International Reading Association, 1987. Various contributing authors deal with such questions as why do we need children's literature in the reading program; how can we use literature with developing readers using whole language routines, including reading aloud, chanting from charts, book discussions, and writing; what are the various ways children can expand their multicultural understanding; how can a teacher use children's books to introduce children to the humanities, including drama, visual arts, movement, and writing.

Fry, Donald. *Children Talk about Books: Seeing Themselves as Readers.* Anthony Adams, ed. Milton Keynes, England: Open University Press, 1985. Fry draws on a series of in-depth conversations with each of six young readers, aged eight, twelve, and fifteen, about their reading.

Hansen, Jane. *When Writers Read.* Toronto: Irwin Publishing, 1987. In this discussion of how recent approaches in the teaching of writing can be used in the teaching of reading, the author explores a response approach in teaching writing that encourages students to take responsibility for their own learning and gives them a sense of control over their efforts.

Hayhoe, Michael and Stephen Parker, eds. *Reading & Response.* Buckingham, England: Open University Press, 1990. The contributors in this book support and investigate the issues of the collaborative link between reader and text.

Jobe, Ron, and Paula Hart. *Canadian Connections.* Markham: Pembroke Publishers, 1991. In this book, teachers and librarians explore dozens of key Canadian books with accompanying activities and related themes.

Kobrin, Beverly. *Eyeopeners! How to Choose and Use Children's Books about Real People, Places, and Things.* New York: Penguin Books, 1988. Parents and educators are offered advice on how to choose non-fiction books that include exciting book-based activities.

MacKenzie, Terry, ed. *Readers' Workshops: Bridging Literature and Literacy: Stories from Teachers and Their Classrooms.* Toronto: Irwin Publishing, 1992. This volume describes classroom environments that enable learners of all ages and abilities to belong to communities of readers.

Meek, Margaret. *On Being Literate.* London: The Bodley Head, 1991. Margaret Meek writes with the intention of reassuring parents and teachers worried about a child's literacy and its importance in a changing society, one in which the word processor has become a symbol of modern literacy and different forms of print confronting us increase every day.

Parsons, Les. *Response Journals.* Markham: Pembroke Publishers, 1990. Concrete examples help teachers implement, organize, and evaluate response journals, including questions for cueing personal response, suggestions for group discussion, sample criteria for evaluation, and sample student responses.

Peterson, Ralph, and Maryann Eeds. *Grand Conversations: Literature Groups in Action.* Toronto: Scholastic, 1990. This book concerns teaching groups of children with real books and describes the meaningful dialogue that develops reading response collaboratively.

Smith, Frank. *Understanding Reading.* Hillsdale, N.J.: Lawrence Erlbaum, 1986. This guide to how reading is learned as an "experience-constructing" activity provides a throeretical analysis of linguistic, psychological, social, and physiological aspects of reading.

Stephens, Diane, ed. *What Matters? A Primer for Teaching Reading.* Portsmouth, N.H.: Heinemann, 1990. *What Matters?* provides access to a broad and complex body of knowledge about teaching reading based on Diane Stephens's twenty years of experience as a reading teacher and on her research with other teachers in their classrooms.

Trelease, Jim. *The New Read-Aloud Handbook.* New York: Penguin Books, 1989. Trelease demonstrates how to begin reading aloud and which books to choose and how reading aloud improves children's language skills and awakens imagination.

Reflections

1 "Many children can read, but few are readers" is almost a proverb among teachers. We have to concern ourselves with the children's attitudes to reading as well as their ability to read. What aspects of a classroom reading program can develop "lifelong readers?" Suggest ways a school might develop a reading profile for each child as a cumulative reading record, giving successive teachers information on which they can build each year's program. What information would you, as a teacher at the beginning of the school year, like to have about your new students' reading abilities and interests?

❷ Young readers need access to a wide variety of reading materials to follow their interests, to discover information, and to help their reading abilities develop. Prepare a list of anthologies, novels, references, folklore, and magazines that you would like to see in your classroom library. How can you collaborate with the school and public libraries to provide new materials from time to time?

❸ We must help children "read the world" in order to "read the word" (Freire and Macedo, 1987). Reading to children can provide the experiences with life and language that children will need in order to meet the challenges of print. List occasions in the class program that can provide you with opportunities to read aloud to the children. What types of resources are most useful when they are shared orally with the children?

❹ Draw up a flexible timetable that allows for each of these occasions for reading in the classroom program:

- a daily silent-reading time, when children select their own books
- opportunities for group reading and interactive response
- book talks by the teacher, by students, the librarian, and/or visitors
- integrating what the children read with their writing
- rehearsed oral reading by the students for real purposes—to buddies, in readers' theatre, and so forth
- reading conferences that will allow you to observe the reading strategies individual children are using and to assess the meaning they are making as they read
- connecting what the children read in any curriculum area to their development as readers

Does your timetable include direct teaching for the whole class and/or mini-lessons for small groups to highlight specific techniques and strategies used by effective readers?

❺ What sort of responses do you expect from children, both as they read and when they have finished reading? Considering your teaching style, how would you enlarge this response repertoire? Would you start by encouraging occasions for journal writing, discussion, retelling, dramatizing, reading aloud, or written reflection? How would you implement this new approach? What other modes of response would you like your students to use?

❻ How do you involve parents in the reading program? Some approaches are listed below. In what other ways could you draw them into the classroom reading community?

- using volunteers in the classroom
- encouraging parents to read to their children
- promoting visits to the public library and bookstores
- holding book fairs and supporting book clubs
- providing information to parents about both the reading program and their child's development in the various aspects of reading

❼ Most programs for enriched or gifted children take place within the classroom community. The children take their enquiries beyond or more deeply into the regular curriculum with the guidance of the teacher or, like Ivey, with that of a resource person. Reading and writing workshops in which children help each other in their work encourage a spirit of community, but they should also allow for individual growth and development. Do you need to rethink your classroom schedule to grant children in need of enrichment a time frame suitable for extensive and involving projects, and their classmates the opportunity to benefit from sharing in their explorations and discoveries?

Becoming a Writer

N
O ASPECT OF TEACHING language arts has received more emphasis in the last decade than writing. Building on Donald Murray's (1979) concept of writing as a process and Donald Graves's (1983) clearly articulated stages of that process, teachers in North America began to change their views of what had long been labelled "creative writing." Suddenly we were past the argument of product versus process into an examination of the process of putting thoughts on paper. In England, James Britton (Britton et al., 1975) and Nancy Martin (Martin et al., 1976) observed students' writing at different levels of experience and concluded that quality and depth of writing depended on how important the topic being written about was to the writer. When they learned of the success of the Manhattan Writing Project (Calkins, 1986), many teachers altered their own writing programs to include conferences during the writing process rather than just marking the final product. Lucy Calkins's further work (1991) stressed the personal notebook as a means of capturing the child's thoughts and as a resource for more extended pieces of writing.

Classrooms have become writing workshops, where everyone is part of the teaching/learning dynamic. Children in groups help their peers improve drafts; they listen to others read aloud their stories as they would to real authors; teachers confer with young writers, asking enabling questions and offering help with editing. The once-a-week writing period is a thing of the past, for writing has become part of daily classroom life (Atwell, 1987). The process lets children see themselves as real writers with something to say to real readers.

Can we help children see writing like painting, where the process is embedded in the product? Can they see revision as a continually changing version of their writing rather than as a separate process? Can we as teachers train ourselves to focus on the stories that the children want to tell? Judith Newman (1989) calls for teachers to think of themselves as writers as well so they will understand the act of writing from inside the process.

What Is Writing?

Every child has a story to tell. The question is, will he tell it to you?
(Harold Rosen)

The literary form children meet most often is story. They listen to their parents' stories of their wedding, to their grandparents' tales of strife and hard luck, to the gossip of adults that drifts up to them when they are in bed but not yet asleep, to the books read aloud by their teachers. They handle storybooks. They read stories for themselves. And for most young children, the most natural form of writing is story.

What stories do children write? Real ones from their own experience; dreams that may seem equally real; family chronicles; personal memories filtered through time; fantasies that carry them out and beyond the real world; adventures that let them take part in the events they conjure up; stories of all types—monologues, tall tales, legends, poems, dialogues, satires.

The stories are there, but for many children, encoding a story in print seems an insurmountable task. (Certainly, very few teachers undertake such a rigorous activity.) The children know they will be judged not just on the strength of their story but also on their ability to transcribe. Will they then forgo story to concentrate on the formalities of print? In our attempts to teach writing, do we destroy the story? How can we maintain the integrity of story and still help children write?

The traditional motivation for writing in the classroom has not been a child's inner compulsion to write, but the completion of assigned writing tasks. Today's writing curricula stress the *use* of writing rather than exercises *about* writing. When writers write in a context that has personal significance, they reach for the necessary skills to explore both content and form.

Writing helps children not only to express their feelings and ideas but to rethink, reassess, and restructure them. As children begin to think of themselves as writers, they discover that they can control the medium to say what they want to say to the people they want to reach. Those first stories lead to the use of all sorts of writing strategies—free writing, journals, interviews, brainstormed lists, letters, announcements, proclamations, petitions, reports, advertisements, and questionnaires. Groups of students can collaborate on a mutual enterprise, collecting data, organizing information, revising, and editing.

Writing at school must not be seen as drill or skill, or as something we do before we can do "real writing." That is why this chapter comes before the one on the problems of transcribing and not after it. The conventions of writing are important, but they must never eclipse the reasons we write. "Many children designated as 'learning disabled' are poor writers," says Donald Graves (1983).

They equate their struggles with handwriting, spelling, and language conventions with a lack of ideas and information worth sharing. The writing-process approach to teaching first emphasizes what children know, then emphasizes the conventions that will help them share their meaning with others in the class. This approach has led to major breakthroughs for young writers, particularly those who have learning problems.

The Writing Folder

A series of self-edited or collaboratively edited writing samples from throughout the year kept in a writing folder provides concrete evidence of progress. Writing from all curriculum areas should be included. When teachers examine dated writing samples, they can pinpoint patterns of development and focus whole-class or small-group "mini-lessons" on needed skills.

Keeping samples of each child's writing at the start of the year is important. It allows students and teachers to see the growth they have made. Photocopies or other writing samples may be sent home at regular intervals to give parents easy-to-understand, concrete proof that their child is learning.

At year's end, Paul Shaw, the principal at Queenston, encourages his teachers to collect three to five pieces of each student's writing to place in a writing folder that is passed on to the teacher for the following year. The samples serve as a reliable assessment tool: by putting pieces of work alongside one another, teacher, parent, and child can recognize growth and development.

A Profile of a Writer
Lois Roy

Dianne's writing folder contains what she considers her "best" writing since kindergarten. She first created storybooks filled with illustrations. Her teacher transcribed the one-sentence stories that accompanied Dianne's pictures. "Colours" was a frequent theme. One book showed her coloured ball, her coloured squares, and a scribbled abstract design that is her coloured world. One of Dianne's later kindergarten entries was an accurate copy of a sentence written by her teacher: "This is a horse and I am petting it."

In grade one, Dianne began writing personal narratives recording adventures with her family. She wrote about her brother or outings with her parents. She had a good sense of spelling conventions by the end of grade one. Her sentences were clear and syntactically correct.

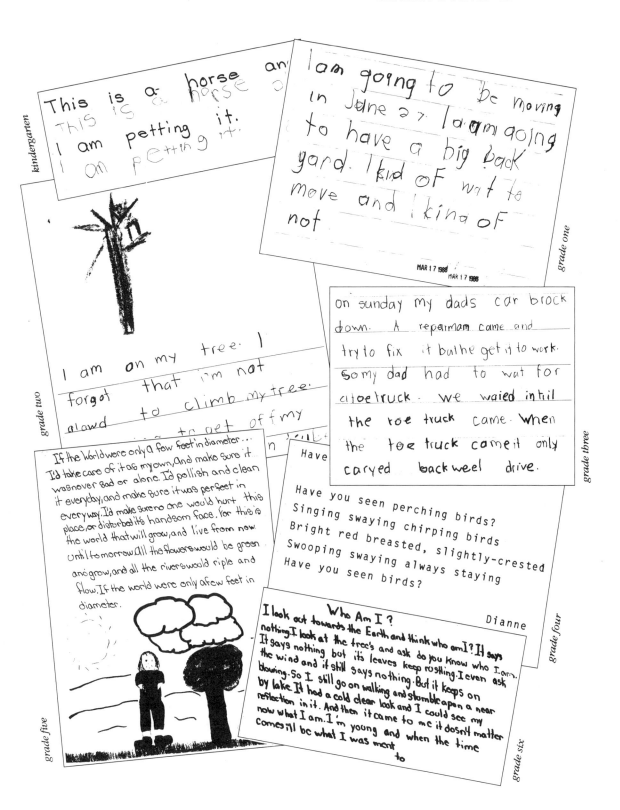

This is a horse an
I am petting it.

I am going to be moving
in June 27 I am going
to have a big back
yard. I kid of wrt to
move and I kina of
not

MAR 17 1988

I am on my tree. I
forgot that I'm not
alowd to climb my tree.

on sunday my dads car brock
down. A repairman came and
try to fix it but he get it to work.
So my dad had to wat for
a toe truck. we waied intil
the roe truck came. When
the toe truck came it only
caryed back weel drive.

Have you seen perching birds?
Singing swaying chirping birds
Bright red breasted, slightly-crested
Swooping swaying always staying
Have you seen birds?

Dianne

If the World were only a few feet in diameter...
I'd take care of it as my own, And make sure it
was never sad or alone. I'd pollish and clean
it everyday, and make sure it was perfect in
every way. I'd make sure no one would hurt this
place, or disturbed it's handsom face. For this is
the world that will grow, and live from now
until tomorrow. All the flowers would be green
and grow, and all the rivers would riple and
flow. If the world were only a few feet in
diameter.

Who Am I?
I look out towards the Earth and think who am I? It says
nothing. I look at the tree's and ask do you know who I am.
It says nothing but its leaves keep rustling. I even ask
the wind and it still says nothing. But it keeps on
blowing. So I still go on walking and stumble apon a near
by lake. It had a cold clear look and I could see my
reflection in it. And then it came to me it dosn't matter
now what I am. I'm young and when the time
comes i'll be what I was ment
to

In grades two and three her journal entries grew longer. She writes about outdoor experiences in the rain, in the park, and climbing a tree. She spelled most words correctly: miscues such as "alowd," "befour,"and "trubel" indicate that she was representing the sounds of words and moving closer to conventional spelling. The entries in grade three were mostly personal anecdotes. She wrote about her father's car being broken and expressed strong feelings about an occasion when her family wouldn't let her watch television. The journal seemed to be important to her, but she was not experimenting with other genres.

In the junior grades, Dianne's writing reflected the theme-based program in her classroom. "Have You Seen Birds?" and "If The World Were Only . . ." were patterned on stories about the environment. She put a great deal of effort into a "published" book about a girl's friendship with a backyard bluejay.

Recent samples of Dianne's writing appear in "Where Does the Wind Blow?"—a book of memoirs and reflections on the people and events in her life. The introduction gives us a verbal self-portrait. She still talks about her family. One poem "Who Am I?" reveals the curiosity and introspection of an eleven-year-old girl, and we are reminded of the five-year-old who wrote about "her coloured world."

When asked about her life "as a writer," Dianne says that she prefers to write poems rather than stories and likes to keep a diary to record the events and feelings of her everyday life. "Most [of my] writing is done in school," she says. When stuck for an idea, Dianne likes to confer with her friends to "get me going." Dianne says that she recognizes the importance of redoing her work and often revises three or four times before considering it complete.

Dianne feels that the computer in the classroom and the weekly session in the computer lab have helped her writing processes. She claims she is not a good speller, but gets help from others. Dianne says that the most important thing that helps her as a writer is having "a teacher who shares lots and lots and lots of stories."

The Writing Process

Children, like adults, have different approaches to the writing process. Some compose a piece in their minds before they put anything on paper. Often their writing comes out quite detailed and "clean." In effect, they do the first draft mentally. Others compose as they write. Their first efforts may be sketchy, needing details added and changes made. The writers know this; it is simply they way they write. We need to learn to recognize which children compose in their minds and which as they write, and they should be allowed to use whatever style of writing is comfortable.

Children should write every day. If they write only once every two weeks, their writing will be predictable and stultified. When they have plenty of opportunities to write, they will take risks: try new subjects, voices, language, and forms of organization. Some experiments will work; others will not be so successful. The more risks they take, the more the quality of their writing will vary from one day to the next. They should be encouraged to see this as a positive thing and accept it as a natural element in the writing process. It shows that they are reaching for something and are experimenting to find better ways to say what they mean.

From Rough Draft to Polished Product

Most of us learn the craft of writing through revision. As students revise and edit their work, they organize, choose an appropriate format, use language to create effects, sequence information, recognize and eliminate irrelevant material, and become aware of how standard spelling, correct punctuation, and legible handwriting help to convey their message to their readership.

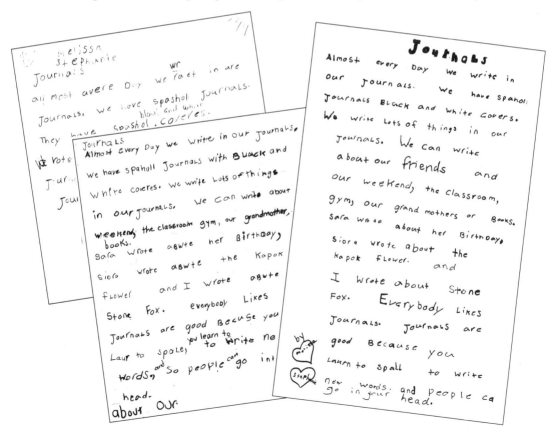

For example, Melissa and Stephanie, in grade three, carried out a series of revisions in going from a draft in their journal to an article in the class newspaper. Collaboration during the writing process encourages students to use a variety of strategies to solve spelling, grammar, and language usage problems.

A piece of writing often requires days to reach completion. Children should see writing as something they can manipulate, rather than something that comes out right the first time. While the teacher may be a facilitator at any stage, it is important for the writer to retain ownership of the piece and make final decisions regarding it.

Not all writing need go through this entire process. Some pieces may be abandoned simply because the writer loses interest or feels the pieces are not going anywhere. Others may go through many revisions before the writer is satisfied. Children need opportunities to share their writings. Publishing, displaying, or reading aloud selected pieces will enable children to see what the results of the full writing process can be. Dated samples of work kept in a writing folder will assist both teacher and child in monitoring progress and planning suitable instruction.

Be aware of emerging patterns in the children's writing behaviour. When, and how often, do they have dry periods? Which children seem to have trouble getting started on a piece of writing? Which children never seem to finish a piece? Which children seem to write on one topic all the time? You will soon realize which children need a writing conference and at which stage they need the most assistance.

The Writing Conference

As classroom teachers, we are honing our skills of talking to children about their writing. The secret is in listening as adults who are actually interested in what is being said, commenting as readers and writers who have faced similar challenges, and developing the wisdom to guide the young writers into revealing more than they thought they could. The next step is to offer our experience during the editing so that others can read the piece easily and, at the same time, help the writer become aware of the conventions of writing.

We learn to confer with children by making the attempt, by thinking about the results of our conversations, and by finding out how other teachers, such as Lucy Calkins, Nancie Atwell, Judith Newman, Mary Ellen Giacobbe, and the teacher across the hall have grown and developed. I propose questions such as the following, suggested by these educators, as signposts to successful writing conferences.

- What are you writing about? Why did you choose this topic? Why is this topic important to you?
- What are you discovering as you write this piece? Has anything surprised you?
- What's the most important thing you are trying to convey?
- How do you feel about your writing so far?
- What is working so well that you would like to develop it further?
- What can you build on? What doesn't fit?
- Do you have enough information for your piece? Too much?
- Can you use examples to help the reader understand what you want to say?
- How does this draft sound to you when you read it aloud?
- What changes have you made from your last draft? What will you do in the next draft?
- What problems are you having? Can I do anything to help you?
- Tell me your best line.
- How does your title fit your story?
- Are you happy with your beginning and ending?
- How does this piece compare to others you have written?
- Have you read a book called _____? Your work reminds me of that. Can you use the form the author chose for that piece?

Questions like these help us use writing conferences to help children generate and organize ideas before the writing, to consider what they are composing while the writing is in progress, or for revising and editing after a first draft. Conferences can take anywhere from two and ten minutes. They are more productive when the child feels at ease and knows what to expect. The child will gain confidence if the teacher sets up a special place for talking about writing and sits beside the child as a collaborator rather than across the desk as an instructor.

During the conference, we can encourage children to talk about the piece of writing and perhaps come up with other ideas or more detail to include in the piece. We want the child to see revising as a normal part of writing and what is already on paper as only a draft. Pieces intended for publication or display may go through more revisions before the child is satisfied, but even a piece that is not designated for publication may benefit from a second look.

We should not take ownership of writing by asking leading questions or making specific suggestions. Our students will see such actions as attempts to make their writing match our intentions rather than their own and render them dependent on us for approval. Broad, open questions that draw out more from students extend the process of making deliberate choices, of experimenting, of adding detail, and invite young writers to choose what is important.

We also want young writers to learn to ask themselves questions. Lucy Calkins (1991) suggests that students switch between the roles of "involved writer and detached critic" in order to "re-see" their work. Calkins also reminds us that we need not relinquish our own identities in order to give students ownership of their craft. If we have a tip to give students about good writing, why not give it? If we think students need instruction in how to use quotation marks, why not teach them? We mustn't be afraid to teach, but we do need to think carefully about the kinds of teaching that will be helpful.

Teacher-selected topics are a poor writing stimulus. We need rather to make students realize that their lives, including their dreams and fantasies, are worth writing about. Then they will want to write. Our task is to help our students choose topic, form, and audience, thus setting the process in motion. The act of writing springs from the need to "frame selected moments in our lives, to uncover and to celebrate the organizing patterns of our existence" (Calkins, 1991).

Writing in Brian Crawford's grades three-to-five classroom is the vehicle that learners use to share their explorations with others in the course of the writing process as well as in the finished product. Writing conferences, both with the teacher and each other, help them experiment with different forms in an environment that values choice and risk taking.

Brian creates this environment from his first meeting with the children when he invites each of them to write down four points of personal interest on an index card. Brian first models by writing his own four ideas, sharing his thoughts aloud as he chooses topics. The children see him struggling to come up with the third and fourth ideas.

The children talk of things they have experienced or have knowledge about and piggyback ideas with their classmates. One boy mentions learning to ride his bicycle, which triggers a girl's memory of learning to tie her shoes. Once the children have chosen their four topics, they begin to confer with one another about their "stories." In a few minutes, the room is full of the sound of pencils leaving behind records of thoughts. Brian himself writes for about ten minutes and then gets up and moves from child to child asking, "How's it going?" or "Tell me about your writing." The brief interactions that follow may last from fifteen seconds to a minute or two.

Brian connects with writers in his class in such teacher/student conferences daily. The students, by their comments, set the direction that the conferences will follow. At first, Brian does not look at the children's work; he has the children read it to him. This puts him into the role of listener/responder and ensures that his mental red pencil does not mark what the children have written.

In the following days, teacher and children explore other ways to confer. At the beginning of the year, the children meet once a week in teacher-assigned groups to share their writing, though each child is not expected to bring a piece of work every time. Those who do talk about their writing identify the type of feedback they need from their listeners. Brian's general rules are that responders first give at least three positive comments. Then they ask questions, often for clarification, that may lead the writer to consider changes in future drafts. The usefulness of these groups disappears as the first term progresses, and they are replaced by the children's own informal peer conferences, usually in groups of two or three. The children use the procedures that they learned in the teacher-assigned groups and in conferences with the teacher.

As the children take on the role of responders, Brian is freed to have longer conferences with individual children. For example, Greg brought his paper airplane experiments to a conference and wanted to talk about how to present his new knowledge. Teacher and child explored together some possible ways, and then Greg made the final decisions. Derik had been to see *Phantom of the Opera* and decided to use the premise of the play for a story of his own but to create new characters. When he had written several pages, he decided he needed a conference because he wasn't sure where the story should go next.

Editing conferences occur only for pieces that are to be published. Teacher and child make changes that are required to polish a piece of writing. From these discussions, Brian notes points of concern in spelling, punctuation, and grammatical conventions to work on during the next week with those children who require this type of assistance.

Whole-class sharing times provide the children with another setting in which to gain feedback about their writing. The children and Brian also use this time to discuss writing by professional authors just as they do their own. Here the learners begin to make the connection between reading and writing and to see themselves as a community of both readers and writers.

A Conference with Sara
Brian Crawford

The following transcript is of a conference with Sara, a grade five student, discussing a story she has just written about twins.

Teacher: I'd like to start by saying that it really helped by hearing both John and Chris speaking. It seemed to come alive. You didn't just use the word "said." I particularly liked when they "plopped" into a chair. I could just see them sinking. Your story reminded me a lot of other books about twins or people switching positions, such as *The Prince and the Pauper* and *The Whipping Boy*. You also made me think about what it might be like to have a twin. You bring out some of the bad things. What I'm wondering about is where you got the idea for this story?

Sara: This week I've been watching movies about twins. I saw *The Parent Trap*, this Disney movie where two girls change places. And oh yes, we just got two new twins at our school across the hall.

Teacher: You know, there are some parts of your story that sound real. I loved the fact that you've included your character "Super Pig" into this story. Is this your first draft?

Sara: No, I've rewritten this already.

Teacher: When you went from draft one to draft two, what did you do?

Sara: I read it over to myself and some parts didn't make sense. When I said that Chris went into his pyjamas and John went into his pyjamas, nobody would understand it, so I had to change it to "they switched."

Teacher: After you finished draft one, did you find an audience to read it to?

Sara: I like to let my mom read it, but she wasn't home, so I gave it to my brother but he doesn't give me many comments except "It's good."

Teacher: Then what did you do?

Sara: I just read it to myself and became my own audience.

Teacher: What do you think you're going to do with it?

Sara: I'd like to publish it. I want to change some of my sentences around and maybe tell another adventure that the twins had.

Teacher: Is there something that you think I might be able to help you with?

Sara: I'm having trouble with the parts where they talk. Do I have the quotation marks in the right place?

Teacher: Maybe if you read it aloud to me again, I can help you with the dialogue.

A Conference with Travas
Larry Swartz

Travas, a grade three student, was stimulated to use the first poem and accompanying painting in *Aska's Animals* by Warabé Aska and David Day for a story in his notebook. When Travas finished his draft copy, he shared it with the class and then asked for a conference to help him prepare a revision.

Teacher: That's quite a powerful story, Travas. It's like a circle story. I like the way the horses came from the sea, galloped to find food, and then returned to the sea, except you don't say "sea," you say "Davey Jones' Locker." Where did you get the idea to use that expression?

Travas: Well, I read a book last week called *Sea Witches* and the author says that they killed some sailors and left them in Davey Jones' Locker. I remembered that and decided to use it in my story because it was also about the sea.

Teacher: How did you get your idea for the story? The poem in the book doesn't talk about the horses going for food and going back to the sea.

Travas: The picture in the book shows water and reflecting horses. I thought that they must be going somewhere, so I thought I'd write a story.

Teacher: What words do you like?

Travas: I like the "watery beach" and "thousands of horses galloping."

Teacher: You've painted quite a picture for those who haven't seen the book. I like the way you've begun like a real author— "Long, long ago." What are you going to do with the story now?

Travas: I'd like to publish it. I'll fix up some words and maybe add an idea.

Teacher: What would you like to fix up specifically?

Travas: I think that the part where it's overnight and then the morning doesn't make sense.

Teacher: Did the class make any suggestions that might help you?

Travas: Jeffrey said I should put a hunter in it. I think Samantha said I should tell how the horses changed. I might add that.

Teacher: Are there any spelling words you'd like help with?

Travas: Did I spell "usual" right?

Teacher:	"Usual" is a hard word. You have the beginning right "u-s.".. Here's what it looks like: "u-s-u-a-l." There's the "w" sound but there's no "w" in that word.
Travas:	Okay.
Teacher:	I'd like you to look at "galloped." You've put a "t" on the end. It has a "t" sound but it ends in "e-d." Do you remember that word puzzle we did when we added "e-d" to "talk" and "walk"? Often when you write words in the past, you add "ed." That's why it's "g-a-l-l-o-p-e-d." Look, you have the word "formed" correct. It's the same ending even though it doesn't sound exactly the same.
Travas:	I think I need some periods. I don't have any.
Teacher:	Well, let's read it aloud one more time and every time you think you stop, you can put in a piece of punctuation.
Travas:	*(reads story)* They found a barn to sleep overnight in the morning they went back to the sea.
Teacher:	Where do you think the period goes? The meaning changes depending where you put the period.
Travas:	I think it goes after "in."

Horses 1991 NOV 22
Long Long Ago In a Watery Beach Lived
Thousands of Horses that had galloped out
Of The Sea. The Sea Horses formed into
Their Real forms And They Looked for Food
They found A Barn to Sleep over Night
The morning They Went Back Sea and
formed into There ushel form and They
Lived Happly ever after in Davy Jones 'ock
Locker

Travas
Grade 3

Teacher:	*(reading)* "They found a barn to sleep overnight in." Or do you want to begin your next sentence with "in the morning"?
Travas:	I'm going to put it here after the word "overnight."
Teacher:	You know how to put in a capital letter automatically. That's good, Travas.
Travas:	I think I'll rewrite this.
Teacher:	Do you think your story could be a picture book?
Travas:	Yes, I could put a sentence and a picture on every page.
Teacher:	I think it'd be interesting to draw the pictures that you've described. Do you think this conference helped you with your story?
Travas:	Yes. I think I'll fix some mistakes. Then maybe I'll write chapter two.
Teacher:	What do you think would happen in chapter two?
Travas:	Well, there's going to be a hunter who captures a tiger and the horses come out of the sea again.
Teacher:	It sounds like you could write many chapters and use other animals from the original book.
Travas:	Good idea.
Teacher:	Maybe you can talk to somebody at your table to help you. Good luck.

The Relationship of Reading and Writing

What does writing do for the reader? What does reading do for the writer? All acts of language are interrelated, but story holds a special place in a child's development. Writing activities that promote story, interpret story, alter story, or generate other stories, provide true learning for children, not only as readers but also as writers. In Brian's and Larry's classes, I see children borrowing from their reading as they write, writing like readers, and reading like writers. The teachers have made available many models of reading and writing for their students because "what an individual can learn, and how he learns it, depends on what model he has available" (Papert, 1980). When they write, children draw both consciously and unconsciously on the stories they have heard and read—for concepts, characters, events, themes, issues, words, patterns. That writing, in turn, reveals their insights into those stories. The two vital processes, reading and writing, are thus linked together as children integrate their feelings and ideas about stories in their reading, in their writing, and from one to the other.

Children can journey further into a story and write the meanings that accrue for them. As they strive for a fuller understanding of what is happening in a story, their writing becomes more complex and their language more sophisticated. In "I Wonder What Kind of Person He'll Be?" Jane Hansen (1991) tells of Colin, who reads a lot of fantasy—the Arthurian legends, J.R.R. Tolkien's *Lord of the Rings*, and Ursula Le Guin's *Earthsea* trilogy. He writes of a man carrying "a staff taller than himself, the staff twisted and turned so that if it was stretched straight it would grow three feet taller," who leaves "a child dressed in a regular childs garb [who] looked big, strong, and very smart for his age . . . with a very dignified look" with an old couple on the island of Sillen. He tells them, "'His name is Arsintar but do not ever speak the name for it will bring death and distruction on to your village. Keep him hidden for nine days . . .'" Colin is not sure how Arsintar will turn out because he is "only on the fourth page." When Hansen asks him, "What character in a book you've read is like Arsintar?" Colin thinks for a long time. "The one I think of is King Arthur 'cuz of the way there's the wise man. There's the wise man Merlin. There's the kid Arthur. There's the parents dead. I didn't think of it till now."

As Hansen tells us, Colin has a fuzzy but realistic plan. He knows that his character will become his own person and that he, Colin, can't control this. He writes to learn, to find out. As he starts to know what kind of person Arsintar is, the plot will emerge. Colin knows about the evolution of characters because in group discussions and in conferences with teachers and friends he has shared his thoughts about story characters and how character and situation influence each other. He knows that characters can't make decisions that are inconsistent with their life situations. Colin will create his character's childhood in order to determine what kind of person he is.

Modes of Writing

Collaborative Writing

Many modes of written discourse are available even to very young children when they work in groups because they can leave the actual writing to those who are comfortable doing so. The teacher may ask a group to start from a literary pattern, as we saw Jo Phenix do in Chapter 3, record a class experience, note down ideas from a brainstorming session, or organize information. Children can represent their ideas in captions, diaries, letters, notes and memos, and personal narratives.

When children collaborate, they talk, plan, and negotiate before and during the writing. As they make suggestions and discuss changes, they

often learn composing and transcribing skills from one another, using a variety of strategies to solve spelling, grammar, and usage problems. When group writing is published, all the students in the group can experience the pride of authorship.

Creating Stories

Writing a story is a complex process, which children can deepen and extend throughout life. Some children from their first days as writers can create stories that are involved and well-structured. Others will take time to develop this talent.

When children write stories, they begin with their own selves in fictional settings, trying on situations for size and sensing from the stories they have heard and read how authors combine imagination and real life. Their stories may depend on flights of fancy or revisit and retell the happenings of their own neighbourhoods. As they build narrative, children see how stories work, how sequence and cause and effect play upon plot, and how characters are developed. In the following story, a ten-year-old child brings all her experience with story as she works within the folktale structure and plays with words and images drawn from her reading.

Yukuto Chung
Lisa, age 10

Once upon a time in China, there lived a man named Yukuto Chung. He was extremely artistic but did not know it. One day his fiancee, MaiLee, went up to him and said "Yukuto! You are a very good artist! PLEASE, draw, paint, do whatever but, put your talent to use!"

"I am not a good artist" Yukuto replied and, without another word, walked away. Later, in MaiLee's chambers she talked silently to God.

OH
MAKE YUKUTO BELIEVE HE IS A FANTASTIC ARTIST!
MAKE HIM BELIEVE!!!!

That night Yukuto had a strange dream. He dreamt he was outside. He was flying a kite He looked up straining his eyes from the sun. It was a beautiful kite! It was the color of the sky at sunset. It was pink, blue, grey, all colors! And then, at the bottom of the kite was a gorgeous ball of fire. I have to make that kite! Yukuto thought.

As soon as Yukuto awoke, he set to work. He started with a rag, as a rough draft. He mixed together blue and pink. No way! he thought. He took another rag and started again. All through the day he started and finished another rag. Nothing seemed right. Days went by, weeks, months, years. Fifty years later he was still working on it. He was eighty years old. He wife was seventy. He worked and worked. First grey, blue and orange, then red, yellow and green. On the night of Yukuto's eighty-fifth birthday, he had the dream again. This time he looked with his wide eyes and saw every color of the world mixed in. That night at 9:00 he died. MaiLee was upset and she refused to even meet anyone else. She cried for weeks.

One day she was going through Yukuto's stuff when she found the hundreds of rough drawings he had done. They were all so beautiful! MaiLee also had artistic talent. She decided to finish off Yukuto's project. She worked hard. She wasn't lonely at all for, Yukuto's spirit guided her through the days. Finally, years later (MaiLee was ninety and very healthy) she finished the kite. It was so colorful and almost exactly the same as the one Yukuto had seen in his dreams, but yet MaiLee had never had the dream herself. She would not sell the kite. One man offered here 1 million "Yuans"* but, that kite was the only thing that reminded her of Yukuto and the good times they had had together. MaiLee always kept Yukuto's side of the room neat. She believed that Yukuto's soul lived in the house.

It remains a mystery!

THE END

* Yuans is Chinese money.

Writing Non-Fiction

Dealing with non-fiction is such a standard function in school that we may fail to recognize its potential as a vehicle for teaching writing. In the past, non-fiction was seldom used to develop writing skills. Today, we recognize possibilities for helping children to write as a natural response in every area of interest.

In the primary years, natural curiosity can lead to lots of writing as children record and present new-found information so their classmates can learn from their discoveries. As they take responsibility for giving information, they will notice the need for revision and editing. Other children will help the authors to present their information effectively.

As much as possible, children should be encouraged to write in their own words rather than copying the writing of adults. More often than we like, children hand in reports that sound as though each word were copied directly from a text. We need to coach and guide students when they set out

Effects Of Acid Rain

Throughout ontario and most of eastern canada a thousand of lakes and rivers are strugling to survive the effects of acid rain and many are losing the fight. Some have already made the acidified stage and others are reachi[ng] the critical stage in the fight agai[nst] acid rain. In the vast of the canadia[n] sheild they do not give there lakes alkine leaving them able to die of rain. How quickly a lake acidifies depends on it's natural chemistry [and] it's geography. Each lake has it'[s] unique ecosystem. As the ecosyst[em] out it's ability to support an[imals] it's ecosystem is inposable th[at] the animals will die. This has happened to some lakes of our[s] happen to many more unless w[e do] something about it soon. As [lakes] start to acidify the diversit[y of] animals decline. As the animals die algue, mougeotia, zygogonien and zygnema

wich thrive acid to appear more otfen. As the animals have died out in the lakes it causes major effects on the food chain. Experaments on the algue, chysochromunila and berturrita that tiny explotions will happen under water causing noxise odurs even in not too polluted lakes. In the 1960's the lake of La Clodre Monlar in the region of Ontario lost veriaty of fish and trout died out very fast as the lake acidafied. While hardier fish such as yellow pearch lake chub survived just a little longer. Fish populations vanished when reproduave falure. Acid rain is nown to erode buildings and monuments and is also suspected to be make life harder for people with diseses. Some of the things acid rain is endangering are fishery, courism, agricalture and forestry in a area of eastern Canada it measures 2.6 millon square miles.

to write a report and to observe the processes they follow (Graves, 1991). There is no linear sequence of steps, but we can ensure that the students understand that writing a report usually entails choosing a research area and beginning to focus on a specific topic in order to become an "expert" on it; analyzing the information they gather, which usually leads to more research; preparing for writing—reading, studying models, rehearsing for writing; making drafts, conferring, editing, and publishing.

To gather information, children can advertise within the school for books, pictures, and resource people. They can take notes at museums, interview those more qualified, as well as use the library for reference books and related fiction. Children need to learn how to read for information, how to prepare the questions they want answered, how to skim, and how to take notes. Note-taking in particular should be taught in a number of ways to accommodate different learning styles.

Organizing information can take other forms than writing a traditional article or essay. Children can write announcements or memos, set up displays, annotate pictures, label diagrams, create charts and webs. These approaches to non-fiction are often easier for children because they serve a more direct, and therefore more meaningful, function.

Writing Poetry

A poem allows us to say things in a special way. Many children are convinced that poetry always has to rhyme and follow a rhythmic pattern, since playground verse tends to do so. Hearing lots of poems read aloud will help children appreciate the variety of forms open to them.

Manipulating chants and cheers by substituting words and lines is an easy way to begin working with poetry. Imposing a slightly unusual pattern, such as that of an acrostic, in which the initial letters of each line form a word or phrase, or a cinquain, in which each stanza has five lines, can help distract the children from the artificial constraints of rhythm and rhyme. Some, however, will immediately see free verse as an effective means of expression.

Teachers can help children sense the aesthetic power of a poem, in a special word being used, a particular image created, or a pleasing juxtaposition of words. When children begin to notice the affective side of language, they are coming to an understanding of poetry.

Children as Poets
Larry Swartz

My students seem to enjoy playing with words and they are often honest about exposing their feelings. Of course they struggle to use poetic language effectively, to write their thoughts in "acceptable" poetic form, to convey an image or emotion artistically. But I feel that it is the simplicity of their prose that allows them to come to a poetic sensibility, particularly in free-verse style. For example,

It's a mask,
No, it's a coloured mask
No, it's a cursed coloured
mask
     Ricky

My mask is
a magic mask
all bad wishes will
disappear
The world will be
calm
     Sunil

my mask has

sharp teeth
triangle eyes
and small nose

filled with magical spirits
wear the mask
and live forever.
Don't let it touch fire
Do not wear it long
It will take your soul
     James

In my classroom, I have used three basic ways to have the students write as poets. I suggest poetic patterns and structures on which to hang their own ideas:

Books are like barbecued steaks
  Sometimes tender
  Sometimes juicy
  Sometimes well done

How do you like yours?
Me?
I like mine with
  lots of spice
  lots of flavour
  lots of meat
  lots to savour.
    Liza

A bird without wings,
A world without sky,
A clock without hands,
Is like a reason without why.

A picture without paints,
A group without a leader.
A song without notes,
Is like a book without a reader
    Matt

I ask them to use poetry as a form for expressing thoughts and feelings:

The loss of my country
I'm truly sad
The death of my heart
I'm totally mad
I can't help my self
My
  heart
    lives
      in
        The United States
    Matthew

My dog is
  dead
My favorite dog
  is dead
My favorite dog
  is dead
    in Japan
      Kuni

I show them that they can restructure their words into a poetic frame. For example, one day Harveen struggled for half an hour to write a poem about baseball and finally cried out, "I'm not a poem guy! I'm a sports guy!"—which he later transcribed into a two-line poem. Shannon and Greg broke and reordered prose paragraphs to highlight the moments of intense feeling in their writing:

My great grandpa was
great
I cannot remember him
very well
I only remember
his sea-blue
eye
Yes!
I am talking about my great
grandpa.
     Shannon

I once had a grandmother
   I don't know what happened
but she's not here any
MORE
I once had a grandmother
     Greg

In February I purchased hardbound books with twenty-four blank pages to be filled and gave one to each child to publish poems that he or she wrote throughout the year. I explained to the students that the books should be finished in June, and that I wanted them to select their poems carefully for "publication," to edit and revise their work, and to pay close attention to the poems that they were most fond of.

I invited them to choose a favourite poem to introduce the book and to extract from that poem a few words to serve as a title. They chose titles such as "A Flock Full of Crows," "Forests Live on Me," "Fried Crispy Bookworms," "Don't Be Polite," "Life Ain't No Piece of Pie," "Flowers Lift Their Heads," and "Enjoy the Earth Gently."

I suggested they record in their anthologies poems from their notebooks or response journals, or poems that they had written in response to a theme, a novel, another poem, or a personal experience. Several students wrote about environmental concerns:

My darling,
  You are so beautiful
  You are like the pearl of my dreams
  Your cheeks are so bright
  Your eyes are so reflecting like the
    setting sun
  Your face gleams in the sunlight
  I am very sorry
  about what I've done to you
    I love you,
      dear world,
    Angela

The earth is water
The earth is soil
If you pollute it,
The Earth you'll spoil

The Earth is green
The Earth is blue
If you pollute it
You'll hurt me
and you
    Christi

The earth is like a diamond
so perfect and intelligent
The earth is like a
    diamond
It is hard to break
    but we are earth miners
and we are breaking it
If the diamond breaks
only 8 of the jewels
and there will be no diamond
Forever
    Matt

The world is like a crystal
If the crystal fall
It will break.
But if you can take care of the
world
it will gleam
Like a CRYSTAL
    Jamie

Liza expressed her feelings after listening to *The Wall* by Eve
Bunting:

All
I
see
is

war   war

    war

All
I
think
about
is
peace
peace
peace

Lisa and Janine often enjoy writing poems together:

Sometimes I wonder . . .
What are we doing to our world?
Sometimes I wonder . . .
How could we do what we are doing?
Sometimes I wonder . . .
Why do I wonder so much . . .
Sometimes I wonder . . .?

All the books you've read make a
library in your mind
Sometimes you forget about a shelf
Sometimes shelves get musty
But sometimes you might dust off a shelf . . .
     To remember . . .
     To revisit . . .
     to renew . . .
A favorite friend

Sunil's spelling miscue "poemtry" prompted him to write three poems entitled "Poemtree #1, Poemtree #2, Poemtree #3":

Today I discovered a new word
Poemtree
I wonder if my poemtree grows leaves
Or my leaves grow poems?
If I plant letters in the ground
Will they be poems?
Will they be stories?

The children's writing of poetry is balanced by their reading of and listening to poetry. We have met a poem each day; we have discussed images in poems, considered the feelings that a poem elicits, and looked at words and images in the works of significant poets. They have responded through talk and writing to discover meanings of poems; they have tried to define poems; they have read poems into tape recorders, to their buddies in the grade one class, and to their parents at a holiday concert; they have written poems to accompany their artwork, to express their feelings about reading, and to reflect on world events; they have written poems on the computer, in their notebooks, on the bulletin board, on small file cards, on the blackboard, on chart paper, and on overhead transparencies. Some poems remained in their notebooks, some were developed into published pieces, and some were chosen to include in a classroom anthology entitled *The Poets in Room 203.*

Audiences for Writing

All writing is meant to be read, if only by the writer. The audience for a piece of writing depends on its function and the reasons for sharing it. Journals, notes, and first drafts, for example, are private and personal. The child may decide to discuss some pieces with a trusted adult—a teacher, a classroom volunteer, or a parent—who will respond to the content in an interested and supportive way. Other pieces will be read by peers—at a draft stage, in a group conference, in the process of collaboration, or in the published or displayed finished work. Children also write for unknown audiences—recipients of letters, readers of the school magazine, students in other classes who read the children's published books, or chance passers-by who glance at a bulletin board display. Each of these situations can give the author a sense of the various functions, styles, and conventions of writing and the importance of accuracy and neatness.

Having the children read their writing aloud to a small group can give them useful audience reaction at an early stage in their writing. While leaving most of the discussion to the group, the teacher can model the kinds of comments and questions that might be helpful to the author. After the conference, the writers should discuss what they found helpful in the group's comments. In this way, children will become more aware of how to help each other and perhaps more aware of the kinds of questions they can ask themselves when revising.

Classroom Publishing

Publishing the children's writing has several purposes. Student newsletters, polished stories and booklets, and researched information can be shared with others in the school and with parents in the community to celebrate the children's learning and validate the teaching program. Letters to the editor, book reviews, surveys of classmates' attitudes, and poems written on a theme are examples of writing for others to read.

Creating books to be shared with wider audiences both at school and at home provides an authentic reason for revising and editing special pieces of writing that require celebration. The teacher can act as editor, helping the children to attain the high standards required for published works. A special corner in the room can be devoted to child-authored materials. At Queenston, Sue Checkeris has an entire shelf in the school library devoted to works by young authors.

Young authors can use a variety of formats for their published works. The various designs and production strategies we saw at this school—for example, printing on the computer, laminating pages, or stitching pages together—demonstrate the endless ways children can develop their aesthetic ideas to complement their writing. With help from volunteers—parents, older students, other teachers—classroom publishing can add a powerful dimension to the desire to become readers and writers. Ivey was in grade eight when she created her book *Who Stole the Cookies from the Cookie Jar.*

As a general rule, one out of every four or five pieces of a student's writing might be considered for publication, either as an individual book or as part of a group collection. Teacher and child can select suitable pieces during writing conferences, taking the intended audience and desired format into consideration.

On Monday morning, Joey worked hard on his picture. He drew his mom, dad and baby sister. He made them all smile. Joey showed his masterpiece to Miss Morrison, his grade one teacher.

Miss Morrison smiled. Joey liked it when she smiled. Miss Morrison said, "That's a lovely picture Joey! Is that your family?"

Joey nodded. He was happy Miss Morrison liked his picture.

"If you don't mind, Joey, I"ll hang it up." Miss Morrison s "Meanwhile, you can help y self to a cookie from the coo jar."

Joey was delighted! He ha ever got a cookie from the cookie jar!

Joey walked over to the b green cookie jar on the c He opened it and it was

EMPTY

There was not so much crumb left!

Joey's best friend, Josh walked over to where Joey and the empty cookie jar stood.

"What's wrong?" Josh asked. "Miss Morrison's cookie jar is empty!" answered Joey in disbelief.

Josh gasped, "Oh no! Who took them?"

"I don't know, but lets find out."

Joey replied.

"Good idea," said Josh, "let' go."

They went off to find the cookie thief.

They walked over to the dinosaurs in the sandbox. There, they found Annie Amy, the twins. They w building a forest for the dinosaurs.

Joey and Josh left the Cookie Monster and headed for Mr. Bear's cave.

They knocked politely on the door that Mr. Bear always kept over his cave entrance.

"Come in." Mr. Bear growled.

Joey and Josh crawled into Mr. Bear's cave.

"Did you steal the cookies from the cookie jar? Josh asked Mr. Bear politely.

"Who me?" Mr. Bear gru bled.

"Yes you!" Joey said.

"Couldn't be," rumbled Bear, "I was getting rea hibernate."

"Then who?" Joey and asked together.

But Grumpy Mr. Bea not answer. He was a asleep.

Booktalk: Looking Deep Inside
Brian Crawford

"I put myself in someone's shoes by writing about them. All kinds of thoughts fly through my head—it's like looking deep inside them and me at the same time." I discovered this passage in Dale Gottlieb's *My Stories by Hildy Calpurnia Rose*, a fictitious journal in which a young girl fills the pages with stories and drawings about her friends and family. I knew at once that this was a "must have" book that would inspire many children to record in their journals some of the stories and descriptions of the people in their own lives. Recently, I have chosen to buy for my classroom books in a variety of genres that not only provide models for the children's own writing but also lead them to think about their own experiences as writers.

For example, Byrd Baylor's *I'm in Charge of Celebrations* has stimulated many children to carry their notebooks with them throughout the day in order to preserve observations of their world and to celebrate it in the written word. Memoirs such as *Three Names* by Patricia MacLachlan and *Night Noises* by Mem Fox encourage them to journey into their own pasts and share them with others in the classroom community through talk and writing. Nathaniel in Eloise Greenfield's *Nathaniel Talking*, Kate in Jean Little's *Hey World, Here I Am*, and Cynthia Rylant in her autobiographical *Waiting to Waltz* present their reminiscences in poetic form and help the children find the poetry in their own lives.

Some may think letter writing is a dying art, but you would never know that in our classroom. *The 13th Clue* by Ann Jonas, *Two Brothers* by Frank Asch, and *Thank You, Santa*, by Margaret Wild are all books that make the reader the recipient of a series of letters. *Stringbean's Trip to the Shining Sea* by Vera B. Williams is a collection of handwritten postcards from a young boy to his family. This picture book prompted the children to send postcards to pen pals all over North America, and the postcards they received soon decorated our walls; the atlas, travel books, histories, and encyclopedias came into play as the children tried to find out more about the pictures on the cards. *Dear Annie* by Judith Casely, *Dearest Grandmama* by Catherine Brighton, and *The Jolly Postman* and *The Jolly Christmas Postman* by Janet and Allan Ahlberg not only provided the children with models of narrative through letter writing, but encouraged many children to write narratives in the form of letters from the point of view of story characters or to write "real" letters to distant family and friends.

I have three particular favourite books written in this "letter" genre. When I share *Dear Mr. Henshaw* by Beverly Cleary with my class, each child sends a letter to a favourite author; this year, several students went out to buy their own diaries—one student decided that he would write his diary to "Dear Miss Pretend Beverly Cleary," just as Leigh Botts addressed his private thoughts to "Dear Mr. Pretend Henshaw." *The War Began at Supper: Letters to Miss Laura* by Patricia Reilly Giff prompted Liza and Heidi to write letters to the prime minister of Canada expressing their views of war. *Nothing But the Truth: a Documentary Novel* by Avi, which won the 1991 Newbery Medal, offers an interesting twist on this genre: it tells through transcripts, journal entries, school announcements, and letters the story of a boy's suspension from school.

Sometimes an idea from a story or the way an author has told a story strike chords for particular people. Soon after I had visited the optometrist to order a pair of glasses, I came upon *Glasses, Who Needs Them?* by Lane Smith. Two students in the class wrote about their own experiences with new eyeglasses, and one girl wrote a poem about a teacher who started to wear glasses. The pattern of *If You Give a Mouse A Cookie* by Laura Joffe Numeroff inspired Stephanie's *If You Give a Cat a Candy*, just as *On the Day You Were Born* by Debra Frasier provided the model for Kristina's published book conjuring events on the day she was born ("On the day I was born, the sea creatures danced"). Twisted fairytales such as Jon Scieszkas's *The True Story of the Three Little Pigs, The Frog Prince Continued,* and *The Stinky Cheese Man and Other Fairly Stupid Tales,* Fiona French's *Snow White in New York,* and Tony Ross's *The Boy Who Cried Wolf* led to many new versions of familiar fairytales.

Suggested Reading for Teachers

Some Day You Will No All About Me. Markham: Pembroke Publishers, 1990. Beginning with five-year-olds, the book follows an exchange of their letters over a two-year period. The letters are reproduced and provide an opportunity to explore the spontaneous and unassisted writing of very young authors.

Atwell, Nancie, ed. *Coming to Know: Writing to Learn in the Intermediate Grades.* Toronto: Irwin Publishing, 1989. Written by teachers of grades three to six who asked their students to write as scientists, historians, etc., in order to use writing-as-process to discover meaning.

Atwell, Nancie. *In the Middle: Writing, Reading and Learning with Adolescents*. Toronto: Irwin Publishing, 1987. Nancie Atwell discusses her eighth-grade students in Boothbay Harbor, Maine, and what she and they have learned together as collaborating writers and readers.

Calkins, Lucy McCormick. *The Art of Teaching Writing*. Toronto: Irwin Publishing, 1986. The author includes chapters on poetry, fiction, and report writing, as well as sections on reading-writing connections, writing development, and teacher-student conferences.

Calkins, Lucy McCormick. *Living Between the Lines*. Portsmouth, N.H.: Heinemann, 1991. Calkins demonstrates the teaching of writing and reading through using personal notebooks.

Ewoldt, Carolyn. *Speaking of Writing. New Directions*. Toronto: Scholastic, 1989. Through the voices of a grade eight student and her teacher, the author provides information on such things as the importance of creative ownership, the role of teacher and peers, evaluation and self-evaluation.

Fulwiler, Toby, ed. *The Journal Book*. Toronto: Irwin Publishing, 1987. This book demonstrates that journals are valuable in school as dialogue journals, learning logs, and diaries, as children work their way through real concerns with interest and intent.

Graves, Donald H. *Explore Poetry*. Portsmouth/Toronto: Heinemann/Irwin Publishing, 1992. This book presents a variety of ways to respond to children's poetry and gives suggestions for spreading poetry throughout the curriculum.

Graves, Donald H. *Investigate Nonfiction. The Reading/Writing Teacher's Companion*. Toronto: Irwin, 1989. This volume explores the richness of reading and writing non-fiction for and with children in meaningful, productive ways.

Phenix, Jo. *Teaching Writing: The Nuts and Bolts of Running a Day-to-Day Writing Program*. Toronto: Pembroke Publishers Limited, 1990. The practical do's and don'ts of the latest theories of writing instruction including organizing time, space, and students.

Robinson, Brent. *Microcomputers and the Language Arts*. Milton Keynes, England: Open University Press, 1985. Aimed at teachers, this book explores how and where a microcomputer might have applications or implications for a language arts curriculum.

Rosen, Michael. *Did I Hear You Write?* Toronto: Scholastic, 1989. Michael Rosen's book, like his anthologies of poems, celebrates the language patterns of children and presents ideas and strategies for helping youngsters create poems from their life experiences.

Reflections

❶ Helping the children take ownership of and responsibility for their own writing can be as simple as letting them retain physical control of their papers while conferring with you. Which of the following strategies are you using in your classroom?

- having the children keep various drafts of their writing in folders so that you and they can see how their work develops
- helping the children to choose their own topics for personal writing so they will feel a commitment to writing it well
- letting them make their own decisions about changes to their writing
- organizing peer conference groups where children read, share, revise, and discuss before final publishing
- expecting children to participate in assessing their writing with you

❷ Which of the following ways of helping children with the revision process do you use in your classroom practice? Which could you usefully introduce in the near future?

- allowing for an incubation or pre-writing period—which may at first seem to have little to do with writing (Graves, 1983)—in which art, discussion, or journal entries help the children focus on a topic and generate ideas and language
- conferring with them during the early composition stages in order to help them develop their ideas
- resisting the itch to evaluate first-draft writing for spelling, handwriting, and usage problems
- allowing them to discard pieces of writing that they don't feel is going anywhere
- encouraging them to revise and improve their work through successive drafts
- offering them time-saving revision strategies, such as editing in a different colour, crossing out, inserting words and letters by writing them above the line and using a carat, and cutting and pasting to insert and deleting sentences and paragraphs
- having them edit each other's work in a group or read the piece to an audience

- expecting the children to proofread, as far as they are able, before writing a final draft
- expecting a final draft only if the writing is to be published

❸ Often, teachers expect their students to write but provide no model of what the writing process is about. Plan ways to model the writing process for your students, by sharing your own writing and your reasons for writing with them. You might demonstrate strategies for revision by writing in draft form on the blackboard or on an overhead transparency and verbalizing your inner dialogue as you make revisions to the draft.

❹ The integration of language arts with "content" curriculum provides opportunities to engage the children in activities in various areas and follow these up with collaborative group writing. Plan activities in math, science, social studies, or even literature where the ensuing writing can be used as another learning experience—a chart of the group's explorations, a summary of a science experiment, a group poem in response to a drama lesson.

❺ In the past, writing in other curriculum areas was often not treated as composing but merely as note taking (a skill which was often not specifically taught at all or, conversely, was treated as an end in itself). Plan how you can integrate the writing process with what are often labelled "content areas" of learning.

❻ The use of journals and notebooks is being stressed in many classrooms, both as a means for the children to reflect on significant events from their lives and from the books they read, and as a resource of ideas for their own future writing (Calkins, 1991). How can you ensure that the children do not see journal writing as a chore, but that they recognize and value their personal writing as a way of learning? How can you ensure the children's privacy, so that they can select for your eyes only the pieces in their journals that they wish to share with you?

Transcription: Writing Words Down

W HEN CHILDREN TRANSCRIBE their thoughts into print, they are engaged in the co-ordination of spelling, punctuation, and handwriting. Helping children learn the skills of transcription requires a delicate balance: we run the danger of restricting their opportunities to compose if we focus too insistently on details of form. As a result, many teachers are uncomfortably aware that they may be neglecting the mechanics of writing (Wilde, 1992).

How can we present techniques and strategies that will help children write down their ideas as easily as possible, encourage independence, and make the written document a means of effective communication (Phenix and Scott-Dunne, 1992)? As children take on responsibility for the many aspects of their writing, their recognition of the need for transcription skills grows. When they compose a first draft, we do not want children to waste creative energy by focusing on the demands and constraints that the act of transcription imposes; rather, they should be free to make educated guesses. But during the revision and editing phases, they can develop their skills of punctuation, spelling, and handwriting (Scott, 1993). While the children should know that we will not be judging early drafts, we can use them to diagnose problems that will become the focus of coaching for individuals or mini-lessons for a group of children at a more appropriate time. Jane Hansen (1987, p. 165) says that we should teach the skills that the children themselves know they need. Our role is "to find out what students know, affirm for them what they don't know, ask what they want to know next, and track it."

As teachers, we need to view the theories of how children learn, not as textbook courses for our certification credits, but as prerequisites to determining what and how we will teach (Stephens, 1991). And we need to be sure we resolve analysis into synthesis. Academic analysis breaks processes into discrete elements. Further analysis of a few individual elements may then lead to ignoring the others. In earlier years, teachers of writing concentrated on the more obvious and easily definable aspects of writing—spelling, handwriting, and syntax. More recently, our interest in child development has led to more or less exclusive attention on the act of composition. Both approaches tended to remove the "skills" from the "content," creating two separate spheres of learning, when what we really need is a larger context in order to practise the small components that structure the event (Tarasoff, 1992).

To make an analogy, learning to swim requires water and an understanding of what it is like to move in water. The very nature of the medium affects our efforts. Though we may occasionally practise the techniques briefly on shore, the movements made by our arms and legs will have no meaning for us until we do them in the water. The coach's basis for pointing out our weaknesses is to observe us in action in the water, the context for swimming. Similarly, filling in blanks, underlining parts of speech, memorizing spelling lists, and completing worksheets are dry runs that rarely equate with the acquisition of literacy or even of transcription skills. We need to find methods of helping young people to become better readers and writers from "inside" the medium. They deepen their awareness of story both through close reading and interactive response and through polishing their writing with care and vigour so that others will draw as much as possible from reading their work. Young people think and learn through reading, writing, and talking.

Preschool children are different from adolescents—ask any parent in any culture. It makes little sense that children attempt the same decontextualized skill sheets for eight years, and yet Goodlad's study (1984) indicates that many children are forced to do just that. How we design learning situations for different children that encourage careful transcription will depend on the needs of the learners (Adams, 1990).

A Context for Skills

"Composition" concerns the ability to generate ideas, organize information, express opinions, and use language effectively for a variety of purposes. "Transcription" involves the ability to write down ideas and information in legible, standard English, following the conventions of spelling, punctuation, and capitalization. But these processes are intertwined. The skills of transcription grow from the writer's need to communicate ideas effectively to others. When children revise and edit their writing, they practise these skills and they begin to understand the use and value of the conventions of print.

Language-based classrooms do focus on parts of words, parts of sentences, and parts of paragraphs, but always within a context. Good language teachers are not afraid of teaching "about" language but they understand that it is through "using" language that children grow in their ability to grasp what the individual elements of language are and how they work. The fact that some children have limited transcribing skills, however, should not deter the development of their composing ability nor take away from the joy of authorship. Children can be helped to develop skills in transcription by collaborating with others, beginning with invented spelling, or using a typewriter or word-processor. In fact, composing and authorship generate the need for transcription and consequently motivate children to grow in their ability to "want to write words down well." James Moffett (1986) suggests activities that give children excellent practice in all encoding skills at once—handwriting, spelling, and punctuation—as they take down dictation from classmates, younger children, or the teacher, act as scribe for a group, write down from memory songs, jokes, recipes, and proverbs, proofread each other's spelling and punctuation, check with other people and the dictionary when unsure of spellings, or tape-record an item and transcribe it afterwards.

Mini-lessons (Calkins, 1986) are short, direct teaching sessions, occasionally with single students but more often with a group or the whole class, that focus on a particular craft or skill. Mini-lessons allow teachers to share their expertise and give students valuable information when they need it— and in amounts they can absorb. The teachers at Queenston use mini-lessons frequently: whenever the need arises to clarify procedures, such as how to record books taken home from the classroom library, to explain a specific convention, such as when to use capital letters, or to demonstrate techniques used by writers, ranging from how to use carats to add information when revising a first draft to how poets use words that sound like the things they are describing. "Showing students writers' techniques has the same effects and benefits as demonstrating artists' methods in art class. Both help kids begin to develop a repertoire of their own strategies. Eventually, as students discover how and when to apply them, the strategies become second nature. In mini-lessons I introduce information about techniques and styles and in conferences I help kids learn how to apply it to their pieces and intentions" (Atwell, 1987, p. 131).

Nancie Atwell has no fear that the mechanics of writing will be lost to her students. She has drawn up a list of the topics covered during editing conferences throughout the year in her class (1987, pp. 110-111). They include "tricks of the trade," such as editing in a different colour from that used in the draft, putting the date and draft number on every piece, and cutting and pasting; organizational concerns such as paragraphing (are the paragraphs too long and complicated? too short and choppy?), consistent use of pronouns (is the hero "I" or "she"? can the reader tell who "he" refers to?) and tenses (did the story happen before or is it happening now?), the form and placement of items included in a letter (return address, date, greeting, closing), the punctuation of sentences, and how to handle words people say out loud; and transcription skills such as the use of apostrophes, word splits at the end of lines, a few rules of thumb for spelling ("I before E except after C"), and how to proofread and use a dictionary to check when the spelling is in doubt.

Yet some "process writing" teachers do indeed expect students to learn writing skills vicariously. This puts many students, especially those who grow up outside the dominant culture, at a disadvantage. We must make explicit the knowledge and skills we expect (Delpit, 1987). There is a fallacy that "whole language teachers don't teach skills." Curt Dudley-Marling and Don Dippo (1991) think those of us who talk or write about language-based theory and practice

may inadvertently send implicit, contradictory messages about the role of skills in whole language practice. The use of contrasts, for example—for purposes of explanation—phonics/whole language, skills/process, process/product, behavioral/holistic, may encourage the view that they are dichotomies. . . . It does not matter that these dichotomies may have been intended to serve merely as contrasting examples. Too often it is the dualistic thinking reflected in the form of the example itself that is seen as important. This kind of talk about whole language theory and practice invites and encourages the view, often held by supporters and critics alike, that whole language instruction is essentially anti-phonics. . . .

Perhaps, then, we need to find new ways to talk about what it is we do.

Spelling

They took our bread and have given in return but a stone. The bread even though a little stale was much more wholesome than the stone. . . . Pupils are turned loose on society to shock it by their bad spelling, and disgrace the schools which they attended, and in which they should have been taught. [In a Civil Service Exam in England] no less than 1,861 out of 1,972 failures were caused by spelling (from the preface to The Practical Speller, *Gage and Company, 1881).*

And still today, nothing causes more consternation between teacher and teacher, parent and teacher, child and teacher than the thorny issue of the teaching of spelling. Teachers concerned with developing holistic, language-based classrooms have appeared to delegate the formal teaching of spelling to the past. The "back-to-basics" movement sees spelling as its rallying point. Questions still plague us: Will children learn about spelling through the processes of reading and writing? What benchmarks can help us monitor a child's progress? Are dictionaries and spelling texts a support or hindrance to a child's spelling awareness? Does invented spelling lead to strength with the tricky problems posed by standard English?

In chairing a committee for the Ontario Ministry of Education on the assessment of language arts, I ran into difficulty when broaching the topic of spelling. I was advised it would be politic to leave any discussion of it out of the document, since to include it might give support to those educators who still believed in the formal teaching of spelling. However, four of the advisers to the project, Ruth Scott, Ethel Buchanan, Jo Phenix, and Doreen Scott-Dunne, were teacher-researchers in spelling, and over the years of working with them, I have come to realize that information about the transcribing of words can bring power to young people as they learn to become literate. Of course we can help children to develop as spellers when we connect orthography to purposeful communication, to the love of words, and to the knowledge of what words can do. Jo Phenix points out that much of the traditionally accepted methodology of spelling instruction in the past has been seriously flawed. It has not taken into account the real nature of our orthography; nor has it capitalized on what we know about how children learn language.

How We Have Taught Spelling in the Past
Jo Phenix

My earliest memory of spelling in school was the weekly spelling bee. Three children stood up at the front and spelled words out loud. If you made a mistake, you had to sit down. Only the good spellers got to participate in this, perhaps as an example to the others. I don't imagine this taught us much about spelling, as we learned nothing new, only paraded knowledge we already had. Moreover, as spelling is primarily a visual skill, and we never got to see the words at all, important information about spelling patterns had no chance to become imprinted on our minds.

Later on, learning to spell was a matter of correcting all the errors we made in our writing. Recognizing which groups of letters are possible, which are probable, and which are impossible in English is an important part of learning to spell. We need to be able to recognize when a word is right and when it is wrong. We never learned to do this, however; the teacher was the one who did all the proofreading, marking errors with a "sp" in the margin. You don't learn anything by having someone else do it for you all the time.

Newer methods of instruction recognize the visual nature of spelling by teaching study steps, such as the following: look at the word; picture it in your mind; look away and write the word; look back and check. While this is useful for some words that don't seem to fit any pattern, it asks the student to rely entirely on rote memory and focuses attention on learning words in isolation from one another.

Some researchers tell us that the best way of handling a spelling list is by a pre-test/study/post-test sequence. This means that on the first day students are tested to see which words they can spell already. Then they study the others for a later test. On the face of it this seems sensible; why spend the week studying words you already know? But doesn't this mean that students who are good spellers have a short list to learn, while students who find spelling difficult have a longer list? Does this really make sense? Neither group is getting appropriate help.

We have sometimes tried to make sense of spelling by grouping together words that are constructed in similar ways, to make "word families." This makes sense, because we can help students see patterns and relationships, and make connections among words. But lists in spelling texts are commonly not based on word families at all, but on lists of high-frequency words that have no logical spelling connections.

Many of us who felt that none of these methods were really helping students came to feel that plenty of reading and writing were enough to ensure growth in spelling. Certainly reading and writing must play a large part in learning to spell. But we know that many students and adults who are good readers and writers are very poor spellers.

A hundred years ago the predominant learning strategy for all subjects in school was rote memorization. "Saying your lessons" played a large part in the classroom. In spelling, nothing has changed. Many children are still "saying their lessons," just as their great-grandparents did.

Researchers such as Charles Read (1975) argued that learning to spell is a complex intellectual activity closely related to the development of the child's own general language system. Children do not learn to spell by rote memorization. Indeed, memorizing isolated words is the most difficult way to learn to spell. Rather they attempt to find underlying rules, perceiving patterns in the appearance of words, noting prefixes, suffixes, root words, and irregularities. They move from approximations to the use of standardized forms. They select from their experiences and instruction the information appropriate for them at the time. Each new piece of information they gain about spelling alters their existing perception of the language and the encoding system. A child will even seem to regress and misspell a word in the attempt to apply all the information gleaned from the latest acquisition of how words function.

We need to help children master the various layers of the English spelling system and to see spelling as a process of discovery, categorization, and generalization that they can apply them to the increasing range of words they want to write.

Invented Spelling

If children write only those words they can spell, their writing will be extremely limited. Rather than stop the flow of language by asking for correct spellings, children should use approximate spellings in their early writ-

HumPOY DemteY Set
on a wall humPOY
Demtey haDa Gret
Fall all the Kings
and all his men Codet Pet
housis humPOY to gateral san

HUPtY dUPtY SAt oN tHe WI
HUPtY dUPtY HAD A GRAt FoL
OL tHE CKINgS TOt STE ANP OL
tHE CKINgS MIN KOD Not Pot HAM
Pto GAtR A GIN

ing, based on their ideas of how spoken and written words correspond. We should encourage them to write any words that are part of their speaking vocabulary. Children who invent spellings develop a better understanding of how words and letters fit together, as they can begin to write words down as soon as they know a few consonants. They usually move toward standard spelling through some progression, first using an initial consonant to represent each word, next an initial and final consonant, and then using vowel markers with consonants, representing syllables, and using more correct vowels as they approach standard spelling.

When experimenting with print, a child is learning the rule-governed nature of phoneme/grapheme correspondences rather than merely producing errors. Invented spellings show that the student is learning phonic relationships (Gunderson, 1989). Jo Phenix points out that in reading, children can bring all the cueing systems to bear as they unlock meaning, but when they begin to spell, the only information they have is their knowledge of letter names and sounds. When children sound out words in order to spell them, they not only develop detailed knowledge about sound-symbol relationships, they also learn strategies to use in word construction. The concept that spelling is a skill of building, not one of memorizing, gives writers "an appreciation of what the task really is, confidence to try new spellings, and power to make reasonable attempts. As a side effect, the child who has struggled to construct words through phonics has no problem at all using this information automatically while reading."

Children's Approaches to Spelling

Most children start school as non-spellers. They have some knowledge of the alphabet but no understanding of letter-sound relationships. Their "writing" is a random stringing together of letters of the alphabet, showing no grasp of the concept of a word as a discrete unit.

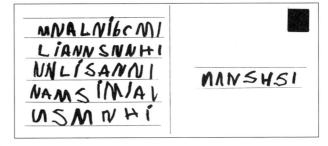

The way children move toward standard spelling depends on the features of words and letters that draw their attention. Some children enjoy puzzles and bring logic to bear on the rules and conventions of spelling almost from the start; some absorb the spelling of whole words more or less

Dear Ms. Hill, I am fine. How are you today? I love you. From Adam.
(Adam demonstrates his knowledge that a telephone number is important information by including one in the address.)

unconsciously; some are happy simply to be told how to spell words they have not met before.

Children often go through a stage of "early invented spelling," when they grasp that sounds can be associated with letters. They have a more or less complete knowledge of the alphabet and use the names of letters to represent sounds when they write. They frequently omit vowels, especially short vowel sounds for which a letter-name strategy does not work. They encode only some parts of a word, often just the first letter. They have an emerging grasp of the concept of a word, breaking letter strings at some word boundaries. (Examples: N for nose, BD for bird, SWM for swim.)

Purely phonetic spelling is based strictly on letter-sound correspondences. Children will encode all parts of a word, often using a letter-name strategy for long vowels. They frequently omit "unheard" vowels and nasals before consonants. By now, the concept of word is well-developed. (Examples: KRI for cry, BRD for bird, BREJ for bridge, PLAT for plant.)

Children using mixed phonetic and visual spelling go beyond one-to-one encoding of sounds with letters. They pay attention to familiar visual configurations of letters and to word parts such as prefixes and suffixes. They are aware that there may be several conventions for encoding a single sound, but not always use the correct convention for a given word, nor remember the correct order of letters in the conventional spelling. Short

Dear Ms. Hill, I know how to read and my teacher's name is Ms. Clegg. I like grade one.

> This is me and I am playing outsoud and I am besid samo treeps and they are brown. What are you playing? I am playing skiping

vowels are usually used correctly. They know many of the basic conventions of English spelling, such as placing a vowel in every syllable. (Examples: THAY for they, ALLSO for also, KITTON for kitten, BRID for bird.)

Each new term, the primary teachers at Queenston are careful to explain to parents how children work through various approaches to spelling so that they can enjoy their child's writing in full appreciation of the child's level of development. The teachers were also very interested in a demonstration by Doreen Scott-Dunne, a resource teacher in Peel, illustrating that students' writing is invaluable in assessing the approach to spelling each child takes. Her suggestions, which follow, for the type of instruction that would be useful confirmed the teachers' own beliefs and practices.

Diagnosing Spelling Miscues
Doreen Scott-Dunne

Note with a Message!
Kim
isa
dumey

What the writer knows:
- the power of the pen to write an insulting message
- the importance of not signing a nasty note
- the name of the person to whom the message is directed
- the correct spelling of the high-frequency words *is, a*
- the fact that *ey* occurs at the end of words as a vowel combination

What can reasonably be taught:

- that there are gentler ways of dealing with anger than writing nasty letters to the object of your anger—perhaps a Personal Journal could be started to record only feelings, such as anger, joy, and sadness; then feelings could be expressed without hurting anyone
- word awareness—that each word has a space, and that *is* and *a* are separate words
- that "dumey" is an excellent spelling prediction for this word, and that we do use *ey* in chimney, monkey, donkey, hockey, turkey, valley, and many other words. Unfortunately, *dummy* does not fit this pattern, but is like gummy (as in gummy bears!—children associate well with food references), Mummy, yummy, and tummy.

Follow-up:

- Give the student many writing opportunities, and point out when letters and little notes could be written.

Snow White (Amy, age 7)

Snow White
One day there was a.
Evil Witch and Her sevrint.
and she had a maigc morrier.
and she said morrier morrier.
on the wall who's the Fairit's.
one of all and all the time.
the morrer reple'dy Snow whIte.
and the witch got mad

Story = 46 words + title
Number of words spelled correctly = 38
Number of spelling miscues = 8

What Amy knows:

- how to retell a section of a well-known fairy tale
- how to spell over 80 percent of the words in her story correctly
- how to handle contractions: *who's*
- how to attempt to punctuate for pause, except that there is some confusion between the uses of periods and commas
- how to spell extremely well

What can reasonably be taught:

- the sight word *mirror*, since it is critical to the story, and accounts for four of her spelling errors

Follow-up:
- This student should be given many opportunities to share work with her peers. She is a talented writer and a very good speller, so she would provide excellent modelling of the writing process for others.

The World is Blue and Green (Jason, age 6)
I lik To see the waD kan
Bie klan ot amp wah my Fands
the waD is Blao anD gana
(I like to see the world clean.
By cleaning it up with my friends,
the world is blue and green.)

What Jason knows:
- how to write a meaningful message about pollution
- how to write a message that is almost in poetic mode
- how to spell high-frequency words: *I, to, see, the, my, and*
- how to get the correct initial consonant sound (not always the correct letter as in kan = clean)
- how to use blends *bl* and *kl* (substituted for *cl*)

What can reasonably be taught:
- high-frequency words: *it, like, with, is*
- the colour words *blue* and *green* as sight words
- that apart from Klondike and Kleenex, we do not see *kl* at the beginning of words—in English we use *cl* for that sound

Follow-up:
- Jason should be given feedback that he would find it easy to write poetry, and he should be given many opportunities to express himself in the poetic mode.

Moving toward Standard Spelling

In trying to spell a word, children must use simultaneously all the cues they have about spelling to achieve the best possible approximation. Proficient spellers have developed a range of cues that help them to spell conventionally when they write. Poor spellers need to focus their attention on a very small amount of information at a time until they have stabilized it. We must help them examine their attempts to see how closely they have approximated the conventional forms. This is, of course, the starting point for further learning. Often the teacher's assistance is needed in locating and correcting misspellings. By dealing with a few errors at a time, we can help children develop strategies for spelling the words correctly. If poor spellers are faced with writing corrections for a large number of errors, they are likely to be swamped with too much information and be unable to concentrate on learning the correct forms.

We should be especially careful not to instil fear; I have seen children using a simple word rather than a complex one for fear of making an error. This is not how writers should work. As Jo Phenix says, "The student who never tries to write a new word will never learn to spell any new words. Learning involves risk-taking, and spelling can be a very risky business." We help children extend their information about language and the range of their cues for spelling as we familiarize them with the patterns, generalizations, and exceptions in the spelling system. Many times, children come to these understandings on their own.

The true measure of learning is transference: can the children take the information they have learned in one context and apply it in another? In the end, children must spell independently; they must find words they need to write but don't know how to spell and check the spelling of words they are uncertain about. We can present games and activities that promote careful attending to words. We can have our classrooms full of resources for correctly spelled words: charts, labels, signs, word banks, dictionaries, reference books, even outdated telephone directories. But what must we do to ensure that the children are aware of these as tools in making meaning? Jo Phenix has some thoughts for us on spelling and writing, which is the learning context for spelling—and some sobering arithmetic.

A Context for Spelling
Jo Phenix

For learning to be effective, new information must be linked to what is already known. This is why context is so important in reading. If we have little or no prior knowledge of the subject we are reading about, we cannot comprehend. The same is true of spelling. It is easier to figure out the spelling of a word if we can link it to another word we know.

The importance of context has led to some misconceptions about what context means in spelling. When we read about a mouse, our understanding depends on how much we already know about mice. To help children comprehend a mouse story, we might initiate some discussion, look at some pictures, and have the children share ideas and knowledge about mice before reading. If we want the children to learn how to spell "mouse," it is less than useful to put it in a word list with "cheese" and "hole." What is helpful is to link it with other words that share a spelling concept—an initial consonant perhaps, or a rhyming pattern. Context in spelling involves making spelling links. Just as context in reading means using what you already know about the subject, so context in spelling means using what you already know about spelling. Theme lists do not place words in spelling contexts, nor do contrived reading passages written to contain all the words on the spelling list.

Writing is the only reason for spelling, so it logically provides not only the medium for using spelling, but also a context for learning to spell. But it is not enough just to write. It is of little importance if I make spelling errors on my shopping list, or when I write the first draft of an article. For these purposes, the only important thing is whether I can read it. To provide motivation for correct spelling, the writing must be intended for another person to read. Then I know that if my spelling is poor, I will make a bad impression. For writing to be a significant factor in learning to spell, the writer must be writing for a real audience. No one wants to look silly in print.

If we want students to understand the stages of the writing process, spelling should not be taught at the first-draft stage. If we start talking about spelling at this stage, then the student will learn that spelling is an important factor in first-draft writing and must therefore be a focus at that time. This is not productive in the process of getting writing done successfully, nor is it productive in the teaching of spelling. There is a time in the writing process when spelling will likely be a major focus. At this stage, we may evaluate it, talk about it, teach about it, and expect a student's full attention on it.

Help given during a writing conference is personal and immediate. We must capitalize on any opportunity to teach a spelling concept at the time a child needs it. There are, however, two major problems with trying to teach spelling through children's writing. The first involves the question of context. Of course it is a good idea to give the students words they need for writing in progress; we know that if they need the words, they are more likely to learn them. But picking out words and using them to make a personal spelling list reduces spelling to a rote-memory skill. Since we know that rote learning is the hardest way to learn anything and is the most short-lived, this is not a productive strategy. It is no better than trying to learn a list from a spelling text; in fact it is often more difficult, as students do not restrict themselves to words at some arbitrary "grade level" but will try to spell any words in their spoken vocabulary. A group of words taken from a student's writing will not necessarily provide a spelling context to help the students learn them. Words must be placed in spelling contexts before they can form the basis of any spelling instruction. This means placing a misspelled word in a group with other words that share a spelling pattern or share a spelling concept. To do this effectively, we may choose only one or two misspelled words and help the child make the necessary contextual links. Words children misspell must not be used to create lists to memorize.

A second problem is simply one of logistics. First, consider how many writing conferences you can do each day. If, for example, you do six, this means you have an opportunity to speak to each child once a week for perhaps eight minutes. (This is a long time, but it's only for the purpose of the example.) We know we will not talk about spelling during first-draft writing, or when the major focus is on planning or organizing the writing; we do not want spelling to interfere with other aspects of writing. Most of the writing children do is first-draft or exploratory writing. This means that in many conferences there will be no opportunity to mention spelling at all. Let us suppose that at every second conference there is an opportunity to spend a third of the time on spelling. This makes a maximum of three minutes every two weeks. Over the course of a year, this adds up to a total of 60 minutes of spelling instruction. In the old days, we spent more time than this every week—and this is not allowing for the Christmas concert, the trip to the zoo, and the day the nurse came in. Throughout the whole of grades one to six, students might get the equivalent of one day's spelling instruction. Even if we spend twice as much time as this, can we really think it is enough?

It is important to talk about spelling during writing conferences when opportunities arise. However, this incidental teaching cannot, by itself, constitute a complete classroom spelling program.

Many of us abandoned the daily spelling period. We were tired of spending so much time having the children work through activities that did not seem to bring about any change in the way they spelled in their own writing. We developed the idea that systematically teaching spelling works against our real purpose, composition, and that if we wait long enough the children will catch it like the measles, although the evidence of our own eyes told us many of them did not. The problem was, when we cancelled the spelling period we didn't quite know what to replace it with. We relied on incidental teaching (or was it accidental teaching?) when we saw opportunities and put our main energy into encouraging composition.

Spelling is not an intrusion into writing; it is a part of the writing process that needs its own focus at the right time. Nor is spelling boring. Words are interesting. The more we know about words, their origins, their histories, and how and why they go together the way they do, the more fascinating a subject it becomes. We do our students no service when we push spelling into a corner and treat it as a necessary evil of writing.

There is nothing intrinsically wrong with a spelling period. The problem with the spelling period lay in the content, not the concept. Why not take a brief time each day, or two or three times a week, and make words the major focus? Each period can be devoted to a particular spelling concept—a phonic generalization, a rhyming pattern, a Greek prefix, a historical anecdote. Through these mini-lessons, students can not only come to discover orthography as an interesting piece of our history and share their teacher's fascination with words and language, but also gradually accumulate a store of knowledge about words that they can use every time they write. By working together as a class or in small groups to investigate words, they can develop strategies for solving spelling problems. Language is not a solitary activity; why should spelling be different?

Similarly, many of us abandoned spelling texts because they did not seem to be helping the students become better spellers. Spelling texts typically have two major flaws. One is that they present memorizing lists of words as the major strategy in learning to spell. The other is that while they do present many of the important spelling concepts students need to know about, they lose them in lists of unrelated words. The key to an effective spelling lesson, whether it is done in a writing conference, in a class or group mini-lesson, or from the page of a book, is focus. When students know which concept they are learning about, and when the words they collect and categorize and manipulate all share the same spelling concept, they have their best chance to recognize patterns and make generalizations. It is this knowledge of patterns that will enable them to figure out the spelling of words in the future, or at least to make reasonable predictions. Generalizations are the raw material for solving spelling problems.

Like the spelling period, there is nothing philosophically wrong with the concept of a spelling text; it is generally the content that is wrong. Along with valid purposes for writing, and plenty of practice, children also need information to help them make decisions and solve problems. A good spelling text could be a reference as valuable in the language program as the dictionary and thesaurus. Such a reference book would not present prescribed lists of words to be learned, but would lead children to discover and explore words, their construction, and their history. It would help students see the logic and pattern of spelling and give them a range of strategies for constructing words.

Punctuation

Punctuation helps translate speech to print and print to speech. Commas, semi-colons, question marks, and periods convey pauses and intonation. During oral reading, when children read aloud dialogue, stories, poems, or favourite excerpts, or their own writing, they must translate punctuation marks into meaningful oral language. We can help them see where sentences end, where there should be pauses, and how they can show them in their writing. The difficulty that many children have in identifying sentences and putting periods in the right places reflects the fact that the printed sentence does not adequately indicate for them the linguistic structure that defines the unit of meaning. When we discuss reading with children, we can draw attention to the devices an author uses to produce certain effects and the ways in which punctuation is used to alter pace, build suspense, introduce surprise, and list items. Children can experiment with such techniques. When children discuss and share their writing with others, they will become aware of the need for the punctuation marks that indicate questions, surprise, fear, or excitement.

Donald Graves's research (1983) has demonstrated that children learn punctuation marks in the order in which they discover they need them, and that they learn to punctuate more effectively through genuine writing rather than through drills and exercises. For example, in her discussion of primary students' writing in Chapter 3, Jo Phenix mentioned that quotation marks are often the first punctuation children learn—they use a lot of conversation in their stories. As children compose, revise, and edit their work in conferences with peers and the teacher, they become aware of the value of punctuation in communicating their ideas. Mini-lessons can help them refine their skills.

Grammar and Usage

Many children, especially in a school such as Queenston, arrive with rich vocabularies and vivid oral language patterns that may vary considerably from what we have come to know as "standard English." We need to cherish these usages—but at the same time recognize our responsibility to teach them the form of English used and sanctioned by the wider world.

Language is a social activity, but it is also personal. It allows us not only to communicate with others, but also to claim and display membership in particular social and cultural groups. All languages and all dialects have their own forms of grammar and patterns of usage. Successful speakers and writers learn when to use standard English, informal English, dialects of English, or other languages depending upon the context of the situation. The question is always one of appropriate usage, rather than of correct usage.

Indeed, standard English is simply another dialect of this powerful language that has spread so far around the world. Since children's usage is influenced by the speech communities in which they live, they will learn the standard "school" dialect in the same way they learned their "home" dialect, and for the same reason—to be a participating member of the speech community. We can immerse children in an environment full of positive standard English models—our own speech to emulate, books to read or to listen to, poems to join in with, stories to retell or to use as a springboard for writing. None of this labels the children's home dialect wrong or substandard, but rather treats standard speech and writing models as useful extensions of the language repertoire.

Children learn to use language effectively and appropriately through interaction with the people around them, from listening to others read, and from learning about language in the context of their own writing. There is no evidence that they are helped to speak, write, or think by studying the rules of prescriptive grammar. To some extent, children may gain facility in writing and understanding of syntax by practising changing tenses, using synonyms, and making transformations in sentence structure, but, as a general rule, competence is best acquired through the comparisons and corrections that children make in their own writing. For example, children's attention can be drawn to standard language through comparing interesting differences in language patterns, discussing a range of possible usages when problems recur in their writing, and examining appropriate usage by characters in books and in the children's own stories.

They can, if interested, undertake comparative and experimental investigations of their own language by considering the kinds of words that are normally used together or that occur in the same place in a sentence or by studying the ways in which changes in sentence and word structure change meaning. Children seem to learn best when they are given a chance to play with new ways of using language, to make comparisons between usages, and to explore the effects of words, word patterns, and idioms. In writing, however, where usage is more stable and where non-standard forms may be a barrier to effective communication, the teacher should help the children develop standard forms by working from their own writing. By surveying the usage differences that are found in children's talk and writing, the teacher can identify significant problems and build a list of ten to fifteen items to focus on during the year.

When should the analytical study of grammar begin? In the junior grades, children can identify name words, action words, and describing words—and learn to call them nouns, verbs, and adjectives if they are interested in that sort of classification. Few children have sufficient metacognitive awareness of the way they form sentences to comprehend such abstractions as subject and predicate much before they are teenagers, so the formal study of syntax is best left until then. This does not mean that younger children are not beginning to grasp the fundamentals of what makes a sentence—and perhaps in a more holistic fashion than a grammar textbook would allow.

Single Words Can Be Sentences
Larry Swartz

Children can develop an awareness of both standard and non-standard grammar through their reading and writing.

Sunny: Wait a minute . . . You said every word means something . . . What does the word "is" mean?

Christi: It's just part of the sentence.

Sunny: But what does it mean to you?

• • • •

Sunny: In Gary Paulsen's book *Hatchet*, remember how he always describes one-word sentences?

Ryan: Oh yeah . . . to explain how.

Heidi: It goes "Locked," "Secret," or "Hungry."

Ryan: It's his thoughts . . . to explain what he feels.

Heidi: Yeah . . . one word leads to the whole sentence . . . like "Secret." . . . You want to know the whole secret.

Sunny: You don't need the whole sentence to make sense.

Ryan: It's like Paulsen can put down one word and you can make a sentence in your head.

Sunny: You know what the author means by it.

Heidi: "Secret."

Liza: "Hatchet." . . . "Fire."

Heidi: You think where is the fire?

Liza: . . . and how do you make a fire?

These ten- and eleven-year-olds are thinking about words, meaning, and communication. They may not be aware that a sentence should have a subject and a predicate, but they certainly know what a sentence is, that Paulsen's usage of single words makes sentences in the context of *Hatchet*, and that other contexts would require other usages.

Capitalization

When children begin to write, they often use only capital (upper case) letters. Capitals are easier to form because they are made up largely of straight lines and circles or parts of circles (Scott-Dunne, in Jack Booth et al., 1993). For example, "M" is easier to write than "m." Capitals are also easier to distinguish from one another. "B" and "D" are much more clearly different from each other than the mirror images "b" and "d."

Most printed material, of course, appears in both upper and lower case. As children begin to read, it is interesting to see how soon they recognize that there are two forms for each letter. They often enjoy matching games that let them display and consolidate their knowledge. It is usually some time before they begin to transfer this understanding to their writing. Some children seem to make a conscious decision to start writing "like grown-ups" and with them the switch may come almost all at one time. With most, the change comes more gradually, and some letters still appear in upper case long after the lower-case forms of others have been mastered. Often a gentle reminder when a piece is being prepared for publication will nudge the writer into paying attention to the conventions of upper and lower case.

For most children, the basic rules of capitalization are almost instinctive. They regard capital letters as "big" and lower-case ones as "small." It is not much of a step from there to notice that we use a capital—a "big letter"—to mark the beginning of something special, such as a person's name. As the children gain a more sophisticated, if still subconscious, understanding of the concept of proper nouns, they will recognize that places, days of the week, months of the year, names of organizations, and titles of books, magazines, and movies also require capitalization. The syntactic concept of a sentence as a complete thought is reinforced by the capital letter at the beginning, as well as the period or other closing punctuation at the end.

Children see words all in capital letters in signs and advertisements in the world around them and love to use "big letters" for emphasis in their own writing. They find the fact that the most important person in one's life—oneself—is written as a single, satisfying, capital letter a boost to self-esteem. Thus the pronoun "I" is often a good starting point for a discussion of how we use capital letters and small letters. As children notice the different patterns they make to form the two versions of each letter, they are taking one step in developing a handwriting style.

Handwriting

Even from the small sampling of student writing in this book, it is obvious that handwriting styles vary from person to person. It is neither possible nor desirable to attempt to impose a uniform style. But is important that clear handwriting be valued and that a pleasing and legible style be developed.

One acquaintance of mine started school in the 1950s in France, where an elegant and flowery script was demanded even from kindergarten children. Her family next moved to India, and she entered the Elisabeth Gauba School. Gauba had studied with Maria Montessori, and her teaching methods were loosely based on the Montessori system. Here, my friend was expected to write a story every day, first copying the words that she had dictated to

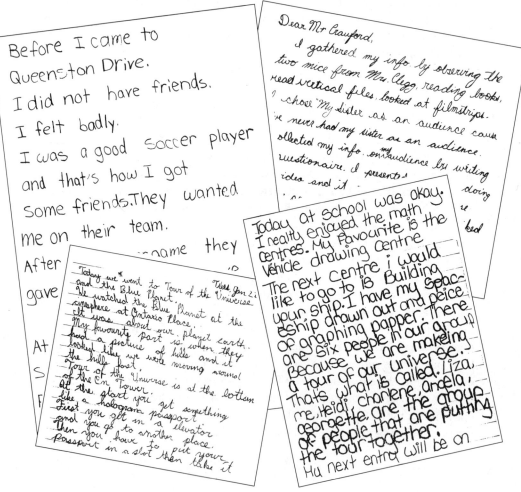

Handwriting styles of Queenston students, age 10–11

Japanese New Year

Author / Illustrator
Kiyoko Ike

After 12 O'clock, we go to shrine to pray for the whole year and then the bell rings. Then we eat buckwheat

In the day, children play with tops and kites and they visit neighbour's houses. They sometimes give them New Year's gift which is money. Parents and grand — parents give them some too.

the teacher. Soon she was printing her own stories without help. She still remembers the delicious feeling of accomplishment when she and her desk-mate decided they would "join up" their letters, just like the bigger children. She maintains it was the moves from school to school and country to country after those two years in India that spoiled her handwriting as she was forced to change from italic to script and back again. Even today, her handwriting is slow and jerky: she often needs to stop in the middle of a word as she consciously decides how to form the next letter.

We must guide each child toward legibility within that child's individual style. Certain requisite qualities need to be promoted and developed— legibility, speed, ease of style, and aesthetic form. Teachers can help some children by demonstrating how letters are formed. Children soon develop a functional and aesthetic awareness of such elements as spacing, margins, and capitals. Children can be encouraged to improve their handwriting by publishing their best stories, recording discussion ideas for others to read, and copying favourite poems and songs. Experimenting with writing as an art form and learning calligraphy for graphic design will give them options to work on to develop their personal style.

Children should understand that their handwriting style depends upon the situation: jotting down information for their own use requires a different approach from writing a letter of sympathy to a friend. Children should become aware of their "handwriting repertoire" and know which style is appropriate to a particular task.

Handwriting is important; illegible or poorly formed letters may cause words to appear misspelled or inappropriate. The quality of the handwriting can affect the reader's judgement of both the writing and the writer.

Transcription Skills and Communication

Children will not learn the skills of transcription, nor much else, if they do not find them relevant. We must foster children's need to communicate easily and gracefully. If we do not let them know where they are failing, we are failing them.

Celebration of a child's creativity is good for self-esteem, but without some guidance, it may not lead to further development. Some children know that work that is important to them needs polishing; others are so taken up by the initial writing process that the first draft is indeed perfect in their eyes. Often, leaving a piece of writing for a period of time allows these children to come back to it with eyes blinded by emotional commitment, and they are able to begin the revision process.

Perhaps Jo Phenix deserves to have the last word.

The Teacher as Editor
Jo Phenix

Students in my grade five class astonished me by the amount of editing they would accept. Under normal circumstances when responding to their writing, I would select a few points of content, some of organization, and some of transcription to focus on at various stages. Often many errors or weaknesses went undiscussed. What changed this was classroom publishing. Many of the students printed their own final copy for books, and they soon discovered that if they still had errors in a final draft, it was not final at all, but needed to be done again. I set myself up as editor and invited students, when they had done as much as they could by themselves, to ask for help. If they asked for editing, I did what a copy editor would do—I marked every spelling error, every paragraph, every punctuation omission I could find. The amazing thing was that they were grateful! They saw what I was doing as a helpful strategy that would save them work at final draft stage. In 25 years of teaching, I never had a student come and ask me to mark every error in a piece of writing. What I did as a copy editor was exactly that; the only difference was in the students' perception of the purpose of proofreading and correcting.

Booktalk: Noticing Words and How They Work
David Booth

L is for Frog: Why?
Because a Frog Leaps.

What do you call a kangaroo that wakes you up every day?
A kangarooster.

These excerpts (from *Q Is for Duck* by Mary Elting and Jack Folsom and *Zoodles* by Bernard Most) are typical of the sort of language play that twists words inside out and upside down and helps children to think about, listen for, and see the shapes and meanings of words and sentences. Many picture books, joke and riddle books, poetry anthologies, and reference books contribute to the understanding of technical aspects of language such as phonics, spelling, homonyms, derivations, and idioms. These books, of course, are popular with the children not because they "teach" but because the bare bones of language hold surprise and delight.

Marvin Terban has written a series of books that celebrate word play: *Superdupers!* explores more than 100 terms such as "wishy-washy," "okey-dokey," and "razzmatazz" that have become part of our everyday vocabulary; *Eight Ate: A Feast of Homonym Riddles* laughs at the vagaries of English spelling ("What will a foot doctor do to you? He'll heal your heel."); *In a Pickle* examines the origins of idioms such as "a chip off the old block" and "a frog in his throat"; *Funny You Should Ask* helps children use word play to compose their own jokes and riddles. The titles of other books in the series are self-explanatory: *I Think I Thought and Other Tricky Verbs, Your Foot's on My Feet and Other Tricky Nouns, The Dove Dove: Funny Homograph Riddles, Too Hot to Hoot: A Collection of Funny Palindrome Riddles.*

Charles Keller gives the children more than 100 examples of word-craft in *Daffynitions*. In *Flapdoodle*, folklorist Alvin Schwartz brings together a collection of parodies, spoonerisms, word plays, and "punctuation rhymes." Like Terban, Keller and Schwartz have produced other books about words that children will enjoy seeking out. Fred Gwynne's books of puns and idioms, *The King Who Rained, Chocolate Moose for Dinner*, and *The Sixteen Hand Horse*, have hilarious illustrations.

Children love puns and expressions that conjure up amusing images. Riddle and joke books are excellent resources for integrating listening and speaking with reading and writing. Starting the year with such word play, perhaps with the children paired to read a joke book together and then creating their own riddle and joke books to share with others, indicates that words and how they go together are an interesting focus for learning. *King Kong's Underwear* by Mike Thaler, *Zoodles* by Bernard Most and the pop-up book *Knock! Knock!* by Colin Hawkins have been recent favourites.

Many books teach skills by focusing on a particular theme or language concept. For example, *CDB and CDC* by William Steig, challenges the reader to think about the sounds of words by solving rebus puzzles. Author/illustrator Ruth Heller uses rhyming text and richly detailed paintings to provide young readers with some basic concepts about parts of speech. In *A Cache of Jewels and Other Collective Nouns*, Heller introduces children to such words as a "batch" of bread and a "fleet" of ships; in *Kites Sail High*, the children explore the variety of uses and meanings a single verb can have. *Weird!: The Complete Book of Halloween* by Peter R. Limburg, discusses definitions and the historical background of words associated with Halloween. Norman Juster's *As . . .* demonstrates similes in rhyming text. Bernard Most has children dissect words into letters to look for words inside words in *There's an Ant in Anthony and Pets in Trumpets*. Alphabet books such as *Animalia* by Graeme Base and *Q Is for Duck* by Mary Elting and Jack Folsom also help children identify letters as they inspect words. Counting books such as *One Watermelon Seed* by Celia Lottridge and *One White Sail; A Caribbean Counting Book* by S.T. Garne not only help children with numbers but also encourage an understanding of the use of the singular and plural.

Books such as these draw children into the fun and delight of words. Their riddles, rhymes, and puzzles sharpen the children's reading, spelling, and thinking skills. As the children laugh, they cannot fail to take time to notice the puzzles and tangles and peculiarities of the English word jungle.

Suggested Reading for Teachers

Bolton, Faye, and Diane Snowball. *Springboards: Ideas for Spelling.* Toronto: Nelson, 1989. *Springboards* provides a rationale for the teaching of spelling based on the nature of the English language and the natural development of children's spelling ability. Spelling is dealt with in the context of writing—not just writing as an isolated area of the language arts, but writing in all areas of the curriculum.

Booth, David, ed. *Spelling Links.* Markham: Pembroke Publishers, 1991. Leading educators including Richard Gentry, Robert and Marlene McCracken, and Carol and James Beers discuss alternatives to the weekly spelling list as they explore the role of spelling in a whole language classroom.

Buchanan, Ethel. *Spelling for Whole Language Classrooms.* Winnipeg: Whole Language Consultants Ltd., 1989. The author discusses developing spelling skills in context, as a tool with a meaningful purpose, as a process within language learning, rather than as an end in itself.

Foster, Graham, Judy Mackay, and Claudette Miller. *Skills Instruction in a Language Arts Program.* Markham: Pembroke Publishers, 1992. Using a question-and-answer format, this book addresses questions posed by teachers and parents about skills instruction within a holistic language program.

Gentry, J. Richard. *Spel . . . Is A Four Letter Word.* Toronto: Scholastic, 1987. A parent-teacher guide on learning to spell. Invented spelling is described and strategies for teaching spelling are included.

Phenix, Jo, and Doreen Scott-Dunne. *Spelling Instruction that Makes Sense.* Markham: Pembroke Publishers, 1991. This book dispels the many myths and misconceptions that surround the teaching of spelling. Practical ideas will help teachers plan classroom programs that help students learn to spell.

Scott, Ruth. *Spelling: Sharing the Secrets.* Toronto: Gage Educational Publishing, 1993. The author presents a framework for placing spelling in the context of active learning. The book is a bridge between spelling research and classroom practice.

Tarasoff, Mary. *A Guide to Children's Spelling Development for Parents and Teachers.* Victoria: Active Learning Institute, 1992. Using spelling samples, this book explains how children learn to spell, how to teach spelling strategies, evaluating progress and integrating spelling into language activities.

Wilde, Sandra. *You Kan Red This! Spelling and Punctuation for Whole Language Classrooms, K-6.* Portsmouth, N.H.: Heinemann, 1992. This book discusses how teachers have begun to rethink how children learn about spelling and punctuation, and what the role of the school should be within that process.

Reflections

❶ Do you differentiate between the acts of composing and transcribing both in instruction and in assessing? Are the children you teach aware of this differentiation? Do they understand the need for transcribing skills and careful editing when writing is to be shared?

❷ Create a file of strategies and activities drawn from or inspired by various books and articles on spelling and punctuation to help you with the problems individual children are having with writing words down.

❸ When working with groups or the whole class, what mini-lessons could you teach, demonstrations could you conduct, or games could you play that would promote an interest in and a love of words and how they are put together?

❹ Write a letter to parents about your programs in spelling, punctuation, and handwriting in order to involve them in the writing process, encouraging them to respond to content and ideas first and to help their children with the revision process when appropriate. Would an evening meeting for parents to discuss these issues be useful in your school? Plan what you would say, how you would demonstrate the process, and what samples of work you would display.

❺ What further background in spelling do you need if you are to assist children in seeing patterns, generalizations, and clusters of information in words that will help them to spell other related words? Make a list of eight to ten such items you might draw to the children's attention over the next month or so. Include strategies for introducing them in a meaningful context—and, of course, be prepared to grasp any opportunities for other discussions of spelling as they arise.

❻ What strategies would you add to this list for promoting spelling in a language-based context?

- helping children work through the stages of invented spelling
- letting them see some of their own writing in standard spelling

- drawing their attention to spelling patterns in their reading
- having a variety of dictionaries available
- teaching children to spell as part of the writing process

7 Children are interested in words and how they fit together in sentences. For a given grade level, what parts of speech or aspects of syntax would you expect to discuss over the course of the year? What games or explorations can you devise to help children discover how language works?

8 Analyze the good and poor aspects of your own handwriting. Can you use these strengths and weaknesses as discussion points when talking to the children about their handwriting styles? What sort of models and resources for the children to use in developing their personal styles would you like to have available in the classroom?

Talking to Learn

C HILDREN'S TALK HAS been "traditionally so often seen as inimical to the educational process (stop talking and get on with some work)" (Knowles, 1983). Although the skills of oral communication and group dynamics are perceived as essential in business and in the community at large, thoughtful, interactive talk has rarely played much part in the official structure of classroom activities. For centuries, education has stressed literacy as the key to knowledge and understanding. Today, the ever-widening scope of oral and visual media brought to us by electronic technology is forcing us to recognize that teaching "oracy" (Wilkinson, 1971) is as important as teaching literacy and numeracy.

Research literature is helping us to focus on the relationship between language and thought, theories of language acquisition, the nature of language, and the various uses of language. School should be a place where we can hear the full sound of the conversation of humankind. Joan Tough (1981) points out that language skills are not developed in isolation from learning but are an integral part of it. Children do most of their important learning as talkers, questioners, arguers, gossips, and chatterboxes (Barnes, 1976). Gordon Wells (1986) suggests that children will learn most effectively when they have frequent opportunities for talk, both with teachers and with fellow students.

Children need to work out for themselves the way in which language is organized. For this, they need the collaboration of partners in conversation to provide feedback that will lead them to understand what they are thinking, what they are saying, and the appropriateness of the language they are using to say it. In true classroom conversation, the talk does not feed through the teacher because the children, not the teacher, are the focus of attention. In small or large group discussions, they engage in types of talk that encourage intense thought processes such as comparison, interpretation, judgement, discrimination, and prediction.

Talk enhances the development of literacy. It is not a subject, but rather a condition of learning in all subjects. Talk has many functions: it leads children to understand new concepts; it enables them to communicate clearly as active learners with others; it lets them consider a diversity of viewpoints; it helps them develop a critical tolerance of others. Without talk, thinking concepts through is difficult, if not impossible (Jones, 1988).

In this chapter we examine talk as a medium of learning. We look at its relationship to the classroom, to the teacher's role of instructing and questioning, and to the variety of children's learning styles. We look at the strategies various teachers have devised to ensure that negotiating, collaborative, analytical talk occurs. We watch children think aloud, test hypotheses, and risk voicing ideas, engaging in true conversation about the world. We watch teachers talk to each other and listen to children, treating talk as a way of learning in every classroom activity.

Talking Allowed

Not too long ago, a teacher's worth was measured by the silence in the classroom. The principal mode of talk was "question and answer," and the students' formal talk time was made up of show-and-tell in kindergarten and public speaking in grade eight. Today, schools are full of the sounds of children talking, and educators recognize the function of speaking and listening in the process of learning.

When people talk, we not only tell the stories of our lives, we also make them real. We assimilate our experiences and build them into a continuing picture of our world. The responses we get from others profoundly affect both the world picture we are creating and our view of ourselves. All talk, purposeful or random, helps us understand the human race in all its variety (Barnes, 1976). Children need to talk in order to symbolize, structure, regulate, and give meaning to experience. As teachers, we need to understand the nature of classroom talk so that we can harness its impact on the lives of children.

A recognition that talking can be a means of learning; that its effectiveness as such a means relies on a relationship of mutual trust between those taking part in the talk; and that the onus for establishing that relationship in the classroom lies first with the teacher—all this clearly assumes an interactive view of learning; and this in turn has important implications for our view of curriculum. (Britton, 1976).

At Queenston Drive Public School, the teachers see themselves as participants in the classroom community—engaging in chit-chat; in significant dialogue; in interviews with individuals; in sharing stories, personal and literary, with the whole class; in moderating disputes; and in building the curriculum with the children.

Brian Crawford has created a rich environment for talk by opening up opportunities for independent, group, and whole-class activities in his family grouping of grades three-to-five children. He encourages them to claim ownership of the planning of events and involves them in organizing the classroom, planning field trips, and interviewing guests. By giving his children a choice of activities, he capitalizes on their interests and encourages them to talk to each other as they exchange information, share feelings, and plan experiments. By having children talk, share, and reflect upon their learning experiences, he maximizes interaction and allows scope for independence of action and participation.

Jim Giles's primary family-grouped classroom is also full of healthy talk for learning. Jim navigates the room, contributing to the learning with groups and individuals, observing and developing personal insights into their lives. He encourages the process of talk by joining in conversations, encouraging children to think and reflect, and conveying his appreciation of the topics under discussion. As Jim chats informally with children about their experiences or before and after tasks, he expands on their utterances in ways that encourage the conversation to continue, adding to the breadth and depth of meaning; he occasionally offers alternative wording in standard or accepted usage. He thus helps the children manage their own talk behaviour; he accepts their questions and comments and leads them to find rules for discussion, such as respecting the opinions of others. Groupings in Jim's classroom are flexible and change frequently; this helps children develop a variety of effective working relationships.

At Queenston, teachers spend virtually no time at their desks (in many classrooms, the teachers' desks have been removed to make more space for work tables). They meet to talk with a group at specified times—and also when the group requests it. They focus on what the children have to say.

The Talk Curriculum

The talk curriculum is not a series of skills to be conquered; it cannot exist in a weekly timetabled session for speaking and listening. Talk is a dynamic medium for learning in all areas and at all levels of schooling, a tool that will increase not only students' knowledge, but their ability to enquire, argue, reflect, and make sense of information. School must be a place where children are permitted and encouraged to talk their way into learning, where thoughtful exploration is valued, and where conversation is a necessary mode of exploration (Bruner, 1983). We need to develop strategies for making the most of classroom talk, to build a talk curriculum where children

- choose both words and language style to suit the context
- note the effect of what is being said on the listener or audience

- find a personal voice that informs and connects to what others are saying
- use talk as a precursor to written work
- become involved through talk in a group task so that they can accomplish more
- appreciate that talk is central to making sense in all learning situations
- reflect on their own participation in talk events

Schools can use the talk curriculum, then, to develop students who use talk to think, to communicate, to reflect, and, most of all, to belong.

Young children acquire their knowledge of language primarily through speaking and listening. From their earliest years, they listen to language models (parents, siblings, acquaintances) and use language as they need it. In the primary grades, much of children's language development comes from listening and reading and from their use of speaking and writing in situations that have meaning for them. Growth in language is nearly always related to the desire to communicate effectively. In other words, children speak and write because they need to describe their world and tell others what they think about it. Talk that fosters learning is exploratory, unstructured, and tentative. It provides the opportunity for learners to try out ideas, to get feedback, to build on each other's insights, and to construct knowledge collaboratively.

Talking to Clarify a Concept
Barbara Clegg

The skills and strategies of the language arts program cannot be separated from other areas of the curriculum. Talking, reading, and writing are essential elements of math and science learning. In my grade one class, I expect children to extend, enhance, and clarify their understanding through talk.

Here is how three six-year-olds experimenting with wooden blocks and other materials came to understand the geometric concept of "arch." Through conversation during the activity as well as in the sharing of results, "balance," "support," and "symmetry" became familiar terms as they built their way into learning.

Jamie:	Here's symmetry.
Mandeep:	That's not symmetry. Symmetry means it's something that's cut in half.
Jamie:	It's the same size on both parts.
Phillip:	The farther one stands up better but they don't have symmetry.

Mandeep: I got this idea from a book.

Phillip: Where are the magic crystals? They make the house magic. The mountains are not magic.

Learning appears to be most effective when the children carry out inquiries. However, Philip is moving into story building from the symmetry discussion. This is constructing meaning in the most integrative of fashions: the children are exploring and thinking in any mode that works for them at the moment, not confined by the idea that they should think in compartments called subjects.

I asked the children to record their results in a notebook. In their writing, the children reflected on problems they encountered during the mathematical exploration and outlined some details of the process they went through. Many had written stories about their structures, and because each child's ability and understanding was individual, these notebooks were an excellent vehicle for assessing their progress and knowledge.

When young children use concrete materials to build things, they are naturally inclined to tell stories about their creations. Children can express their imagination and feelings as they build and invent. After the class's work with structures, I read *Leanna Builds a Genie Trap* to them, and then in a drama activity the children worked as inventors to

help Leanna solve her problem. They also designed their own genie traps from materials in the classroom, and I videotaped them at work. These transcripts demonstrate the story making that accompanied the mathematical explorations.

> Kim *(ESL student, working with Lego):* This is the master of the bad guys and he tells the worker and he wants to get the powerful gun. This castle has a powerful gun and told him to go get it. He opens the door. He think this is the way to go inside the castle. So when he gets trapped this thing starts to ring and this thing goes up.

> Kevin *(working with plastic interlocking pieces):* I made a genie trap and this is the genie with one eye. And when it spots the cookies it goes into the trap and the thing automatically closes . . . by the lock and it locks it up by turning it . . . by taking it off and it locks and it can't get out.

> Nicole *(working with sand):* The genie comes out and he walks up 'cause he smells the candy and then he sees the golden ring. He's ready to sink. . . . And then he walks in and he sees a golden ring. He goes in and he hears this noise. He looks behind him and . . . Oh my god . . . locked him in then I dig out and there he is all buried. And then he gets back up . . . Then he appears with the stone in his hand. Right here but he's . . . Bring him back and then he goes back to his farmhouse.

Social Talk

Social talk is the conversation we engage in most of the time, and it is vital to our well-being. A child who is isolated from others in a class, for whatever reasons, sounds a warning bell because healthy children need interaction. Through social talk, we learn to appreciate the people we want to know and to get along with the people we have to know. All the rituals of social behaviour are included in social talk—greetings, goodbyes, chatter, gossip, jokes. Social talk is sharing in the lives of others.

Often, classrooms have directly discouraged social talk, but children found occasions for friendly chit-chat during the school day—at recess, during lunch, or walking home after school. Such social exchange should be part of the curriculum as well, not as a focus, but as a natural feature of classroom activities. In this way, the environment for talk models that of the family, the workplace—and life. Children naturally recount personal experiences to each other as they work in groups, often as counterpoint to task talk. Tidying up after a project, preparing for a change of subject, welcoming visitors, sharing after story time, chatting with the teacher about the week-end—all of these moments are social talk.

Teachers who are unable to accept the role of social talk create an artificial situation for communication in the classroom. We need to be aware of how personal talk fits in the teaching/learning spectrum. Children can take responsibility for monitoring their own talk patterns as they complete their tasks. Certainly, times for attentive silence, for respectful quiet, for focused listening are necessary, but the more "normal" the classroom's conversational environment, the more time the teacher will have to interact with the children in enabling and fruitful ways.

Task Talk

Children in school are not always given time to think out loud and talk themselves into understanding. Douglas Barnes (1976) calls this groping toward meaning "exploratory talk" and says that it is usually marked by frequent hesitations, rephrasing, false starts, and changes in direction. Talking helps children make sense "out loud" as they come to grips with new ideas. It is the bridge that helps them explore relationships that arise between what they know and what they are coming to know. As they put their knowledge into words, they reflect on that knowledge. How different this meaning making is from the formal giving of right or wrong answers!

Joan Tough (1981) concluded that three factors help children reach their full language potential: dialogue with an empathetic adult, opportunities for imaginative play, and an enabling environment in which the child encounters a variety of language experiences. Teachers may have to alter the communication patterns of the classroom and use a number of approaches to talk to ensure that all three factors are present.

We can encourage talk within limits that allow for a maximum of expression and a minimum of thoughtless or self-indulgent behaviour. Children can best express their thoughts and feelings within a social dynamic where the context rather than the teacher does the controlling. When we act as involved listeners rather than as detached evaluators, we open up a whole range of communication strategies. Children talk not only to express their ideas but to reflect on them and refine them. The responses of listeners are an important indicator of their success. By listening and talking with children in casual conversation and by creating opportunities for significant dialogue, we can help children both to find new meanings in their experiences and to communicate those meanings.

A World in a Poem
Larry Swartz

In a unit of study on environmental concerns, I presented my grade five students with "There Was Once a Whole World in the Scarecrow" by Brian Patten. The poem details how a farmer dismantled an old scarecrow. As he took away each part, he destroyed a creature's home until the field was empty and all the creatures, their world, the scarecrow, were gone. The students broke into groups of four or five to respond orally to the poem and then shared their ideas with the rest of the class before the end of the period. The following is from a transcript of one group's discussion.

Teacher:	Matthew, you say it's about the world. How do you think it's about the world?
Matthew:	Um . . . About it . . . like being gone, everything's going and like the world—everything's going.
Heidi:	Yeah—by pollution!
James:	It's like um . . . the animals . . . like . . . like some parts are being demolished and put into apartments and houses and all that, so it's like the scarecrow being taken apart.
Heidi:	Maybe it's sort of like . . . the world . . . that's sort of like . . .
All	. . . like the world's being taken apart!
Heidi:	And all the animals . . . And everything is gone.
Sunny:	And, the scarecrow is their world.
Heidi:	And the animals . . .
Sunny:	That means like the humans have like destroyed the earth.
Liza:	And we're taking . . . when we build the houses here for us to live . . . we're taking away their property, sort of.

Matthew begins the conversation, making an analogy between the scarecrow and the whole world. Sunny recognizes the farmer as representing all humans who might be destroying the Earth. Very quickly the group relates the poem to their own experiences. At this point, the talk helps the students look at the whole meaning of the poem, before breaking it down into little bits.

Matthew:	*(reading)* "The farmer has dismantled . . . "
Sunny:	. . . "the old scarecrow"
Matthew:	. . . "the old scarecrow"

Sunny: That means he has taken it apart.

Matthew: He has taken it apart.

Sunny: The straw is the only thing that's being blown away.

Liza: Yeah.

Heidi: Yeah.

Sunny: . . . and the mouse once . . .

Matthew: The scarecrow means life!

Liza: Yeah.

Heidi: Yeah . . . the scarecrow means life and . . . the wind's taking the . . . well, we're sort of like the wind taking their homes and life.

Sunny: Yeah, the straw's the life of the scarecrow.

Heidi: 'Cause like in hunting season when they . . . when they shoot the animals it's like they're taking their lives away.

Liza: So we're taking the scarecrow away.

Matthew: We're taking advantage of it.

Liza: Yeah.

Matthew: We're using it.

Sunny: We're using it unwisely.

Matthew: Use it wisely . . . *(dramatically)*

Sunny: . . . young man . . .

Heidi: Use it while you can!

Liza: So, do you think that straw will be used for anything?

Matthew: Straw heart . . . ? *(reading)* . . . "a mouse once lived in the straw heart."

Sunny: Why are you asking questions?

Heidi: I don't know. She feels like it.

Matthew: Just explain what you feel—no, you don't ask questions! *(dramatically)* How do you feel? *(laughs.)*

Heidi: *(reading)* "A mouse once lived in its straw heart." I never knew scarecrows had hearts. They don't have brains. They don't have hearts.

Liza: The world has a heart!

Matthew: The wizard of . . .

Liza: The world has a heart!

Sunny: Everything has a heart, Matt.

Heidi: I don't understand it. It goes *(reading)* "now . . . now the field is empty." It's sort of like . . . the world is empty!

James:	Yeah, but that will come really soon.
Liza:	But that straw can make more hearts.

As the students discuss the poem, they are

- describing (Sunny: The straw is the only thing that is being blown away)
- making analogies (Heidi: Yeah . . . the scarecrow means life and . . . the wind's taking the . . . well, we're sort of like the wind taking their homes and life.)
- reasoning (Liza: So we're taking the scarecrow away. Matthew: We're taking advantage of it.)
- questioning (Liza: So, do you think that straw will be used for anything?)
- instructing (Sunny: Everything has a heart, Matt.)
- explaining (Heidi: It goes "now . . . now the field is empty." It's sort of like . . . now the world is empty!)
- speculating (Liza: But that straw can make more hearts.)

Heidi:	What did you say, Liza?
Liza:	Well um . . . the galaxy has a heart—it's the sun!
Heidi:	Yeah I guess you're right, sort of . . . in a way.
Liza:	Because all the planets circulate the sun . . .
Heidi:	Like all our blood circulates around the heart . . .
Liza:	. . . and it goes "poom" . . . and it goes out again . . . and "poom" *(Liza joins in)* . . . and out again!
Matthew:	Okay . . . Where are all the animals that are gone? . . . that are going . . . that are going to be gone!
Heidi:	They're probably going to be gone.
Matthew:	I always . . . had . . . I have a feeling everyday that I'm about to die . . .
Heidi:	I don't! I have . . .
Matthew:	I'm walking down the street . . . and I feel like I'm going to die.

Through talk, the group has worked inside the poem, discussing the dismantled scarecrow, the mouse in a straw heart, and a world that has all gone. They have also gone beyond the words of the poem as they discussed the planets circulating the sun, the blood circulating the heart, and the extinction of animals. The atmosphere was supportive enough for Matthew, who had earlier felt a need to overdramatize, to reveal some very real fears about dying.

As the students discussed "There Was Once a Whole World in the Scarecrow," they looked carefully at what the poet was trying to say and how he was trying to say it, and they were making connections to their own lives and to their concerns with the environment. More significant, however, the discussion demonstrated to the students that the poem might have several meanings depending on personal perspective, and that significant dialogue is one of the chief means we have of constructing meaning.

Rehearsed Talk

When children report on information they have researched, introduce a guest speaker, or read a group of poems aloud, they are giving voice to words that they have previously thought about. The audience receives their message "live at the moment" but understands the premeditation that has occurred. This is rehearsed, often scripted, talk.

We can develop opportunities for children to explore all types of scripted talk. We often ask children to recount past experiences or retell a story, allowing them time to go over incidents and information and to work out a sequence of events before they present their narratives. Reviewing a book or a film, reporting the outcome of a group task, summarizing the results of a project, giving instructions for a game, and making announcements on the public address system are all occasions for planning what to say. When children read aloud their own writing, they often manipulate the text on the spot, changing words, omitting others, rephrasing as they speak to adjust to the needs of the listeners.

Children usually find that reading aloud, after exploring their own responses and rehearsing the text, is a satisfying mode of communication. It lets them share their reading comprehension and try on new language styles, voices, and patterns of speaking. Oral reading verifies print and helps silent readers to "hear" dialogue. Small groups can come together for oral reading, or older children can read stories they have prepared for younger listeners. Children will grow as oral readers if the situation calls for skilful interpretation for true listeners rather than for teachers intent on the public correction of errors and mispronunciations that can only stifle them.

Scripted talk is talk influenced by print. When children who recognize the power of the words they read or listen to speak or interpret, they begin to understand the reciprocal nature of speaker and listener. Children who revisit words they have read before through storytelling, reading aloud, or improvising, they become aware of the subtext, the layers of meaning, the associations that lie below the surface.

Formal Talk

Formal talk traditionally meant the public speech given once a year. This resulted in little or no growth as a speaker. Many children developed a great fear of such events and an aversion forever after to speaking in public. The chief characteristic of joint exploration through talk—the leapfrogging of listening and speaking—is not available to the child who is called upon to talk alone to an audience in a context that is neither enabling nor supportive.

He has to supply everything almost from his own intellectual and emotional resources and in addition he puts himself "at risk" in front of listeners who, even if they are sympathetic at heart, also exercise a critical function (Britton, 1975).

Formal talk is hardly the most common or significant mode of interaction, but it can be a basis for learning if it is surrounded with authentic contexts and opportunities for exploration beforehand. There are many strategies that will build a healthy and nurturing atmosphere for encouraging talk in formal situations. We can use the curriculum to create low-threat learning contexts that encourage sharing work in progress and presenting completed ideas and information. When children share ideas first with partners or small groups instead of immediately with the whole class, they develop confidence as speakers with something to say. Helping children use notes and various aids such as overhead transparencies or blackboard diagrams can support their attempts at formal presentation. We can also encourage children to rethink and rework their ideas afterward, thus leading them to see such occasions as opportunities for making meaning rather than as exercises undertaken to get good marks.

The everyday experiences of children always come to school with them. A child's particular interest in a subject is a gift to the teacher. Twelve-year-old Kim is in grade six and is hearing-impaired. I observed her in a small-group sharing session where the previous day one child in each group had volunteered to be "the expert for the day." Kim had no hesitation in taking on this leadership role even though she knew I would be videotaping the session. She simply asked me to wear an amplifier so that she could hear my "stage directions" more clearly. Her topic was her pony and her love of riding. Although her pronunciation of some words indicated the challenge oral language offered her, her presentation flowed easily, with plenty of information for us, and her own pleasure in her knowledge of her subject and her ability to hold the interest of the group demonstrated the satisfaction we can gain from telling about something that matters to us.

An Expert on Horseback
Kim

My expertise is horses. And I wanted to bring some pictures of the pony I have. He's my fifth pony, I've had five horses, and this is my fifth. His name is Silver, and here's a picture of me and my best friend on Silver.

He's fourteen hands high and he's eight years old. Silver is a really sweet pony. He can open his door—he takes his lips and he opens his door. And he gives kisses and hugs, and he can bow. I would ride him almost every day in the week, and in the summertime I take him way down back into the fields. My favourite thing to do on Silver is swimming. There's a big stream that goes down back, and we would go real, real deep, and he would swim along and I would be on his back. It was a lot of fun.

This is a bridle. This is what goes on the horse's head, and this is what goes in the mouth—it's the bit. And this is to protect his mouth, to keep it from getting pinched. You have to learn how to put this bridle on, and to slip this over his head, and do up some buckles and put the reins over his head. You have to learn the brushing—what their names are and where to put the brush on the horse. Then, the first thing we learn about getting on a horse is how to mount him, then walk around and sit. And then we learn to trot. You can do "trotting poles" where they have poles on the ground and you trot over them.

You mount on the left side, and you mount with your left foot. You put it up in the stirrup and you swing your right leg over and put your feet in the stirrups. They used to do that, I think, because a long time ago the men who were in the war, when they first started riding, they had their knives or whatever—those long swords down one side—so it was easier for them to mount on one side so that's why.

The Guided Tour
Brian Crawford interviews Ruth Wyman

I was very interested in an event for parents designed by our kindergarten teacher, Ruth Wyman. Her young students were the knowledgeable ones on this occasion, in charge of explaining their kindergarten work to their parents. In this formal talk situation, the children were secure and comfortable with their role as "speakers."

Brian: Can you tell us about the child-guided tour that you and the children planned together?

Ruth: When I visited my own daughter's classroom, we were told that the parent/teacher interview would be conducted by my daughter and not by the teacher. This seemed like a very interesting idea, and when my husband and I arrived, she "wrote" her report card and then "read" it to us. She and her teacher had made a plan, and she showed us some of the things she had learned. The teacher was available to help her. The interview ended with a social time for the teacher, the four sets of parents who were there, and the children. The atmosphere was tremendous and very, very empowering for the children. I asked the teacher's permission to adapt this idea, and she thought that would be terrific.

Brian: How did you use the idea with your children?

Ruth: The established reporting procedure at our school didn't allow me to use this method exactly as it had been used in my daughter's school though that is what I'd really like to do if I had it all my own way—

Brian: Me too.

Ruth: —but Education Week was approaching. Often children, especially in kindergarten, have difficulty in talking about school to their parents. I thought, if Education Week is about showing parents what their kids are doing, what better way than to have the kids lead them on a tour? I sent a letter home to the parents and told them that during Eduction Week, they would be welcome to come in and their child would take them on a tour of the classroom.

Brian: How did it work?

Ruth: I made a very definite structure for this tour. Many parents responded, and I decided to have only four or five tours going on at a time and found that it worked out well. We had to do the tours after school or in the evening.

Brian: What happened on a tour?

Ruth: The child read a book or told a story, showed the parents a drawing and writing book with work from September to April, taught the parents a math or computer lesson, and demonstrated a favourite school activity. We then all had juice and cookies together.

Brian: Did the children do it all in the same order? For example, did they read the book and then show them the drawing?

Ruth: That's a good question. I helped plan the tours during class time. We devoted a good chunk of time to this. I usually took two or three children at a time, and together we agreed on a plan. I transcribed the plan for the kids, using pictures along with words so they would be able to refer to it easily. I expect I led them to do it in a certain order because I worked through the plan the way I had thought of it. Sometimes they decided what they wanted to do next and the order would change. If I did this again, I think I would ask what they would like to do first, and then allow them as much freedom as possible while still giving them some strategies to work with.

Brian: Did you hear any comments from the children or their parents after the tours were conducted?

Ruth: The children really enjoyed doing the tours but didn't make a lot of comments afterwards. My feedback came largely from watching the tours in progress. There was an atmosphere of great power in the children's hands; they had poise and dignity and it gave them tremendous self-esteem. With one exception, they all treated this very seriously and did an excellent job of showing their parents what they were learning in a very direct way. It's all very well for me to write it down on a report card!

Brian: Yes, I think it's extremely important that the children have the control, and now the parents have seen the children actually engaged in learning, they can make connections when they do get a written report.

Ruth: The parents did ask a lot of questions and are thirsty for this kind of information. They felt very proud and interacted with their children in a very absorbed way.

Brian: Did you talk to the children afterwards about it—what they would change or do the same next time?

Ruth: No, I didn't do much follow-up, and maybe that would be the challenge for the next time. I would like to have much more discussion afterwards.

Brian: The parents must have been amazed at what children of this age can do. I think this idea could be built into our evaluation of the children to supplement some of the other things that we do.

Ruth: I made some notes after the parents had left while things were fresh in my mind.

Brian: An evaluation tool—I feel this could be one of the key components of evaluation.

Ruth: Yes. I received a letter of thanks from one parent who wrote, "Whenever I entered your classroom I felt an unrepressed atmosphere which was rich with possibilities. Evan proved this on that wonderful day when he took me on a tour and happily tackled all the opportunities he could, showing me proudly what he had learned." When this mother thinks back over the year, this is what stands out in her mind as a parent, a rare opportunity for parent and child to share something very wonderful.

Drama Talk

As a collaborative social activity, drama allows children to speak and listen to each other within contexts that demand concentration and response. As the children explore ideas and plan and debate events through improvisation and role playing over several days, they are using all they know about communication and persuasion, and their reflections and writing, talk and art will reveal the power of real language in imaginary situations. The possibilities of drama are explored further in Chapter 8.

Patterns of Interaction

Children talk their way into learning in a nurturing classroom environment that challenges them to explore both new concepts and more complex uses of language. A rich and varied curriculum, with ample opportunity for exploratory talk as children encounter new ideas, leads to greater experimentation with language and encourages confident and effective language use. With whom does a child interact in the classroom, and how can we ensure that the most learning possible comes from each type of interaction?

Interacting with Adults

The teacher's major role is to enable children to refine and expand the ways they use oral language. Teachers must create situations in which children need to use language for various purposes. Talk can be encouraged by such simple matters as the physical arrangement of the room: areas can be provided for private conversation with the teacher, for pairs of children to collaborate, for small groups to play and work, and for large groups to come together. Each child needs opportunities to participate in classroom talk in a variety of communication patterns.

Wherever appropriate, the teacher should appear as an interested participant. The teacher's most direct involvement is in child-to-teacher conversation. (Sadly, student teachers tell me that they remember very few opportunities in their school years when they had real conversations with a teacher.) Individual children can relate personal experiences to the teacher at suitable social opportunities. More formally, every child in a well-organized and caring classroom receives some form of individual instruction, whether it be a two-minute confirming conference or a special session with a classroom assistant. Carefully guided questions at less structured moments can help a child bring meaning to a story or grasp a mathematical concept. In *The Whole Story* (1988) Brian Cambourne describes six phases of teacher response to children, which I summarize here.

1. Seeking clarification of the learner's intent. "What are you doing?" "What are you trying to do?" "What are you supposed to be doing?" This helps the learner verbalize the task or reveal strategies or problems.
2. Listening to the learner's response. The message to be communicated to the learner is "I find your response worthwhile and I am listening to it."
3. Focusing on a gap in the learner's knowledge or skill and responding with a quick demonstration then and there.
4. Extending the child's frame of learning into new areas. "What else will you (could you, should you) do now?"
5. Refocusing the direction of the work if the child is unclear about it.
6. Redirecting the learner when the work does not match the expectations the teacher holds. "I think you should just work on getting the ideas organized in the right order now, and handle the difficult spellings later."

Interacting with Peers

Children converse naturally on a one-to-one basis. They tell each other about personal experiences at recess or during moments of interaction at learning centres. Dramatic play situations also present opportunities for authentic conversations. Partners can collaborate on problem-solving activities in various curriculum areas. After the teacher has shared a picture book, they can retell the story to each other, examining the pictures carefully.

Talking to and with a small group of fellow students is a little more demanding. Children can collaborate on a puzzle or a game. One child can demonstrate a problem-solving strategy in a complex mathematical situation using three-dimensional objects. A child can tell a small group about an interesting personal experience such as seeing a film. The children can discuss the results of an experiment. One child can organize a presentation of researched information.

The teacher must probably devise opportunities for individual children to speak to a large group. The teacher can invite a child to report on a holiday trip with the family. After a guest has spoken to the class, children can contribute their own experiences. During organized dramatic play, a child might speak in role as a villager to persuade the other residents (the rest of the class) to choose a plan of action. Formal class meetings allow children to debate problems of organization and management, such as preparing for a prospective field trip.

Some children are able to speak easily in a whole-class setting, offering personal thoughts and feelings unimpeded by the numbers of people listening and responding. However, only one person speaks at a time in such a forum, and true dialogue seldom emerges. Whole-class situations may be more useful for introducing units, listening to stories, watching films, or sharing findings.

Interacting in Groups

For co-operative and collaborative learning that promotes true language development, then, the most effective social dynamic is the small group. Group talk has its own special qualities. Children can learn so much when the structure of the classroom uses the energy generated by group talk. We work in groups because they make it easy to interact. Children must not be sent off in groups without a clearly defined task and without a plan of how they will bring their work back to the class. The focus must be on the learning that grows from the talking and the thinking going on as children make decisions, solve problems, create a diagram, or engage in peer editing. Established routines will assist children in group talk, so that the focus can be on the endeavour rather than on management.

Group talk is concerned with getting things done, exploring, questioning, and arriving at conclusions no one child could have reached alone. Children can clarify and modify their ideas in this natural and effective forum. Their skills in interaction will grow as they build on the talk of others to carry the discussion forward. They will learn to mediate and resolve their own conflicts as they look for alternative solutions that suggest new lines of discussion. Healthy group talk allows children to experiment with the roles of leader and participant at different times.

Sometimes students will choose their own groupings; at others the teacher will assign them to groups. To ensure that group learning is effective, the teacher needs to ensure the group is appropriate for the particular situation and then monitor the interaction so as to be ready to intervene to focus and refocus the talk if necessary. The teacher can be both a participating and an enabling group member, helping students to describe and summarize ideas. Group activity should be promoted across the curriculum. The work of groups can be integrated into and shared with the whole class.

Most conversations between teachers and children take place during small-group or activity time. We interact in the group, listening and responding in an undirected fashion; we can engage children in ways that will develop positive attitudes and self-concepts. A collaborating adult brings another kind of wisdom and expertise to the group discussion. Small-group work provides us with optimal "teaching moments," and the children will come to realize that working with other children helps them learn and that the teacher is committed to facilitating and participating in their growth.

Group work offers the teacher the opportunity to observe children in interaction. Peer relationships are known to be an important influence on whether a person develops high ego strength and personal autonomy; acquires appropriate attitudes and values; engages in positive social actions; and achieves in school and at work. Being isolated from peers is a major signal of psychological distress and maladjustment. The ability to decide what groups to join, with whom to associate, and with whom to be friends is an important skill for children in ensuring a fulfilling life.

Interacting with Older and Younger Children

One natural pattern of interaction missing almost by definition from many of our classrooms is talk between older and younger children. Marie McLay teaches grade one and Jill Jones grade five. They have gone beyond the walls of their own classrooms to introduce their students to each other. Jill and Marie decided initially to buddy their children for reading, but found the program idea mushroomed until they were combining their classes at least once a month over the year for a variety of large and small group activities and special events. They wrote about the results for the Peel TALK Project.

Buddy Talk
Jill Jones and Marie McLay

My buddy is Ryan. Every time I say Hi to him, he smiles at me. He reads stories to me and I know where he lives . . . At recess I watch him play football. He read Arthur's Halloween *to me. I liked when they went into an old lady's house and their friends thought it was a witch's house.*
   Maria

Maria talked a lot about how much she liked her grade five buddy, Ryan. Her little dictated story expresses the quality and characteristics of our buddy program and the warmth and sharing that grows between two friends of different ages. At the Awards Assembly to recognize special happenings in our school, we took this opportunity to highlight our buddying program by giving Maria and Ryan awards for "best buddies."

Last year, we arranged for three grade five students each to take a mat out into the hall to sit with two grade ones and read them a story. We wanted minimum disruption in classroom routines, and this eliminated the problem of children wondering what to do when some were finished while other groups were still reading.

We both believe that buddying children of different ages is an ideal way of extending learning for both groups. The buddy program facilitates growth at both age levels. The older ones gain a new purpose for reading, and all the children can discuss their likes and dislikes following a story. Reading and discussing a book without the presence of a teacher enables our children to perceive themselves as reasonably competent and efficient individuals.

This year, we determined to proceed on a more ambitious basis. We revised our plan and decided that each older student would read to his or her own buddy only. In September, each student from both classes chose a book from the library, and we stored these books in our buddy library. A pair of buddies choose their story for the day from this collection. They sit on a couch in the library to read their story just as they would if they were reading with a family member at home. Then the grade five student delivers the younger buddy back to the grade one classroom. The buddies are gone for about five to ten minutes. When books need changing, we all meet together to choose new ones. This system runs itself, and we do only minimal monitoring.

Shared enthusiasms evolve as the children interact with books. The trust that develops between buddies encourages risk taking and allows maximum opportunity for feedback and praise. The younger children enjoy the one-on-one attention, as well as simply being read to. When a grade five buddy arrives at the door and the grade one buddy is absent, others beg to fill in.

We have made some amusing and informative videotapes. Through these, we can observe at our leisure how individual pairs and groups of children interact. We have discovered the use of different kinds of talk among the children. The following is part of a transcript of a discussion that took place between buddies about the story *Great Cat*. Erin and Tara are grade five students and Carmen and Andrew are their grade one buddies.

Erin: What do you think it looks like, Carmen? *(questioning)*

Carmen: A big tiger . . . A boy pulling something on a rope. *(hypothesizing)*

Erin: Pulling something from a rope . . . *(accepting. To Andrew)* What do you think it is? *(questioning)*

Andrew: I think it is something like a kite and 'cause . . . *(exploring)* uh . . . the tiger pulled it and it's falling off the tree and then . . . uh . . . he's trying to get it out.

Tara: I think they fell from a boat or something. *(imagining)*

Erin: I think, personally . . . I think a little boy's . . . *(hypothesizing)* . . . pushing . . . like an animal somewhere . . . it looks like a big thing . . . it looks like a boat or something.

Tara: I think he had a kite and it got stuck up in the *(imagining)* trees and whatever animal it was it was trying to pull it . . . out of the trees.

Erin: . . . uh ... do you have any more ideas, Carmen? *(questioning)*

Carmen: uh . . . if I knew what that big thing was . . . uh . . . *(exploring)* the tall thing, I'd say that a boy has captured a big animal and he's pulled the thing.

Erin: It's a very good thought. *(accepting. To Andrew)* Do you have any more ideas? *(questioning)*

Andrew: I think, like . . . uh . . . it was a windy day and then *(imagining)* they . . . uh . . . the kite came there and there was some string hanging down and he was pulling it . . . the tiger came and he decided to rest . . . then he saw the boy there and he was pulling the kite.

Erin: We all agree it's pulling something, and it's a *(collaborating)* boat or something.

Erin keeps pulling ideas from the younger children and then responds with "It's a very good thought." No teacher could have done it better. Note the change from "I" to "we" as the children come to see their ideas as a group consensus, rather than as a set of individual suggestions. The positive encouragement and the collaboration between the different age groups is astounding.

The one-on-one shared reading in a relaxed and informal setting is only one part of our program. The second is that at least once a month, groups of buddies work together on a common theme. We plan individual conferences, small group settings, whole group discussions, and activity-based centres. We take advantage of special events and outings to allow the buddies to spend time together in a relaxed atmosphere. In the fall, we went together to the Royal Winter Fair. At our Winter Carnival and Summer Play Day, we placed buddies on the same teams; we found this reduced the competitive quality of the events and led to more co-operative play, as well as giving the little ones a sense of security. We planned buddy activities for a large portion of the hectic week before the winter break, and noise levels were lower and involvement higher than we normally expect at this time of year. It has been interesting to see the co-operation and support between buddies even when they were engaged in different activities.

We have noticed positive changes in the friendship patterns in the school. Older buddies develop a sense of responsibility and become protective toward the younger ones. (After a playground altercation, one small child was asked by the principal, "What would have been a better way of handling the situation?" and replied, "I should have found my buddy.") In some cases, behaviour problems disappeared as the interaction caused the children to be less self-centred.

Two of the families in our neighbourhood have formed a friendship as a result of the buddying relationship. We are constantly being reminded by our students that it is time for the buddies to get together again. Cards and letters from buddy to buddy fill the gaps between sessions.

As teachers, we have found our group lessons extremely stimulating because we brainstorm together to find the best methods of presentation and we each get an overview of a different age group. With two adults observing, our evaluations, both of our students and the program, become more objective. A day seldom passes when we do not seek each other out before school, even if only to say, "Good morning," which acts as a reliever of stress. We see the time we spend together as valuable to the development of our friendship, to the growth of the children, and to our own growth as professionals.

Timetabling is difficult, because we have to work around physical education, music, French, and various withdrawal programs. We are constantly rescheduling around other interruptions, such as extra music practice for concerts, visits from the nurse and from the firefighters, and student teaching practice. We have had to persist to make it work. For buddying to be successful, teachers must believe strongly in the importance of the program and have similar philosophies about how children learn, a willingness to co-operate, and supreme flexibility. The more involved we become, the harder we work.

The Teacher's Voice: Exploring and Modelling Language

And what of the teacher's own art with language? How important are our own skills of speaking and listening? What types of talk behaviour do we demonstrate for our students during our time with them? Do they learn the art of talk from us by simply observing, interacting with, and listening to us? Dorothy Heathcote (Wagner, 1984) feels that we must be ever aware of the power of language and the pleasure and inspiration it can bring to children. Even though few of us have trained voices, when reading aloud, we can read with integrity and commitment. We can develop an ear for effect, a wide range of tone, effective volume and pitch, and an awareness of the reactions of the children.

Our own language abilities are important resources in teaching. We should be able to rework classroom talk where necessary—elevating, correcting, elaborating, extending, focusing, altering the mood or the tone; and always encouraging both the participation of the children and the quality of their language and thought. Our personal language goals should remain constant: to communicate appropriately and effectively; to understand the needs of those listening and participating; and to be free enough to become involved in the making of meanings, both private and public. The art of language is the heart of teaching. It provides an opportunity for us as teachers to learn along with the children and lets us share in their exploration.

Booktalk: Opening the Floodgates of Memory
Lois Roy

When I share books with children, I hope they will discover something of themselves inside. This doesn't happen automatically: the catalyst that leads the children to uncover their personal stories is talk. I like to introduce a variety of picture books on the theme of memoirs to help the children revisit the snapshot memories of their own lives. As they build these personal experiences into coherent narrative, they are making sense of and find meaning in their worlds.

James Stevenson's *July* is an excellent vehicle for stimulating personal narrative in the classroom. Stevenson recalls moments and memories of his youth—"when each month was like a glacier slowly melting"—of summer months visiting Grandma and Grandpa, playing with friends and swimming at the beach. The boy playing baseball in the story helped Brodie to think about the time he went to a baseball game with his father; the description of marshmallows led Karen to talk about a time she shared with a good friend back in Hong Kong;

the car accident helped Melissa reveal the story of her father's motorcycle accident and death. Stories begat stories, which begat stories. Reading *July* together was a significant event not only because it allowed the children to unpack their memories, but because through sharing these narratives, we changed the classroom into a community of storytellers and meaning makers. Other titles in Stevenson's memoir series are *Higher on the Door, When I Was Nine,* and *When My Dad Went to War.*

Some books describe special memories of a parent or grandparent. In Jane Yolen's *Owl Moon,* a young child remembers winter nights spent owling with her father, a tale that helps the children to discuss the special things they do with close relatives. *Tar Beach* by Faith Ringgold, describes Cassie Louise Lightfoot's fantastic dream of flying around her Harlem neighbourhood one night in 1939 and the memories the dream evoked. *Tar Beach* led to stories about our parents' jobs, our neighbourhoods, and our own dreams. Cynthia Rylant's stories about family gatherings, *When I Was Young in the Mountains, The Relatives Came,* and *Appalachia,* prompted stories about family visits, rituals, and celebrations.

I began to collect books that were illustrated as if by photographs. *Grandpa's Slide Show* by Deborah Gould, *Grandma's Bill* by Martin Waddell and *The Red Ball* by Joanna Yardley invited the children to think about the visual records of their own lives. They began to bring in photographs from home and tell the stories behind the pictures—the trips they had taken, their adventures with pets, and family celebrations of special events. *This Quiet Lady* by Charlotte Zolotow, in which a young girl comes upon photos of her mother, made the children ponder their own parents' lives.

Home Place by Crescent Dragonwagon, *The Auction* by Jan Andrews and *Time to Go* by David and Beverly Fiday, led the children to talk about the places they have lived. Discussion ranged across such themes as homes, changes, moving, and the loss of friends. Similarly, books such as *Some of the Pieces* by Melissa Madinsky, *Always Gramma* by Vaundra Micheaux Nelson and *Badger's Parting Gifts* by Susan Varley allowed the children to share stories about death, loss, and remembrance.

Stories about telling stories was another popular genre. In Montzalee Miller's *My Grandmother's Cookie Jar,* a young native girl learns about her heritage as her grandmother pulls out from a jar both cookies and stories. Children learn about their grandfathers' past in *Knots on a Counting Rope* by Bill Martin Jr. and John Archambault and *The Old Old Man and the Very Little Boy* by Kristine Franklin. *The*

Lemon Drop Jar by Christine Widman, and *The Rag Coat* by Lauren Mills tell of mementos that hold special stories.

As a response to *Wilfred Gordon McDonald Partridge* by Mem Fox, I invited the children to play a storytelling game we called "That Reminds Me." One child was to begin a conversation by telling a personal anecdote suggested by the story. As the children listened, they were to put up their hands and when called on would begin to tell a story suggested by the one being told. As the game continued, children's hands were continually being raised as they thought of stories to share. When the bell for recess rang, many hands were still in the air, and when I suggested that the children go outside, Samantha asked, "Hey, don't you want to listen to my story?"

Books such as these engage the children in the stories of their lives. Through talk, they open their stories to inspection and celebration.

Suggested Reading For Teachers

Barnes, Douglas, James Britton, and Mike Torbe. *Language, the Learner and the School.* 4th ed. New York: Penguin Books Ltd., 1986. The central theme of this book is that teachers communicate both information and values to their students almost exclusively through the medium of language.

Booth, David, and Carol Thornley-Hall, eds. *Classroom Talk.* Markham: Pembroke, 1991. Based on classroom teacher experience, this book includes ideas as diverse as peer leaders in group discussion, talk and the quiet child, talk and peer conferences, talk and computers, communication through body talk, current events as a springboard to talk, talk as a way of learning in all areas, the role of talk in drama, and talk and the ESL student.

Booth, David, and Carol Thornley-Hall, eds. *The Talk Curriculum.* Markham: Pembroke, 1991. Eight leading educators, including Yetta Goodman, Gordon Wells, and Judith Newman, share their experience, research and commitment to talk as a medium for learning. From practical suggestions on observing talk, story talk and drama talk, the essays lead to a thoughtful examination of assessing and researching talk.

Brissenden, Tom. *Talking about Mathematics: Mathematical Discussion in Primary Classrooms.* Oxford: Basil Blackwell Ltd, 1988. This book offers help to teachers wishing to break out of the traditional, teacher-led, question-and-answer pattern and provides a program of self-development for primary teachers in the teaching skills needed for discussion-based learning of mathematics.

Brownlie, Faye and Susan Close. *Beyond Chalk & Talk: Collaborative Strategies for the Middle and High School Years.* Markham: Pembroke Publishers, 1992. Through a series of classroom vignettes, this book demonstrates the use of case studies to involve students in collaborative learning and problem solving.

Dwyer, John, ed. *"A sea of talk."* Portsmouth/NSW Australia: Heinemann/PETA, 1991. This book focuses on talking and listening aspects of language and relates talk to the whole program.

Gibbs, Jeanne. *Tribes: a Process for Social Development and Cooperative Learning.* Santa Rosa: Center Source Publications, 1987. This book shows educators how to create a positive learning environment in which students can build on the experience of success.

MacLure, Margaret, Terry Phillips, and Andrew Wilkinson, ed. *Oracy Matters.* Milton Keynes, England: Open University Press, 1988. "Oracy" concerns competence in talking and listening. This book contains selected papers from the International Convention on Oracy at the University of East Anglia in 1987, including the latest work of some of the leading scholars and teachers in the field.

Newkirk, Thomas, and Patricia McLure. *Listening In: Children Talk about Books and Other Things.* Portsmouth, N.H.: Heinemann, 1992. Understanding occurs only when the children "speak over" the words of the authors they have read; their talk, jokes, and stories are an integral part of the learning process. This book highlights for teachers the opportunities for talk in their classrooms.

Reflections

❶ In your own elementary school education, which of the following ways of talking were disapproved of and which were nurtured?

- conversation
- interviewing
- asking questions
- solving problems
- reading aloud
- retelling
- explaining

How successful do you think the approaches to talk taken by your teachers were? With a group of teachers, discuss your own approach to children's classroom talk.

❷ Sketch out occasions you can create in your program for children to interact formally and informally with a variety of audiences: friends, younger or older buddies, members of the community.

❸ Record on tape a conversation between yourself and one child or a group of children. Listen to it with a group of teachers. Did you extend their use of language without interfering with the flow of ideas? Did you act as an interested partner in the dialogue to help the child or children to report on their experiences or voice their thoughts? Did you rephrase and restate ideas from your point of view as listener, thus modelling language usage?

❹ Are contributions from the children expected and welcomed in your classroom? Are there situations that require students to talk in pairs, small groups, and as a class, so that the listening and speaking grow naturally from activities that the children regard as real and important?

❺ What would you include on an observation list to use as you watch the children engaged in talk so that you can reflect upon their behaviour and patterns of conversation as you set up other effective situations?

❻ How can you relate talk to reading aloud for the children, so that they come to understand the importance of interpreting the written word, either their own or that of others, as if they were actually talking? Which of the following opportunities for reading aloud do you use in your program and which others could you most easily introduce?

- reading aloud the stories they write
- rehearsing a picture book for a small group
- joining in chorally with a poem
- reading aloud a story with a partner
- reading with an older or younger reading buddy
- finding in a text and reading aloud a sentence that contains particular information or expresses a particular emotion
- sharing a favourite passage with a group who has read the same story
- reading school announcements or letters written by pen pals to the class
- acting as herald with a royal proclamation in a dramatic context
- reading a prepared speech in an official class debate
- with a group, reading a script or dialogue from a story
- planning, preparing, and taping an interview about a topic in which they have a special interest

❼ Kim, who so loves horses, has a physical impairment that in another time might have meant she would have gone to a special school. The integration of children with physical challenges into regular classrooms has given all children opportunities to expand their personal horizons. We met Kim as she gave a formal talk, but many and more natural preceding interactions had given her the confidence to speak in that situation and to that group. As teachers, how can we develop classroom patterns of interaction that encourage personal development and collaborative experiences for all?

The Role of Drama

I N 1917, CALDWELL COOK published *The Play Way* in England, advocating that students experience literature through drama in order to sense the power of the creative artist at work. The study of drama as an integral part of classroom activity, as distinct from a performance on stage for an audience, had begun. Since then, Brian Way (1967) has described the security that lies in working in role for children when they are free from audience demands. Richard Courtney (1980) has drawn together the theoretical connections between child play and child drama, and dozens of books have been written attempting to define the goals and methods of using dramatic art with young people in educational settings.

The impetus for classroom drama has come from two directions. In the United States, educators have followed up perhaps more directly on Cook's work. They have drawn attention to the greater depth of understanding of story that "acting it out" can bring. Winnifred Ward (1957) encouraged children to improvise in drama, using the plot of a story as a guide. In Britain, the focus has been on the social and psychological learning that can come through role playing. Dorothy Heathcote (1984) altered the position of drama in education forever. She stressed that confronting social issues in a dramatic context leads children to develop empathy as they discover from within how people feel and behave in exacting situations. They also clarify their own ethical viewpoints as, in role, they determine the direction of the drama. Gavin Bolton (1984) has also examined the cognitive and affective growth that comes from taking part in drama as a collective meaning-making activity.

Drama is a springboard for all types of language experiences. It provides opportunities for children not only to talk as they take on roles in the central dramatic event, but also to read, write, and reflect, individually, in groups, and as a community, as they ponder problems posed by the drama and come to recognize the power of the art form.

Jonothan Neelands (1990) and Cecily O'Neill and Alan Lambert (1982) offer practical help to the classroom teacher. Neelands describes a range of dramatic forms and theatrical conventions on which teachers can base strategies to use in collaborative drama. O'Neill and Lambert develop a series of lesson formats for building drama in a number of contexts.

At Queenston Drive Public School, the teachers use drama in every subject area—and for all the purposes suggested here. Indeed, the school provides us with special opportunities to study young people involved in drama. Several of the teachers have taken graduate courses in drama in education, written articles on it, and taken part in classroom-based research. In these classrooms, we can see educational drama in action and the role it plays in social, cognitive, and language development.

Learning in Role

Role play allows children to explore the world without risk; to step outside their own skins and into the skins of others—a cave dweller making fire, a blind person meeting a young kitten, a bully in the schoolyard, an alien landing on Earth from space, a parent of a sick baby—and to discover what these others think and feel. It allows them to try on roles they may assume later in life—scientist, paramedic, civil rights worker, police officer—and to live through events they may fear or hope for all in the knowledge that they can come back at will to the protected and immediate classroom environment. When they improvise, children respond as if the events conjured up by the imagination were actually occurring, however unfamiliar the context and far removed the time and place. As the participants create their roles, they see situations from other people's points of view and can stand back and examine how people's actions, including their own, affect what happens and what might happen next.

Language is one means we use to make things happen in our lives. Drama and dramatic play can provide a setting for all kinds of language explorations. The children are inside the event, using language to express the ideas and feelings they discover there as they work together to create the drama. As they speak in role and listen to other participants, they have reason to notice the inflections and gestures that extend meaning and the strategies that can clinch an argument. Role play also lets them try out different language usages that may lie outside their normal range as they alter their language patterns to approximate those of their characters.

Drama is a medium for "out-loud" thought in which students are free to talk themselves into believing the fiction. In the give and take of dialogue, the statements and ideas expressed demand careful listening, analytical response, and constant clarification. The immediacy of grappling with the tensions and nuances of persuasion, negotiation, witnessing, and narrating creates new understandings of the ways people can use language. The participants express the thoughts of the characters they play, thoughts that are—and yet are not—their own. This process forces them to reframe their own world view as they recognize the truth of what the characters are saying through their own mouths. As they stand in the midst of the action, they see how the very language they use determines that action and brings the reality out of the fiction.

Drama and dramatic play allow children to grow and learn spontaneously. They are vehicles through which children can express their thoughts, develop their imaginations, explore language, and organize and make sense of their experiences.

Dramatic Play

Dramatic play is a natural childhood activity that depends upon language. Talk shapes the theme of the play and helps the participants gain new understandings through interactive feedback. As children get inside their roles, the feeling of the role gives them new ways to gain experience, perception, and insight. Language is not just a by-product: it grows from the play, and forms the play, both together.

Children can use dramatic play to explore possible responses to a particular situation. Many kindergarten and grade one classrooms encourage such play with facilities such as a drama centre; a well-equipped house corner; and boxes, cloaks, hats, toys, and models that stimulate exploration in role.

Exploring through Dramatic Play
Jim Giles

Daniela: *(to Grandma asleep in her chair)* Grandma, can I go to the park? Grandma, wake up, wake up! I thought we were going to the park.

Grandma: Tomorrow we'll go. I have to get my sleep.

Daniela: I thought we were going today! Oh Grandma, come here. I have something to show you. *(Daniela takes her sleepy Grandma by the hand and leads her to an imaginary window.)*

Grandma: *(bored)* Oh, it's just another fire . . . *(She returns to her chair and flops back to sleep.)*

This excerpt was part of a larger work created by two grade one students, Leanne and Daniela. In our family grouping classroom, dramatic play is yet another way through which children make meaning of their world. By stepping into the shoes of other people, they can explore many types of verbal communication, such as questioning, reporting, and justifying. In our room, you can observe this type of play emerging not only at the drama and house centres, where Leanne and Daniela created their "sleepy Grandma" play, but also at centres with puppets, sand, water, blocks, and toys.

Here is an example of dramatic play from a grade two student, Caitlin who was playing alone at the playhouse with four figurines, "Rebecca," "Sally," and two "mothers."

Rebecca: *(Caitlin holds Rebecca figurine)* Mommy, can I go play with my friends?

Mother I: *(She holds Mother I figurine)* Sure, but be careful.

Sally: I'll call my mom. Mom, can my friend Rebecca stay over?

Mother II: All right, as long as you're good.

Sally: My mom said you can!

Mother II: It's time for dinner.

Sally: What are we having?

Mother II: Spaghetti with meatballs!

The girls: Yum yum.

In this short transcript, a child has used her knowledge and experience of home life and friendships in dramatic play. Caitlin's language demonstrates that she knows how to conduct a conversation, reconstruct a relationship, and project her own life into her play. Such dramatic play often becomes the rough draft for ideas that later become practised and polished into short dramas that are shared in class. Many students also take the ideas that arise in their dramatic play and use them in their own story writing.

Dramatic play is a natural activity. We can promote it by giving children opportunities in class and ample time to work through their ideas. If dramatic play is given a prominent place in the activities of the day, the children will use it more and more as a means of exploring and learning.

With appropriate intervention, teachers can help children expand both the language and the themes of their play. They can guide the action, ask the children about what is happening, and even take on roles in the play themselves. Reading stories and poems can stimulate dramatic play. If the class is working on a thematic unit, teachers and students can redesign the dramatic play centre for the theme to encourage particular situations (Paley, 1992).

Much dramatic play takes place naturally; teachers may intervene when necessary, but the children determine the direction of the activity. In Evelyn Bruno's class, the children take dramatic play very seriously and will put a great amount of time and effort into preparing for it. Evelyn Bruno, a teacher at another school involved in the Peel TALK Project, describes as typical the way one group of grade one children planned roles, costumes, and props and reminded each other of the story line before playing out "The Three Little Pigs and the Wicked Witch," which was their own version of the fairy-tale. She points out that children must do a great deal of thinking and talking in order to construct and co-ordinate meaning in shared dramatic play. "We have to work hard," comments one of the children she observed. For children, dramatic play is important work as they use it to make sense of the world. Observing this play will help us plan more formal drama lessons based on their experiences.

Drama and Learning

The distinction between dramatic play and drama is blurred. Drama in the classroom involves elements of play, but the approach is more structured. Roles may be assigned and maintained for a longer period. Planning is more deliberate; the children may work within a specific framework. Imaginative response through movement to narration, simple dialogue, questions and answers in role, and work with puppets may bridge play and classroom drama. After both play and drama, the children can share individual experiences and feelings—further opportunity for language growth.

Directed activities in drama will let children experiment, consider alternatives, and order their environment. Careful structure and intervention can support and guide the children's work without diminishing their own creative direction. Taking on another person's perspective, or "role," trains thinking and the controlled use of emotion. It requires children to translate their learning into statements and actions others will understand. The ability to see from the perspective of another is useful in many situations throughout life.

Drama is the playing out of story. Begin to look at the stories, poems, and books you read your children a little differently. Ask yourself, "Is there a situation I can use to involve the children in the story?" Formulate other questions that may be implicit but unanswered in the story:

- Is there a problem to be solved?
- Are there characters you would like to learn more about?
- Is there action that lends itself to movement or improvisation?
- Can a small detail be the beginning of another story?

- Do the illustrations promote more storytelling?
- Is there a story within the story?
- Are there unexplained events that can be explored?
- Is there a role for you, the teacher, in the story?

Questions like these can lead to role playing, which propels the children into thinking, exploring, and interacting within a framework of attitudes that may differ from or cast a new light on their own. When improvising scenes that arise from a story or poem, they take part in—and expand on—the story's issues, themes, conflicts, and relationships.

Finding the Drama in Your Literature
Sue Ann Checkeris

I have a wonderful memory of sharing a picture book, *The Magic Fan*, with a class of six-year-olds this year. The story is of Yoshi, a young Japanese boy who loves building but who is sad because he believes there is nothing left for him to build. As he sits by the sea, he finds a fan that gives him ideas for new things to build. In the end, Yoshi discovers that the magic of the fan is really his own talent.

These children did not know me, and I was not sure how they would react, but I believed that the beauty of the illustrations and the wonder of the words would captivate them. I had prepared a list of "good" questions to begin the discussion, but a magic of its own happened. At the very moment I finished the story, an eager hand shot up in front of me. Jason announced, "I think we all have magic inside but we just forget it sometimes." Gone was my list of questions!

I asked, "What do you think your magic is?"

"Right now, it's hockey," Jason replied proudly. Six-year-old hands became a sea waving in front of me.

"My magic is dancing."

"My magic is drawing."

"My magic is soccer."

"My magic is puzzles."

Jason had discovered the heart of the story and directly linked it to his own experiences. He dictated how the learning from this story would happen. It was far more relevant to these children than the questions I had planned. Each child began to show me, using movement, what his or her magic was. The children were experts in their magics and wanted to help others learn them. Drama had grown from one piece of quality literature.

Later, their teacher read with them other stories and poems about people with different types of talents. When I returned to this class a month later, the children were eager to share the "magic" books they had written.

Look at the ending to this story by Jason.

On the last day of April Robert watched very carefully all day long, but he didn't see a single rabbit.
Anywhere.
That night, a frog followed him home.

Then, remember Jason and rediscover the magic inside you and your students.

Role playing may also occur in the context of everyday life, as well as in story. The children can imagine themselves members of a community with individual histories, jobs, and relationships. We can let them work toward a solution of a special problem in a community meeting and improvise interviews with the media on the issue. We can ask questions about their roles: "How long have you lived here?" "Where did you learn your job?" Writing in role—a petition to the mayor, a scientist's report—can help clarify and share their understanding of a character they have played.

The Teacher in Role

The dynamics of a drama set up alternative communication patterns, and the context of the drama determines the right to control talk. A teacher who joins in as a member of the ensemble becomes a "true listener" rather than an "evaluator." This alters the communication systems of the classroom and the children's expectations about language suitable to the context. When in role, the teacher has a whole new range of communication strategies available beyond the traditional options of instructor, narrator, and side coach.

The teacher's task within the drama framework is to assist the children in focusing, defining, and structuring events. The teacher thus monitors the learning from within the activity. Role taking by the teacher opens up the language, thought, and social patterns of the class. The initiative for communication is in the hands of the children, and they can select the language that most closely fits the requirements of the situation. Drama allows children to express thoughts and feelings within a social context where they speak and act without personal risk. They are in control of the decisions, from the safety of role. In role, they have the power to practise language codes very different from those dictated by society. Drama demands both emotional and cognitive commitment, which provide stimulus for language exploration.

Exploring Social Conditions through Drama
Larry Swartz

When we were exploring the issue of segregation through Jerry Spinelli's *Maniac Magee*, I decided to use Jonothan Neeland's approach to help the students gain a perspective on the issue through drama. I decided to base the dramatic activity on a real historical event, the moment on December 1, 1955, when Rosa Parks refused to give up her seat on the bus to a white man in Montgomery, Alabama. I started by reading aloud Eloise Greenfield's account of the incident.

I asked the students to think about the visual images and words that had affected them as they listened to the story and then to brainstorm scenes they might dramatize in order to examine the prejudice that Rosa encountered and to appreciate the implications of her actions. The students compiled this list.

- Rosa's day at work
- Rosa's trial
- facing people at work upon release from jail
- scene of the bus—before "No!"/after "No!"
- protest
- church meeting
- media interview with Rosa
- Rosa at home
- Rosa's friends talking about her
- what Rosa thinks about in jail
- convincing someone to take the bus during the strike
- what happens a month later/year(s) later

Because the class felt very strongly about Rosa's "No!" they decided to dramatize the tension of that moment and Rosa's decision to hold to her convictions. One group was assigned the task of creating the bus that Rosa rode, while another prepared the roles of the people who rode the bus that day. Georgette, a young black girl, assumed the role of Rosa, Robbie the role of the bus driver, and Jason and I the roles of the policemen who forced Rosa off the bus. (Casting myself in this way made sense to the students; the teacher is an authority figure. At the same time, being paired with a student brought me fully into the drama and helped them accept me as a role taker just as they themselves were.) After the scene was played, the class discussed the points of view presented by "the blacks" and "the whites."

To move the children into a more poetic frame, we next depicted a scene with Rosa in the jail cell. This time I asked them to create the scenes that ran through Rosa's head as she awaited her trial. I gave the children some time to prepare these as tableaux, and then as Georgette ("Rosa") sat in her "cell," the rest of the class brought the images to life one by one upon a signal from me. We repeated the activity, this time adding words, phrases, or sounds that Rosa might have been thinking to create a soundscape.

In a final discussion, the class shared stories about prejudice and injustice. Some related the East Side and West Side communities described in *Maniac Magee* to the Rosa Parks incident. For the children, Rosa's refusal to move off the bus was analogous to Maniac's determination to stay on the East Side, even though he didn't "belong" there.

Planning for Drama

At Queenston, drama is used by several teachers as a way of learning in many areas of the curriculum, for example, social sciences, physical education, music, and art, as well as language arts. A dramatic activity may take as little as five minutes; a drama-oriented theme may extend over a month.

Teachers may feel they cannot use drama effectively because the classroom provides insufficient space. But many drama activities can be played at or around the children's tables or desks, and this gives children a sense of being on home ground. When the work requires more space, tables can be moved against the wall or even into the hall. If the school timetable permits, working in the school gym encourages flexibility and spontaneity. In suitable weather, the playground can also be used. Wherever drama lessons take place, the circle is an excellent management technique. The teacher has a complete view of the class and can speak to each child directly; the group has unity; everyone has equal access to space; demonstrations can take place in the immediacy of the centre of the circle.

At various times during a drama unit, children can work as partners, in small groups, and as a whole class. Drama lessons fare best if the entire class is involved, even if the children are working individually. Work in pairs or in small groups will stimulate and support thinking and discussion. Drama is for the participants, rather than an outside audience, but the groups may share with each other to demonstrate their work. When the children work as one large group, in a problem-solving, in-role improvisation, they learn to compromise, co-operate, think from the point of view of the whole group and avoid power struggles and personality conflicts.

Some children participate in drama naturally and immediately and should be led to discover more through deeper involvement. Those who prefer simply to observe should not be pressed into activity they find uncomfortable, but should be encouraged to try to learn from the situation—to act as more than "just an audience." Eventually, most will want to participate.

During a drama lesson, the teacher must invite and encourage physical and verbal activity, yet still contain the children's contributions within a meaningful framework. The children must be able to be adventurous and creative and yet work within the rules of the classroom. Teachers must develop their own management strategies in order to help the children make maximum use of drama for learning. Of course, the best management device is to provide content that is interesting and relevant to the children, offering them scope for both emotional and aesthetic satisfaction. Children learn best when they feel committed—when they decide to take up a challenge and reach a goal. To do so, they must understand and accept the plan for attacking the problem. If they contribute to the planning, and if the teacher demonstrably takes account of their contributions, the children will come to own the drama. Co-operative interaction takes time to learn: the group will have a mind of its own, constantly growing and changing.

Various techniques can be used for special purposes. The children can work in slow motion, as in a dream, to govern movement, improve concentration, and increase involvement. Interrupting the action of the drama may help clarify instructions, redefine the focus, build belief, or deal with conflicting emotions. Children can switch roles in order to explore the perceptions of various characters and contrasting facets of the issue being dramatized. They can also take turns in more and less dominant roles. Replaying a drama lesson refines and polishes the ideas that have been explored and allows for new perceptions in the final synthesis. Drama should be approached with energy and the aim of new learning rather than as a rehearsed scene.

Role playing and drama help students discover why people behave as they do. Larry Swartz is a former drama consultant for the Peel Board of Education and uses drama to help make real to children in his class the issues, conflicts, and relationships that arise from a story or poem.

Drama from a Nursery Rhyme
Larry Swartz

Ring a ring a rosie,
A pocket full of posies,
A-tishoo! A-tishoo!
We all fall down.

As a starting point for finding out how a community makes decisions and problem solving in role, I presented this familiar rhyme to the children in my grade four class. (You will recognize a number of the names: many of the children stayed with me for grade five.) We first explored various ways of reading the poem chorally.

I then asked the children what they thought the rhyme meant. What did they know about the circumstances behind it?

Laurie told us that one of her teachers had explained that the rhyme was from a long time ago when people were very sick and died and that's why they all fell down. I added that historians believed that the "ring a rosie" referred to a red ring of rash that appeared on the wrists of people who had been struck by the plague about 300 years ago. They would keep "a pocketful of posies" to ward off any bad luck. "A-tishoo, a-tishoo" was the sneezing that was one of the symptoms of the disease, and "all fall down" meant that the victims couldn't get up again and died.

Patrick said that he was born in Ireland and when he went there a few years ago, people were sick and he had to leave. Ricky told a story he had heard about his great-grandmother who died in Germany, suggesting that she might have died from the plague. (Their offerings demonstrate that young children often have a shaky sense of chronology.) Laurie gave us more details about what she had learned about the plague. Building on these three stories, I explained that the plague had begun in London, but quickly spread to other parts of England.

We then moved toward the drama. I asked the students if they wanted to find out more about the plague and if they were willing to try something that might be very hard to do. "Do you think you can handle it?" I have found that questions like this build commitment. They challenge the students and lure them into the drama experience. In this case, the students were going to have to work at believing that the classroom was the village of Eyam at the time the plague struck and that they were the villagers.

Beginning the Drama

Each table became a house in the village and the students who sat at the table a family or group of people living there together. One table was empty. I asked the class what had happened there.

Sunil replied that the people there had all died.

I asked, "Who lived there?" and they answered, "Jonathan, John, and Carson." In room 208 in 1989, the table did belong to Jonathan, John, and Carson. This led to giggles, and I emphasized that everybody would have to believe that the tables were old houses on a street long ago, but I did not dismiss the names they had suggested. Students often have difficulty choosing names for their characters, and Jonathan, John, and Carson could indeed have been people in Eyam 300 years ago. The challenge was whether the students could build roles around these names or would stick to the identities of the ten-year-olds they knew.

I asked Johanna to look through the window of this house and tell what she saw. She was to imagine that she wasn't a student in a classroom but a villager from 300 years ago.

Teacher: As you walk by the house and gaze in the window, who do you see?

Johanna: I see Jonathan, John, and Carson *(giggles)*.

Teacher: What are they doing?

Johanna: They are eating supper around a table.

Teacher: Who was cooking the supper?

Johanna: Jamie *(a girl in the class)*.

Teacher: What do you know about Jamie Clarkson?

Johanna: She was sick. This was the last meal she served.

In this small bit of improvisation, Johanna was moving from the real world to a fictional world. She could have chosen any names, any characters to reveal, but she kept with the names the class had given her. When she said she saw them eating dinner, she was entering the long-ago "as if" world of drama. Their appearance, the meal, the atmosphere would be conjured up in her mind and the minds of all who listened to her story. Further details did not need to be added or explained. Johanna might easily have answered questions about what they were eating, how the characters were related to each other, or what they might be saying.

Instead, testing their suspension of disbelief, I asked the people in the other houses, "Who knows something about Jamie —have you seen her, or talked to her?" thus building the story of Eyam. Laurie said she had seen Jamie two weeks ago, and she was just starting to get sick with red spots on her wrist. Sunil saw her through the window three days ago, and she was lying down. Ryan said that Jamie was dead.

I brought the students together on the rug and had them clarify the "story" they were creating. As they talked about Jamie dying, about an empty household, about the "scene through the window" they consolidated the experience of the past ten minutes. I then entered the circle in the role of a "wanderer" who had left London two weeks before and needed a place to stay. The children offered to take me to the empty house, though some worried that I might get the plague. When the "wanderer" acted surprised, they tried to downplay the disease and said that I'd be all right there. But I said that I didn't want to take any chances and that I'd be off. The children watched me leave.

Reflection

Out of role, the group discussed how they thought the village should deal with the plague. Where should sick people be kept? How would they feel if a stranger came into their village? Would they be worried about giving him the plague? about him giving them the plague? Would they provide food for him? They agreed that maybe the people would have said nothing about the plague.

I asked if they wanted to replay the scene (a useful technique in drama) and they cleared away the space for me as I entered the village. There was no hesitation about admitting me. When I explained that I was looking for refuge, Ricky said, "You can't stay here, there's the plague." The drama stopped immediately. The children were angry at Ricky for revealing the "secret." We used this circumstance to talk about how people in those times had choices to make: about keeping a secret or getting help.

A Dilemma

Next I told them I was going to try a different role and we would see what happened. This time, I entered the village as a government official taking a census to make sure that no diseased people were being hidden. I commanded each family group to stand and repeat "I swear there are no people in this village who have the plague." I approached Patrick (who didn't seem to take the oath too seriously), made him stand, and told him that if he was caught lying, the blame would fall on his head and he would be dealt with by the king. As a final constraint, I gave the order "No person shall be allowed to leave the village for any circumstance until the plague has been cleared up. We cannot take any chances that the disease will spread. Anyone caught will be returned immediately to their village."

When I approached Sunil's group, Sunil confessed that he was sick. I then built with the children the image of Sunil in his house, dying. Liza put Sunil to rest, tenderly giving him a pillow and covering him with his jacket, Sunil was now the "symbol" of those who were about to meet their death.

Making a Decision

The students now had to think about what they should do with the sick people: Should they put them all together in one house? Who would feed them? Should they ever be allowed to come out of their houses? How could the healthy villagers stay healthy?

The students, as villagers, said that they wanted the sick left in one house. I said that I wouldn't go near them. Some argued that they couldn't be left to die, something had to be done. Johanna, in the role of the doctor, said that she might be able to find a cure. The children argued with her, saying that she could not do anything to heal the diseased people. They worried that she might become infected herself.

As the discussion evolved and points of view were taken, many who had been withdrawing from the drama came back into it to present their arguments.

"We don't care if others die . . . "

"Somebody has to make a sacrifice . . . "

"How long can we wait to find a cure . . . "

"They're going to die anyways . . . "

"Let the doctor take care of them all . . . "

As the discussion grew more intense, I forced the students to take sides: (a) those who wanted to take care of the sick, to stay in the village, to give them food; (b) those who wanted to have no part of helping others, to let the sick die of hunger, and to leave the village.

The children split to either side of the rug. Jonathan and Michael, however, would not take sides. The two boys then walked down a "conscience alley" as each side shouted out its arguments. They eventually came over to the side who wanted to help the sick.

More Reflection

In a final discussion, I asked the students what they thought about their decisions. What could the people have done? Did they have any choices? How did they feel in the drama?

The children discussed the problems of coming to a joint decision and how we handle issues when we don't agree with one another. The learning was taken to another level, which had little to do with the plague, but everything to do with the social dynamics of room 208, which after all was one of the prime objectives.

I asked the students to write to me about how their individual contributions and their work with each other made the drama work successfully. They were to consider three questions: What part or parts of the drama did you like? When did you think it was "drama"? What did you do in the drama? Here are some responses:

Dear Mr. Swartz
I relly enjoyed the Drama a spasaly the Plague. It was like it was hap-pening. right here. My favrit part was when we had to take sides and see what we wanted to do. Not help or help, i pickt i well help . . . It was like i was relly happening. Because i relly happed and the class and Mr. Swize made it realistic. Cause we did almost what relly happed in reel life. I was relly in to it. Because i that it was interesting even as i didt answer every questions.
     Jamie

Dear Mr. Swartz
I thought that you and Joanna were into the drama most. When I was relly in to it was when we were arguing. And I don't just mean you and mean, I mean the hole class. And the most exiting part in the drama was when one of my best friend was on the other side and I was arguing.
     Trevor

Dear Mr. Swartz
My favorite parts were the argument and the decions. The part I did not like was when we were in the families. To tell you the truth I did not dis-like enything. I would like to do the argument over again because they were fun. I think the decions were hard because everybody has to make decions in there life. I think this was a good one for drama. I didn't talk much in the argument but sometimes in the a did let out my feelings.
     Ryan

During the course of the morning I had been listening to the ideas the students expressed, both in role and out of role, and observing how each child accepted or rejected the ideas of others. As a final activity, I roughed out a chart on the board to demonstrate how each person's contribution might be analyzed.

Category 1: Those who were committed to the drama throughout, offering ideas during discussions and understanding the role that was required of them.

Category 2: Those who said little throughout the morning but could be "heard" thinking. These people were listening well and seemed to be working hard to solve the problem for themselves.

Category 3: Those who were in and out of the drama. Sometimes they contributed ideas, at other times they were outside the drama, perhaps fooling around or giggling.

Category 4: Those who contributed little and were reluctant to take the drama seriously. These children might call out comments that weren't useful, or they would play with a neighbour or giggle.

Category 5: Those who seemed to be committed for only a short block of time either at the beginning, in the middle, or at the conclusion of the drama. For these short periods, they would reveal their thoughts, or would pay close attention to the discussion.

This chart seemed to help the students think about their involvement. Many asked which category I thought they fitted in. I used these as examples to help them see what I meant but went on to explain how a person's input can vary for different dramas, for different reasons. This discussion also let the students know that I was doing lots of "kid-watching" and that in drama, everyone must consider how his or her behaviour might affect the work of the group.

The drama exposed them to the possibilities of role playing and provided them with the experience to challenge, within role, make decisions, and communicate their ideas.

Extending the Drama

I referred the students back to the "Ring a ring a rosie" rhyme and asked the groups to create a new chant for the villagers of Eyam to use to frighten away the plague. They discussed what the chant might be, how they might repeat words, some thoughts about the plague that they'd like to describe, and how the chant might be a spell to ward off the plague.

On another day, I conferred with each group, suggesting the repetition of a phrase or the editing of some words to make the piece work as a chant. The groups then shared their chants, and suggestions for revision came from the larger group. They then prepared a final copy.

1.*The plague, the plague*
 We better run, we better hide
 We better lock ourselves inside
 It's coming to get us
 The plague, the plague

2. *People get trapped by the plague*
   Black rats, red spots
   People are dying, victims are lying
   Black rats, red spots
   Children sneak out to play tag
   Black rats, red spots.

3. *We won't play outside today!*
   We won't break the rules today!
   We won't run away today!
   Today the plague scares us away

   We will play outside today
   We will break the rules today!
   We will run away today!
   We will scare the plague away!

4. *Magic magic magic*
   Let the hungry hungry cats
   Get the black black rats

   Magic magic magic
   Let the victims in their beds
   Escape from the dead

5. *A place full of people*
   A pocket full of tears
   Ah tishoo! Ah Tishoo!
   A village full of fears!

Interpreting the Words of Others

If improvised drama encourages children to make discoveries using their own language, reading aloud can help them do so using the language of others. However, the skills of oral interpretation are complex, to say the least. Can we as teachers help children accept the challenge of bringing someone else's words to life? Teachers need to re-examine their motives and strategies for including or excluding oral reading in the language programs of their classes.

Although reading aloud is not necessary for proficient comprehension, it can stimulate learning. It lets children demonstrate their understanding and encourages them to try out new language styles and patterns. Oral reading also verifies print, helping silent readers to "hear" dialogue and trains their eyes and ears in the rhythms of language. Reading a poem aloud can reveal its heart and core. As the cadences of natural speech, alliteration, onomatopoeia, repetition, or rhyme emerge, the children will come to realize that any of these qualities can create poetry.

Before the development of drama in education programs, the dramatic script seemed the most natural vehicle for reading aloud. Unfortunately, reading the script of a play is extremely difficult, especially if it is long or complex. Dorothy Heathcote (1984) points out that it requires students to penetrate someone else's written words and illuminate those words from their own experience. Then, using their memory, observation, and perception, they have to invent characterizations, while remaining true to those suggested by the writer. They also have to memorize and deliver the script to an audience, sounding as if they were creating the lines spontaneously.

To enjoy the script's content and style and to relate it to their own life experiences, not only must the students be able to read the script, but they must not feel locked into one meaning. They must understand that much of the meaning of a play is in the subtext, that which lies beneath the apparent logic of the words. Just as in life, actions and words seem to have an obvious and unambiguous meaning, but underneath there may be a whole range of motives and impulses that support or conflict with the surface.

In any case, few good playscripts for children are available (the writers of children's literature generally choose other genres). However, novels, poems, and picture books written for children are excellent sources of good dialogue that may easily be adapted for oral reading activities. Children can work in pairs or in small groups, reading the dialogue silently and then aloud. Teachers can have the children exchange roles, change the time period, or introduce new settings or new tensions to help them dramatize the selection so that they can discover new meanings in it.

Reading aloud can be connected to drama in four other ways: by sharing well-known selections that have dramatic possibilities, by reading aloud selections that have already been explored and dramatized; by reading aloud in-role items (letters, proclamations, points of debate, songs, and chants) within a dramatic activity; and by reading aloud reflections about a drama from personal journals or from poems and related materials that may lead to further understanding of it. The dynamics of improvised drama thus provide support and real reasons for reading aloud.

"Shared reading" is today's approach to what many of us knew as "choral speaking," with the goal of interpretation rather than performance. Through shared reading, the children can explore the sounds and rhythms of language in poems, songs, chants, and prose excerpts. To enjoy the experience of shared reading, many children need the extra incentive of dramatizing the selection with role play, movement, and improvisation, which help them feel the music and meaning of the words as they bring the author's ideas and themes to life.

Choral Dramatization
Larry Swartz

Construction
by Virginia Schonberg

WHAM!
Comes the wrecking ball.

WHAM!
And the bricks fly.
I see where people lived
In rooms with pale blue walls,
Pale green, pale rose.

WHAM!
A whole wall crumples,
Sinks into red dust.
I see where people have lived.

WHAM!
I see old tables
And a bed.
Where did they go,
The people who lived
In the rooms with the pale blue wall,
Pale green, pale rose?

I prepared this shared reading lesson plan with a junior grade class, and it was included in *Shared Reading 4* in the *Impressions* series. The goal was for the children to explore the poem "Construction" aloud by assuming various roles and to use the poem as a source for improvisation.

We first read the poem in unison. Then I asked the students to read the poem in small groups, varying the pace (slow, fast, with pauses) and the type of voices (loud, soft, excited, sad), and to decide how to share the lines among themselves: which were to be spoken solo, which with a partner, and which in unison.

After they were familiar with the lines and various approaches to them, I instructed the students to read the poem first as if they were construction workers who were tearing the building down and then as if they were the people who once lived in the rooms of the building.

The children discussed which reading they thought was more effective and divided into groups. After time for preparation, I had the groups pair up and exchange presentations. Next the whole class came together and combined their ideas, sharing the lines so that everyone had a part. I suggested they consider the following questions as they prepared the reading:

• Are you all going to be construction workers?
• Are you all going to be the people who have lived in this building?
• Are you going to be a combination of construction workers and tenants?
• Are you going to freeze in position or do mime as others read?
• Can you create some sound effects to add to the construction scene?
• Does it work better to have sound effects being made by some members of the group as the poem is being read by others, or can you find other ways to add appropriate sound effects?

After the class had read the poem together, groups of three or four students prepared short improvisations about the people who had lived in one of the apartments in the building. Group members had to decide who they were, what their jobs were, and how they felt about being evicted. The improvisation was to show the "family" on the day they received the notice of eviction or on the night before they moved out of the building.

The groups shared their improvisations, one group bringing their conversation to life while the others "eavesdropped." We next moved the drama to the moment where the tenants were leaving the building for the last time. I asked everyone to remember one special thing about living in the building or one thought about moving out. I read the poem aloud a line or two at a time as I moved among the students and when I tapped individual students on the shoulder, they interrupted with their thoughts.

Teacher: WHAM!
            Comes the wrecking ball.
Student 1: I was born in this apartment 30 years ago.

Teacher: WHAM!

Student 2: How can I afford to move my family?

Teacher: I see where people lived.

Student 3: I loved reading by that window.

Writing and Drama

Imaginative involvement in drama can be a powerful stimulus for writing, and that writing in turn can serve several different purposes in building and developing an imaginative thematic unit. The best drama, and the most opportunity for linking writing with it, emerges over extended periods, during which children have time and incentive to work their way into a unit, to refocus and change direction; and to edit and present their creations to trusted and understanding others.

The experience of drama itself can affect writing. When children work in role in invented worlds and unfamiliar contexts, their perspective changes. They themselves are creating the learning and are responsible for what occurs. Because drama is an art form that progresses in the classroom as a story does on paper, the process of drama is similar to that of writing. And when children move from drama to story writing and base their ideas on this first-hand experience, they bring new insight and involvement to the play with language that writing requires.

Educating the imagination is a slow process when children work in the written mode. Drama is a catalyst the teacher can use to help children tap resources they may not have known were there. As they enter into problems and conflicts, they imagine themselves as other people, thinking their thoughts, and feeling their responses. They begin to view situations from outside themselves and see the consequences of actions from a new perspective. Once the setting is in their mind's eye and reflected in the lives of the characters they have created, they can transfer these processes to their writing.

Traditional motivations for classroom writing have often not dealt with inner compulsion or felt need, but only with the completion of writing assignments. When writing is embedded in a context that has personal significance for the writer, writing skills will be enhanced. The writer explores meaning through both content and form in a feeling/thought mode, learning through writing, just as children learn through drama. If children are engaged in the expressive and reflective aspects of drama and live through here-and-now experiences that draw upon their own life meanings, the writing that grows out of the drama may possess the same characteristics and qualities.

Writing in role or as a result of role playing lets children enter a new set of attitudes and feelings and at the same time keep their own in mind.

Through the process of writing, participants can give form to their feelings and ideas and learn not only to express their views but to re-examine and reassess themselves in light of the reading audience and its needs. They begin to think of themselves as writers who control the medium in order to say what they want to say to the people they want to reach.

In their writing, students can use their imaginations to travel further into the dramatic situation and let meanings that accrue in the drama reveal themselves. As they try for a more elaborate imaginative understanding of the events of the drama, their writing becomes more complex and their language deepens. And the fact that the writing is often to be used within the drama itself or to be read or listened to by others provides a built-in reason to proofread and edit.

A Medieval Drama
Brian Crawford

The children in my grades three-to-five family grouping had been exploring a medieval theme. I read to them three novels: *Robin Hood* by Sarah Hayes, *The Stained Glass* Window by Penelope Lively, and *The Dragon's Boy* by Jane Yolen. The children kept asking if they could "do a drama" about the period.

They decided that their drama would take place in a castle. To begin, I assumed the role of a leading citizen and conducted a meeting to find out what they knew about castles. The other "citizens" realized that they needed to find out much more if they were to construct their castle. The drama, therefore, had already initiated a "real" need for research. The children compiled lists of questions and gathered information from resource materials. Over a two-day period, construction paper and paint transformed the classroom into a castle.

When the castle was complete, the children felt that they needed to know more about the people who lived in castles. Several volunteered to become "masters" and used the library to find out what they needed to know for their roles. With this knowledge, they prepared training programs for groups of "apprentices." Working in groups of two, three, or four, the masters told their apprentices about their responsibilities. The apprentices were invited to ask questions to get more information about their role (for example, how a page helped a knight train for a joust, what the cook needed to know to prepare a feast).

As the training programs progressed, I borrowed an idea Larry Swartz had used very successfully in his class and, in role as a stranger, I called a meeting of all those in the castle and announced that several deaths had been reported from a mysterious plague that had arisen in the land. The citizens asked some questions, but the "stranger" had few answers and soon departed. At that point, the students began discussing what precautions, if any, they should take and began planning for their future. To end the session, the students wrote a diary entry that their character might have written that night to reflect on their experiences of the day and their concerns about the plague.

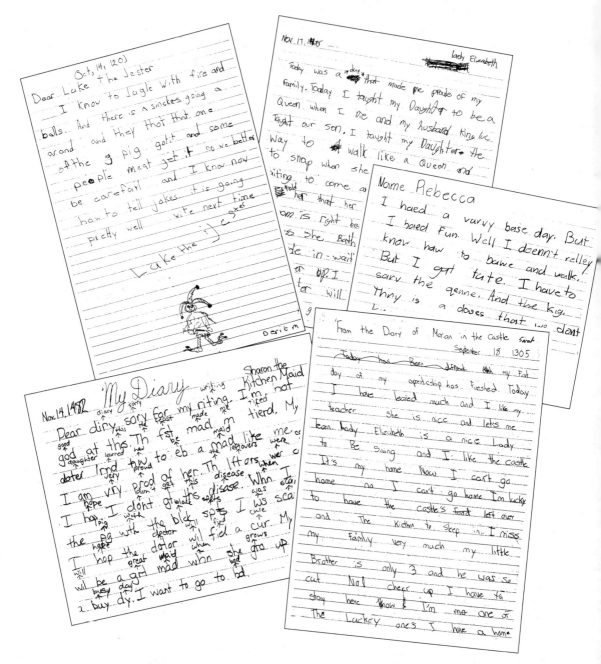

Thus, drama can act as a strong stimulus for writing in an embedded and meaningful context. In drama, the students can explore all of the strategies open to the writer—free writing, journals, letters, interviews, brainstorming, and so on. Many opportunities for collective writing, in which groups collaborate on a mutual enterprise, will also arise. The students can co-operate in collecting data, organizing information, revising and editing within an authentic context for learning.

Reflecting through Drama

It is easy to see that when students distance themselves from the drama for a moment to ponder the implications of what is happening, they will need the tools of reflective language. The implications and applications of the students' words can be articulated legitimately as part of the drama itself (Verriour, 1984). Whatever techniques the teacher uses to promote reflection, they must not interfere with the drama as perceived by the children, but rather allow them to reflect upon it from within the activity. For example, the teacher can freeze the moment, change the setting, or introduce other roles to provide a new viewpoint. As they reflect on their experiences from within the drama, its metaphor reshapes their perceptions of reality at a higher level of abstraction. The impact of the drama leads to a more universal understanding of their own world.

Reflective discussion afterward provides opportunities for children to revisit and rethink the issues and concerns raised in the drama. As children think aloud, they grapple with the language they need to express their evolving ideas and changing opinions. They analyze the motives and behaviour that emerged during the drama and seek reasons and implications for assumptions and decisions they made in role. (Sometimes children will be so involved with the drama that they find themselves still in role when they discuss what happened.) The thought, discussion, and writing that occur after the drama may be as important to learning as what happened during it. As the children look back on what they have done, the teacher can make the learning that has occurred explicit by questioning and deepening their reflections on the implications and consequences of their actions in role. Students may also use drama as the source for private writing in a journal or for visual artistic expression.

Reflection offers a chance to be heard, an opportunity to express ideas and feelings, an occasion for language. While drama is an active, "doing" medium, the reflective mode allows children to make meaning by examining and understanding their thoughts and perceptions both as spectators and participants. "Analogous reflection," as Gavin Bolton (1984) calls it, transpires when students relate the information and feelings gleaned from a drama experience to another situation. This generalization may occur much later and be revealed informally in a seemingly unrelated context.

Drama allows children to use language in the classroom for a greater variety of purposes than many areas of the curriculum allow. Its very nature encourages children to imagine, predict, hypothesize, and evaluate as they explore situations, solve problems, make decisions, create new contexts, interpret new information, and reassess previous attitudes.

In classroom drama, the participants use a variety of thinking/feeling language functions—arguing, persuading, explaining, mediating, and organizing—in an intimate atmosphere free from audience tensions. As dramatic work grows in depth, the students may choose to move into more public and formal modes of speaking in role—addressing the townspeople, speaking to the king, arguing at a council meeting, or presenting their work to an audience. For affective learning to occur, the children must have the power to shape the action and have some say in the outcome of events. Children must recognize that they are using drama in a real context as a true shared learning experience, in which both they and the teacher recognize the importance and value of what they are contributing to the learning situation.

Drama: This Year and Next
Sarah, grade five

1. I learned that when we all are diffrent people it works Better, and when we chosse what to do (witch drama) it works Better and when we are give lots of time to organize.
2. My favourite drama was the movie one Because we could Be any one make any move and lot of time to organize
3. Next year I want to inpove getting into roll this year I was not as good and goofed of Sometimes. Usally I still acked like a 10 or 9 year old when I was supost to be 20.

Stephanie, grade four

1. I learned that we are all Diffrent in Drama, all of us act Diffrent. Some people take it seurouis some Don't. Some people get right in to it and some don't.
2. The Best Drama this year has been the homeless people in the airport, Because I was pertending at times that I was homeless and now I know how some homeless people live and I got right into it.
3. I want to inprove next year is, to put more exsperince next year and to really put my mind on Drama and Drama can really really fun.

Gita, grade five

1. I learned theat Drama is a groups work and you each have to add your own part or it doesn't work. I also learned that any body can act not just people on T.V. and the third thing I learned was to be able to get into role and learn my character
2. The drama I liked best was the movie becuase it let every one have thier own part and it was fun to play grown-up
3. The thing I would improve about was have more time to do drama

Presenting and Performing

Occasions will arise when sharing work with an audience is appropriate. However, presentation is only one particular form of dramatic activity—and a somewhat limiting form at that. Children must be given plenty of opportunities for dramatic exploration in a thinking/feeling mode before they face the problems of communication with an audience. Experiencing, expressing, and performing are different parts of the drama spectrum. For example, experiencing the role of an apprentice pastry cook and expressing that role in interaction with other members of the castle staff requires dialogue with others and in front of others, but without the pressure of being there for their entertainment. The child works in role, and those listening and watching are in role too. The difficulties of performing in "theatre mode" for presentation to people who have not been part of the drama experience must be fully taken into account.

We tend to think of a performance as a polished production for parents. But presenting and performing are also involved in the informal sharing of various groups' work and even within the group. In presentation, the external qualities of the drama for the audience take precedence over exploration and internal growth by the students. The performers must, by definition, be concerned with those who are watching and listening. The language that arises from performance-centred drama tends to be concrete, interactive, and in the present tense with simpler syntactic structures (Parsons, 1984). The pressures of how the performers look and sound also direct the type of language used—the tone and the choice of words. Clarity of speech is paramount (those in the audience must to be able to hear the dialogue). In other words, the children's language will be driven by their need to demonstrate, not by exploring and "living-through" ideas. Formal communication rather than exploratory thought and feeling become the main goal of the work.

Improvised drama makes special cognitive and linguistic demands on children. As children present "themselves" in a fictional context, they must develop both powers of self-expression and communicative strategies. By working inside the drama and in a presentational mode at the same time, they can increase their sense of audience and gain immediate feedback within the imagined context. Thus it may be useful to work in the presenting mode at various points in a drama session. For example, a group may wish to demonstrate its solution to a village problem to the whole class in the role of other villagers. The information presented can be used to further the next phase of the drama work. Meanwhile, the children are exploring the attributes of the actor/audience relationship. For example, when they persuade, argue, or cajole in role within the drama, they must be aware of how others involved in the drama are receiving their message. They must assess the social needs of language—the degree of formality, the choice of words, and the types of sentence structure. They are speaking in public, in front of an audience, from the safety of role.

Booktalk: The Story Leads to Drama
Larry Swartz

The story structure found in picture books, poetry, folk tales, myths, and novels suggests ideas for action, engages the imagination, sets creativity in motion, and stimulates thinking. I rarely teach drama without using literature as a starting point.

When I began teaching drama, one of the first picture books I used was Ralph Steadman's *Two Donkeys and a Bridge*, not only because I found opportunities in the story for movement, interviewing, designing, storytelling, and problem solving, but because it provided the children with an opportunity to understand how a democratic society works and experience how wars might begin and be prevented. The sources that I choose for drama usually invite the children to become members of a community that is forced to make some kind of a decision, whether about a horrible thing that is coming their way (*The Judge* by Harve and Margo Zemach), about a strange creature seeking its identity (*The Bunyip of Berkeley's Creek* by Jenny Wagner), or about an alien society in distress (*Future Story* by Fiona French). *Two Islands* by Ivan Gantschev allowed the children to play citizens of two societies, a utopian one named Greenel and an industrialized one named Greynel, and to solve the problems that the two societies encountered when they visited one another. Ruth Brown's *The House that Jack Built* has no human characters ("This is the meadow where the trees used to grow/ next to the factory that Jack built"), and so the children became members of the community surrounding the factory. By going forward and backward in time through drama, they were able to invent stories about the creation of the factory, the reaction of people to the factory, and the exploration of alternatives to having the factory operate.

Often I choose a source for the many questions it raises. I love the opportunity for exploring stories with a story. Drama allows the children to invent roles to answer the questions a story presents and to weave narratives that extend a particular incident. For example, the illustrations in Chris Van Allsburg's *Mysteries of Harris Burdick* invite speculation. The students assumed the roles of detectives trying to discover the whereabouts of the disappearing author and raised many questions, discovered many roles, and built many new stories. Nursery rhymes, such as "One Misty Moisty Morning," Maurice Sendak's *Hector Protector* are a good sources. The first page of *The Dancing Skeleton* by Cynthia de Felice ("Aaron Kelly was dead and nobody cared.") and excerpts from novels such as *The Iron Man* by Ted Hughes ("The Iron Man came to the top of the cliff/ Where did he come from? Nobody knows.") open the doors to inquiry and storytelling.

I like to take on a role to help the children get inside a story or to challenge them to solve a problem presented within it. For *Weasel* by Cynthia de Felice, I played Willie, who had to decide whether or not to commit an act of violence. The children first played the roles of Willie's friends offering him advice and later that of his "conscience" as he wrestled with his decision. I find the role of a stranger ("I'm new to this community and would like to find out more about . . .") is another convenient way to help the children develop the story line. For instance, I assumed the role of a visitor who wanted to find out more about Lonesome John whose only friend is a scarecrow (*The Scarebird* by Sid Fleischman). Another time I played a visiting relative who wanted to discover what the villagers knew about their neighbour, Miss Moody, who had discovered a mysterious bottle on a beach (*Do Not Open* by Brinton Turkle).

When I choose a source for drama, I look for holes in the story that demand extension or elaboration of the text. When we read *Tillie and the Wall* by Leo Lionni, the class was curious: why had the wall been built to separate the two communities of mice? *Window, Mirror, Moon* by Liz Rosenberg made us wonder why a woman would be stopped in her car examining photographs of her baby.

Recently, I read aloud *The Wretched Stone* by Chris Van Allsburg to a group of grade three children. They were surprised and puzzled when I reached the last page. I asked the children what they wondered about in the story, and Samuel answered, "There are too many things that the author didn't explain. It must be a drama book!"

Suggested Reading for Teachers

Bolton, Gavin *New Perspectives on Classroom Drama.* Hemel Hempstead, Hertfordshire: Simon & Schuster Education, 1992. An alternative guide for the drama teacher, this book highlights classroom drama and offers insight into the basic understanding students need in order to produce a school play.

Booth, David. *Games for Everyone.* Toronto: Pembroke Publishers Limited, 1986. More than 200 imaginative games to help students learn to co-operate, collaborate, and communicate.

Courtney, Richard. *Drama and Intelligence.* Montreal/Kingston: McGill-Queen's University Press, 1990. This book looks at dramatic action as an intellectual and cognitive activity in a way that uses a variety of analytic tools that cross disciplines to focus on dramatic activity.

Courtney, Richard. *Play, Drama & Thought: The Intellectual Background to Dramatic Education.* 4th, Revised. ed. Toronto: Simon & Pierre Publishing Ltd., 1991. Newly revised, this text focuses on the intellectual and theoretical background to drama and the relevance of drama in education.

Hughes, Fergus P. *Children, Play and Development.* Boston: Allyn and Bacon, 1991. The book is written primarily from the perspective of developmental psychology, and the goal in its writing to blend the major theoretical perspectives on play with up-to-date reviews of the research literature.

Neelands, Jonothan. *Structuring Drama Work: A Handbook of Available Forms in Theatre and Drama.* Ed. Tony Goode. Toronto: Irwin Publishing, 1990. This is a practical handbook for drama teachers offering a range of theatrical "conventions" to help initiate, focus, and develop dramatic activity—whether in a workshop situation or as part of an active exploration of texts.

O'Neill, Cecily, and Alan Lambert. *Drama Structures: A Practical Handbook for Teachers.* London: Hutchinson, 1982. This book provides fifteen developing lesson structures on different themes involving pupils in a range of drama and learning activities.

Ontario Ministry of Education. *Drama in the Formative Years.* Toronto: Ontario Ministry of Education, 1984. This teacher resource moves through the different areas of drama in education for young children from goals and aims to drama and play, from classroom management to drama and language, from drama and integrated learning to evaluation procedures.

Paley, Vivian Gussin. *The Boy Who Would Be a Helicopter.* Cambridge, Maine: Harvard University Press, 1990. The author focuses on the challenge posed by the isolated child to teachers and classmates alike in the unique community of the classroom. It is a close documentation of one child's journey from isolation to connection and safety.

Peterson, Ralph L. *Life in a Crowded Place: Making a Learning Community.* Richmond Hill: Scholastic Canada, 1992. This book demonstrates to teachers how to bring students together to create a learning community and discusses how that community functions to influence the quality of learning and life in the elementary and middle school.

Swartz, Larry. *Dramathemes.* Markham: Pembroke Publishers Limited, 1990. The author presents practical lessons in ten thematic units that explore major literacy modes and techniques of drama from games to storytelling to whole-class improvisation.

Tarlington, Carole, and Patrick Verriour. *Role Drama.* Markham: Pembroke Publishers Limited, 1991. In this handbook teachers will discover what role drama is and how it can work successfully in their classroom.

Reflections

❶ Plan ways to incorporate drama into your program so that the children extend and enrich their language and social development by working in role:

- in language contexts to dramatize a poem or story
- in social studies contexts to dramatize particular societal problems and issues
- in response to an overall theme through all the arts—drama, movement, song, painting, and modelling

❷ Share effective starting points for drama with your colleagues, in order to build a set of stimuli for dramatic activity. You might include provocative ideas or questions, scenarios related to—but adequately distanced from—the children's own lives; news items that have moved the children; picture books that require group problem solving; poems that act as cheers, chants, or work songs; themes from history that can be a basis for improvisation.

❸ Analyze and reflect on a specific drama lesson you have conducted, using this checklist to help you reassess your teaching strategies:

- Did the drama engage the interests of the children?
- Did the lesson provide opportunities for the children to work together in a variety of ways?
- Did you take part in the drama yourself in role? Were you able to inject new ideas or refocus the drama from within your role?
- Did you use the available space effectively? Would it strengthen the work to move to another location such as the gym?
- Did you allow the children time for reflection and celebration at the close of the lesson?
- Did you have the children use other language processes, such as reading or writing, in preparation for, during, or in reflection on the drama?

❹ Consider the methods you used to influence the course of the drama lesson and other aspects that affected it.

- What kinds of questions did you use?
- What functions did you yourself play—did you set the scene, act as narrator, monitor the action, work in role?
- Did you change the focus or direction during the lesson? Was the change effective?
- What signals did the children give you that helped you redirect the work?
- What outside considerations governed the drama—time, space, interruptions, disruptive behaviour?
- What changes occurred in class groupings?
- What learning areas did you identify for exploration in future lessons?

❺ Assess the effectiveness of the drama lesson.

- Did the drama stimulate lively discussion in role and reflection after the lesson?
- Was the relationship between teacher and children reasonably relaxed and yet dynamic enough to accomplish the different tasks?
- How committed to the work were the children? How much were they challenged by it?
- How might you use the drama in subsequent lessons?

❻ Drama is often a very good way to bring children with behavioural difficulties further into the classroom community. Consider a child you know who has trouble interacting effectively with other students. What type of role might you ask this child to undertake in a drama that would be within the child's capacity and thereby increase his or her self-esteem?

Such children often make giant strides when school, home, and the wider community work together to help them. How can we develop a school culture that welcomes these children into mainstream classes and offers them enough support to ensure some measure of success in their learning?

Assessing Language Growth

Self Evaluation

DATE NAME

1. Think of one or two pieces of writing that you've done this year.

a. What have you discovered about your writing (at least three things)

b. What has helped you the most with your writing? (at least three things)

2. Think of 1 or 2 books that have meant the most to you this year.

a. What have you discovered about reading? (at least three things)

b. What has helped you the most with your reading? (at least three things)

Roald Dahl

ASSESSMENT AND EVALUATION have always posed problems for language arts teachers: How do we find out if the children are really gaining proficiency with language as a result of our teaching? The traditional approach was to test what was easy to test: understanding of phonographemic relationships, oral reading, grammar, handwriting. In recent years, "it has been increasingly evident that assessments of component subskills are not reliable measures of performance in English, but the effect of these examinations has been to hamper the growth and productive developments of English language arts curriculum" (Tchudi, 1991, p. 5). Such tests provide only partial information—and they provide it too late to be of much use in redesigning a program that has already failed to serve the child. Teachers need assessment tools that will inform their efforts to help young people learn. We also need to be able to describe to parents and administrators what our students actually do with language as a result of the program they are following.

Queenston Drive Public School is developing assessment and evaluation policies for its various divisions. Several staff members contributed to the Assessment Instrument Pool for Language Arts in the Junior Years (1990) for the Ontario Ministry of Education. The ministry is also establishing a series of explicit and detailed "benchmarks" of student accomplishment and a number of staff members are collaborating on the language arts portion of the project. Benchmarks is a term devised by David Jackson (1983, p. 239) to describe specific indicators that offer a clear profile of what children of a certain age can generally do. John Dixon (1987) uses the term "staging points" to describe a similar concept, in which the things a child does with language are viewed as staging points for the next step. Such indicators allow the teacher to focus on the potential for new growth.

This chapter examines techniques for monitoring children's development, selecting effective teaching strategies, and reporting children's progress to parents. The observation guides, checklists, and profiles presented as examples are from *Assessment and Evaluation 1–3* (Booth, Booth, and Phenix, 1991) in the *Impressions* series. The parent-teacher conference records and report card formats are those used at Queenston Drive Public School.

Assessment and Evaluation

We use the term *assessment* to refer to the collection of information about a child, both informally through observations and conferences and formally through inventories, checklists, and tests. Assessment allows a teacher to make well-grounded decisions about what approach to take with a child. *Evaluation* refers to the value judgements the teacher makes when considering this information. The teacher can evaluate the children's progress over a period of time or their level of achievement at a particular point of the school year.

Assessment is an ongoing process of observation and analysis of the children's language behaviour. Children come into the classroom with varying degrees of language ability and progress at different rates. It is, therefore, difficult to establish expectations for the achievement of children at a particular age or grade level. However, all children progress through a series of identifiable developmental stages and patterns of behaviour. Language growth is a continuum, and each child's progress can be monitored along this continuum. From the time the child first comes to school, notes based on observation and assessment should be kept every year to build an individual portfolio: a full record of growth and development (Graves and Sunstein, 1992).

In order to appreciate each child's language competence, needs, and learning potential, the teacher should have as much information about the child as possible. Contact with the home through visits, conversations, and letters will help build a larger picture. The teacher can observe and talk with the children individually in various classroom situations, using these observations to record accomplishments, skills, knowledge, attitudes, language growth, and interests. Marks and rankings achieved in test situations offer little practical help in the assessment of individual children, but formal reading and writing conferences for assessment purposes, reading logs, and folders of writing samples are invaluable.

In the light of our understanding about the ways language is used and of the developmental learning stages children pass through, the teacher can then use this amalgam of information to evaluate the child's progress. The difference in intent between assessment and overall evaluation means the teacher should maintain a balance between daily observations that focus on the child's needs in the classroom and record keeping as the basis for making reports or recommendations about the child to parents, administrators, and other teachers.

We assess the children's reading in order to identify their strengths and needs and to monitor their reading progress. To develop a comprehensive assessment of a child's reading performance, the teacher should observe and

I read a newspaper because

Newspapers a Reading Adventure

Kid thinks newspaper is for adults
Different headlines
Different stories
Different everyday
Read intresting things
Index
Diffent Sections
Art Book Reviews, Classified Ads,
Puzzle entertainment, Home, S
Travel, weather
Different on every page

News stories, editorials
Around Worth
Things that happened
Editors figure out
Reporters get facts
Research
Write story
Reporter tell where you
from
Don't need to read whole article
Headlines tell what story about
Style upside
First paragraph called lead
has all five questions answered

Editorials
Opinions about news
Tells opinions
Other points of view
Write Editorials
Letters to Editors

Features
To Entertain
Inform you
people, science, how
to do things

Syndicated art
Advertisements
Individuals
Weather on late
Tempature in ot
Important
You get inform
other parts
and you car
date to wh
in the world.
And I like
page and
You can find
is for Sale

There are diffent stories
There are intresting articles
You can see the
of other people opinions
There are diffent Sections
They have a variety of

Importance of a newspaper

A news paper is important because
you can get information from other
parts of the world.
In advertisement it is good because
you can save money.
A newspaper has a variety articles
Editorials is good because you can
find out what other people's opinions
are.
Features are to inform and entertain
you
There are different things in features
like people science, hobbies, how to do
things, and comics.
News Stories tells you about
things happening around the world.
Headlines tell you what the
story is about

record data that demonstrate a child's reading growth and his or her reading strategies and then develop an effective reading program for that child. Reading assessment should consider the child's progress and development as a reader; the quality, range, and quantity of material the child reads across the various curriculum areas; the pleasure and involvement the child finds in reading, alone and with others; the strategies the child uses in reading; and the child's ability to reflect on what he or she has read. The child's knowledge of the reading process and self-assessment of his or her reading proficiency should receive particular attention. Teachers' records and observations of children also contribute to overall reading program assessment and plans for the future.

In assessing writing, teachers need to be aware of the approach individual children take to the writing process. Do they work things out mentally before writing or do they, like James, put any and all ideas down on paper and then edit and revise? Knowing which approach a child favours can alter the teacher's perceptions. Early drafts may provide insight into a child's difficulties with writing, but of course, the final version is what the writer intends should be read, and in evaluating writing, the teacher should give most weight to that. An emphasis on errors will not help children develop competence as writers; the teacher should rather document and praise their use of various problem-solving techniques. Assessment of children's development as writers should consider not only the understanding the children demonstrate of the conventions of composing and transcribing, but also the confidence and independence they show when writing alone and collaboratively with others, the range and quality of their writing in various curriculum areas, and the pleasure and involvement they find in writing material of all types—stories, poems, letters, non-fiction.

Speaking and listening assessment should consider how the children talk in different social and curriculum contexts, the ways they use conversation and discussion for learning and thinking, the range and variety of oral expression available to them in particular situations, their confidence in speaking in various settings, and their ability to listen to, understand, and appreciate the words of others.

We want children to see role playing as a natural extension of the world of play. We also want them to recognize drama as an art form—with power and strength in making personal and collective meaning—and to learn to work with the subtleties of role in communicating their ideas and feelings. We can assess children's growth and development in drama in the following areas: their participation in the drama, their ability to work co-operatively, their use of language, their understanding of the issues being explored, and their growth in sharing ideas and feelings in role. However, assessing all the information that comprises learning in drama is extremely difficult. Drama is an internal and personal process as well as an external and public form, and teachers may find themselves trying to single out, observe, and assess individual students in the midst of a busy and confusing shared activity. Videotaping drama will allow a more leisurely examination of the activity.

Assessing Both Children and Program

Assessment is an ongoing process in which all members of the classroom community participate. The teacher helps students to become conscious of the learning process and to take an active role in monitoring progress and in making plans for the future. At the same time, the teacher is also evaluating the success of his or her own teaching and monitoring student needs and interests, and the programs and resources available to meet those needs. As teachers and students assess progress, they can modify the curriculum appropriately.

Effective assessment strategies are holistic; they are concerned with the child's actual work in order to avoid fragmenting either the language or the learning process. We assess natural language activities in contexts that are meaningful and relevant to the learners, drawing on what they can do so that the assessment reveals their competence and helps us plan curriculum. Assessment must allow for variations in the background and development of the learners in the class, and be "consistent with the best scholarship on language, learning, teaching, and curriculum" (Goodman and Hood, 1989).

Each child should be assessed as an individual and his or her growth carefully documented. The teacher can gain important information regarding a child's growth and consequent needs through individual and group conferences. The information gathered during observations and conferences provides the basis not only for individual, group, or whole-class instruction, but also for drawing up with the children learning contracts that actively involve them in their learning as they negotiate the tasks they are to accomplish.

When we think about assessment and evaluation, we should keep Walter Loban's warning in mind: "The curriculum inevitably shrinks to the boundaries of evaluation; if your evaluation is narrow and mechanical, that is what your curriculum will be" (1986). Assessment has a profound impact on all aspects of learning and teaching. It directly influences a student's perception of learning and commitment to the goals of the program. Consequently, to contribute to a strong and vibrant language arts program, the techniques of assessment must reflect the actual learning situations of the classroom. The converse is also true: to provide meaningful assessment and evaluation, the learning situations must reflect a broad curriculum connected to real-world experiences.

Two important aspects of the students' learning are self-assessment and peer assessment. If the children are taught to react to their own work, they may provide insights into their own learning that are not visible to the teacher as "kid-watcher." In a healthy environment, children are encouraged to talk, to read, to write, and to collaborate with others; in taking ownership of the work, they monitor and assess it with one another, learning and growing from the discussion and group feedback.

Effective assessment tracks and records a child's development and progress in practical ways. It includes frequent opportunities for recording significant observations about a child's special qualities, unique or apt comments and ideas, and personal discoveries. Making extensive use of self- and peer-assessment techniques helps ensure that the form of assessment is appropriate to the task, the kind of learning, and the stage of learning and that it focuses on the child's actual use of language rather than performance on standardized tests.

Assessment in the language arts includes assessment of the program itself. We need to ask, "To what extent are the goals of our language arts program being realized in my classroom?" The information that we collect to evaluate the children's progress can also be used to evaluate the program's effectiveness; we can assess the program through observation, recording, reflection, and analysis and make adjustments accordingly. Although a teacher can undertake a program assessment independently, it is often helpful to invite colleagues or administrators to participate. Networking can provide great insight.

Everyone involved needs to understand the process of evaluation: children need to know beforehand how, when, and for what purposes they are being assessed; parents need to understand the details of the evaluation system, to receive immediate information about unusual developments in their child's progress, and to discuss and contribute to the evaluation at regular intervals; teachers working with the same children need to agree on common principles, to ensure that evaluation procedures remain consistent, and to confer regularly; principals should be kept informed, especially about individual children at risk. Teachers should emphasize positive feedback to all concerned: to children through response journals, notes, conferences, and casual conversations; to parents through telephone calls, notes, newsletters, and meetings; to other teachers and principals through regular meetings, notes, and conversations.

In a language-based classroom, then, assessment de-emphasizes formal measures of the mastery of skills in favour of observation of the children in the context of meaningful language use. The teacher looks for "error" not as a sign of failure but as a clue to the better understanding of the child's stage of language development and a guide to what to do next. Thus, ongoing observation becomes the basis for planning instruction. The teacher accumulates information about the child through student writing folders, conferences, and the use of observation guides and checklists.

Observing Children

Observation is the link between theory and practice. Theory and research form the knowledge base that guides teachers' observations and assessments. Observation gives us an immediate impression about the students' talking, reading, and writing abilities, their awareness of books and their social development. Impressions formed during observations can be recorded and kept along with dated samples of work in each child's portfolio. When teachers work in team situations, each can refer to the portfolio as well as share and discuss their observations. Samples of work serve to provide not only teachers and parents but also the child with evidence of day-to-day victories and long-term progress. Queenston teachers use two common techniques: observation at a distance and close-in observation when the children are reading and writing.

Observation at a distance involves periodically taking five minutes or so to stand to one side and watch the children as they go about their activities. The teacher explains the procedure to the children so that they know they should not interrupt at this time. When observing reading, the teacher can consider both individual children's reading behaviour and the way the overall reading program is working: Do the children select appropriate books easily? How many are actually reading? How long do they read? Do some of the children get out of their seats? What do they do? Similar concerns can be addressed when observing writing activities at a distance: Are the children using writing materials effectively—paper, writing instruments, and resource books? Do they feel free to get out of their seats to help or request help of others? How many are actually writing and do those who are not doing so seem to be engaged in productive pre- or post-writing activities?

Close-in observation of a single child involves observing and noting the child's behaviour for five minutes or so while he or she is reading or writing. When conducting close-in observation of reading, the teacher can consider whether the child shows interest in the book; what reading strategies the child appears to be using; which aspects of reading seem to come easily and which seem difficult; what the child does when the book is finished. Observing a single child engaged in writing allows teachers to consider how the child uses the page; whether the child composes while writing or pre-rehearses the piece mentally; how the child handles problems of transcription or composition; and which aspects of writing seem to come easily and which with difficulty.

Assessment cannot be an isolated event that takes place at the end of the year or just before report cards are sent home. Observations should be made and recorded in various learning situations throughout the year. This requires planning: too many teachers discover in mid-November that they have records of observations on six individuals out of a class of 35. If they are to provide an accurate picture of each child's progress, teachers should plan to record observations on one or two children each day or to set aside one day a week or one week a month to concentrate on observation while the children continue their normal activities.

Gathering Information for Portfolio Assessment

In the classroom, students should be aware that both they and the teacher have reasons for keeping records. Students need to keep records in order to keep track of the books they have read, the pieces they have written and published for the classroom or home audience, and the tasks they have completed and to plan the tasks they need to complete. They should understand that the teacher keeps records in order to monitor all students' progress and to be aware of individuals' needs and interests—and that these records will be used to plan instruction, set tasks, provide materials, organize groups, and, last but not least, report to parents.

Shared task-setting and record-keeping responsibilities create a more functional language environment. Both teacher and student are engaged in recognizing needs and in acknowledging success. A carefully documented assessment system provides the teacher and student, as well as parents and administrators, with useful information concerning each student's program.

Assessment of a child's understanding of literacy and speech can be based on a comprehensive individual portfolio of both the teacher's and the child's observations along with the child's work—lists of books read, photocopies of reading response journal entries, writing samples, and art. Such a portfolio allows the teacher to demonstrate each child's interests and level of functioning and also to identify any difficulties the child may have in order to provide appropriate action. Teachers need to use a variety of tools to gather the necessary information so it will be readily accessible. Page references in the sections that follow are to *Assessment and Evaluation 3*.

Inventories and Profiles

Inventories can reveal a child's feelings and attitudes toward various aspects of the language arts and help build a complete picture of each child's background by revealing activities and interests, both in and out of school. This information provided by the children themselves may suggest ideas for theme activities or topics for discussion, drama, and painting. The children, with help from their parents, can first complete an inventory such as "About Me" (pp. 53-59) when they start school and then update it at the beginning of each year. The children can provide a great deal of more specific information about their tastes, feelings, and attitudes through reading and writing inventories (pp. 67–68, 161–162), and teachers can record the types of material the children actually read and write in reading and writing profiles (pp. 69–70, 163–164). These instruments help the teacher get to know the chil-

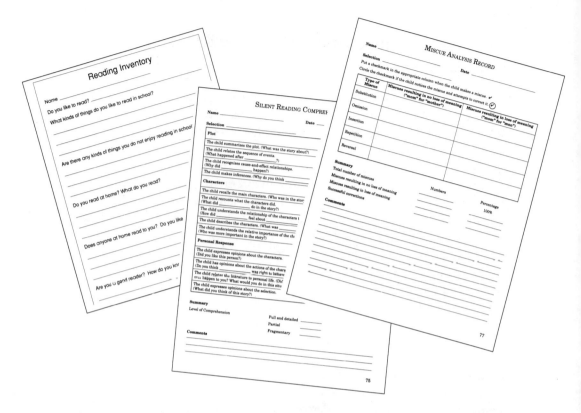

dren, who may themselves find it interesting to review the comments they made in previous years to see how their views have changed. During the year, children can analyze their own interests, strengths, and problem areas through records such as "My Reading" and "My Writing" (pp. 149–150, 181). More spontaneous response journal entries will pour light on information gathered from other methods of assessment. Teachers can also consult with the school librarian and the children's parents about reading habits outside the classroom. The children's own thoughts about how they can make their writing better add to their own awareness of the writing process and to teachers' understanding of the pleasures and difficulties they find in writing.

Anecdotal Records

In-depth anecdotal observations about the day-to-day interactions of children can serve as a record of how and what they are learning in the classroom. Many teachers keep at hand index cards or a conveniently sized note pad to capture these moments so that records over a period of time can be included in the portfolio.

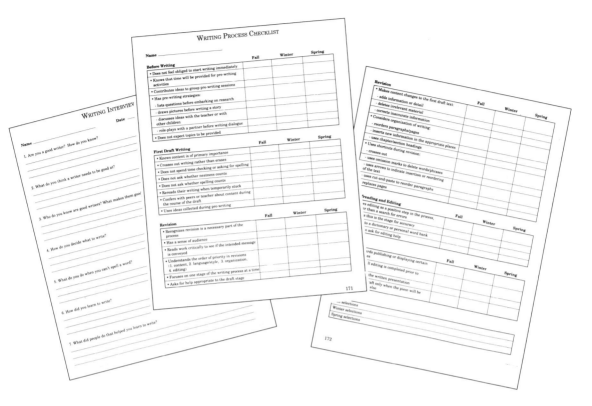

Audio and Videotapes

Analyzing audio and videotapes of the children's work can help the teacher gain insight into the dynamics of a discussion group and become aware of individual children's strengths and weaknesses. Teachers find it particularly useful to review auditory and visual records when they have been participating in classroom activities such as drama because these records allow them to assess their own actions and their effects as well as those of various students. Tapes can also help teachers to assess their skills in conducting conferences.

Observation Guides and Checklists

The teachers can use observation guides to note each child's language behaviour and level of functioning, as well as to plan appropriate activities and experiences. Checklists and observation guides used several times over the year can enhance observations by reminding the teacher to consider all aspects of language proficiency and by demonstrating the students' development over time. For example, reading and writing observation guides (pp. 73–74, 167) provide a framework for observing children's reading and writing

behaviour and their understanding of the processes and strategies involved. At first, few children are likely to exhibit many of the behaviours listed in the guides, but trends will emerge over time. Speaking and listening and drama observation guides (pp. 61–62, 191–192) provide a similar framework for observing children's behaviour, use of language, and comprehension in various speaking, listening, and expressive situations. Successful talk and effective drama are largely matters of experience: children's abilities will develop as they explore through talk and drama in a supportive environment.

Checklists are indicators only. For example, it is unlikely that any one child will fall neatly into one stage or another of reading development at any one time (pp. 147–148), but the check marks will tend to fall in one stage or another. The writing process checklist (pp. 171–172) assesses children's knowledge of the steps involved in producing a piece of writing. As children take different approaches to writing, however, no one child is likely to exhibit all the behaviours listed; in addition, some behaviours will "disappear" as the children internalize them, while others become more prominent. The checklist is useful, though, because it allows teachers to consider various stages of the writing process at various times and help children to focus on appropriate aspects of their work so they will not be discouraged by wasting time and effort. Assessment of story writing (pp. 173–174) cannot be regarded as a formula for good story writing—no story will demonstrate all the features listed—but the information may lead to useful discussions during writing conferences and also form the basis for an evaluation of a child's ability in story writing. Summaries of each child's growth in story writing can then be made at the end of the year.

Some checklists are meant to be used with some children only. The writing behaviour profile (p. 169) examines how a child works on a specific piece and is designed for periodic use with children who do not seem to write productively. One way to use the profile is to select a small number of children for observation, record what each child is doing at intervals of about five minutes, and note whether the activities are constructive to the task at hand. For example, sitting silently may mean the child is planning the writing—or avoiding it.

Transcription skills lend themselves to the sort of quantitative assessment that checklists can provide, but teachers must interpret them with care. The spelling observation guide (pp. 175–176) is useful for recording progress from the time that children's spelling can be easily read and understood. Tallies to indicate the children's understanding and use of conventions of print (p. 177) can contribute to reports on children's achievement and progress and to plans for appropriate instruction.

Checklists are also useful for program assessment and planning (pp. 63, 65, 157–158, 159-160, 187–188, 189–190). They provide a visual record of the opportunities the children have had with various language experiences and thus help the teacher plan which areas to stress in coming weeks and point out possible deficiencies in the program that might be the topics for discussion with other teachers or further professional exploration.

Miscue Analysis

Conducting a miscue analysis (p. 77) may offer the teacher more information about children who seem to have difficulty with reading comprehension. It allows for detailed observation of the strategies children use when they read and highlights how successful they are in using the pragmatic, semantic, syntactic, and phonographemic cueing systems. The most common miscues are a result of the substitution of another word for one in the text, the omission of a word or phrase, the insertion of a word or phrase where none appears in the text, or the reversal of words or phrases. The teacher should be wary of the temptation to interpret results too rigidly: miscues can reveal reading strengths when, for example, the reader substitutes "mom" for "mother," having grasped the meaning before pronouncing the word. Such an analysis should always be interpreted in the light of an assessment of the reader's overall comprehension of the story.

Conferences

The teacher should meet with each child informally to assess language growth and to share the child's reading log and writing folder. Keeping a comprehensive record of all reading and writing conferences in the portfolio can provide insightful information about the child and suggest topics or points of interest for further consideration. The teacher may wish to conduct diagnostic reading and writing interviews (pp. 71–72, 165–166) during conferences with children who are having limited success.

Writing Folders

Folders containing a range of writing over time enable the teacher to monitor writers' growth and development, identify their strengths and needs, and plan appropriate instruction for an effective writing program. Folders also provide significant information to share with parents. It is, of course, much more valuable to assess work written in a natural context for a real reason than work written for the sole purpose of being evaluated. Therefore, writing folders should contain writing from all curriculum areas. Writing folders are discussed in more detail in Chapter 5.

Student Self-Assessment

Children should be involved in the assessment process through conferences, response journals, and reflective discussions about feelings and attitudes with peers and teachers. Knowing that their own opinions contribute to assessment puts children on the path to autonomous learning. It helps them become aware of their own development, to know exactly how much they know, and to establish realistic learning objectives. The teacher should seek the child's permission before making and keeping copies of personal journal entries in the portfolio.

Formal and Informal Tests

In most classrooms, formal testing also occurs, but if the information that tests provide about a child's development does not largely confirm what is already known to the teacher from daily observation, there is an obvious mismatch. Either the test is not relevant to the program, the teacher's skills in observation need to be honed, or the program itself is inadequate.

Tests can only be useful in assessing the features of learning that are measurable and can be reduced to some sort of score. This makes them

SELF EVALUATION - FALL TERM (Family Grouping)   Grade: 1 / 2 / ③   Fall Term

Chris Q

P Part of the time   **N** Not Yet

J Almost Always

1. I am a good listener — A
2. I try to do things by myself first — A   A
3. I follow instructions — A
4. I play and get along with my friends — A
5. I am polite and use manners — A
6. I am tidy — A   A   P
7. I am responsible — A
8. I ask questions in school — A
9. I share my ideas in class and during carpet time — P
10. I always try my best — A

11. I enjoy reading and books — A
12. I practise my reading everyday — A   A
13. I can write and spell words by myself — A   A
14. I enjoy writing time (stories, letters etc.) — A
15. My printing can be easily read by others — A
16. I enjoy math and science — A   P
17. I can solve most of the problems I have — P

18. My favourite activity is — LEGO
19. I am good at — MAth
20. My favourite story is — the ALevth AWR
21. The one thing I want to do better is — RedIn

Chris
(signature

What does one have to do in order to be a good writer?

To be able to not worry about time. And be able to express his/her feelings on a piece of paper.

In the past six weeks, how have you changed or grown as a writer? What have you discovered about yourself as a writer? What have you discovered about your writing?

I discovered I wasn't as dry as I thought I was. I also learned I never lost the knoweg to make a magazine.

What has helped you the most in your writing?

I think conferences and brainstorming. Conferences help you get other peopl's opinions. And brainstorming helps you get organized.

What does one do in order to be a good reader?

To not worry about words he/she does not understand.

In what ways are your reading and writing connected? How does one affect the other?

This is an easy one. You read something an it triggers a memory or an idea. Reading gives you lots of ideas.

---

at math centre Andrea Boby chris and I were making a citty out of patrn blok's afte recec. Whne wewer tideing up I got a bit mad becos ↑ Andrea did not clen mr g. is side to clen up yor centr yor resoncab for so I spok to Andrea and She Saide nono ng the

At math centre Andrea, Bobby, Chris, and I were making a city out of pattern blocks. After recess when we were tidying up, I got a bit mad because Andrea did not clean up. You're Mr Giles said to clean up your centre. You're responsible for [it]. So I spoke to Andrea and she said no no no, the centre [is] your group[']s].

I have not done to good in spelling but the minny lesons really helped me to understand how to spell them but I sometims think that there boring and I yoused to think they were a waiste of time but they relly helped me in my reading and spashly my writing and I don't have to do as much editing with the teacher and I don't have to wast oter time and get it done faster so I can have a publeshed piece.

Yours Truly

Cameron

more useful in "content" areas than in language arts and other aesthetic areas of learning. For the most part, they can examine only specific, often isolated, language skills. They must therefore be interpreted with care and in the context of the full language program. The teacher must also be aware of reasons why individual students may perform poorly on a test given at a set time—reasons can range from sore fingers to emotional problems at home to excitement over tickets to the ballet or tonight's baseball game.

The results of external tests are particularly equivocal. There may be valid reasons why a class does not perform according to the norm or the criterion for such a test (for example, a large proportion of children in the class for whom English is a second language), but these should be identified—and, if necessary, teaching and/or observation methods adjusted accordingly. Less formal tests devised by the teacher may help establish whether certain immediate goals of the language arts program are being met.

It is important to ensure that children understand that the teacher uses tests as a double-check on the program rather than on individual students. If the teacher can establish this, tests will be viewed in a co-operative rather than competitive spirit.

A Language Growth Profile for Each Child

Using the strategies described in this chapter, teachers can collect for each child's individual portfolio data that will enable them to develop a comprehensive language profile as the basis for more formal assessment and evaluation—reporting to parents, determining the need for special resources, informing next year's teacher, or developing a special program for the child. Once a system for cumulative information is in place, recording findings and observations will become part of the normal routine, offering teachers resources for effective and professional assessment.

For assessment to be useful, teachers need to be aware of what they are looking for. A detailed profile of the behaviours that demonstrate language growth thus clarifies the goals of assessment. I offer the following suggestions as starting points for teachers to develop their own language profile outlines. To ensure continuity, teachers within a particular school division or even the entire school should arrive at such profiles together. Queenston includes parents on its assessment development committees to ensure that evaluation procedures meet their needs and will have community support.

A Reading Profile

A child who is involved with books and other print resources
- is aware of a variety of reading materials, in language arts classes, other curriculum areas, at home—books, environmental print, etc.
- listens to and appreciates literature read aloud, at home and at school, "live" and on tape
- distinguishes between different kinds of reading materials—fiction, non-fiction, etc.
- participates in shared reading
- looks for favourite authors and illustrators
- has a positive attitude toward reading, at home and at school
- chooses books appropriate to reading ability and interests
- selects books by browsing, reading the first few pages, etc.
- uses a variety of cues for choosing—number of pages, length of book, size of print, format, difficulty, ratio of dialogue to narrative, etc.
- checks with previous readers of the book
- selects books for enjoyment and satisfaction
- increases the volume of reading
- has books on hand—owns books, visits public library
- rereads favourite books
- reports about reading books at home

A child who is demonstrating successful reading behaviour
- focuses on print (directionality and word awareness)
- reads silently for meaning
- uses pragmatic, semantic, syntactic, and phonographemic cueing systems
- uses more than one strategy with new words
- predicts, using informed guesses
- self-monitors reading and self-corrects where appropriate
- chooses to read voluntarily
- is not interrupted by minor distractions
- reads intensively for an appropriate period of time
- demonstrates sustained engagement with books and other texts
- persists with challenging texts
- wants to continue reading when time is up
- reads with independence and confidence
- responds with suitable emotion—laughs, cries, smiles
- reads alone, in small groups, with the whole class

A child who is making personal connections with text
- shows personal involvement in conferences and in the reading response journal
- discusses books, magazines, and other print materials
- expresses strong feelings about issues and events in a book
- gives opinions about the characters' actions and statements
- seeks meaning in both pictures and text
- draws on personal experiences and earlier reading experiences in making meaning
- gossips about books and recommends them to others

A child who is making textual connections
- compares a work to others of the same and different authors
- asks questions and seeks out the help of others to clarify meaning
- predicts and anticipates what will happen in the story
- attends to multiple levels of meaning
- searches out and values the perspectives of others
- verifies and clarifies ideas by quoting from or referring to the text
- modifies interpretations in light of new information
- infers relationships in the text
- contributes tentative ideas to a discussion and is ready to benefit from feedback
- goes beyond plot summaries in writing and talking about the text

A child who understands the art of reading
- uses techniques found in reading material when writing
- is able to offer an assessment of personal reading strengths
- enjoys and participates in reading conferences
- is aware of how text structures work—story, poem, essay, etc.
- is intrigued by how authors present material
- refers to the author's techniques when discussing text
- reads critically—appreciates and evaluates wider meanings
- reads at variable speeds, rereading for clarification or pleasure and skimming and scanning to locate information
- uses the table of contents or index to find pertinent information
- abandons a text after a fair and appropriate attempt to read it
- seeks to find meaning in text that at first seems ambiguous or contra-dictory to personal experience
- chooses to read aloud for a group, interpreting characters and mood
- confirms meaning drawn from text by responding in a variety of modes—retelling, writing, painting, etc.

A Writing Profile

A child who is interested in writing
- understands the relationship between talk and writing
- shows an understanding of the structure of stories
- is aware of written language—environmental print, messages, books, etc.
- shows an understanding of the conventions of writing words down
- demonstrates pleasure and involvement in the act of writing

A child who is demonstrating successful writing behaviour
- voluntarily chooses to write
- is confident and relaxed when writing
- writes with reasonable speed
- contributes to group writing
- sees the value of keeping a journal
- chooses to share writing with others–publishes and displays writing

A child who understands the writing process
- demonstrates a wide range, quantity, and variety of writing in all areas of curriculum—writing stories, messages, notes, lists, reports, etc.
- uses a variety of pre-writing strategies—discussion, research, role playing, etc.
- understands how to approach a first draft—gets down ideas, confers, etc.
- understands the function of revising—reads work critically, makes content changes to the first draft, reorders paragraphs, etc.
- takes pride in the presentation of the final draft—proofreads and edits, confers, and uses dictionaries, word banks, etc.
- uses diagrams and drawings to accompany the writing
- understands when neatness and correctness are important
- is aware of the audience in developing the writing
- relates the writing to recent reading material
- has a grasp of the conventions of spelling and punctuation

A child who is growing as a writing
- uses a widening range of forms
- works toward more complex narrative and non-narrative forms
- shows an increasing control of form—in stories, poems, research reports, etc.
- displays an increasing confidence in writing
- is developing a personal voice as a writer
- is able to manage the writing of longer and more complex text
- reveals a developing sense of the reader's needs
- is developing control of standard spelling and punctuation
- learns by experience how to lay out a text attractively on the page
- is developing control of handwriting and a personal style

A Talk Profile

A child who is comfortable in social (listener-related) situations
- enjoys the company of others, and shows confidence and ease in a variety of speaking and listening situations
- talks about personal experiences and reveals feelings
- interacts with others at recess, on the way home, at lunch
- welcomes visitors, etc.
- initiates conversation with the teacher
- works co-operatively and collaboratively with other people in various settings
- listens to stories read aloud by peers, teacher, and on tape

A child who works well in co-operative (task-related) situations
- talks in the process of learning and thinking
- takes turns during talk
- asks relevant questions
- brainstorms and explores themes
- builds on the talk of others
- recognizes points of view
- justifies decisions and actions
- mediates and resolves tensions
- looks for alternative solutions
- suggests new lines of discussion
- carries the discussion forward
- relates new to known information
- modifies and adapts ideas
- accepts or adopts the role of group leader when appropriate
- organizes activities
- interviews school guests effectively

A child who is comfortable in communicative (audience-related) situations
- presents information to groups and the class
- gives instructions
- makes announcements
- tells stories and personal anecdotes
- summarizes and reports on group work
- offers a personal interpretation when reading aloud
- gives book talks and reviews
- works well with younger or older partners
- recognizes the factors that make communication effective

A Drama Profile

A child who is exploring ideas and feelings in role
- accepts the confines of working in role
- participates in drama activities verbally and non-verbally
- represents ideas and feelings in role
- identifies with the attitudes of the role
- demonstrates engagement with and committment to the drama

A child who responds to and communicates with others through dramatic play and classroom drama
- focuses attention and energy
- explores various modes of drama
- responds with appropriate behaviour
- accepts and supports the contributions of others
- works well in small and large groups, adapts, and shows flexibility
- views self as part of the ensemble
- develops role through interactive involvement
- accepts teacher in role within the drama
- negotiates to build meaning
- questions, persuades, interviews, and clarifies in role
- uses voice appropriately and effectively
- maintains an appropriate mood and atmosphere
- understands the effect of an audience on the drama
- uses various forms of drama
- selects, shapes, and presents ideas through drama
- uses masks, costumes, properties, and instruments
- understands that learning can be aesthetic and affective

A child who reflects in and out of role
- contributes, receives, and modifies meanings
- recognizes the implications of the drama
- reveals and shares insights
- questions the concepts within the drama
- connects the drama to personal experience
- assesses own participation in the drama
- responds in role to the teacher's signals
- considers personal contributions
- reflects upon the emotional response
- examines the form of the dramatic exploration
- uses insights from the drama for other activities—journal writing, painting, etc.

Reporting Children's Progress

Many parents have expectations of evaluation that they express in variations of three common questions (Mickelson, 1980). As teachers, we should not dismiss such questions as wrong-headed simply because we do not feel they are relevant to a language-based program. Parents' concerns are valid, and we need to address them.

- *How is my child doing?* Parents may be looking for numbers or letters that reflect "marks." We may need to explain how real work samples, audiotapes, videotapes, "published" books, records of books read, and writing folders all provide clear demonstrations of growth. If we show parents concrete evidence of their children's progress, they will be far less inclined to be concerned about absolute marks. We can also point to the interest and enthusiasm children show when they are doing work that is important to them. We may wish to include children in parent-teacher conferences; it is not unusual for them to become involved in assessing and demonstrating their own progress for their parents.
- *How is my child doing compared with other children?* We may need to explain to parents that the way a score on a test compares with the scores of children in other schools, cities, or countries or even in the same classroom will not tell them very much about their child. What really matters is how the child is developing according to the circumstances and environment in which she or he is living. The focus of parent-teacher conferences should be positive, and discussion should centre on how parents, teacher, and child can work together to ensure continued growth.
- *Will my child pass?* Many parents tend to think of learning as mastering an identifiable body of content sacrosanct to a particular "grade." The concepts of "passing" or "failing" assume an absolute, required standard of performance in this content before a child can depart for the next "grade." We need to help parents understand that children do not "pass" or "fail." They grow and develop through experience and coaching— some more rapidly than others. Teachers may need to redirect the focus of this question: it might more appropriately be rephrased as "In what room, with which people, might this child do best?"

Teachers need to present a thoughtful account of the children's language strengths to parents and school administrators. Not only can the teacher collect insightful information to offer parents, but the child can also play a part in creating the evaluation, so that reporting student progress becomes a three-way communication system.

Letter to Parent/Guardian

A letter can establish rapport between the teacher and the home early in the school year. This letter and any other teacher-parent communication should be jargon-free. Terms such as "environmental print," "whole language," "self-directed learning," and "individualized instruction" are a useful shorthand that has meaning for us as teachers because we have discussed and absorbed the philosophy behind these concepts; we have seen how they affect classroom work; we have understood the implications. We cannot expect the same grasp from those not involved in the classroom on a day-to-day basis any more than we would expect fully to understand all the jargon that speeds up communication between workers in a steel foundry or the air traffic control tower.

The letter should describe the aspects of the language arts children will encounter in the classroom and how they will be assessed. It might also suggest ways in which parents can assist children's development—for example, by encouraging children to share favourite picture books with parents or siblings; by listening to children discuss their writing; by telling children family stories, folk tales, and nursery rhymes so that they learn that both young and old can enjoy stories and poems. The letter should be phrased so that it does not seem to demand the impossible of parents whose reading skills are poor or whose proficiency with English is limited. Indeed, it can point out that in families whose home language is not English, appreciating the richness of the home culture and language will enhance the children's appreciation of English. The letter should focus on the child's abilities and achievements and the pleasure that both parents and child can gain from sharing them.

Parent-Teacher Conferences

A parent-teacher conference allows us to convey our observations of a child and to illustrate a child's development in various aspects of literacy through a folder of student work. It allows parents or guardians to contribute their own insights to the picture of a child's language development. A good conference will help the teacher to understand the child, and parents to appreciate the language arts program. For example, parents may be bothered by what they see as a child's lack of expertise in spelling. A glance at dated writing samples will demonstrate how the child is progressing and illuminate the teacher's explanation of the journey from invented to standard spelling.

The Report Card

The report card must not be a mere summary of a teacher's records, but an interpretation of those records for the benefit of parents. The evaluation should be based upon the portfolio of work, checklists, and brief anecdotal comments gathered over a period of time, and, where applicable, specific tests or projects.

The goals of reporting must be clear if we are to develop effective assessment strategies. Queenston has a report card that presents drafts of its report card form to all parents and invites questions and constructive comments in order to ensure that the report card will tell parents what they need to know. The report card format shown here emphasizes the importance of a framework for evaluating progress in language. It indicates the child's progress and development in language and allows teachers to identify children's strengths and note growth points.

A Reporting Procedure
Diane Carter

As our teaching practices and our understanding of the learning process changed, the staff at Queenston became increasingly dissatisfied and frustrated with our report cards and our reporting procedure. We no longer felt honest about the "Above or Below" achievement scales used in the primary and junior levels or the letter grades assigned to intermediate students. After all, what does an "A" or "B" mean? Moreover, how do judgmental grades help students to improve their behaviour, attitudes, and skills? And if the students don't know at what they are successful, with what they need assistance, or what is interfering with their achievement, what part do report cards play in promoting further learning?

The teachers also felt that parents needed to be more actively involved in the reporting process. We recognized that parents were, in essence, a child's first teacher and had a great deal of information and observations that they could share with the teacher. We felt the need to build on parents' knowledge and insight throughout the years at school, and so we developed a system to enrich communication and "report" information from home to school and from school to home.

We established an in-school report card committee with two teachers representing each of the primary, junior, and intermediate divisions. The committee examined various systems of reporting from other schools, both inside and outside the Peel Board of Education, and began to develop a reporting process that comprised more than an

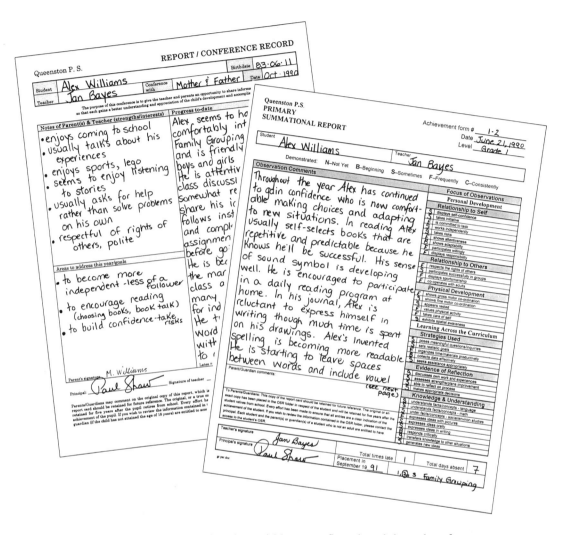

end-of-term report card and would better reflect the philosophy of child-centred learning being practiced at the school. Keeping in mind that the reporting process is a mutual responsibility, the committee devised a scheme that involved face-to-face communication, where both parents and teachers could have input.

The committee suggested the following process, which was further shaped by the staff.

1. Early fall: Conference with parents. (The student is invited to attend.) During a half-hour session, parents and teacher discuss a child's strengths, talents, and interests and establish three to five learning goals. Information is recorded on a conference sheet.

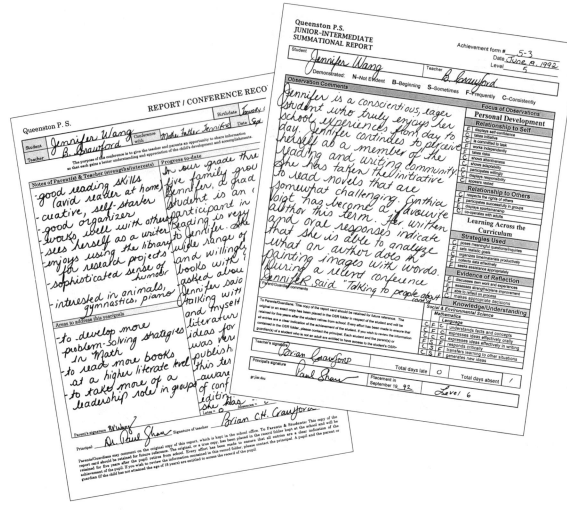

2. December: Anecdotal reports. The teacher outlines the student's progress toward the learning goals.
3. March: Conference with parents. (The student is invited to attend.) During a half-hour session, parents and teacher discuss the student's progress and set new goals.
4. June: summative report, including a checklist with anecdotal comments that outlines personal growth in terms of self, working relations with others, academic reflection, strategies, and understandings.

The committee did not disband once the school had adopted the process. Rather, it continues to review and revise the invitation form sent to the parents in the fall, and the summative report indicators. It has also created a comprehensive handbook to assist teachers in assessing students and in writing comments. The aim is to develop a common approach and a common language for reporting throughout the school that will be understood and appreciated in the community.

We have found that the implementation of this reporting system at Queenston has increased communication between home and school, helped teachers become more professional in their approach to teaching and learning, and put the whole child at the centre of the whole process.

Suggested Reading for Teachers

Baskwill, Jane, and Paulette Whitman. *Evaluation: Whole Language, Whole Child.* Toronto: Scholastic, 1988. Strategies are presented for "kid-watching"—observing, recording, and interpreting what children are doing and saying on a daily basis. Useful and manageable alternatives are offered to formal testing procedures.

Booth, David, Jack Booth, and Jo Phenix. *Assessment and Evaluation 1-3. Impressions Series.* Toronto: Holt, Rinehart and Winston, 1991. These books include a set of masters designed to provide a range of assessment and record-keeping measures to provide guides for observation and checklists for noting specific strengths of the children and the program.

Centre for Language in Primary Education. *The Primary Language Record: Handbook for Teachers.* London: ILEA, 1988. Distributed in Canada by Pembroke, in Markham, Ont. This practical handbook for teachers provides a framework for enhancing teacher record keeping and observation skills through observation diaries, work samples, detailed record of discussions, etc.

Goodman, Kenneth S., Yetta M. Goodman, and Wendy J. Hood, ed. *The Whole Language Evaluation Book.* Toronto: Irwin Publishing, 1989. The authors of this book—classroom teachers from all over North America, representing kindergarten through adult education—discuss the strategies they use in evaluating students' growth across many curricular areas, including reading, writing, and second language growth, and suggest alternatives to standardized tests in mainstream, resource, and special education programs.

Graves, Donald, and Bonnie S. Sunstein, ed. *Portfolio Portraits.* Portsmouth/Toronto: Heinemann/Irwin, 1992. Twelve contributors from all levels of education share experiences with portfolios as an alternative to traditional grading and assessment methods

Jaggar, Angela, and Trika Smith-Burke, ed. *Observing the Language Learner.* Newark, Del.: International Reading Association, 1985. These editors have gathered a collection of articles by leading researchers, representing the best current thinking about language learning both in and out of the classroom.

Johnson, Terry, et al. *Evaluating Literacy: A Perspective for Change.* Toronto: Irwin Publishing, 1991. Since more and more teachers have come to embrace a philosophy of integrated, holistic instruction, the authors have attempted to bridge the gap between how children learn and how we evaluate them with well-researched theory and practical suggeastions.

Johnston, Peter H. *Constructive Evaluation of Literate Activity.* New York: Longman Publishing, 1992. Based on the premise that evaluation's main purpose is to improve children's learning, this text presents an approach grounded in reflective practice.

Ontario Ministry of Education. *Assessing Language Arts.* OAIP: Ontario Assessment Instrument Pool. Toronto: Ontario Ministry of Education, 1990. The OAIP is an extensive collection of assessment evaluation materials, designed for use in elementary schools for instructional and evaluation purposes. The materials include assessment/evaluation approaches, strategies, and instruments, based on Ontario curriculum guidelines and other curriculum documents.

Tierney, Robert J., Mark A. Carter, and Laura E. Desai. *Portfolio Assessment in the Reading–Writing Classroom.* Norwood, Mass: Christopher Gordon Publishers, 1991. This book presents a discussion of how teachers might implement portfolio assessment in their classrooms.

Reflections

❶ Queenston is developing a school assessment and evaluation policy that clarifies for teachers, administrators, and parents the relationship between the program in language arts and the evaluation procedures in the school. How could your school begin to examine its policies and articulate a similar plan for assessing the progress of children in the various divisions? How would you enlist the help of parents in such an endeavour?

❷ The better teachers can describe children's development in language arts, the more support and assistance parents will provide the teacher and the school. Collect materials created by departments of education, district school boards, and educational publishers to develop an assessment resource package for your class or school. Decide which checklists, observation guides, strategies, and techniques will be most useful as a starting point for frequent assessment of each child and for writing evaluative reports to parents about their children's achievements in language.

❸ For conferences with parents, some of the teachers at Queenston prepare in advance demonstrations of the child's growth using writing folders, reading logs, and videotapes of classroom activities. Sometimes they include the child in the conference. Which of these ideas can you use in your own approach to parent-teacher conferences? Can you use the questions that arise during these conferences as the starting point for further communication through personal letters, newsletters, copies of articles, or self-assessment reports from the child?

❹ New materials—books, articles, documents—are being created as you read this book. How will you keep aware of new research and practice? Could teams or committees of teachers monitor changes in assessment philosophy and methodology, informing colleagues of new information?

❺ Can your school conduct occasional reading and writing assessments across the whole school, perhaps even using standardized tests? How can the staff ensure that these events occur without measuring teacher against teacher and child against child—that the staff see the results as information, rather than as grades? Can you use what you learn through such school-wide assessments as the basis for discussion about the children's language competencies and potential? Can you establish benchmarks for anticipated language growth through further interpretation of this material?

How Teachers Learn

COMPLACENCY ABOUT the teaching we offer our students has never been good enough, neither in "the good old days" nor in today's language-based classrooms. No one will ever be able to prescribe the best language arts curriculum for any one school or even any one student. Teachers know that they will spend the rest of their professional lives finding out more about children and learning, developing their expertise, honing their skills.

Language Arts Teaching Today

We have, of course, learned many things about successful language arts teaching. There are certain constants that teachers must be aware of. Every teacher faces these, and each works with them in his or her personal and individual fashion.

Allowing the Time

Children need to devote time—large blocks of time—to reading and writing, speaking and listening if they are to become real readers and writers, speakers and listeners. Constant interruption and demands for attention from the teacher try the children's patience and impede learning. Reading is a significant activity and even after children have mastered its technical aspects, it deserves time on the daily schedule. Some teachers like to provide a sustained silent reading time for the entire class; others integrate the personal reading into thematic units or small group reading workshops. Writing is a time-consuming task: the students need to consider topics that are meaningful to them, shape their initial ideas and concerns on paper, try out drafts with their peers, confer about the progress of the piece with the teacher. Meaningful, deeply felt conversation does not arise from quick question-and-answer routines between teacher and class. It grows out of situations and events that demand to be talked about, where participants can present concerns, listen to different viewpoints, and think aloud, hitchhiking their own words on the words of others as they make the deepest, most personal meanings possible.

Ensuring a Sense of Ownership

"People think hardest and best when it is about something that matters to them, when they have an investment, when there's something at stake. People learn in meaningful contexts" (Atwell, 1991, p. 42). Learners need to feel that they have some control over the curriculum areas that fill their days; they need to have input into what happens in the classroom. When participants care about what they are doing, when school activities seem to relate to their own lives, they will have that sense of ownership. In our teaching, we need to present our students with opportunities to read the books they want to read, to choose the writing topics that matter to them, to speak their minds about events under discussion, and to try on roles they wish to play or need to work through in the safety of classroom drama.

Teaching at the Right Moment

Discerning teachers challenge and nudge when necessary, provide the organization and resources that assist learning, build on what the children know, and find ways to help with specific areas of concern. Teachers must help children to learn, not simply tell them that they have or have not learned. Many of us need to change the focus of our efforts. Instead of seeing our function as that of examiner of the work after the children have completed it, we have to make time to help children while they are writing, while they are reading, while they are deep in conversation, while they are working in role. We have to teach as participants from within the action in the classroom, not as intervenors descending from above; we have to attend to the writer's attempts at making meaning, not to the mistakes. Knowing that the message is important to us will lead the writer to care enough about reaching us and others to revise and edit and proofread. As we change our approach to teaching, we must remember that many children will need to change their approach to learning. Children whose past experiences with reading and writing have had no intrinsic meaning for them, where marks were the reasons for completing a task and competition was used as a goad, will need time and reassurance to make the transition to collaborative and supportive learning.

Participating in the Learning

Over the years, I have worked with hundreds of teachers and student teachers who were striving to understand how children learn language, how children learn through language, and how children learn about language. Today we have a fundamental change in our view of professional growth. We have come to realize that teachers must see themselves as language learners and language users—as real readers and writers—if they are to understand how children become literate. In other words, they must work from inside the reading and writing processes, from inside the conversation.

This approach changes not only how teachers view their students, it also changes the way they themselves behave in the classroom. Children see their teachers as participants in the literacy activities of the classroom, discovering and sharing stories, revelling in the rhythm and images of a poem, writing down an important thought, reading what children write with interest, enjoying a real conversation, exploring how words sound in the air and how they appear on paper. They recognize that this is what literate people do; they want to become literate people themselves. They learn by example to value books and writing and talk; they view projects and themes and units as sources of excitement and commitment; as individuals, they feel part of an authentic, language-rich learning community.

Many of the teachers at Queenston are active readers and writers alongside their students. They provide a model of literacy, but more importantly, they find these activities bring them great personal satisfaction. These teachers read for themselves—novels, poems, books about teaching by and about other teachers, newspapers, and magazines. They read to the children not only children's stories, poems, and non-fiction but also extracts from their personal reading. They read with growing interest what the children write: poems, stories, journals, records of school activities, research reports on topics of their own choice, letters, sometimes personal and private, written to their teachers.

The teachers use writing to communicate and know the satisfaction writers feel when their message is received. They write letters to their students; they respond to comments in the students' dialogue journals; they draw up information sheets to help students with organizational strategies; they record anecdotes for assessment; they report their observations to parents. They fulfil their own needs through writing: they jot down their thoughts in their own journals; they compose their own poems and stories; some write books; they write personal letters to loved ones.

The teachers talk to their students about children's books, about authors they enjoy personally, about how they themselves read and write. They respond to their students' comments in one-to-one conversation, in group discussion, in the classroom, in the hall, at recess, and after school. They find themselves dealing with their own approach to literacy: this in itself is a model for their students.

We ask our students to keep journals as records of their lives and observations and learning. Teachers who do the same may find it a useful and rewarding activity.

From a Student Teacher's Journal
Julie Wilkins

I kept a journal while working as a student teacher with Jim Giles and Jan Bayes in their primary family grouping classroom. The journal gave me a day-to-day opportunity to reflect on my teaching experiences, to raise questions and comments—and to describe my frustrations about what happened in the classroom. As I glance back through the pages, I can see my own progress and development. At the time, it allowed open discussion between me—the apprentice—and the supervising teacher—Jim Giles—away from the bustle of classroom activity.

January 8
Dear Jim,
Observing Children was very interesting and would be a valuable reference book. It reinforces the fact that you can't push children into doing something they're not ready for—but with such a wide range among children, how does one know when and for what a child is ready? *Play* also looks interesting and I'd like to keep it for a bit longer if I can. When I can, I'll order my own copy—it looks like it might be a very worthwhile investment. With 46 children altogether, how do you keep track of who's who—how long did it take to learn everyone's name? How do you and Jan track and monitor them to make sure they are going to all the centres they need to go to? Do you both keep records for all of the children or do you each concentrate on your own class? But it's early yet and I'm sure a lot of my questions will be answered as I spend more time in the class. I'm looking forward to it. . . .
Julie

January 13,
Jim,
Here we go! I've been working like crazy on this environmental studies unit and it seems to be finally coming together. Still can't seem to get the trip arranged, though. I've been trying to get through to the person at Superwood (the plastic recycling place) but she's not in 'til tomorrow (Monday). Will have to try again! Let's hope it all comes together. I've put together a tentative timetable for the activities but it really is tentative, flexible, etc. I found it was helpful to circle the ones that I felt were of higher priority. I'd also like you to look at the teaching sheets I've designed and see what you think of them (it's yet another requirement of this project for my faculty instructor). Would the kids want to fill them in?
Thanks, Julie

Taking Responsibility

As teachers, we make time for what we feel is important. Therefore, we must be sure of our priorities in language learning. Everything we do in the classroom is founded on a set of assumptions about learning and teaching, about knowledge, about literacy. These beliefs and values, however, are all too often tacit and unacknowledged. We need to uncover and examine them if we—and our teaching—are to change and grow and develop. One way of doing this is to look at our current instructional practices. We can analyze "critical incidents"—those special moments in our teaching experience when we and our students know that real teaching and real learning are taking place. We can observe and learn from our students' responses and then reflect on our teaching, our setbacks, and our successes with colleagues who, like us, want to become better teachers. We can accompany our own classroom research by reading books and articles by other professionals on work that illuminates, strengthens, and redirects our own approach to teaching. We need to see ourselves as learners.

The Staff Room
Lois Roy

The one thing I find at Queenston in contrast to some other schools is that there is always an interesting dialogue going on—sometimes positive, sometimes negative—but always discussion. You don't walk into the staff room and hear a lot of conversation about the baseball game last night; it's beyond that. I think the teachers here probably have more investment in doing classroom research on their own, too. You have to be thinking about where you are going in your own process of learning as well. If you want your students to be risk takers, you have to learn to be a risk taker as well. I've been astounded at how many teachers out there are not risk takers.

We can't have apathy in education—that's happened for far too long. This school is never apathetic. There are lots of strong individuals with lots of strong ideas.

Demonstrating Success

Once teachers develop and articulate a theory of language learning and teaching that they truly believe in, they must be able to demonstrate its success to administrators and parents. At Queenston, the teachers report to parents by explaining the children's progress as shown in their reading journals and writing folders and by maintaining lists of reading and writing conventions and skills that the children have mastered during group and whole-class direct instruction, group workshops and mini-lessons, and individual conferences. Both parents and administrators need to know that we know what we are doing; we must be informative, not defensive.

Lifelong Learning

How do teachers continue to grow and develop professionally? When I began teaching, there were very few methodology courses for teachers, few reference books on classroom theory and practice, and often a single text-book in each subject for every child in the district. To keep up to date, I relied heavily on associates, consultants, and the occasional in-service program. Even so, I felt very much alone, with little to measure the success, or lack of it, of my teaching. Today, teachers have a wealth of materials and resources to assist them, yet some still have difficulty knowing where to turn for information on appropriate and effective strategies for helping children learn and advice on what will be most useful in their classrooms.

As I talked to the teachers at Queenston about their work, three patterns in professional development emerged:

Further Education

Conscious reflection on their own teaching practices and planning their own future growth often lead teachers to identify thin spots or even gaps in their understanding. The teachers at Queenston continue to take summer and evening courses in education, in psychology and sociology, and in curriculum content areas. They know that significant change seldom occurs incidentally or accidentally.

Professional Reading

Seminars, courses, and personal reading provide an informal reference library. The teachers pass on articles they have read that they know will attract wider interest. They lend or even buy one another books that they feel will strengthen and support their colleagues in particular areas of concern or exploration.

To keep abreast of significant developments that will help us in teaching, we must be on the lookout for the latest publications—books, articles, and newsletters. Today's language-teaching experts give us plenty of opportunities for professional development. Both we and our students will benefit as we cruise the world through reading, visiting schools in New Zealand,

Australia, Britain, the United States, and Canada. We come to know the writers as our colleagues; we sit in their classrooms; we appreciate their practices; we recognize their successes.

If our reading is wide, we can quickly select those authorities whose work applies to a particular challenge we face. Of course, this requires knowing where to turn: for example, if you find you are bogging down in reading conferences, you need to be aware that those Australians David Hornsby and Deborah Sukarna are among the pioneers of the conference approach, and that they may have some pointers for you in *Read On: A Conference Approach to Reading*. We need to know who the reliable writers are in the areas of education that specifically interest us and be on the lookout for their publishing ventures. By recognizing the language arts specialists who inspire us, we can build our own personal philosophy of language teaching by interacting with their ideas.

However, many teachers attempt blindly to replicate the recipes offered in professional writings. Others react defensively to what they see as an unrealistic vision of the teaching experience. The classroom activities and the context in which they are presented on paper often imply a coherence few teachers meet in their own work. They are sometimes overwhelmed by the disparity and dissonance between these "perfect" classrooms and their own. I have met and worked with teachers who, for various reasons, have frozen their teaching in time; I have met others who continue to seek significant change and progress all their lives. Reflective teachers are always expanding their professional knowledge base and developing their philosophy of teaching, so that the strategies and activities they employ benefit the children with whom they have been entrusted.

Networking

A series of intricate networks are in place at Queenston: teachers work with other teachers in grade groups; they team-teach in multi-grade family groupings for several consecutive years; they collaborate on projects for professional development courses they are taking together; they discuss new children's books during planned book-talk lunch sessions; individual teachers prepare schoolwide in-service sessions based on the expertise they personally bring to the school and the classroom.

Growing as Teachers
Katie Thurston and Catherine Florian

Katie Thurston and Catherine Florian recently began their teaching careers at Queenston. Katie has taught grade one for two years.

Catherine has moved from teaching a grade four class to a combined grades three and four class. Katie and Catherine talked to me about their growth as teachers and revealed some thoughts about their own learning.

David: You both began teaching last year. How did you come to the decision to have a comprehensive reading time and a process writing program?

Katie: For me, a lot of it was the example of the other teachers on this staff. Seeing the results of what they've done, you can't help but want to do it too, because you want the same results for your kids. I feel fortunate to be among these teachers at Queenston.

Catherine: I think, too, that the kids I had last year, the ones who were in grade four, already had wonderful reading and writing times, and they expected more and they let me know that!

David: If guests came in to your room this year, what's something you would like them to see?

Katie: I think I'd say our author's chair. To me that's an exciting part of our program because now the children are in charge. I keep turning around and finding different children occupying the chair and talking about books they've read or stories they've written. It's spontaneous and now seems to be intrinsic to the program.

Catherine: I would choose the whole writing process from rough draft to publication. We have a conference table with editors-of-the-week. Everyone seems to get involved at different levels whether they're trying to get ideas, edit their work, or design a cover. It's an exciting routine, especially since the kids have started to rely on each other.

David: Is there anything you've felt uncomfortable about in your teaching?

Katie: For me it's the conferences. When children bring their literature or writing to me, it's always a challenge to extend them further and ask the right questions that will move them more deeply into the work. I'm looking for the best methods and I've learned a lot from being at Queenston where I could go to Brian or Barb for advice about conferences.

Catherine: I think I'd like to do more drama activities. For one thing, the writing the kids do inside drama seems to be more successful, and they enjoy it. I often borrow an idea from others who have tried it with their classes to try it with mine. I would like to learn more from the teachers in this school who seem to be experts at drama.

David: You've said you've learned a great deal from being at Queenston. What stands out?

Katie: That in order for children to learn they must have a certain degree of ownership in what they're doing. It's one thing to read about it in books, but when you're surrounded by teachers who are striving to give their children more choice, you think about your own philosophy of teaching. For instance, when I came away from a professional growth session, "Negotiating the Curriculum," I reflected on my own teaching theories and practices. I don't think I'd get that same interaction in some schools.

David: It seems that you have both grown as teachers. How might you continue to grow?

Katie: I think that in order to grow you still have to get out and see what's there—visit other teachers—even classrooms in your own school. Sometimes we get so busy that we don't get to see different activities that are happening down the hall that we can incorporate into our own programs.

Catherine: I've grown a great deal since I've started teaching. In the beginning I wanted to do everything for my students. And it's letting them make decisions and mistakes that has taught me that we learn from others. . . . Many teachers in the primary division have been very helpful and supportive at showing me how literature can be used meaningfully for writing and for talking. Many teachers here know so much about the books they have suggested for my kids to enjoy—their enthusiasm has been contagious.

Katie: I remember the time that Camille in my grade one class wrote her first sentence in her journal. Well, I started skipping down the hall with Camille's notebook, showing Dale and Brian and Barb her writing, which for Camille (and me) was a terrific achievement. Teachers sometimes tease me about how silly I looked that day, but I think that's what's been special about being at Queenston— teachers really understand your frustrations and celebrate your accomplishments.

As teachers, we can determine our own future. We can stay informed about research and techniques for helping children develop their language potential. We can create classrooms where making meaning is central to learning language. We can structure an environment in which each child is a member of a community of language learners. We can observe the children, assess their learning, and intervene when necessary. We will then move schools into a position in the lives of children that parents will find necessary and vital.

The Teacher as Researcher

Over several years, many teachers at Queenston have changed their way of teaching. With the support of a network of colleagues and the encouragement of a caring and enlightened administration, they began by examining their own behaviour as teachers. Teachers need to take responsibility for their own professional growth. The classroom is the best site for research into teaching, and the teacher is at the core of the research team. As they examine their own classrooms and tell their stories about their children, teachers begin to gain an understanding of how children develop and how social needs determine language.

Research in the Classroom
Paul Shaw

When I first came to Queenston, I suggested that we hold literacy interviews, conversations with individual students about their reading and writing, where the students bring the book they are reading and something they've written. The idea was that through dialogue, we would come to understand the experience that the children have had with print and the value they placed on reading and writing. For example, do they read and write at home? We asked each teacher to choose a range of readers and writers and do six of these literacy interviews. We discovered that about 70 percent of the children claimed that they read a book only when the teacher made them. That was quite alarming to me. It was an opportune time for us to share some images that people had of literate people.

We know that literate people read and write because they want to. We looked at some of the strategies that literate people use when they read and write, and we tried to find evidence of the kids in this school using them. We decided to observe individual children reading and to identify the strategies that the kids used when they came to a word that they didn't know. Did they sound it out? Did they read ahead? Did they comment? Did they repeat? Did they give up? We found there was a range of strategies, and we tried to draw comparisons between the competent readers and the less able ones. We saw patterns emerging. We talked about how we might help our less able readers use the same strategies as our gifted readers.

That one simple task set us on our way. The teachers now had some data to reflect on. They wanted to see if we could effect change in the school. We were beginning to develop an inquiry culture, which became more and more persuasive.

A typical professional growth session lasts at least two hours. Our professional growth committee works out a question for the staff to focus on: for example, they might request that everyone gather some type of information from the classroom—a piece of writing or a summary of all the different kinds of writing that went on during a certain week. Then we gather together and begin to talk about our classroom experiences, about the data that we have to share. Our sessions always start with the classroom experience, where teachers are. Then we move ahead to where they would like to be, back that up with what the experts are saying, and then the dialogue begins.

And it's conversation based on experience in the classroom. Periodically, we take stock or run into a question to which we have no answers. At times we speak to people from various universities or to some of our consultants. For example, one year we focused on writing genres for six months, from January to June. We had moved from a discussion of writing genres to a tighter focus on getting kids to write things other than straight non-fiction. We arranged a teleconference with Donald Graves. Ahead of time, we read some pieces about writing that he sent along to us, and just before the conference we met in groups for about an hour and a half and discussed the issues he raised. These discussions helped us generate very specific questions for him. It was an exhilarating experience to sit around the speaker phone and ask this leading authority questions that were pertinent to the work we are trying to do and have him respond in the hearing of everyone in the room. The following year, we arranged a similar teleconference on assessment with Jane Hansen.

The teleconferences are special, but what I am really pleased with is how the sustained, focused conversations in our regular professional growth time extend beyond those formal sessions into partnerships and mentoring and further dialogue. A significant number of staff members have undertaken their own personal inquiries. Many are keeping their own reflective journals. A number of people are forming

interest groups, meeting together to look at certain aspects of programs—we've one group working on mathematics. Personal inquiry,
and eventually group inquiry, can only add to the professional growth
process. It changes the conversations in the staff room and in the hall-
ways. New books and new information pass through the school. If
someone finds something, whether it is a new children's literature
book or an article pertinent to some of the things that people are talking about, then others will soon be sharing the information.

The TALK Project

Reclaiming the Classroom (Goswami and Stillman, 1987) suggests that teachers should control their own learning. For many of us—teachers, teachers of
teachers, and researchers—this concept comes as a breath of fresh air. Carol
Thornley-Hall, who headed the Peel TALK teacher-research project run by
the Peel Board of Education and at first sponsored by a grant from the
Ontario Ministry of Education, agrees wholeheartedly:

*How can teachers transmit a sense of worth to their children if they do not
have it themselves? Most professional development activities have been organized and often mandated for teachers by others, a phenomenon that does
not seem to occur in any other profession. This leaves the teachers with the
feeling that they have been "professionally developed" rather than that they
have expanded their own professional expertise and knowledge. Workshops
and presentations, traditional forms of professional development, are stimulating and informative but have short term or little effect on the classroom.*

*There are other disadvantages to such top-down, laid-on programs for
implementing curriculum change or new ideas. Teachers often respond
wearily with the comment "What next?" or "Now, what's coming down the
tube?" They dutifully try to assimilate the new knowledge but frequently find
the changes required in adjusting their practice to fit new ideas can be dis-
couraging and lower self esteem. The uncomfortable business of changing
patterns and procedures which have been successful over the years can make
some feel, temporarily at least, utterly defeated (Thornley-Hall, 1992).*

It is easy to see that the inquiry culture at Queenston fitted smoothly
into the TALK Project in which Carol Thornley-Hall invited teachers in the
district to participate in classroom-based research inquiries. Consultants such
as Gordon Wells, Bob Barton, and I helped the teachers both to come up
with questions that were significant to them as teachers, and to develop
research models for gathering and interpreting their data. The results were
so stimulating that many teachers have continued their classroom inquiries

after the project was officially wound down. I have been involved in the TALK project and the inquiries at Queenston for four years now.

The teachers in the Peel TALK Project have created booklets, run workshops, and made videotapes showing what they tried to do in their own classrooms, what they had thought about, observed, and concluded. Many have shared their personal inquiries with the larger community of teachers and encouraged others to use their own classes as resources for research. Many of the voices we have heard in this book are those of teachers involved in this project, sharing their journeys as they grow professionally.

The Peel TALK Project sponsored two international conferences on classroom talk. The conferences included presentations from the local teacher-researchers as well as those from various guest educators. In their evaluations of the first conference, other teachers attending suggested that the next year they wanted to spend much more time with the teacher presenters. The voices of our peers pull us so much faster into new contexts for learning. When our colleagues ask us to join them, somehow the challenge of change and the risk of growth implicit in classroom-based research seem to fade. What we hear is the excitement found in developing as teachers together with other teachers and through the help of our own students. Steven Lieberman, a resource teacher for the Peel Board of Education, saw the process at work at Queenston and found it contributed to his own growth as a teacher.

Queenston as a Research Community
Steven Lieberman

Teachers' own investigations, demonstrations, and articles are the heart of the TALK project. As a resource teacher working in several Peel schools, I enjoy being part of Queenston's pleasantly open learning community. I have been invited to professional dialogue sessions as a fellow researcher, not an outside expert. I have been with the staff on a retreat at which Gordon Wells was a guest, and I also participated in a teleconference between the staff and Donald Graves. The teachers had planned these events carefully, preparing ahead of time individual and group questions based on their readings and classroom experiments and therefore were able to make the most of the time available. Each session ended with a period for reflection and discussion.

At Queenston, regular grade and division level meetings take place as well as full staff meetings. These meetings address normal business items, but a large portion of time is always set aside for professional dialogue. This is a formal opportunity for teachers to listen to each other and learn from each other's experiences. Pairs or small groups of teachers naturally discuss items of interest and develop mutual support networks on a more casual basis at any time.

Queenston teachers expect their resource teachers to make themselves useful, so I've worked with the staff in many situations. I have coached teachers who want to develop better techniques for conferring with their students. I have been asked for information and supplies. Since family grouping classrooms present teachers with special challenges, at the instigation of Queenston teachers, I have helped establish a network of family grouping teachers across a number of schools in the area.

Meanwhile, when I go to the university for graduate courses, I keep meeting Queenston teachers in the halls. They may be taking update or specialist courses or working toward a master's or doctoral degree. Some are instructing courses for other teachers. The climate at Queenston Public School tends to be infectious. Learning, for students or staff, does not stop once they leave the building. The spark continues; the gift has been given.

A TALK Inquiry

Inquiries in the TALK Project were shared among the staffs at all the participating schools. As might be expected, the teachers at Queenston were particularly interested in *I'm Not Alone: Teacher Talk, Teacher Buddying*, produced by Betty Ferri and Mirella Aglio, teachers at Silverthorn Public School, in 1990. The two began an informal mentor relationship—Betty is an experienced teacher, and Mirella was just beginning her career. They met at the beginning of the school year and as both were teaching grade three, they decided to share classroom ideas and expertise. Betty and Mirella chose the term "buddying" to describe the relationship that developed over the year. The following introductory remarks and excerpts from their journals illustrate how their relationship moved from one of mentoring to a more equal partnership.

Teacher Buddying
Betty Ferri and Mirella Aglio

Our collaboration grew informally and naturally. We shared a common grade level but were not required to team-teach. The relationship was highlighted when we were asked to reflect on it as teacher researchers examining talk in a school setting, within the Peel Board of Education TALK Project. Through personal journals we gathered our thoughts on "buddying" and the value of teacher talk.

The focus for our inquiry in the project was professional talk between colleagues. As partners, we found we were talking in the halls, classrooms, staff rooms and restaurants. We were talking during recess, planning time, staff meetings and lunch hours. We were talking, talking, talking.

The journal entries reflect our feelings at the time that they were written. Whether the entries are about one another or written to each other, they always show insight into our relationship. Teaching does not need to be an isolated individual journey. Through sharing and communicating, it can become more effective.

Mirella: October 12. Talk. There certainly is enough talking in my room. My children are always talking even during silent reading time. Their talk is not always "chit-chat." They have important messages to get across and they do. I have noticed that forcing children to be silent is equivalent to draining all their enthusiasm away.

I am a very talkative person. I need to talk and I recognize this in my classroom. Oral language facilitates learning. Learning seldom happens if the communication is only one way. Interaction needs to take place.

Betty: October 12. I am excited and interested in the [TALK] project. At the moment, I am not totally receptive to changing my philosophy about "talk" in the classroom and am a little sceptical of the "change." I have always prided myself on a quiet, well-run classroom where the students appeared to be learning in spite of the quiet. Now the question arises, "Will talk in the classroom really promote and facilitate learning, and will the students actually become more literate?"

Mirella: November 14. As a first-year teacher right out of teachers' college, I have the latest ideas on whole language, drama, active and co-operative learning, but I'm not sure how effective they are or how well other teachers will receive them. I'm not saying that more experienced teachers are not open to new ideas, but change comes slowly.

(After several months of journal writing, we spontaneously began to write our entries to each other.)

Betty: December 7. I felt scattered today, but following our talk I felt much more reassured and relaxed. Especially after we concurred that a totally activity-based program was not easy to set up by any stretch of the imagination and that it was a gradual process, not an overnight thing. During our planning session today, you reminded me of what one of your professors kept emphasizing—that it is better to work on one subject area at a time. When you are happy and comfortable with the way it's working, then work on another subject area. It makes sense.

I'm coming to realize that "talk" is definitely a medium for learning and change, but perhaps I'm trying to implement too many changes this year. I've also come to realize that "listening" is a very important part of "talk." I've learned a great deal from you, Mirella, by listening to you talk about a student-directed classroom, whole language, co-operative learning, problem solving, etc., etc. I'm overwhelmed by all of these ideas, but you've definitely got me thinking about my teaching philosophy. I find I'm constantly reassessing my strategies and program and am constantly running across the hall to ask yet another question, bounce another idea off you, or simply seek reassurance. You are always patient, encouraging, and complimentary. Change is never easy and certainly seems to become more difficult as one grows older.

Betty: January 19. Our planning time talk was so helpful today. When I start feeling a little insecure about something new I'm trying, just talking to you about my concerns is reassuring. Our focus today seemed to be individualized reading. Is it a good idea to make students responsible for their own learning? We both agreed that children don't automatically grow up to be decisive, responsible adults. They must be provided with lots of opportunities along the way to make choices and take responsibility. They also need to be encouraged to take risks, fail and try again after learning from their mistakes. I feel I am now providing many more opportunities in my classroom for the students to try these things. It really helps to listen to you talk about the problem-solving, risk-taking situations that you provide in your class.

I have learned so much from our "talk" sessions that it has become very obvious that talk facilitates learning not just for kids but for teachers as well.

Mirella: January 22. Betty, your notes are so thorough! That is something else that I am learning from you—organization! I always feel more confident after one of our planning meetings. These meetings give me a chance to discuss my concerns and anxieties.

It's funny how you keep saying "whole language" is so new to you and ask me for advice. I am equally insecure about the program. At university we discussed whole language and all its benefits, but I have never seen a good whole language program working. I like to believe what I am doing is best for the children, but I need reassurance from the "outside." That's where you come in. You continually tell me

I'm doing a good job, and even more important, you let me know what I should be doing. You have given me guidance. You have made my first year so much easier than I expected it to be. THANKS!

Betty: January 25. After several "talk" session with you regarding spelling, I've finally thrown out the grade three speller and am trying some of the ideas we discussed. The class now brainstorms for words that they would like to learn as a group. These words are from their personal writing or reading activities, or simply words they would like to learn how to spell. The kids are highly motivated because the words are meaningful and they are able to work co-operatively in a group to learn them. The students are feeling good about themselves and perceive school as a fun place to learn. Mirella, all your suggestions for the independent reading program seem to be bringing about similar results.

Mirella: May 20. Betty, I have spent a lot of time with the teacher-mentor articles. The main problem is that the articles discuss very formal types of teacher-mentoring programs. We don't have that and we are not looking to have that. Our relationship is quite unique, but not necessarily unreproducible.

Betty: May 21. Our two classes work very well together and the benefits of having two teachers in the classroom as well are endless. While each of the groups were busy creating and writing songs and chants based on the book, there were two of us to circulate, help, and encourage the students.

One of the observations I made while all of this was happening was that you are a very effective questioner. Your questions stimulated the students' thinking and creativity. My questioning ability is somewhat weak and could use some work. That will be something for me to focus on next year. I think by having more opportunity to observe your questioning style and to talk about your style, I can improve in this area.

Betty: June 8. You have certainly changed my way of thinking and my approach to planning units. My themes are becoming less teacher directed and more student directed. The enthusiasm and motivation, not to mention the learning taking place, are surprising since it is now June. I owe a lot to you, Mirella, for exposing me to so many new ways to make teaching better and more fun for the kids. Your support and encouragement gave me the confidence to try them.

Mirella: June 10. Silverthorn School does not have a formal mentoring program, but the principal does try to connect people. A couple of weeks into the school year the principal called me into his office. He explained how he liked to link new teachers on staff with another member of staff to make the year easier. He explained that he normally tries to link teachers that share a grade level. He then went on to say that he did not have to do that in the case of Betty and myself because it happened naturally and very early in the year. It was nice to know that our relationship had been noticed and accepted as very healthy.

I knew the relationship was helping me a great deal, but at first I wondered if I was being a leech. If the relationship had been one way, I don't think I could have been comfortable. However when Betty began telling me how much she was getting from me it felt good. As others told me how lucky I was to be working with Betty, I was really appreciative. Our relationship had mutual benefits and the benefits were being noticed by us and others.

The benefits of the buddy relationship that Betty and I share are threefold. I benefit, Betty benefits, and the school benefits. Working closely with Betty has provided me with many opportunities to question and evaluate myself and my program. I have always done this, but now I have an honest, objective opinion to help me. I am not just questioning myself now—I am finding answers. My program is shaping up and I feel I am becoming a more effective teacher.

I also strengthen my beliefs and theories as I attempt to explain them to Betty. In vocalizing and sharing them, I have clarified them. Sometimes, speaking a thought out loud helps me to see the importance of or the lack of importance in my thoughts.

Having Betty as a role model has helped me to become a risk taker. Betty and I do many things together. If I fail or succeed I am not alone. Betty is always there to pick up the pieces or to help celebrate. I am not afraid to take chances. Betty helps me to make good decisions and feel confident in what I do. Without her I do not think that I would have done as much this year as I have.

I am still trying to evaluate the benefits the school has received. The children benefit a great deal. They benefit from joint programming and sharing of materials. They benefit from being taught by two separate personalities. The children also benefit from observing the positive sharing and co-operating that takes place between two adults.

The Logic of Learning and Growing

I want us to go inside language, using it to know and shape our worlds—but my practices evolve as the children and I go deeper. What I learn with these students, collaborating with them as a writer and reader who wonders about writing and reading, makes me a better teacher—not great maybe, but at least grounded in the logic of learning and growing (Atwell, 1987, p. 3).

In this book, I have attempted to focus on the philosophical and practical issues teachers must confront if they are to help young people develop as users of language and as makers of meaning. If we are true professionals, we need well-researched strategies on which to build our language arts curriculum. We need to continue to investigate language learning and teaching. And in the end, good teaching is not the materials and resources we have accumulated to assist our students; it is not a methodology that we lift from the pages of Nancie Atwell, Lucy Calkins, Donald Graves, or Jerome Harste; it is the dynamic of the interaction between teacher and student and between student and student within a language-based classroom where what each person says and feels counts. It looks outward to the real world of family and the wider community. We listen to our students and we learn from our students so that we can challenge them to grow and develop—and move on.

The Value of Taking Control
Paul Shaw

If you want teachers to become empowered then you have to trust them to make decisions wisely, to spend their money wisely, to communicate with parents wisely. The fascinating thing is that when teachers take control they become more committed, they work harder, they become more knowledgeable; when they take part in sustained, focused dialogue, they become more confident with parents, who in turn become more convinced that our school is doing a good job; when teachers begin to articulate their view of the children's learning and their view of their own learning and see parallels, the control is moving from the office to the teachers, from the teachers to the students.

The spinoffs of the inquiry culture in this building are quite enormous. I used to be the person who held the purse strings, made the decisions, wrote the timetable, directed everything. Now the budget is being spent more wisely, the timetable looks better, we have better and more interesting extra-curricular events, and our teachers work harder and with commitment. I'm quickly moving to a stage where I make a very few decisions in this building outside of hiring and firing people. The people I hire, who are critical to our future, to where we go, are people who are ready to reflect and to question and to examine, and who are open to change.

As a principal, I now participate in teacher growth workshops, not just administration seminars. When I attend the International Reading Association's annual conference, the number of administrators there is minimal. Where do all my colleagues go? They go to the principals' conference or the administrators' conference or the conference on supervision. They do not go to the reading or the math or the science teachers' conferences. This has a lot to do with what's valued in educational leadership. Historically, our principals have not been educators. They've been managers. School administrators that really valued knowing a lot about children and curriculum were quite rare. We're slowly breaking away: I'm excited by some of the young people who have recently been appointed principals. But even now, it seems the higher you go, the less you will see true educators in the hierarchy, and that's disappointing. I'm sure we can change that.

In this last section, we have listened to the voices of teachers as they analyze, implement, and adapt to new ideas and new directions in the teaching of language arts. Such thoughtful curriculum development can happen only when teachers are empowered to do it; as professionals they need time and resources to examine their own programs, to study other programs, and to plan and try out new approaches.

Booktalk: School Days
David Booth

It hit a little close to home when I read that Margaret Narwin, the ninth-grade teacher in Avi's *Nothing But the Truth*, was considering taking a summer course in whole language because she found herself unable to relate to the young people in her English classroom. How dare an author of books for young people move onto my professional turf! And yet, during my career, I've encountered—and found bits and pieces of myself in—hundreds of teachers in children's books. This time, the image stared back at me from the page and I couldn't look away.

How close to us as teachers are the characters drawn from the imaginations and life experiences of the writers of children's literature? Do children build their images of us from Lego the way a writer creates a composite story teacher? When they grow up, what bits of us will be left in the toy box, what bits taken on the journey?

Not all teaching in books is what we would choose. Have I made a child disappear as Mr. Rawlings did in Kin Platt's *The Boy Who Could Make Himself Disappear*, when he asked Roger aloud in class whether he had ever thought of doing something about his speech defect? Roger had an answer for that. Have I been as unaware of my students as the experimenters who flashed phonics on a screen in Robert O'Brien's *Mrs. Frisbee and The Rats of Nimh*? The rats learned much faster than their instructors suspected and soon began decoding the notes written for the lab technicians. Did I assign book reports as a young teacher? Does my son do book reports now? In *Dear Mr. Henshaw*, Beverly Cleary slams the book report again and again as Leigh Botts reports on the same book for four years in a row. Was I sure I knew the newest and best system for teaching, without reference to my students? In Harper Lee's *To Kill a Mockingbird*, Miss Caroline Fisher taught Scout's class ignoring their knowledge and advice because as Scout's brother Jem pointed out, she was teaching by the Dewey Decimal System.

Whose side am I on? Didn't I join in the cheer that went up when the biggest student in the class thrashed the bullying new master in Ralph Connor's *Glengarry Schooldays*? Don't I still taste Anna's terror in Jean Little's *Listen for the Singing* when the role-call stopped after her name as the jingoistic and sadistic Mr. Lloyd singles out those students with German backgrounds just after World War Two? Didn't I hide a secret grin when the hero of Paula Danzinger's *The Cat Ate My Gym Suit* gave her thirtieth excuse for not bringing her phys-ed uniform to class with her? Who got my sympathies in Louise Fitzhugh's *Harriet the Spy* when Harriet rudely told Miss Elson that she wasn't going to be an onion in the school play?

Who are the teachers, anyway? In Virginia Hamilton's *The Planet of Junior Brown*, it's the janitor, Mr. Pool, who helps Buddy Clark. I remember the caretaker who taught me drama in grade eight. And so much learning goes on outside the classroom. Katherine Paterson leads me across *The Bridge to Terabithia* to meet Miss Edmunds, who takes Jess to the Smithsonian, on her own time, and alters his life forever.

Perhaps I'll retreat more than a century to the prairies and look at the schoolroom through the eyes of Laura Ingalls Wilder. After all, I too boarded with a farm couple in my first two years of teaching as Laura does in *These Happy Golden Years*. But I did not suffer as she did when the school day ended: she had to go back to a home where the husband was abusive. And yet I know it happens—in teachers' homes, in students' homes. Where shall we find the ideal setting for our teaching dreams?

Beginning readers, of course, rest safely with Leatie Weiss in the knowledge that *My Teacher Sleeps in School*. But Harry Allard and James Marshall make them realize that *Miss Nelson is Missing!* And teachers are human: has Eve Bunting told them that *Our Teacher's Having a Baby*? And once they've learned from James Howe about *The Day the Teacher Went Bananas*, how can we wipe it from their minds?

The pages of these books play tricks on me; they keep revealing glimpses of my face, my class, my colleagues, shadows of my life. Did I teach Roger, Leigh, Harriet, and Junior Brown? Was I so blinded by my own preconceptions that I saw children as physical defects, as Nazis, as onions? And the students, how do they remember those years? Do they remember all of our times together, or just the mean ones, the ones that hurt—the ones that are just plain funny?

These writers were children once, students in my classroom. What are they saying about schools and teachers and students? Would these stories be so gripping, for teacher as well as child, if there were not truth within them? And how would I know who I was if there were no more children—and writers—to tell me? When I recognize that truth, I am already moving on. Yet my reality is still formed by these books that have been part of my life with school children and with my own son. I smart from the sharp jabs some writers have given me; I am soothed by the honeysweet images of teachers depicted by others.

I think I'll take my chances with Ernestine Blue in M. E. Kerr's *Is That You, Miss Blue?* Students at Charles, a conservative religious school, had their days brightened by her unusual yet effective teaching methods. However, when her own, unorthodox relationship with Jesus began to dominate her life, she was asked to leave, and the girls realized their enormous loss. As an adult, one of them recalls her years with Miss Blue, and like all of us who mourn the passing of a loved one, conjures her image into the crowds on the streets of New York, and longs to be recognized in return: "'Miss Blue,' I say. 'It's me. Is it really you?'"

We find ourselves in story, as does everyone who looks. The picture is always slightly out of focus, and we have to adjust our rose-coloured glasses. For teachers, looking in the mirrors of our classrooms and struggling to make out the often distorted reflections provided by the children—and the artists writing for the children—is our starting point for tomorrow. We must therefore read with the children, noticing the story and the writer and the children and ourselves—all at once. Or else, who will conjure us up when we have made ourselves disappear?

It's me, Miss Blue. You're me, Miss Blue. I'm you, Miss Blue. We're all Miss Blue. I'll miss Miss Blue. Will Miss Blue miss me? Will you?

Suggested Reading for Teachers

Atwell, Nancie. *Side by Side: Essays on Teaching to Learn.* Portsmouth/ Toronto: Heinemann/Irwin, 1991. In this volume, Atwell explores the conditions that make it possible for children and their teachers to become writers and readers.

Boomer, Garth. *Negotiating the Curriculum: A Teacher-Student Partnership.* Sydney: Ashton Scholastic, 1982. This book presents reports from more than twenty teachers who have conducted successful classroom experiments in negotiation in which teachers invite students to negotiate what and how they are going to learn.

Duckworth, Eleanor. *The Having of Wonderful Ideas & Other Essays on Teaching & Learning.* New York: Teachers College Press, 1987. Eleanor Duckworth brings together her wide-ranging writings on Piaget and teaching. Each of these essays supports the author's belief that "the having of wonderful ideas is the essence of intellectual development" and the focus of teacher education should be on the learner's point of view.

Fullan, Michael G. and Susanne Stiegelbauer. *The New Meaning of Educational Change,* 2nd ed. New York: Teachers College Press, 1991. A reference volume for change in education, this book looks into the change process and its impact on teachers and students, with suggestions and strategies for implementing change.

Newman, Judith M., ed. *Finding Our Own Way: Teachers Exploring Their Assumptions.* Toronto: Irwin Publishing, 1989. The articles in this book were written by practising teachers who have examined some of the uncertainties and problems they encountered when moving from a traditional to a holistic perspective in their teaching.

Pinnell, Gay Su, and Myna L. Matlin, eds. *Teachers and Research: Language Learning in the Classroom.* Newark, Del.: International Reading Association, 1989. The message of this book is a call for classroom-based research to examine the conditions under which learning can most effectively and constructively occur.

Smith, Frank. *Insult to Intelligence: The Bureaucratic Invasion of Our Classrooms.* Toronto: Irwin, 1986. Smith distills twenty years of research and firsthand work with teachers and students to launch a powerful attack on the widespread drill approach to teaching that is used in classrooms across the nation.

Weaver, Constance, and Linda Henke, eds. *Supporting Whole Language: Stories of Teacher and Institutional Change.* Portsmouth, N.H.: Heinemann, 1992. Stories of the successes and the struggles of individual educators and institutions as they have worked to change the traditional educational paradigm.

Reflections

❶ With a group of teachers, brainstorm to create the best possible language arts curriculum you could ever hope for. What resources would you need to support your program? What would the students achieve? How could you as teachers facilitate their development? Analyze the principles embedded in your suggestions to find out just what your team wants to accomplish.

❷ Examine the curriculum each division in your school is asked to follow.

- How do individual teachers establish their timetables?
- What materials are used? Do they form the basis for the curriculum or are they seen as resources?
- How integrated is the school day?
- Are reading, writing, and talking the centre of the curriculum?

Hold a discussion with teachers in the division about changes that you would like to see. Over which potential areas of change do you, as teachers, have control?

❸ At Queenston, the teachers choose a focus of concern each year, amass articles and books about it as support, and plan classroom inquiries. Does your school carry out similar projects? Could a small team in your school begin a classroom-based research project? Could staff members share areas of special interest and expertise with others on staff in a planned and organized fashion?

❹ Queenston sees communicating with parents as a significant goal and sends out newsletters and articles throughout the year to keep parents informed. Plan an issue of an annual, term, or even monthly newsletter. Include highly readable items on current topics in language arts, synopses of a couple of articles from educational journals, and reviews of books that parents might find interesting.

❺ How can your school ensure that it stays abreast of current understandings and trends in language arts education?

- Read educational journals and check with your school board and department of education to discover what educational conferences are taking place next year. Canvass the staff to find out which conferences individual teachers are particularly interested in attending and reporting on. Draw up a feasible schedule for attendance at these conferences, taking logistical and financial considerations into account.
- How can the learning achieved by staff members who have taken in-depth summer courses in writing, children's literature, or drama in education be most profitably shared with others?
- What mechanisms does your school have in place for sharing and discussing books and articles of interest? How could these be made more effective? Are there sources of information on the teaching of language arts that the staff is overlooking? Is discussion sufficiently focused? Do teachers actually try out in the classroom the good ideas found in these resources?

6 Most school boards have in-service and support staff, but the school must make good use of the time these professionals can allot to its teachers. Can the staff at your school take ownership of the next series of in-service workshops and plan the series so that you will want to participate and the events will be significant for your program.

7 Parents want to take part in choosing the material their children will read. Compose a letter to parents inviting them to recommend books that they have enjoyed with their children. With the librarian and a group of parents, plan ways to involve parent volunteers in the library to shelve books, review new materials, and read with children.

8 Some schools have used parents as researchers, involving them in drawing up questionnaires, holding interviews, and analyzing results and reactions. As a result, parents become informed about the school community and the programs being implemented. Can you organize a project for your area that would include parents in a significant way?

References

Adams, Marilyn Jager. 1990. *Beginning To Read: Thinking and Learning about Print. A Summary.* Urbana: University of Illinois.

Ashton-Warner, Sylvia. 1965. *Teacher.* New York: Simon and Schuster.

Atwell, Nancie. 1987. *In the Middle: Writing, Reading and Learning with Adolescents.* Portsmouth/Toronto: Heinemann/Irwin.

Atwell, Nancie. 1991. *Side by Side: Essays on Teaching to Learn.* Portsmouth/Toronto: Heinemann/Irwin.

Barnes, Douglas. 1976. *From Communication to Curriculum.* New York: Penguin.

Barrs, Myra, and Anne Thomas, ed. 1992. *The Reading Book.* London: Centre for Language in Primary Education.

Barton, Bob. 1986. *Tell Me Another: Storytelling and Reading Aloud at Home, at School and in the Community.* Toronto: Pembroke.

Barton, Bob, and David Booth. 1990. *Stories in the Classroom: Storytelling, Reading Aloud and Role-Playing with Children.* Markham, Ont.: Pembroke.

Baskwill, Jane. 1989. *Parents and Teachers: Partners in Learning.* Toronto: Scholastic.

Bennett, Jill. 1979. *Learning to Read with Picture Books.* Stroud, England: Thimble Press.

Bissex, Glenda. 1980. *GNYS AT WRK: A Child Learns to Read and Write.* Cambridge, Mass.: Harvard University Press.

Bolton, Gavin. 1984. *Drama as Education: An Argument for Placing Drama at the Centre of the Curriculum.* London: Longman.

Boomer, Garth. 1982. *Negotiating the Curriculum: A Teacher–Student Partnership.* Sydney: Ashton Scholastic.

Booth, David, Jack Booth, and Jo Phenix. 1991. *Assessment and Evaluation 1–3. Impressions* series. Toronto: Holt, Rinehart and Winston.

Booth, David, Jack Booth, Jo Phenix and Doreen Scott-Dunne. 1994. *Word Sense: Spelling, Punctuation, and Handwriting Skills for Young Writers.* Levels A, B, and C. Toronto: MeadowBook Press, a Division of Harcourt Brace & Company, Canada.

Booth, David, Larry Swartz, and Meguido Zola. 1987. *Choosing Children's Books.* Toronto: Pembroke.

Britton, James. 1976. *Language and Learning.* London: Penguin.

Britton, James, et al. 1975. *The Development of Writing Abilities.* Urbana, Ill.: National Council of Teachers of English.

Brownlie, Faye, Susan Close, and Linda Wingren. 1990. *Tomorrow's Classroom Today: Strategies for Creating Active Readers, Writers, and Thinkers.* Toronto: Pembroke.

Bruner, Jerome. 1983. *Child's Talk.* Oxford: Oxford University Press.

Butler, Dorothy. 1980 *Cushla and Her Books.* Boston: The Horn Book.

Calkins, Lucy McCormick. 1986. *The Art of Teaching Writing.* Portsmouth/Toronto: Heinemann/Irwin.

Calkins, Lucy McCormick. 1991. *Living Between the Lines.* Portsmouth/Toronto: Heinemann/Irwin.

Cambourne, Brian, and Jan Turbill. 1987. *Coping with Chaos.* Toronto: Irwin.

Cambourne, Brian. 1988. *The Whole Story: Natural Learning and the Acquisition of Literacy in the Classroom.* Toronto: Scholastic.

Clark, Margaret. 1976. *Young Fluent Readers.* Portsmouth, N.H.: Heinemann.

Clay, Marie M. 1975. *Writing Begins at Home.* Portsmouth, N.H.: Heinemann.

Clay, Marie M. 1985. *Reading Recovery Diagnostic Survey.* Portsmouth, N.H.: Heinemann.

Clay, Marie M. 1988. *The Early Detection of Reading Difficulties.* 3rd ed. Toronto: Irwin.

Cook, Caldwell. 1917. *The Play Way.* London: Heinemann.

Courtney, Richard. 1980. *The Dramatic Curriculum.* London, Ont.: University of Western Ontario Press.

Delpit, L. 1987. "The Silenced Dialogue: Power and Pedagogy in Educating Other People's Children." *Harvard Educational Review* 58:280–298.

Dixon, Barbara, and Lilian Lane. 1992. *Our Present: Their Future.* Toronto: OISE Press.

Dixon, J. 1993. "Students Exploring Literature across the World." In *Fifty Years of Literature as Exploration.* Urbana, Ill.: National Council of Teachers of English.

Doake, David. 1988. *Reading Begins at Birth*. Toronto: Scholastic.

Donavin, Denise Perry, ed. 1992. *Best of the Best for Children*. New York: Random House.

Dudley-Marling, Curt, and Don Dippo. 1991. "The Language of Whole Language." *Language Arts* 68:548–54.

Dunn, Sonja. 1987. *Butterscotch Dreams*. Markham, Ont.: Pembroke.

Dunn, Sonja. 1990. *Crackers and Crumbs*. Markham, Ont.: Pembroke.

Ferri, Betty, and Mirella Aglio. 1990. *I'm Not Alone: Teacher Talk, Teacher Buddies*. Peel TALK Project. Peel, Ont.: Peel Board of Education.

Fox, Mem. 1987. "The Teacher Disguised as Writer: In Hot Pursuit of Literacy." *Language Arts* 68:548–54.

Freire, Paolo, and Donaldo Macedo. 1987. *Literacy: Reading the Word and the World*. South Hadley, Mass.: Bergin and Garvey.

Fullan, Michael G., and Susanne Stiegelbauer, 1991. *The New Meaning of Educational Change*. 2nd ed. New York: Teachers College Press.

Giacobbe, Mary Ellen. 1986. "Learning to Write and Writing to Learn." *National Society for the Study of Education Yearbook* 85:131–147.

Goldberg, Natalie. 1986. *Writing Down The Bones*. Boston: Shambhala Publications.

Goodlad, John I. 1984. A Place Called School: Prospects for the Future. New York: McGraw-Hill.

Goodman, Kenneth S. 1986. *What's Whole in Whole Language*. Toronto: Scholastic.

Goodman, Kenneth S., ed. 1973. *Miscue Analysis: Applications to Reading Instruction*. Urbana Ill.: National Council of Teachers of English.

Goodman, Kenneth S., Yetta M. Goodman, and Wendy J. Hood, eds. 1989. *The Whole Language Evaluation Book*. Toronto: Irwin.

Goodman, Yetta M., Wendy J. Hood, and Kenneth S. Goodman, eds. 1991. *Organizing for Whole Language*. Portsmouth/Toronto: Heinemann/Irwin.

Goodman, Yetta. 1990. *How Children Construct Literacy*. Newark, Del.: International Reading Association.

Goswami, D. and P. R. Stillman, eds. 1987. *Reclaiming the Classroom*. Portsmouth, N.H.: Boynton/Cook–Heinemann.

Graves, Donald H. 1983. *Writing: Teachers and Children at Work.*
Portsmouth/Toronto: Heinemann/Irwin

Graves, Donald H. 1989. *Investigate Nonfiction. The Reading/Writing
Teacher's Companion.* Portsmouth/Toronto: Heinemann/Irwin.

Graves, Donald H., and Bonnie S. Sunstein, eds. 1992. *Portfolio Portraits.*
Portsmouth/Toronto: Heinemann/Irwin.

Griffiths, Alex, and Dorothy Hamilton. 1984. "Parent, Teacher and Child:
Working Together." In *Children's Learning.* London: Methuen.

Gunderson, Lee. 1989. *A Whole Language Primer.* Toronto: Scholastic.

Halliday, M.A.K. 1975. *Learning How to Mean: Explorations in the
Development of Language.* London: Edward Arnold.

Hansen, Jane. 1987. *When Writers Read.* Portsmouth/Toronto:
Heinemann/Irwin.

Hansen, Jane. 1991. "I Wonder What Kind of Person He'll Be."
In *New Advocate* 4:89–100.

Hardy, Barbara. 1977. "Towards a Poetics of Fiction: An Approach through
Narrative." In *The Cool Web,* Margaret Meek et al. London: The Bodley Head.

Harste, Jerome, Kathy Short, and Carolyn Burke. 1988. *Creating
Classrooms for Authors: The Reading-Writing Connection.* Toronto: Irwin.

Harste, Jerome, Virginia Woodward, and Carolyn Burke. 1984. *Language
Stories and Literacy Lessons.* Toronto: Irwin.

Hart-Hewins, Linda, and Jan Wells. 1990. *Real Books for Reading: Learning
to Read with Children's Literature.* Toronto: Pembroke.

Harwayne, Shelley. 1992. *Lasting Impressions.* Portsmouth, N.H.:
Heinemann.

Heard, Georgia. 1989. *For the Good of the Earth and Sun.* Portsmouth N.H.:
Heinemann.

Heath, Shirley Brice. 1983. *Ways with Words: Language, Life and Work in
Communities and Classrooms.* Cambridge: Cambridge University Press.

Heathcote, Dorothy. 1984. *Dorothy Heathcote: Collected Writings on
Education and Drama.* Liz Johnson and Cecily O'Neill, eds. London:
Hutchinson.1984.

Holdaway, Don. 1979. *The Foundations of Literacy.* Toronto: Scholastic.

Hornsby, David, and Deborah Sukarna. 1986. *Read On: A Conference
Approach to Reading.* Portsmouth N.H.: Heinemann.

Huck, Charlotte S., Susan Hepler, and Janet Hickman. 1987. *Children's Literature in the Elementary School.* 4th ed. New York: Holt, Rinehart and Winston.

Jackson, David. 1983. *Encounters with Books: Teaching Fiction 11-16.* London: Methuen.

Jaggar, Angela M., et al. 1986. "Research Currents: The Influence of Reading on Children's Narrative Writing (and vice versa)." *Language Arts* 63:292–300.

Johnson, Terry D., and Daphne R. Louis. 1987. *Literacy through Literature.* Toronto: Scholastic.

Jones, Jill, and Marie McLay. 1991. *All This Talk Gives Me an Idea!* Peel TALK Project. Peel, Ont.: Peel Board of Education.

Jones, Pat. 1988. *Lipservice: The Story of Talk in Schools.* Milton Keynes, England: Open University Press.

Knowles, Lewis. 1983. *Encouraging Talk.* London: Methuen.

Kobrin, Beverly. 1988. *Eyeopeners! How to Choose and Use Children's Books about Real People, Places and Things.* New York: Penguin.

Landsberg, Michelle. 1986. *Michelle Landsberg's Guide to Children's Books.* Toronto: Penguin.

Loban, Walter. 1986. "Research Currents: The Somewhat Stingy Story of Research into Children's Language." *Language Arts* 63:608–16.

Martin Jr., Bill. 1972. *Bill Martin's Instant Readers: Teacher's Guide.* New York: Holt, Rinehart and Winston.

Martin, Nancy, and et al. 1976. *Understanding Children Talking.* New York: Penguin.

McCracken, Robert, and Marlene McCracken. 1987. *Stories, Songs & Poetry to Teach Reading & Writing.* Winnipeg: Peguis.

Mickelson, Norma. 1980. *Assessing Language Development.* Toronto: Oxford University Press.

Moffett, James. 1986. *Active Voice: A Writing Program across the Curriculum.* Upper Montclair, N.J.: Boynton/Cook.

Moffett, James, and Betty J. Wagner. 1983a. *Student-Centered Language Arts Curriculum Grades K–13: A Handbook for Teachers.* Boston: Houghton Mifflin.

Moffett, James, and Betty J. Wagner. 1983b. *Writing: Teachers and Children at Work.* Portsmouth/Toronto: Heinemann/Irwin.

Mooney, Margaret E. 1990. *Reading to, with and by Children.* Katonah, N.Y.: Richard C. Owen.

Murray, Donald M. 1979. *Expecting the Unexpected: Teaching Myself—and Others—To Read and Write.* Toronto: Irwin.

Neelands, Jonothan. 1990. *Structuring Drama Work: A Handbook of Available Forms in Theatre and Drama.* Tony Goode, ed. Toronto: Irwin.

Newkirk, Thomas, and Patricia McLure. 1992. *Listening In: Children Talk about Books (and Other Things).* Portsmouth, N.H.: Heinemann.

Newman, Judith M. 1985. *The Craft of Children's Writing.* Toronto: Scholastic.

Newman, Judith M. 1991. *Interwoven Conversations.* Toronto: OISE Press.

Newman, Judith M., ed. 1985. *Whole Language: Theory in Use.* Toronto: Irwin.

Newman, Judith M., ed. 1989. *Finding Our Own Way: Teachers Exploring Their Assumptions.* Toronto: Irwin.

O'Neill, Cecily, and Alan Lambert. 1982. *Drama Structures: A Practical Handbook for Teachers.* London: Hutchinson.

Ontario Ministry of Education. 1988. *Growing With Books: Children's Literature, the Formative Years and Beyond.* Toronto: Ontario Ministry of Education.

Ontario Ministry of Education. 1990. *Assessing Language Arts. OAIP: Ontario Assessment Instrument Pool.* Toronto: Ontario Ministry of Education.

Paley, Vivian Gussin. 1990. *The Boy Who Would Be a Helicopter.* Cambridge, Mass.: Harvard University Press.

Paley, Vivian Gussin. 1992. *You Can't Say You Can't Play.* Cambridge, Mass.: Harvard University Press.

Parsons, B., et al. 1984. "Drama, Language and Learning." Tasmania: National Council for Drama in Education.

Peterson, Ralph, and Maryann Eeds. 1990. *Grand Conversations: Literature Groups in Action.* Toronto: Scholastic.

Phenix, Jo, and Doreen Scott-Dunne. 1991. *Spelling Instruction That Makes Sense.* Markham, Ont.: Pembroke.

Piaget, Jean. 1969a. *The Child's Conception of the World.* Patterson, N.J.: Littlefield, Adams.

Piaget, Jean. 1969b. *The Psychology of Intelligence.* Boston: Routledge and Kegan Paul.

Pinnell, Gay Su, Mary Fried, and Rose Mary Estice. 1990. "Reading Recovery: Learning How to Make a Difference." *Reading Teacher* 43:282–295.

Protherough, Robert. 1983. *Developing Response to Fiction.* Philadelphia: Open University Press.

Read, Charles. 1975. *Children's Creative Spelling.* London: Routledge and Kegan Paul.

Reasoner, Charles. 1972. *Bringing Children and Books Together.* New York: Dell.

Rhodes, Lynn K., and Curt Dudley-Marling. 1988. *Readers and Writers with a Difference: A Holistic Approach to Teaching Learning Disabled and Remedial Students.* Portsmouth/Toronto: Heinemann/Irwin.

Rosenblatt, Louise M. 1978. *The Reader, the Text, the Poem: The Transactional Theory of the Literary Work.* Portsmouth, N.H.: Heinemann

Schwartz, Susan, and Mindy Pollishuke. 1990. *Creating the Child-Centred Classroom.* Toronto: Irwin.

Smith, Frank. 1973. *Psycholinguistics and Reading.* New York: Holt, Rinehart and Winston.

Smith, Frank. 1986. *Understanding Reading.* Hillsdale, N.J.: Lawrence Erlbaum.

Smith, Frank, ed. 1988. *Joining the Literacy Club. Further Essays into Education.* Toronto: Irwin.

Taylor, Denny, and Dorothy Strickland. 1983. *Family Storybook Reading.* Portsmouth, N.H.: Heinemann.

Tchudi, Stephen N. 1991. *Planning and Assessing the Curriculum in English Language Arts.* Alexandria, Va: Association for Supervision and Curriculum Development.

Thomson, Jack. 1987. *Understanding Teenagers' Reading: Reading Processes and the Teaching of Literature.* London: Croom Helm.

Thornley-Hall, Carol. 1988. *Let's Talk about Talk.* Peel TALK Project. Peel, Ont.: Peel Board of Education.

Toronto Board of Education. 1980. *Observing Children through Their Formative Years.* Toronto.

Tough, Joan. 1981. *Talk for Teaching and Learning.* London: Ward Lock.

Tough, Joan. 1983. *Listening to Children Talking: A Guide to the Appraisal of Children's Use of Language.* Portsmouth, N.H.: Heinemann.

Trelease, Jim. 1989. *The New Read-Aloud Handbook.* New York: Penguin.

Vancouver Board of Education. 1989. *External Review.* Vancouver: Vancouver Board of Education.

Veatch, Jeanette. 1986. "Individualized Reading: A Personal Memoir." *Language Arts* 63:586–93.

Verriour, Patrick. 1984. "The Reflective Power of Drama." *Language Arts* 61(2).

Vygotsky, Lev. 1962, 1986. *Thought and Language.* Cambridge, Mass.: MIT Press.

Vygotsky, Lev. 1978. *Mind in Society: The Development of Higher Psychological Processes.* Cambridge, Mass.: Harvard University Press.

Ward, Winnifred. 1957. *Playmaking with Children.* 2nd ed. New York: Appleton.

Waterland, Liz. 1988. *Read with Me: An Apprenticeship Approach to Reading.* 2nd revised ed. South Woodchester, England: Thimble Press.

Watson, Dorothy, Carolyn Burke, and Jerome Harste. 1989 *Whole Language: Inquiring Voices.* Toronto: Scholastic.

Way, Brian. 1967. "Development through Drama." *Education Today.* London: Longman.

Weaver, Constance. 1988. *Reading Process and Practice: From Socio-psycholinguistics to Whole Language.* Toronto: Irwin.

Weaver, Constance. 1990. *Understanding Whole Language: From Principles to Practice.* Toronto: Irwin.

Wells, Gordon. 1986. *The Meaning Makers: Children Learning Language and Using Language to Learn.* Toronto: Irwin.

Wiener, Harvey S. 1990. *Any Child Can Read Better: Developing Your Child's Reading Skills Outside the Classroom.* New York: Bantam.

Wilkinson, Andrew. 1971. *The Foundations of Language: Talking and Reading in Young Children.* Oxford: Oxford University Press.

Wilkinson, Andrew. 1975. *Language and Education.* Oxford: Oxford University Press.

THE QUEENSTON COLLECTION OF

Children's Literature

Many more books, poems, and authors than could be mentioned in this book help form the collection at Queenston Drive Public School. Those that appear in this index without page references are just a few of those that teachers and students find significant.

WHO'S WHO AND INDEX OF

Contributors

READER REPLY CARD

NAME: _____

ADDRESS: _____

_____

_____

PHONE: _____

We are interested in your reaction to *Classroom Voices: Language-Based Learning in the Elementary School.* You can help us improve this book in future editions by completing this questionnaire.

1. What was your reason for using this book?

   ☐ university course ☐ college course ☐ continuing education course
   ☐ professional development ☐ personal interest ☐ other

2. If you are a student, please identify your school and the course in which you used this book.

3. Which chapters or parts of this book did you use?

4. Did you omit any chapters or parts? If so, which?

5. What did you like best about this book? What did you like least?

6. Please identify any topics you think should be added to future editions.

7. Please add any comments or suggestions.

8. May we contact you for further information?

-- fold here --

Comments:

(fold here and tape shut)

0116870399-M8Z4X6-BR01

Heather McWhinney
Publisher, College Division
HARCOURT BRACE & COMPANY, CANADA
55 HORNER AVENUE
TORONTO, ONTARIO
M8Z 9Z9